The Future of the Internet—
And How to Stop It

The Future
of the Internet

And How to Stop It

Jonathan Zittrain

With a New Foreword
by Lawrence Lessig and a
New Preface by the Author

Yale University Press

New Haven & London

Set in Adobe Garamond type by The Composing Room of Michigan, Inc.

Printed in the United States of America by R. R. Donnelley, Harrisonburg, Virginia.

Library of Congress Control Number: 2008942463
ISBN 978-0-300-15124-4 (pbk. : alk. paper)

A catalogue record for this book is available from the British Library.

10 9 8 7 6 5 4 3 2 1

Contents

Foreword by Lawrence Lessig

It has been a decade since book-length writing about law and the Internet began in earnest. Ethan Katsh's wonderful book *Law in a Digital World* (1995) is just over a decade old, and anticipated the flood. My first book, *Code and Other Laws of Cyberspace* (1999), is just under.

Most of these early books had a common character. We were all trying first to make the obscure understandable, and second, to draw lessons from the understood about how law and technology needed to interact.

As obscurity began to fade (as the network became more familiar), a different pattern began to emerge: cheerleading. Many of us (or at least I) felt we had seen something beautiful in the Net, felt that something needed to be protected, felt there were powerful interests that felt differently about all this, and thus felt we needed to make clear just how important it was to protect the Net of the present into the future.

This cheerleading tended to obscure certain increasingly obvious facts (not features, more like bugs) of the Internet. Put most succinctly, there was a growing and increasingly dangerous lot of stuff on the Net. The first notice of this crud pointed to pornography. In response, civil libertarians (the sort likely to love the Net anyway) launched a vigorous campaign to defend the rights of porn on the Net. But as the crud got deeper and more vicious, the urge to defend it began to wane. Spam became an increasingly annoying burden. Viruses, and worse, became positively harmful. Like a family on a beach holiday not wanting to confront the fact that "yes, that is a sewage line running into the water just upstream from the house we have rented," many of us simply turned a blind eye to this increasingly uncomfortable (and worse) fact: The Net was not in Kansas anymore.

Jonathan Zittrain's book is a much-needed antidote to this self-imposed blindness. It changes the whole debate about law and the Internet. It radically reorients the work of the Net's legal scholars. Rather than trying to ignore the uncomfortable parts of what the Net has become, Zittrain puts the crud right in the center. And he then builds an understanding of the Net, and the computers that made the Net possible, that explains how so much good and so much awful could come through the very same wires, and, more important, what we must do to recapture the good.

It is long past time for this understanding to become the focus, not just of legal scholars, but any citizen thinking about the future of the Net and its potential for society. Indeed, it may well be too late. As Zittrain argues quite effectively, the Internet is destined for an i9/11 event—by which I don't mean an attack by Al Qaeda, but rather a significant and fatally disruptive event that threatens the basic reliability of the Internet. When that happens, the passion clamoring for a fundamental reform of the Internet will be—if things stay as they are—irresistible. That reform, if built on the understanding that is commonplace just now, will radically weaken what the Internet now is, or could be. If built upon the understanding Zittrain is advancing here, it could strengthen the very best of the Internet, and the potential that network offers.

Zittrain doesn't have all the answers, though the proposals he offers are brilliant beginnings, and I think this powerfully argued book has more answers than even he suspects. But his aim is not to end a debate; it is to begin it. After providing an understanding of the great power this network promises, a power grounded in the "generativity" of the network, and the civic spirit of a critical mass of its users, he begins us on a path that might yet teach how to preserve the best of generativity, while protecting us from the worst.

This is a debate that all of us need to engage soon. I know of no book that more powerfully and directly speaks to the most important issues facing the future of the Net. I can't imagine a book that would speak to everyone more clearly and simply. You need know nothing about computers or the Internet to be inspired by this book. We need many more than the experts in computers and the Internet to preserve it.

Preface to the Paperback Edition

The venerable Warner Brothers antagonist Wile E. Coyote famously demonstrates a law of cartoon physics. He runs off a cliff, unaware of its ledge, and continues forward without falling. The Coyote defies gravity until he looks down and sees there's nothing under him. His mental gears turn as he contemplates his predicament. Then: splat.

Both the Internet and the PC are on a similar trajectory. They were designed by people who shared the same love of amateur tinkering as the enterprising Coyote. Both platforms were released unfinished, relying on their users to figure out what to do with them—and to deal with problems as they arose. This kind of openness isn't found in our cars, fridges, or TiVos. Compared to the rest of the technologies we use each day, it's completely anomalous, even absurd.

This openness, described and praised in this book in more detail as "generativity," allowed the Internet and PC to emerge from the realms of researchers and hobbyists and surprisingly win out over far more carefully planned and funded platforms. (They were certainly more successful than any of the Coyote's many projects.)

Today the very popularity and use of the Internet and PC are sorely testing that generativity. We wouldn't want our cars, fridges, or TiVos to be altered by unknown outsiders at the touch of a button—and yet this remains the prevailing way that we load new software on our PCs. More and more often that software is rogue—harvesting computing cycles from a PC in order to attack others, stealing personal information, or simply frying the PC. Soon, either abruptly or in slow motion: splat.

The first reaction to abuses of openness is to try to lock things down. One model for lockdown can be drawn from our familiar appliances, which are sealed when they leave the factory. No one but a true geek could hack a car or a fridge—or would want to—and we've seen glimpses of that model in communications platforms like iPods, most video game consoles, e-book readers like the Amazon Kindle, and cable company set-top boxes. Such lockdown was the direction a visionary Steve Jobs—the guy who gave us the first open PC, the Apple II—first took with the iPhone, with which he bet the future of Apple.

Of course, the Internet or PC would have to be in bad shape for us to abandon them for such totally closed platforms; there are too many pluses to being able to do things that platform manufacturers don't want or haven't thought of. But there's another model for lockdown that's much more subtle, and that takes, well, a book to unpack. This new model exploits near-ubiquitous network connectivity to let vendors change and monitor their technologies long after they've left the factory—or to let them bring us, the users, to them, as more and more of our activities shift away from our own devices and into the Internet's "cloud."

These technologies can let geeky outsiders build upon them just as they could with PCs, but in a highly controlled and contingent way. This is iPhone 2.0: an iPod on steroids, with a thriving market for software written by outsiders that must be approved by and funneled through Apple. It's also Web 2.0 software-as-service ventures like the Facebook platform and Google Apps, where an application popular one day can be banished the next.

This model is likely the future of computing and networking, and it is no minor tweak. It's a wholesale revision to the Internet and PC environment we've experienced for the past thirty years. The serendipity of outside tinkering that has marked that generative era gave us the Web, instant messaging, peer-to-peer networking, Skype, Wikipedia—all ideas out of left field. Now it is disappearing, leaving a handful of new gatekeepers in place, with us and them prisoner to their limited business plans and to regulators who fear things that are new and disruptive. We are at risk of embracing this new model, thinking it the best of both worlds—security and whimsy—when it may be the worst. Even fully grasping how untenable our old models have become, consolidation and lockdown need not be the only alternative. We can stop that future.

Introduction

On January 9, 2007, Steve Jobs introduced the iPhone to an eager audience crammed into San Francisco's Moscone Center.[1] A beautiful and brilliantly engineered device, the iPhone blended three products into one: an iPod, with the highest-quality screen Apple had ever produced; a phone, with cleverly integrated functionality, such as voicemail that came wrapped as separately accessible messages; and a device to access the Internet, with a smart and elegant browser, and with built-in map, weather, stock, and e-mail capabilities. It was a technical and design triumph for Jobs, bringing the company into a market with an extraordinary potential for growth, and pushing the industry to a new level of competition in ways to connect us to each other and to the Web.

This was not the first time Steve Jobs had launched a revolution. Thirty years earlier, at the First West Coast Computer Faire in nearly the same spot, the twenty-one-year-old Jobs, wearing his first suit, exhibited the Apple II personal computer to great buzz amidst "10,000 walking, talking computer freaks."[2] The Apple II was a machine for hobbyists who did not want to fuss with soldering irons: all the ingredients for a functioning PC were provided in a convenient molded plastic case. It looked clunky, yet it could be at home on someone's desk. Instead of puzzling over bits of hardware or typing up punch cards to feed into someone else's mainframe, Apple owners faced only the hurdle of a cryptic blinking cursor in the upper left corner of the screen: the PC awaited instructions. But the hurdle was not high. Some owners were inspired to program the machines themselves, but true beginners simply could load up software written and then shared or sold by their more skilled or inspired counterparts. The Apple II was a blank slate, a bold departure from previous technology that had been developed and marketed to perform specific tasks from the first day of its sale to the last day of its use.

The Apple II quickly became popular. And when programmer and entrepreneur Dan Bricklin introduced the first killer application for the Apple II in 1979—VisiCalc, the world's first spreadsheet program—sales of the ungainly but very cool machine took off dramatically.[3] An Apple running VisiCalc helped to convince a skeptical world that there was a place for the PC at everyone's desk and hence a market to build many, and to build them very fast.

Though these two inventions—iPhone and Apple II—were launched by the same man, the revolutions that they inaugurated are radically different. For the technology that each inaugurated is radically different. The Apple II was quintessentially *generative* technology. It was a platform. It invited people to tinker with it. Hobbyists wrote programs. Businesses began to plan on selling software. Jobs (and Apple) had no clue how the machine would be used. They had their hunches, but, fortunately for them, nothing constrained the PC to the hunches of the founders. Apple did not even know that VisiCalc was on the market when it noticed sales of the Apple II skyrocketing. The Apple II was designed for surprises—some very good (VisiCalc), and some not so good (the inevitable and frequent computer crashes).

The iPhone is the opposite. It is sterile. Rather than a platform that invites innovation, the iPhone comes preprogrammed. You are not allowed to add programs to the all-in-one device that Steve Jobs sells you. Its functionality is locked in, though Apple can change it through remote updates. Indeed, to those who managed to tinker with the code to enable the iPhone to support more or different applications,[4] Apple threatened (and then delivered on the threat) to transform the iPhone into an iBrick.[5] The machine was not to be *generative* beyond the innovations that Apple (and its exclusive carrier, AT&T) wanted. Whereas the world would innovate for the Apple II, only Apple would innovate for the iPhone. (A promised software development kit may allow others to program the iPhone with Apple's permission.)

Jobs was not shy about these restrictions baked into the iPhone. As he said at its launch:

> We define everything that is on the phone. . . . You don't want your phone to be like a PC. The last thing you want is to have loaded three apps on your phone and then you go to make a call and it doesn't work anymore. These are more like iPods than they are like computers.[6]

No doubt, for a significant number of us, Jobs was exactly right. For in the thirty years between the first flashing cursor on the Apple II and the gorgeous iconized touch menu of the iPhone, we have grown weary not with the unexpected cool stuff that the generative PC had produced, but instead with the unexpected very uncool stuff that came along with it. Viruses, spam, identity theft, crashes: all of these were the consequences of a certain freedom built into the generative PC. As these problems grow worse, for many the promise of security is enough reason to give up that freedom.

*   *   *

In the arc from the Apple II to the iPhone, we learn something important about where the Internet has been, and something more important about where it is going. The PC revolution was launched with PCs that invited innovation by others. So too with the Internet. Both were generative: they were designed to accept any contribution that followed a basic set of rules (either coded for a particular operating system, or respecting the protocols of the Internet). Both overwhelmed their respective proprietary, non-generative competitors, such as the makers of stand-alone word processors and proprietary online services like CompuServe and AOL. But the future unfolding right now is very different from this past. The future is not one of generative PCs attached to a generative network. It is instead one of sterile *appliances* tethered to a network of control.

These appliances take the innovations already created by Internet users and package them neatly and compellingly, which is good—but only if the Internet and PC can remain sufficiently central in the digital ecosystem to compete with locked-down appliances and facilitate the next round of innovations. The balance between the two spheres is precarious, and it is slipping toward the safer appliance. For example, Microsoft's Xbox 360 video game console is a powerful computer, but, unlike Microsoft's Windows operating system for PCs, it does not allow just anyone to write software that can run on it. Bill Gates sees the Xbox as at the center of the future digital ecosystem, rather than at its periphery: "It is a general purpose computer. . . . [W]e wouldn't have done it if it was just a gaming device. We wouldn't have gotten into the category at all. It was about strategically being in the living room. . . . [T]his is not some big secret. Sony says the same things."[7]

It is not easy to imagine the PC going extinct, and taking with it the possibility of allowing outside code to run—code that is the original source of so much of what we find useful about the Internet. But along with the rise of information appliances that package those useful activities without readily allowing new ones, there is the increasing lockdown of the PC itself. PCs may not be competing with information appliances so much as they are becoming them. The trend is starting in schools, libraries, cyber cafés, and offices, where the users of PCs are not their owners. The owners' interests in maintaining stable computing environments are naturally aligned with technologies that tame the wildness of the Internet and PC, at the expense of valuable activities their users might otherwise discover.

The need for stability is growing. Today's viruses and spyware are not merely annoyances to be ignored as one might tune out loud conversations at nearby tables in a restaurant. They will not be fixed by some new round of patches to bug-filled PC operating systems, or by abandoning now-ubiquitous Windows for Mac. Rather, they pose a fundamental dilemma: as long as people control the code that runs on their machines, they can make mistakes and be tricked into running dangerous code. As more people use PCs and make them more accessible to the outside world through broadband, the value of corrupting these users' decisions is increasing. That value is derived from stealing people's attention, PC processing cycles, network bandwidth, or online preferences. And the fact that a Web page can be and often is rendered on the fly by drawing upon hundreds of different sources scattered across the Net—a page may pull in content from its owner, advertisements from a syndicate, and links from various other feeds—means that bad code can infect huge swaths of the Web in a heartbeat.

If security problems worsen and fear spreads, rank-and-file users will not be far behind in preferring some form of lockdown—and regulators will speed the process along. In turn, that lockdown opens the door to new forms of regulatory surveillance and control. We have some hints of what that can look like. Enterprising law enforcement officers have been able to eavesdrop on occupants of motor vehicles equipped with the latest travel assistance systems by producing secret warrants and flicking a distant switch. They can turn a standard mobile phone into a roving microphone—whether or not it is being used for a call. As these opportunities arise in places under the rule of law—where some might welcome them—they also arise within technology-embracing authoritarian states, because the technology is exported.

A lockdown on PCs and a corresponding rise of tethered appliances will eliminate what today we take for granted: a world where mainstream technology can be influenced, even revolutionized, out of left field. Stopping this future depends on some wisely developed and implemented locks, along with new technologies and a community ethos that secures the keys to those locks among groups with shared norms and a sense of public purpose, rather than in the hands of a single gatekeeping entity, whether public or private.

The iPhone is a product of both fashion and fear. It boasts an undeniably attractive aesthetic, and it bottles some of the best innovations from the PC and Internet in a stable, controlled form. The PC and Internet were the engines of those innovations, and if they can be saved, they will offer more. As time passes, the brand names on each side will change. But the core battle will remain. It will be fought through information appliances and Web 2.0 platforms like today's Facebook apps and Google Maps mash-ups. These are not just products but also services, watched and updated according to the constant dictates of their makers and those who can pressure them.

In this book I take up the question of what is likely to come next and what we should do about it.

I

The Rise and Stall of the Generative Net

Today's Internet is not the only way to build a network. In the 1990s, the Internet passed unnoticed in mainstream circles while networks were deployed by competing proprietary barons such as AOL, CompuServe, and Prodigy. The technorati placed bets on which baron would prevail over the others, apparently imagining that the proprietary networks would develop in the same way that the separate phone networks—at one time requiring differently colored phones on each person's desk—had converged to just one lucky provider.[1] All those bets lost. The proprietary networks went extinct, despite having accumulated millions of subscribers. They were crushed by a network built by government researchers and computer scientists who had no CEO, no master business plan, no paying subscribers, no investment in content, and no financial interest in accumulating subscribers.

The framers of the Internet did not design their network with visions of mainstream dominance. Instead, the very unexpectedness of its success was a critical ingredient. The Internet was able to develop quietly and organically for years before it became widely known, remaining outside the notice of those who would have insisted on more cautious strictures had they only suspected how ubiquitous it would become.

This first part of the book traces the battle between the centralized proprietary networks and the Internet, and a corresponding fight between specialized information appliances like smart typewriters and the general-purpose PC, highlighting the qualities that allowed the Internet and PC to win.

Today, the same qualities that led to their successes are causing the Internet and the PC to falter. As ubiquitous as Internet technologies are today, the pieces are in place for a wholesale shift away from the original chaotic design that has given rise to the modern information revolution. This counterrevolution would push mainstream users away from a *generative* Internet that fosters innovation and disruption, to an *appliancized* network that incorporates some of the most powerful features of today's Internet while greatly limiting its innovative capacity—and, for better or worse, heightening its regulability. A seductive and more powerful generation of proprietary networks and information appliances is waiting for round two. If the problems associated with the Internet and PC are not addressed, a set of blunt solutions will likely be applied to solve the problems at the expense of much of what we love about today's information ecosystem. Understanding its history sheds light on different possible futures and helps us to recognize and avoid what might otherwise be very tempting dead ends.

One vital lesson from the past is that the endpoint matters. Too often, a discussion of the Internet and its future stops just short of its endpoints, focusing only on the literal network itself: how many people are connected, whether and how it is filtered, and how fast it carries data.[2] These are important questions, but they risk obscuring the reality that people's experiences with the Internet are shaped at least as much by the devices they use to access it.

As Internet-aware devices proliferate, questions posed about network regulation must also be applied to the endpoints—which, until recently, have been so open and so nonconstricting as to be nearly unnoticeable, and therefore absent from most debates about Internet policy. Yet increasingly the box has come to matter.

History shows that the box had competitors—and today they are back. The early models of commercial (as compared to academic) computing assumed that the vendor of the machinery would provide most or all of its programming. The PC of the 1980s—the parent of today's PC—diverged from these models, but the result was by no means a foregone conclusion. Internet users are again embracing a range of "tethered appliances," reflecting a resurgence of the initial model of bundled hardware and software that is created and controlled by one company. This will affect how readily behavior on the Internet can be regulated, which in turn will determine the extent that regulators and commercial incumbents can constrain amateur innovation, which has been responsible for much of what we now consider precious about the Internet.[3]

The Internet also had competitors—and they are back. Compared to the Internet, early online information services were built around very different technical and business models. Their designs were much easier to secure against illegal behavior and security threats; the cost was that innovation became much more difficult. The Internet outpaced these services by assuming that every user was contributing a goodwill subsidy: people would not behave destructively even when there were no easy ways to monitor or stop them.

The Internet's tradeoff of more flexibility for less security worked: most imaginable risks failed to materialize—for example, people did not routinely spy on one another's communications, even though it was eminently possible, and for years there were no spam and no viruses. By observing at which point these tradeoffs were made, we will see that the current portfolio of tradeoffs is no longer optimal, and that some of the natural adjustments in that balance, while predictable, are also undesirable.

The fundamental challenges for those who have built and maintained the Internet are to acknowledge crucial deficiencies in a network-and-endpoint structure that has otherwise served so well for so long, to understand our alternatives as the status quo evaporates, and to devise ways to push the system toward a future that addresses the very real problems that are forcing change, while preserving the elements we hold most dear.

1

Battle of the Boxes

Herman Hollerith was a twenty-year-old engineer when he helped to compile the results of the 1880 U.S. Census.[1] He was sure he could invent a way to tabulate the data automatically, and over the next several years he spent his spare time devising a punch card system for surveyors to use. The U.S. government commissioned him to tally the 1890 Census with his new system, which consisted of a set of punch cards and associated readers that used spring-mounted needles to pass through the holes in each card, creating an electrical loop that advanced the reader's tally for a particular hole location.

Rather than selling the required equipment to the government, Hollerith leased it out at a rate of one thousand dollars per year for each of the first fifty machines. In exchange, he was wholly responsible for making sure the machines performed their designated tasks.[2] The tally was a success. It took only two and a half years to tally the 1890 Census, compared to the seven years required for the 1880 Census. Hollerith's eponymous Tabulating Machine Company soon expanded to other governments' censuses, and then to payroll, inventory, and billing for large firms like railroad and insurance companies.[3] Hollerith retained the idea of renting rather than selling, controlling the ongoing computing processes of his clients in order to ensure a desirable outcome. It worked. His clients did not want to be burdened with learning how to operate these devices themselves. Instead, they wanted exactly one vendor to summon if something went wrong.

By the 1960s, the company name was International Business Machines, and IBM dominated business computing. Its leadership retained Hollerith's original control paradigm: firms leased IBM's mainframes on a monthly basis, and the lease covered everything—hardware, software, maintenance, and training.[4] Businesses developed little in-house talent for operating the machines because everything was already included as part of the deal with IBM. Further, while IBM's computers were general-purpose information processors, meaning they could be repurposed with new software, no third-party software industry existed. All software was bundled with the machine rental as part of IBM's business model, which was designed to offer comprehensive computing solutions for the particular problems presented by the client. This model provided a convenient one-stop-shopping approach to business computing, resulting in software that was well customized to the client's business practices. But it also meant that any improvements to the computer's operation had to happen through a formal process of discussion and negotiation between IBM and the client. Further, the arrangement made it difficult for firms to switch providers, since any new vendor would have to redo the entire project from scratch.

IBM's competitors were not pleased, and in 1969, under the threat of an antitrust suit—which later materialized—IBM announced that it would unbundle its offerings.[5] It became possible to buy an IBM computer apart from the software, beginning a slow evolution toward in-house programming talent and third-party software makers. Nevertheless, for years after the unbundling announcement many large firms continued to rely on custom-built, externally maintained applications designed for specific purposes.

Before unbundling, mainstream customers encountered computing devices in one of two ways. First, there was the large-scale Hollerith model of mainframes managed by a single firm like IBM. These computers had general-purpose processors inside, capable of a range of tasks, and IBM's programming team devised the software that the customer needed to fulfill its goals. The second type of computing devices was information appliances: devices hardwired for a particular purpose. These were devices like the Friden Flexowriter, a typewriter that could store what was typed by making holes in a roll of tape.

Rethreading the tape through the Flexowriter allowed it to retype what had come before, much like operating a player piano. Cutting and pasting different pieces of Flexowriter tape together allowed the user to do mail merges about as easily as one can do them today with Microsoft Word or its rivals.[6] Information appliances were substantially cheaper and easier to use than mainframes, thus requiring no ongoing rental and maintenance relationship with a vendor. However, they could do only the tasks their designers anticipated for them. Firms could buy Flexowriters outright and entrust them to workers—but could not reprogram them.

Today's front-line computing devices are drawn from an entirely different lineage: the hobbyist's personal computer of the late 1970s. The PC could be owned as easily as a Flexowriter but possessed the flexibility, if not the power, of the generic mainframe.[7] A typical PC vendor was the opposite of 1960s IBM: it made available little more than a processor in a box, one ingeniously under-accessorized to minimize its cost. An owner took the inert box and connected it to common household appliances to make it a complete PC. For example, a $99 Timex/Sinclair Z-1000 or a $199 Texas Instruments TI-99/4A could use a television set as a display, and a standard audio cassette recorder to store and retrieve data.[8] The cassette player (and, later, PC-specific diskette drives) could also store and retrieve code that reprogrammed the way the computers worked.[9] In this way, the computers could run new software that was not necessarily available at the time the computer was purchased. PC makers were selling potential functionality as much as they were selling actual uses, and many makers considered themselves to be in the hardware business only. To them, the PCs were solutions waiting for problems.

But these computers did not have to be built that way: there could simply be a world of consumer information technology that comprised appliances. As with a Flexowriter, if a designer knew enough about what the user wanted a PC to do, it would be possible to embed the required code directly into the hardware of the machine, and to make the machine's hardware perform that specific task. This embedding process occurs in the digital watch, the calculator, and the firmware within Mr. Coffee that allows the machine to begin brewing at a user-selected time. These devices are all hardware and no software (though some would say that the devices' software is inside their hardware). If the coffeemaker, calculator, or watch should fail to perform as promised, the user knows exactly whom to blame, since the manufacturers determine the device's behavior as surely as Herman Hollerith controlled the design and use of his tabulators.

The essence—and genius—of separating software creation from hardware construction is that the decoupling enables a computer to be acquired for one purpose and then used to perform new and different tasks without requiring the equivalent of a visit to the mechanic's shop.[10] Some might remember global retailer Radio Shack's "75-in-1 Electronic Project Kit," which was a piece of cardboard with lots of electronic components attached to it.[11] Each component—a transistor, resistor, capacitor, speaker, relay, or dial—was wired to springy posts so that a budding Hollerith could quickly attach and detach wires linking individual components to one another, reconfiguring the board to imitate any number of appliances: radio, doorbell, lie detector,[12] or metronome. The all-important instruction manual offered both schematics and wiring instructions for various inventions—seventy-five of them—much like a book of recipes. Kids could tinker with the results or invent entirely new appliances from scratch as long as they had the ideas and the patience to attach lots of wires to springy posts.

Computer software makes this sort of reconfigurability even easier, by separating the act of algorithm-writing from the act of wiring and rewiring the machine. This separation saves time required for switching between discrete tasks, and it reduces the skill set a programmer needs in order to write new software.[13] It also lays the groundwork for the easy transmission of code from an inventor to a wider audience: instead of passing around instructions for how to rewire the device in order to add a new feature, one can distribute software code that feeds into the machine itself and rewires it in a heartbeat.

The manufacturers of general-purpose PCs could thus write software that gave a PC new functionality after the computer left the factory. Some early PC programs were distributed in printed books for buyers to retype into their machines, but increasingly affordable media like cassette tapes, diskettes, and cartridges became a more cost-effective way to install software. The consumer merely needed to know how to load in the cassette, diskette, or cartridge containing the software in order to enjoy it.

Most significantly, PCs were designed to run software written by authors other than the PC manufacturer or those with whom the PC manufacturer had special arrangements.[14] The resulting PC was one that its own users could program, and many did. But PCs were still firmly grounded in the realm of hobbyists, alongside 75-in-1 Project Kit designs. To most people such a kit was just a big pile of wires, and in the early 1980s a PC was similarly known as more offbeat recreation—a 75-in-1 Project Kit for adults—than as the gateway to a revolution.

The business world took up PCs slowly—who could blame companies for ignoring something called "personal computer"? In the early 1980s firms were still drawing on custom-programmed mainframes or information appliances like smart typewriters. Some businesses obtained custom-programmed mini-computers, which the employees accessed remotely through "dumb" terminals connected to the minicomputers via small, rudimentary in-building networks. The minicomputers would typically run a handful of designated applications —payroll, accounts receivable, accounts payable, and perhaps a more enter-prise-specific program, such as a case management system for a hospital or a course selection and assignment program for a university.

As the 1980s progressed, the PC increased in popularity. Also during this time the variety of things a user could do with a PC increased dramatically, pos-sibly because PCs were not initially networked. In the absence of a centrally managed information repository, there was an incentive to make an individual PC powerful in its own right, with the capacity to be programmed by anyone and to function independently of other computers. Moreover, while a central information resource has to be careful about the places to which access is granted—too much access could endanger others' use of the shared machine—individual PCs in hobbyist hands had little need for such security. They were the responsibility of their keepers, and no more.

The PC's ability to support a variety of programs from a variety of makers meant that it soon outpaced the functionality of appliancized machines like dedicated word processors, which were built to function the same way over the entire life of the machine. An IT ecosystem comprising fixed hardware and flexible software soon proved its worth: PC word processing software could be upgraded or replaced with better, competing software without having to junk the PC itself. Word processing itself represented a significant advance over typ-ing, dynamically updated spreadsheets were immensely more powerful than static tables of numbers generated through the use of calculators, and relational databases put index cards and more sophisticated paper-based filing systems to shame.[15] Entirely new applications like video games, beginning with text-based adventures,[16] pioneered additional uses of leisure time, and existing games—such as chess and checkers—soon featured the computer itself as a worthy opponent.[17]

PCs may not have been ideal for a corporate environment—documents and other important information were scattered on different PCs depending on who authored what, and enterprise-wide backup was often a real headache. But the price was right, and diffidence about them soon gave way as businesses could rely on college graduates having skills in word processing and other basic PC tools that would not have to be relearned on a legacy minicomputer system. The mature applications that emerged from the PC's uncertain beginnings provided a reason for the white-collar worker to be assigned a PC, and for an ever broader swath of people to want a PC at home. These machines may have been bought for one purpose, but the flexible architecture—one that made them ready to be programmed using software from any number of sources—meant that they could quickly be redeployed for another. Someone could buy a PC for word processing and then discover the joys of e-mail, or gaming, or the Web.

Bill Gates used to describe his company's vision as "a computer on every desk and in every home, all running Microsoft software."[18] That may appear to be a simple desire to move units—nearly every PC sold meant more money for Microsoft—but as it came true in the developed world, the implications went beyond Microsoft's profitability. Significantly, Gates sought to have computers "all running Microsoft software" rather than computers running only Microsoft software. Windows PCs, like their Mac OS and Linux counterparts, do not insist that all the software found within them come from the same vendor and its partners. They were instead designed to welcome code from any source. Despite Microsoft's well-earned reputation as a ruthless monopolist, a reputation validated by authorities in multiple jurisdictions, a Microsoft PC on nearly every desk can also be interpreted as an ongoing invitation to outside coders to write new software that those PCs can run.[19]

An installed base of tens of millions of PCs ensured the existence of pretilled soil in which new software from any source could take root. Someone writing a creative new application did not need to persuade Microsoft or Apple to allow the software onto the machine, or to persuade people to buy a new piece of hardware to run it. He or she needed only to persuade users to buy (or simply acquire) the software itself, and it could run without further obstacle. As PCs were connected to the Internet, the few remaining barriers—the price of the media and corresponding trip to the computer store—were largely eliminated. People could simply click on the desired link, and new software would be installed.

Networked PCs may have been purchased for a variety of narrow reasons, but collectively they represented openness to new code that could be tried and shared at very little effort and cost. Their manufacturers—both hardware and operating system makers—found their incentives largely aligned with those of independent software developers.[20] The more outside developers there were writing new code, the more valuable a computer would become to more people. To be sure, operating system makers sometimes tried to expand their offerings into the "application space"—for example, Microsoft and Apple each developed their own versions of word processing software to compete with third-party versions, and the Microsoft antitrust cases of the 1990s arose from attempts to link operating system dominance to application dominance—but the most successful business model for both Microsoft and Apple has been to make their computers' operating systems appealing for third-party software development, since they profit handsomely from the sale of the platforms themselves.[21]

*   *   *

The Hollerith model is one of powerful, general-purpose machines maintained continuously and exclusively by a vendor. The appliance model is one of predictable and easy-to-use specialized machines that require little or no maintenance. Both have virtues. The Hollerith machine is a powerful workhorse and can be adapted by the vendor to fulfill a range of purposes. The appliance is easy to master and it can leverage the task for which it was designed, but not much else. Neither the Hollerith machine nor the appliance can be easily reprogrammed by their users or by third parties, and, as later chapters will explain, "generativity" was thus not one of their features.

A third model eclipsed them: powerful desktop PCs that were adaptable to many different tasks and accessible to anyone who wanted to recode them, and that had the capacity to connect to an Internet that was as good as invisible when it was working well. Perhaps the PC model of computing would have gathered steam even if it had not been initially groomed in hobbyist backwaters. But the strength of the Hollerith model and the risk aversion of many commercial firms to alternatives—"No one got fired for choosing IBM systems"—suggest that the idea of user-maintained and user-tweaked computers running code from many different sources was substantially enhanced by first being proven in environments more amenable to experimentation and risk-taking.[22] These backwater environments cultivated forms of amateur tinkering that became central to major software development. Both small and large third-party applications are now commonplace, and major software efforts often include plug-in architecture that allows *fourth* parties to write code that builds on the third parties' code.

The box has mattered. The complex, expensive computers of the 1960s, centrally run and managed by a professional class, allowed for customization to the user's needs over time, but at substantial expense. The simpler, inexpensive information appliances intended for individual use diffused technology beyond large consuming firms, but they could not be repurposed or customized very well; changes to their operation took place only as successive models of the appliance were released by the manufacturer. The PC integrated the availability of the appliance with the modifiability of the large generic processor—and began a revolution that affected not only amateur tinkerers, but PC owners who had no technical skills, since they could install the software written by others.

The story of the PC versus the information appliance is the first in a recurring pattern. The pattern begins with a generative platform that invites contributions from anyone who cares to make them. The contributions start among amateurs, who participate more for fun and whimsy than for profit. Their work, previously unnoticed in the mainstream, begins to catch on, and the power of the market kicks in to regularize their innovations and deploy them in markets far larger than the amateurs' domains. Finally, the generative features that invite contribution and that worked so well to propel the first stage of innovation begin to invite trouble and reconsideration, as the power of openness to third-party contribution destabilizes its first set of gains. To understand the options that follow, it helps to see the sterile, non-generative alternatives to the generative system. The endpoint box is one place where these alternatives can vie against each other for dominance. The network to which these boxes are connected is another, and the next chapter explores a parallel battle for supremacy there.

2

Battle of the Networks

As the price of computer processors and peripheral components dropped precipitously from the days of mainframes, it became easier for computer technology to end up in people's homes. But the crucial element of the PC's success is not that it has a cheap processor inside, but that it is generative: it is open to reprogramming and thus repurposing by anyone. Its technical architecture, whether Windows, Mac, or other, makes it easy for authors to write and owners to run new code both large and small. As prices dropped, distributed ownership of computers, rather than leasing within institutional environments, became a practical reality, removing legal and business practice barriers to generative tinkering with the machines.

If the hobbyist PC had not established the value of tinkering so that the PC could enter the mainstream in the late 1980s,[1] what cheap processors would small firms and mainstream consumers be using today? One possibility is a set of information appliances. In such a world, people would use smart typewriters for word processing from companies like Brother: all-in-one units with integrated screens and printers that could be used only to produce documents. For gaming,

19

they would use dedicated video game consoles—just as many do today. A personal checkbook might have had its own souped-up adding machine/calculator unit for balancing accounts—or it might have had no appliance at all, since the cost of deploying specialized hardware for that purpose might have exceeded consumer demand.

There is still the question of networking. People would likely still want to exchange word processing and other documents with colleagues or friends. To balance checkbooks conveniently would require communication with the bank so that the user would not have to manually enter cleared checks and their dates from a paper statement. Networking is not impossible in a world of stand-alone appliances. Brother word processor users could exchange diskettes with each other, and the bank could mail its customers cassettes, diskettes, or CD-ROMs containing data usable only with the bank's in-home appliance. Or the home appliance could try to contact the bank's computer from afar—an activity that would require the home and the bank to be networked somehow.

This configuration converges on the Hollerith model, where a central computer could be loaded with the right information automatically if it were in the custody of the bank, or if the bank had a business relationship with a third-party manager. Then the question becomes how far away the various dumb terminals could be from the central computer. The considerable expense of building networks would suggest placing the machines in clusters, letting people come to them. Electronic balancing of one's checkbook would take place at a computer installed in a bank lobby or strategically located cyber café, just as automated teller machines (ATMs) are dispersed around cities today. People could perform electronic document research over another kind of terminal found at libraries and schools. Computers, then, are only one piece of a mosaic that can be more or less generative. Another critical piece is the network, its own generativity hinging on how much it costs to use, how its costs are measured, and the circumstances under which its users can connect to one another.

Just as information processing devices can be appliance, mainframe, PC, or something in between, there are a variety of ways to design a network. The choice of configuration involves many trade-offs. This chapter explains why the Internet was not the only way to build a network—and that different network configurations lead not only to different levels of generativity, but also to different levels of regulability and control. That we use the Internet today is not solely a matter of some policy-maker's choice, although certain regulatory interventions and government funding were necessary to its success. It is due to an interplay of market forces and network externalities that are based on presumptions such as how trustworthy we can expect people to be. As those presumptions begin to change, so too will the shape of the network and the things we connect to it.

BUILDING NETWORKS ON A NETWORK

Returning to a threshold question: if we wanted to allow people to use information technology at home and to be able to network in ways beyond sending floppy diskettes through the mail, how can we connect homes to the wider world? A natural answer would be to piggyback on the telephone network, which was already set up to convey people's voices from one house to another, or between houses and institutions. Cyberlaw scholar Tim Wu and others have pointed out how difficult it was at first to put the telephone network to any new purpose, *not* for technical reasons, but for ones of legal control—and thus how important early regulatory decisions forcing an opening of the network were to the success of digital networking.[2]

In early twentieth-century America, AT&T controlled not only the telephone network, but also the devices attached to it. People rented their phones from AT&T, and the company prohibited them from making any modifications to the phones. To be sure, there were no AT&T phone police to see what customers were doing, but AT&T could and did go after the sellers of accessories like the Hush-A-Phone, which was invented in 1921 as a way to have a conversation without others nearby overhearing it.[3] It was a huge plastic funnel enveloping the user's mouth on one end and strapped to the microphone of the handset on the other, muffling the conversation. Over 125,000 units were sold.

As the monopoly utility telephone provider, AT&T faced specialized regulation from the U.S. Federal Communications Commission (FCC). In 1955, the FCC held that AT&T could block the sale of the funnels as "unauthorized foreign attachments," and terminate phone service to those who purchased them, but the agency's decision was reversed by an appellate court. The court drolly noted, "[AT&T does] not challenge the subscriber's right to seek privacy. They say only that he should achieve it by cupping his hand between the transmitter and his mouth and speaking in a low voice into this makeshift muffler."[4]

Cupping a hand and placing a plastic funnel on the phone seemed the same to the court. It found that at least in cases that were not "publicly detrimental"—in other words, where the phone system was not itself harmed—AT&T had to allow customers to make physical additions to their handsets, and manufacturers to produce and distribute those additions. AT&T could have invented the Hush-A-Phone funnel itself. It did not; it took outsiders to begin changing the system, even in small ways.

Hush-A-Phone was followed by more sweeping outside innovations. During the 1940s, inventor Tom Carter sold and installed two-way radios for companies with workers out in the field. As his business caught on, he realized how much more helpful it would be to be able to hook up a base station's radio to a telephone so that faraway executives could be patched in to the front lines. He invented the Carterfone to do just that in 1959 and sold over 3,500 units. AT&T told its customers that they were not allowed to use Carterfones, because these devices hooked up to the network itself, unlike the Hush-A-Phone, which connected only to the telephone handset. Carter petitioned against the rule and won.[5] Mindful of the ideals behind the *Hush-A-Phone* decision, the FCC agreed that so long as the network was not harmed, AT&T could not block new devices, even ones that directly hooked up to the phone network.

These decisions paved the way for advances invented and distributed by third parties, advances that were the exceptions to the comparative innovation desert of the telephone system. Outsiders introduced devices such as the answering machine, the fax machine, and the cordless phone that were rapidly adopted.[6] The most important advance, however, was the dial-up modem, a crucial piece of hardware bridging consumer information processors and the world of computer networks, whether proprietary or the Internet.

With the advent of the modem, people could acquire plain terminals or PCs and connect them to central servers over a telephone line. Users could dial up whichever service they wanted: a call to the bank's network for banking, followed by a call to a more generic "information service" for interactive weather and news.

The development of this capability illustrates the relationships among the standard layers that can be said to exist in a network: at the bottom are the physical wires, with services above, and then applications, and finally content and social interaction. If AT&T had prevailed in the *Carterfone* proceeding, it would have been able to insist that its customers use the phone network only for traditional point-to-point telephone calls. The phone network would have been repurposed for data solely at AT&T's discretion and pace. Because AT&T lost, others' experiments in data transmission could move forward. The physical layer had become generative, and this generativity meant that additional types of activity in higher layers were made possible. While AT&T continued collecting rents from the phone network's use whether for voice or modem calls, both amateurs working for fun and entrepreneurs seeking new business opportunities got into the online services business.

THE PROPRIETARY NETWORK MODEL

The first online services built on top of AT&T's phone network were natural extensions of the 1960s IBM-model minicomputer usage within businesses: one centrally managed machine to which employees' dumb terminals connected. Networks like CompuServe, The Source, America Online, Prodigy, GEnie, and MCI Mail gave their subscribers access to content and services deployed solely by the network providers themselves.[7]

In 1983, a home computer user with a telephone line and a CompuServe subscription could pursue a variety of pastimes[8]—reading an Associated Press news feed, chatting in typed sentences with other CompuServe subscribers through a "CB radio simulator," sending private e-mail to fellow subscribers, messaging on bulletin boards, and playing rudimentary multiplayer games.[9] But if a subscriber or an outside company wanted to develop a new service that might appeal to CompuServe subscribers, it could not automatically do so. Even if it knew how to program on CompuServe's mainframes, an aspiring provider needed CompuServe's approval. CompuServe entered into development agreements with outside content providers[10] like the Associated Press and, in some cases, with outside programmers,[11] but between 1984 and 1994, as the service grew from one hundred thousand subscribers to almost two million, its core functionalities remained largely unchanged.[12]

Innovation within services like CompuServe took place at the center of the network rather than at its fringes. PCs were to be only the delivery vehicles for data sent to customers, and users were not themselves expected to program or to be able to receive services from anyone other than their central service provider. CompuServe depended on the phone network's physical layer generativity to get the last mile to a subscriber's house, but CompuServe as a service was not open to third-party tinkering.

Why would CompuServe hold to the same line that AT&T tried to draw? After all, the economic model for almost every service was the connect charge: a per-minute fee for access rather than advertising or transactional revenue.[13] With mere connect time as the goal, one might think activity-garnering user-contributed software running on the service would be welcome, just as user-contributed content in the CB simulator or on a message board produced revenue if it drew other users in. Why would the proprietary services not harness the potential generativity of their offerings by making their own servers more open to third-party coding? Some networks' mainframes permitted an area in which subscribers could write and execute their own software,[14] but in each case restrictions were quickly put in place to prevent other users from running that software online. The "programming areas" became relics, and the Hollerith model prevailed.

Perhaps the companies surmised that little value could come to them from user and third-party tinkering if there were no formal relationship between those outside programmers and the information service's in-house developers. Perhaps they thought it too risky: a single mainframe or set of mainframes running a variety of applications could not risk being compromised by poorly coded or downright rogue applications.

Perhaps they simply could not grasp the potential to produce new works that could be found among an important subset of their subscribers—all were instead thought of solely as consumers. Or they may have thought that all the important applications for online consumer services had already been invented—news, weather, bulletin boards, chat, e-mail, and the rudiments of shopping.

In the early 1990s the future seemed to be converging on a handful of corporate-run networks that did not interconnect. There was competition of a sort that recalls AT&T's early competitors: firms with their own separate wires going to homes and businesses. Some people maintained an e-mail address on each major online service simply so that they could interact with friends and business contacts regardless of the service the others selected. Each information service put together a proprietary blend of offerings, mediated by software produced by the service. Each service had the power to decide who could subscribe, under what terms, and what content would be allowed or disallowed, either generally (should there be a forum about gay rights?) or specifically (should this particular message about gay rights be deleted?). For example, Prodigy sought a reputation as a family-friendly service and was more aggressive about deleting sensitive user-contributed content; CompuServe was more of a free-for-all.[15]

But none seemed prepared to budge from the business models built around their mainframes, and, as explained in detail in Chapter Four, works by scholars such as Mary Benner and Michael Tushman shed some light on why. Mature firms can acquire "stabilizing organizational routines": "internal biases for certainty and predictable results [which] favor exploitative innovation at the expense of exploratory innovation."[16] And so far as the proprietary services could tell, they had only one competitor other than each other: generative PCs that used their modems to call other PCs instead of the centralized services. Exactly how proprietary networks would have evolved if left only to that competition will never be known, for CompuServe and its proprietary counterparts were soon overwhelmed by the Internet and the powerful PC browsers used to access it.[17] But it is useful to recall how those PC-to-PC networks worked, and who built them.

A GRASSROOTS NETWORK OF PCs

Even before PC owners had an opportunity to connect to the Internet, they had an alternative to paying for appliancized proprietary networks. Several people wrote BBS ("bulletin board system") software that could turn any PC into its own information service.[18] Lacking ready arrangements with institutional content providers like the Associated Press, computers running BBS software largely depended on their callers to provide information as well as to consume it. Vibrant message boards, some with thousands of regular participants, sprang up. But they were limited by the physical properties and business model of the phone system that carried their data. Even though the *Carterfone* decision permitted the use of modems to connect users' computers, a PC hosting a BBS was limited to one incoming call at a time unless its owner wanted to pay for more phone lines and some arcane multiplexing equipment.[19] With many interested users having to share one incoming line to a BBS, it was the opposite of the proprietary connect time model: users were asked to spend as little time connected as possible.

PC generativity provided a way to ameliorate some of these limitations. A PC owner named Tom Jennings wrote FIDOnet in the spring of 1984.[20] FIDOnet was BBS software that could be installed on many PCs. Each FIDOnet BBS could call another in the FIDO network and they would exchange their respective message stores. That way, users could post messages to a single PC's BBS and find it copied automatically, relay-style, to hundreds of other BBSs around the world, with replies slowly working their way around to all the FIDOnet BBSs. In the fall of 1984 FIDOnet claimed 160 associated PCs; by the early 1990s it boasted 32,000, and many other programmers had made contributions to improve Jennings's work.[21]

Of course, FIDOnet was the ultimate kludge, simultaneously a testament to the distributed ingenuity of those who tinker with generative technologies and a crude workaround that was bound to collapse under its own weight. Jennings found that his network did not scale well, especially since it was built on top of a physical network whose primary use was to allow two people, not many computers, to talk to each other. As the FIDOnet community grew bigger, it was no longer a community—at least not a set of people who each knew one another. Some new FIDOnet installations had the wrong dial-in numbers for their peers, which meant that computers were calling people instead of other computers, redialing every time a computer did not answer.

"To impress on you the seriousness of wrong numbers in the node list," Jennings wrote, "imagine you are a poor old lady, who every single night is getting phone calls EVERY TWO MINUTES AT 4:00AM, no one says anything, then hangs up. This actually happened; I would sit up and watch when there was mail that didn't go out for a week or two, and I'd pick up the phone after dialing, and was left in the embarrasing [*sic*] position of having to explain bulletin boards to an extremely tired, extremely annoyed person."[22]

In some ways, this was the fear AT&T had expressed to the FCC during the *Carterfone* controversy. When AT&T was no longer allowed to perform quality control on the devices hooking up to the network, problems could arise and AT&T would reasonably disclaim responsibility. Jennings and others worked to fix software problems as they arose with new releases, but as FIDOnet authors wrestled with the consequences of their catastrophic success, it was clear that the proprietary services were better suited for mainstream consumers. They were more reliable, better advertised, and easier to use. But FIDOnet demonstrates that amateur innovation—cobbling together bits and pieces from volunteers—can produce a surprisingly functional and effective result— one that has been rediscovered today in some severely bandwidth-constrained areas of the world.[23]

Those with Jennings's urge to code soon had an alternative outlet, one that even the proprietary networks did not foresee as a threat until far too late: the Internet, which appeared to combine the reliability of the pay networks with the ethos and flexibility of user-written FIDOnet.

ENTER THE INTERNET

Just as the general-purpose PC beat leased and appliancized counterparts that could perform only their manufacturers' applications and nothing else, the Internet first linked to and then functionally replaced a host of proprietary consumer network services.[24]

The Internet's founding is pegged to a message sent on October 29, 1969. It was transmitted from UCLA to Stanford by computers hooked up to prototype "Interface Message Processors" (IMPs).[25] A variety of otherwise-incompatible computer systems existed at the time—just as they do now—and the IMP was conceived as a way to connect them.[26] (The UCLA programmers typed "log" to begin logging in to the Stanford computer. The Stanford computer crashed after the second letter, making "Lo" the first Internet message.)

From its start, the Internet was oriented differently from the proprietary networks and their ethos of bundling and control. Its goals were in some ways more modest. The point of building the network was not to offer a particular set of information or services like news or weather to customers, for which the network was necessary but incidental. Rather, it was to connect anyone on the network to anyone else. It was up to the people connected to figure out why they wanted to be in touch in the first place; the network would simply carry data between the two points.

The Internet thus has more in common with FIDOnet than it does with CompuServe, yet it has proven far more useful and flexible than any of the proprietary networks. Most of the Internet's architects were academics, amateurs like Tom Jennings in the sense that they undertook their work for the innate interest of it, but professionals in the sense that they could devote themselves full time to its development. They secured crucial government research funding and other support to lease some of the original raw telecommunications facilities that would form the backbone of the new network, helping to make the protocols they developed on paper testable in a real-world environment. The money supporting this was relatively meager—on the order of tens of millions of dollars from 1970 to 1990, and far less than a single popular startup raised in an initial public offering once the Internet had gone mainstream. (For example, ten-month-old, money-losing Yahoo! raised $35 million at its 1996 initial public offering.[27] On the first day it started trading, the offered chunk of the company hit over $100 million in value, for a total corporate valuation of more than $1 billion.[28])

The Internet's design reflects the situation and outlook of the Internet's framers: they were primarily academic researchers and moonlighting corporate engineers who commanded no vast resources to implement a global network.[29] The early Internet was implemented at university computer science departments, U.S. government research units,[30] and select telecommunications companies with an interest in cutting-edge network research.[31] These users might naturally work on advances in bandwidth management or tools for researchers to use for discussion with each other, including informal, non-work-related discussions. Unlike, say, FedEx, whose wildly successful paper transport network depended initially on the singularly focused application of venture capital to design and create an efficient physical infrastructure for delivery, those individuals thinking about the Internet in the 1960s and '70s planned a network that would cobble together existing research and government networks and then wring as much use as possible from them.[32]

The design of the Internet reflected not only the financial constraints of its creators, but also their motives. They had little concern for controlling the network or its users' behavior.[33] The network's design was publicly available and freely shared from the earliest moments of its development. If designers disagreed over how a particular protocol should work, they would argue until one had persuaded most of the interested parties. The motto among them was, "We reject: kings, presidents, and voting. We believe in: rough consensus and running code."[34] Energy spent running the network was seen as a burden rather than a boon. Keeping options open for later network use and growth was seen as sensible, and abuse of the network by those joining it without an explicit approval process was of little worry since the people using it were the very people designing it—engineers bound by their desire to see the network work.[35]

The Internet was so different in character and audience from the proprietary networks that few even saw them as competing with one another. However, by the early 1990s, the Internet had proven its use enough that some large firms were eager to begin using it for data transfers for their enterprise applications. It helped that the network was subsidized by the U.S. government, allowing flat-rate pricing for its users. The National Science Foundation (NSF) managed the Internet backbone and asked that it be used only for noncommercial purposes, but by 1991 was eager to see it privatized.[36] Internet designers devised an entirely new protocol so that the backbone no longer needed to be centrally managed by the NSF or a single private successor, paving the way for multiple private network providers to bid to take up chunks of the old backbone, with no one vendor wholly controlling it.[37]

Consumer applications were originally nowhere to be found, but that changed after the Internet began accepting commercial interconnections without network research pretexts in 1991. The public at large was soon able to sign up, which opened development of Internet applications and destinations to a broad, commercially driven audience.

No major PC producer immediately moved to design Internet Protocol compatibility into its PC operating system. PCs could dial in to a single computer like that of CompuServe or AOL and communicate with it, but the ability to run Internet-aware applications on the PC itself was limited. To attach to the Internet, one would need a minicomputer or workstation of the sort typically found within university computer science departments—and usually used with direct network connections rather than modems and phone lines.

A single hobbyist took advantage of PC generativity and forged the missing technological link. Peter Tattam, an employee in the psychology department of the University of Tasmania, wrote Trumpet Winsock, a program that allowed owners of PCs running Microsoft Windows to forge a point-to-point Internet connection with the dial-up servers run by nascent Internet Service Providers (ISPs).[38] With no formal marketing or packaging, Tattam distributed Winsock as shareware. He asked people to try out the program for free and to send him $25 if they kept using it beyond a certain tryout period.[39]

Winsock was a runaway success, and in the mid-1990s it was the primary way that Windows users could access the Internet. Even before there was wide public access to an Internet through which to distribute his software, he claimed hundreds of thousands of registrations for it,[40] and many more people were no doubt using it and declining to register. Consumer accessibility to Internet-enabled applications, coupled with the development of graphic-friendly World Wide Web protocols and the PC browsers to support them—both initially noncommercial ventures—marked the beginning of the end of proprietary information services and jerry-rigged systems like FIDOnet. Consumers began to explore the Internet, and those who wanted to reach this group, such as commercial merchants and advertising-driven content providers, found it easier to set up outposts there than through the negotiated gates of the proprietary services.

Microsoft bundled the functionality of Winsock with late versions of Windows 95.[41] After that, anyone buying a PC could hook up to the Internet instead of only to AOL's or CompuServe's walled gardens. Proprietary information services scrambled to reorient their business models away from corralled content and to ones of accessibility to the wider Internet.[42] Network providers offering a bundle of content along with access increasingly registered their appeal simply as ISPs. They became mere on-ramps to the Internet, with their users branching out to quickly thriving Internet destinations that had no relationship to the ISP for their programs and services.[43] For example, CompuServe's "Electronic Mall," an e-commerce service intended as the exclusive means by which outside vendors could sell products to CompuServe sub-scribers,[44] disappeared under the avalanche of individual Web sites selling goods to anyone with Internet access.

The resulting Internet was a network that no one in particular owned and that anyone could join. Of course, joining required the acquiescence of at least one current Internet participant, but if one was turned away at one place, there were innumerable other points of entry, and commercial ISPs emerged to provide service at commoditized rates.[45]

The bundled proprietary model, designed expressly for consumer uptake, had been defeated by the Internet model, designed without consumer demands in mind. Proprietary services tried to have everything under one roof and to vet each of their offerings, just as IBM leased its general-purpose computers to its 1960s customers and wholly managed them, tailoring them to those cus-tomers' perceived needs in an ordered way. The Internet had no substantive offerings at all—but also no meaningful barriers to someone else's setting up shop online. It was a model similar to that of the PC, a platform rather than a fully finished edifice, one open to a set of offerings from anyone who wanted to code for it.

DESIGN CHOICES AND THE INTERNET ETHOS

Recall that our endpoint devices can possess varying levels of accessibility to outside coding. Where they are found along that spectrum creates certain basic trade-offs. A less generative device like an information appliance or a general-purpose computer managed by a single vendor can work more smoothly be-cause there is only one cook over the stew, and it can be optimized to a particu-lar perceived purpose. But it cannot be easily adapted for new uses. A more generative device like a PC makes innovation easier and produces a broader range of applications because the audience of people who can adapt it to new uses is much greater. Moreover, these devices can at first be simpler because they can be improved upon later; at the point they leave the factory they do not have to be complete. That is why the first hobbyist PCs could be so inexpen-sive: they had only the basics, enough so that others could write software to make them truly useful. But it is harder to maintain a consistent experience with such a device because its behavior is then shaped by multiple software au-thors not acting in concert. Shipping an incomplete device also requires a cer-tain measure of trust: trust that at least some third-party software writers will write good and useful code, and trust that users of the device will be able to access and sort out the good and useful code from the bad and even potentially harmful code.

These same trade-offs existed between proprietary services and the Internet, and Internet design, like its generative PC counterpart, tilted toward the simple and basic. The Internet's framers made simplicity a core value—a risky bet with a high payoff. The bet was risky because a design whose main focus is simplicity may omit elaboration that solves certain foreseeable problems. The simple design that the Internet's framers settled upon makes sense only with a set of principles that go beyond mere engineering. These principles are not obvious ones—for example, the proprietary networks were not designed with them in mind—and their power depends on assumptions about people that, even if true, could change. The most important are what we might label the procrastination principle and the trust-your-neighbor approach.

The procrastination principle rests on the assumption that most problems confronting a network can be solved later or by others. It says that the network should not be designed to do anything that can be taken care of by its users. Its origins can be found in a 1984 paper by Internet architects David Clark, David Reed, and Jerry Saltzer. In it they coined the notion of an "end-to-end argument" to indicate that most features in a network ought to be implemented at its computer endpoints—and by those endpoints' computer programmers—rather than "in the middle," taken care of by the network itself, and designed by the network architects.[46] The paper makes a pure engineering argument, explaining that any features not universally useful should not be implemented, in part because not implementing these features helpfully prevents the generic network from becoming tilted toward certain uses. Once the network was optimized for one use, they reasoned, it might not easily be put to other uses that may have different requirements.

The end-to-end argument stands for modularity in network design: it allows the network nerds, both protocol designers and ISP implementers, to do their work without giving a thought to network hardware or PC software. More generally, the procrastination principle is an invitation to others to overcome the network's shortcomings, and to continue adding to its uses.

Another fundamental assumption, reflected repeatedly in various Internet design decisions that tilted toward simplicity, is about trust. The people using this network of networks and configuring its endpoints had to be trusted to be more or less competent and pure enough at heart that they would not intentionally or negligently disrupt the network. The network's simplicity meant that many features found in other networks to keep them secure from fools and knaves would be absent. Banks would be simpler and more efficient if they did not need vaults for the cash but could instead keep it in accessible bins in plain view. Our houses would be simpler if we did not have locks on our doors, and it would be ideal to catch a flight by following an unimpeded path from the airport entrance to the gate—the way access to many trains and buses persists today.

An almost casual trust for the users of secured institutions and systems is rarely found: banks are designed with robbers in mind. Yet the assumption that network participants can be trusted, and indeed that they will be participants rather than customers, infuses the Internet's design at nearly every level. Anyone can become part of the network so long as any existing member of the network is ready to share access. And once someone is on the network, the network's design is intended to allow all data to be treated the same way: it can be sent from anyone to anyone, and it can be in support of any application developed by an outsider.

Two examples illustrate these principles and their trade-offs: the Internet's lack of structure to manage personal identity, and its inability to guarantee transmission speed between two points.

There are lots of reasons for a network to be built to identify the people using it, rather than just the machines found on it. Proprietary networks like CompuServe and AOL were built just that way. They wanted to offer different services to different people, and to charge them accordingly, so they ensured that the very first prompt a user encountered when connecting to the network was to type in a prearranged user ID and password. No ID, no network access. This had the added benefit of accountability: anyone engaging in bad behavior on the network could have access terminated by whoever managed the IDs.

The Internet, however, has no such framework; connectivity is much more readily shared. User identification is left to individual Internet users and servers to sort out if they wish to demand credentials of some kind from those with whom they communicate. For example, a particular Web site might demand that a user create an ID and password in order to gain access to its contents.

This basic design omission has led to the well-documented headaches of identifying wrongdoers online, from those who swap copyrighted content to hackers who attack the network itself.[47] At best, a source of bad bits might be traced to a single Internet address. But that address might be shared by more than one person, or it might represent a mere point of access by someone at yet another address—a link in a chain of addresses that can recede into the distance. Because the user does not have to log in the way he or she would to use a proprietary service, identity is obscured. Some celebrate this feature. It can be seen as a bulwark against oppressive governments who wish to monitor their Internet-surfing populations. As many scholars have explored, whether one is for or against anonymity online, a design decision bearing on it, made first as an engineering matter, can end up with major implications for social interaction and regulation.[48]

Another example of the trade-offs of procrastination and trust can be found in the Internet's absence of "quality of service," a guarantee of bandwidth between one point and another. The Internet was designed as a network of networks—a bucket-brigade partnership in which network neighbors pass along each other's packets for perhaps ten, twenty, or even thirty hops between two points.[49] Internet Service Providers might be able to maximize their bandwidth for one or two hops along this path, but the cobbled-together nature of a typical Internet link from a source all the way to a destination means that there is no easy way to guarantee speed the whole way through. Too many intermediaries exist in between, and their relationship may be one of a handshake rather than a contract: "you pass my packets and I'll pass yours."[50] An endpoint several hops from a critical network intermediary will have no contract or arrangement at all with the original sender or the sender's ISP. The person at the endpoint must instead rely on falling dominos of trust. The Internet is thus known as a "best efforts" network, sometimes rephrased as "Send it and pray" or "Every packet an adventure."[51]

The Internet's protocols thus assume that all packets of data are intended to be delivered with equal urgency (or perhaps, more accurately, lack of urgency). This assumption of equality is a fiction because some packets are valuable only if they can make it to their destination in a timely way. Delay an e-mail by a minute or two and no one may be the poorer; delay a stream of music too long and there is an interruption in playback. The network could be built to prioritize a certain data stream on the basis of its sender, its recipient, or the nature of the stream's contents. Yet the Internet's framers and implementers have largely clung to simplicity, omitting an architecture that would label and then speed along "special delivery" packets despite the uses it might have and the efficiencies it could achieve. As the backbone grew, it did not seem to matter. Those with lots of content to share have found ways to stage data "near" its destination for others, and the network has proved itself remarkably effective even in areas, like video and audio transmission, in which it initially fell short.[52] The future need not resemble the past, however, and a robust debate exists today about the extent to which ISPs ought to be able to prioritize certain data streams over others by favoring some destinations or particular service providers over others.[53] (That debate is joined in a later chapter.)

*   *   *

The assumptions made by the Internet's framers and embedded in the network—that most problems could be solved later and by others, and that those others themselves would be interested in solving rather than creating problems—arose naturally within the research environment that gave birth to the Internet. For all the pettiness sometimes associated with academia, there was a collaborative spirit present in computer science research labs, in part because the project of designing and implementing a new network—connecting people—can benefit so readily from collaboration.

It is one thing for the Internet to work the way it was designed when deployed among academics whose raison d'être was to build functioning networks. But the network managed an astonishing leap as it continued to work when expanded into the general populace, one which did not share the worldview that informed the engineers' designs. Indeed, it not only continued to work, but experienced spectacular growth in the uses to which it was put. It is as if the bizarre social and economic configuration of the quasi-anarchist Burning Man festival turned out to function in the middle of a city.[54] What works in a desert is harder to imagine in Manhattan: people crashing on each others' couches, routinely sharing rides and food, and loosely bartering things of value.

At the turn of the twenty-first century, then, the developed world has found itself with a wildly generative information technology environment.

Today we enjoy an abundance of PCs hosting routine, if not always-on, broadband Internet connections.[55] The generative PC has become intertwined with the generative Internet, and the brief era during which information appliances and appliancized networks flourished—Brother word processors and CompuServe—might appear to be an evolutionary dead end.

Those alternatives are not dead. They have been only sleeping. To see why, we now turn to the next step of the pattern that emerges at each layer of generative technologies: initial success triggers expansion, which is followed by boundary, one that grows out of the very elements that make that layer appealing. The Internet flourished by beginning in a backwater with few expectations, allowing its architecture to be simple and fluid. The PC had parallel hobbyist backwater days. Each was first adopted in an ethos of sharing and tinkering, with profit ancillary, and each was then embraced and greatly improved by commercial forces. But each is now facing problems that call for some form of intervention, a tricky situation since intervention is not easy—and, if undertaken, might ruin the very environment it is trying to save. The next chapter explains this process at the technological layer: why the status quo is drawing to a close, confronting us—policy-makers, entrepreneurs, technology providers, and, most importantly, Internet and PC users—with choices we can no longer ignore.

3

Cybersecurity and the
Generative Dilemma

In 1988 there were about sixty thousand computers connected to the Internet. Few of them were PCs.[1] Instead, the Net was the province of mainframes, minicomputers, and professional workstations found at government offices, universities, and computer science research centers.[2] These computers were designed to allow different people to run software on them at the same time from multiple terminals, sharing valuable processor cycles the way adjoining neighbors might share a driveway.[3]

On the evening of November 2, 1988, many of these computers started acting strangely. Unusual documents appeared in the depths of their file systems, and their system logs recorded activities unrelated to anything the computers' regular users were doing. The computers also started to slow down. An inventory of the running code on the machines showed a number of rogue programs demanding processor time. Concerned administrators terminated these foreign programs, but they reappeared and then multiplied. Within minutes, some computers started running so slowly that their keepers were unable to investigate further. The machines were too busy attending to the wishes of the mysterious software.

System administrators discovered that renegade code was spreading through the Internet from one machine to another. In response, some unplugged their computers from the rest of the world, inoculating them from further attacks but sacrificing all communication. Others kept their machines plugged in and, working in groups, figured out how to kill the invading software and protect their machines against re-infection.

The software—now commonly thought of as the first Internet worm—was traced to a twenty-three-year-old Cornell University graduate student named Robert Tappan Morris, Jr. He had launched it by infecting a machine at MIT from his terminal in Ithaca, New York.[4] The worm identified other nearby computers on the Internet by rifling through various electronic address books found on the MIT machine.[5] Its purpose was simple: to transmit a copy of itself to the machines, where it would there run alongside existing software—and repeat the cycle.[6]

An estimated five to ten percent of all Internet-connected machines had been compromised by the worm in the span of a day. Gene Spafford of Purdue University called it an "attack from within."[7] The program had accessed the machines by using a handful of digital parlor tricks—tricks that allowed it to run without having an account on the machine. Sometimes it exploited a flaw in a commonly used e-mail transmission program running on the victimized computers, rewriting the program to allow itself in. Other times it simply guessed users' passwords.[8] For example, a user named jsmith often chose a password of . . . jsmith. And if not, the password was often obvious enough to be found on a list of 432 common passwords that the software tested at each computer.[9]

When asked why he unleashed the worm, Morris said he wanted to count how many machines were connected to the Internet. (Proprietary networks were designed to keep track of exactly how many subscribers they had; the simple Internet has no such mechanism.) Morris's program, once analyzed, accorded with this explanation, but his code turned out to be buggy. If Morris had done it right, his program would not have slowed down its infected hosts and thereby not drawn attention to itself. It could have remained installed for days or months, and it could have quietly performed a wide array of activities other than simply relaying a "present and accounted for" message to Morris's designated home base to assist in his digital nose count.

The university workstations of 1988 were generative: their users could write new code for them or install code written by others. The Morris worm was the first large-scale demonstration of a vulnerability of generativity: even in the custody of trained administrators, such machines could be commandeered and reprogrammed, and, if done skillfully, their users would probably not even notice. The opportunity for such quick reprogramming vastly expanded as these workstations were connected to the Internet and acquired the capacity to receive code from afar.

Networked computers able to retrieve and install code from anyone else on the network are much more flexible and powerful than their appliancized counterparts would be. But this flexibility and power are not without risks. Whether through a sneaky vector like the one Morris used, or through the front door, when a trusting user elects to install something that looks interesting but without fully inspecting it and understanding what it does, opportunities for accidents and mischief abound. Today's generative PCs are in a similar but more pronounced bind, one characterized by faster networks, more powerful processors, and less-skilled users.

A MILD AUTOIMMUNE REACTION

The no-longer-theoretical prospect that a large swath of Internet-connected computers could be compromised, and then contribute to the attack of others, created a stir. But to most, the Morris attack remained more a curiosity than a call to arms. Keith Bostic of the University of California–Berkeley computer science department described in a retrospective news account the fun of trying to puzzle out the problem and defeat the worm. "For us it was a challenge. . . . It wasn't a big deal."[10]

Others perceived the worm as a big deal but did little to fix the problem. The mainstream media had an intense but brief fascination with the incident.[11] A professional organization for computer scientists, the Association for Computing Machinery, devoted an issue of its distinguished monthly journal to the worm,[12] and members of Congress requested a report from its research arm, the U.S. General Accounting Office (GAO).[13]

The GAO report noted some ambiguities and difficulties in U.S. law that might make prosecution of worm- and virus-makers burdensome,[14] and called for the creation of a government committee to further consider Internet security, staffed by representatives of the National Science Foundation, the Department of Defense, and other agencies that had helped fund the Internet's development and operation.[15] At the time it was thought that the Internet would evolve into a "National Research Network," much larger and faster, but still used primarily by educational and other noncommercial entities in loose coordination with their U.S. government sponsors.[16] The most tangible result from the government inquiry was a Defense Department–funded program at Carnegie Mellon University called CERT/CC, the "Computer Emergency Response Team Coordination Center." It still exists today as a clearinghouse for information about viruses and other network threats.[17]

Cornell impaneled a commission to analyze what had gone wrong. Its report exonerated the university from institutional responsibility for the worm and laid the blame solely on Morris, who had, without assistance or others' knowledge, engaged in a "juvenile act" that was "selfish and inconsiderate."[18] It rebuked elements of the media that had branded Morris a hero for exposing security flaws in dramatic fashion, noting that it was well known that the computers' Unix operating systems had many security flaws, and that it was no act of "genius" to exploit such weaknesses.[19] The report called for a university-wide committee to advise the university on technical security standards and another to write a campus-wide acceptable use policy.[20] It described consensus among computer scientists that Morris's acts warranted some form of punishment, but not "so stern as to damage permanently the perpetrator's career."[21] That is just how Morris was punished. He apologized, and criminal prosecution for the act earned him three years of probation, four hundred hours of community service, and a $10,050 fine.[22] His career was not ruined. Morris transferred from Cornell to Harvard, founded a dot-com startup with some friends in 1995, and sold it to Yahoo! in 1998 for $49 million.[23] He finished his degree and is now a tenured professor at MIT.[24]

As a postmortem to the Morris worm incident, the Internet Engineering Task Force, the far-flung, unincorporated group of engineers who work on Internet standards and who have defined its protocols through a series of formal "request for comments" documents, or RFCs, published informational RFC 1135, titled "The Helminthiasis of the Internet."[25] RFC 1135 was titled and written with whimsy, echoing reminiscences of the worm as a fun challenge. The RFC celebrated that the original "old boy" network of "UNIX system wizards" was still alive and well despite the growth of the Internet: teams at university research centers put their heads together—on conference calls as well as over the Internet—to solve the problem.[26] After describing the technical details of the worm, the document articulated the need to instill and enforce ethical standards as new people (mostly young computer scientists like Morris) signed on to the Internet.[27]

These reactions to the Morris worm may appear laughably inadequate, an unwarranted triumph of the principles of procrastination and trust described earlier in this book. Urging users to patch their systems and asking hackers to behave more maturely might, in retrospect, seem naïve. To understand why these were the only concrete steps taken to prevent another worm incident— even a catastrophically destructive one—one must understand just how deeply computing architectures, both then and now, are geared toward flexibility rather than security, and how truly costly it would be to retool them.

THE GENERATIVE TRADE-OFF

To understand why the Internet-connected machines infected by the Morris worm were so vulnerable, consider the ways in which proprietary networks were more easily secured.

The U.S. long distance telephone network of the 1970s was intended to convey data between consumers in the form of telephone conversations. A group of hackers discovered that a tone at a frequency of 2,600 hertz sent over a telephone line did not reach the other side, but instead was used by the phone company to indicate to itself that the line was idle.[28] For example, the tone could be used by a pay phone to tell network owner AT&T that it was ready for the next call. It was not intended for customers to discover, much less use. As fortune would have it, a children's toy whistle packaged as a prize in boxes of Cap'n Crunch cereal could, when one hole was covered, generate a shrill tone at exactly that frequency.[29]

People in the know could then dial toll-free numbers from their home phones, blow the whistle to clear but not disconnect the line, and then dial a new, non-toll-free number, which would be connected without charge.[30] When this vulnerability came to light, AT&T was mortified, but it was also able to reconfigure the network so that the 2,600 hertz tone no longer controlled it.[31] Indeed, the entire protocol of *in-band* signaling could be and was eliminated. Controlling the network now required more than just a sound generated at a telephone mouthpiece on one end or the other. Data to be sent between customers and instructions intended to affect the network could be separated from one another, because AT&T's centralized control structure made it possible to separate the transfer of data (that is, conversations) between customers from instructions that affected network operations.[32]

The proprietary consumer networks of the 1980s used similar approaches to prevent network problems. No worm could spread on CompuServe in the same manner as Morris's, because CompuServe already followed the post– Cap'n Crunch rule: do not let the paths that carry data also carry code. The consumer computers attached to the CompuServe network were configured as mere "dumb terminals." They exchanged data, not programs, with Compu-Serve. Subscribers browsed weather, read the news, and posted messages to each other. Subscribers were not positioned easily to run software encountered through the CompuServe network, although on occasion and in very carefully labeled circumstances they could download new code to run on their genera-tive PCs separately from their dumb terminal software.[33] The mainframe com-puters at CompuServe with which those dumb terminals communicated ex-isted out of view, ensuring that the separation between users and programmers was strictly enforced.[34]

These proprietary networks were not user-programmable but instead relied on centralized feature rollouts performed exclusively by their administrators. The networks had only the features their owners believed would be economi-cally viable. Thus, the networks evolved slowly and with few surprises either good or bad. This made them both secure and sterile in comparison to genera-tive machines hooked up to a generative network like the Internet.

Contrary to CompuServe's proprietary system, the Internet of 1988 had no control points where one could scan network traffic for telltale wormlike be-haviors and then stop such traffic. Further, the Morris worm really was not per-ceived as a *network* problem, thanks to the intentional conceptual separation of network and endpoint. The Morris worm used the network to spread but did not attack it beyond slowing it down as the worm multiplied and continued to transmit itself. The worm's targets were the network's endpoints: the computers attached to it. The modularity that inspired the Internet's design meant that computer programming enthusiasts could write software for computers with-out having to know anything about the network that would carry the resulting data, while network geeks could devise new protocols with a willful ignorance of what programs would run on the devices hooked up to it, and what data would result from them. Such ignorance may have led those overseeing net-work protocols and operation unduly to believe that the worm was not some-thing they could have prevented, since it was not thought to be within their de-sign responsibility.

In the meantime, the endpoint computers could be compromised because they were general-purpose machines, running operating systems for which out-siders could write executable code.[35] Further, the operating systems and appli-cations running on the machines were not perfect; they contained flaws that rendered them more accessible to uninvited code than their designers in-tended.[36] Even without such flaws, the machines were intentionally designed to be operated at a distance, and to receive and run software sent from a distance. They were powered on and attached to the network continuously, even when not in active use by their owners. Moreover, many administrators of these machines were lazy about installing available fixes to known software vulnerabilities, and often utterly predictable in choosing passwords to protect entry to their computer accounts.[37] Since the endpoint computers infected by the worm were run and managed by disparate groups who answered to no single authority for their use, there was no way to secure them all against attack.[38]

A comparison with its proprietary network and information appliance counterparts, then, reveals the central security dilemma of yesterday's Internet that remains with us today: the proprietary networks did not have the Cap'n Crunch problem, and the Internet and its connected machines do. On the Internet, the channels of communication are also channels of control.[39] There is no appealing fix of the sort AT&T undertook for its phone network. If one applies the post–Cap'n Crunch rule and eliminates the ability to control PCs via the Internet—or the ability of the attached computers to initiate or accept such control—one has eliminated the network's generative quality. Such an action would not merely be inconvenient, it would be incapacitating. Today we need merely to click to install new code from afar, whether to watch a video newscast embedded within a Web page or to install whole new applications like word processors or satellite image browsers. That quality is essential to the way in which we use the Internet.

It is thus not surprising that there was little impetus to institute changes in the network in response to the Morris worm scare, even though Internet-connected computers suffered from a fundamental security vulnerability. The decentralized, nonproprietary ownership of the Internet and the computers it linked made it difficult to implement any structural revisions to the way it functioned, and, more important, it was simply not clear what curative changes could be made that did not entail drastic, wholesale, purpose-altering changes to the very fabric of the Internet. Such changes would be so wildly out of proportion with the perceived level of threat that the records of postworm discussion lack any indication that they were even considered.

As the next chapter will explore, generative systems are powerful and valuable, not only because they foster the production of useful things like Web browsers, auction sites, and free encyclopedias, but also because they can allow an extraordinary number of people to express themselves in speech, art, or code and to work with other people in ways previously not possible. These characteristics can make generative systems very successful even though they lack central coordination and control. That success draws more participants to the generative system. Then it stalls.

Generative systems are built on the notion that they are never fully complete, that they have many uses yet to be conceived of, and that the public can be trusted to invent and share good uses. Multiplying breaches of that trust can threaten the very foundations of the generative system. A hobbyist computer that crashes might be a curiosity, but when a home or office PC with years' worth of vital correspondence and papers is compromised it can be a crisis. As such events become commonplace throughout the network, people will come to prefer security to generativity. If we can understand how the generative Internet and PC have made it as far as they have without true crisis, we can predict whether they can continue, and what would transpire following a breaking point. There is strong evidence that the current state of affairs is not sustainable, and what comes next may exact a steep price in generativity.

AN UNTENABLE STATUS QUO

The Internet and its generative machines have muddled along pretty well since 1988, despite the fact that today's PCs are direct descendants of that era's unsecured workstations. In fact, it is striking how *few* truly disruptive security incidents have happened since 1988. Rather, a network designed for communication among academic and government researchers appeared to scale beautifully as hundreds of millions of new users signed on during the 1990s, a feat all the more impressive when one considers how demographically different the new users were from the 1988 crowd. However heedless the network administrators of the late '80s were to good security practice, the mainstream consumers of the '90s were categorically worse. Few knew how to manage or code their generative PCs, much less how to rigorously apply patches or observe good password security.

The threat presented by bad code has slowly but steadily increased since 1988. The slow pace, which has let it remain a back-burner issue, is the result of several factors which are now rapidly attenuating. First, the computer scientists of 1988 were right that the hacker ethos frowns upon destructive hacking.[40] Morris's worm did more damage than he intended, and for all the damage it did do, the worm *had no payload other than itself.* Once a system was compromised by the worm it would have been trivial for Morris to have directed the worm to, for instance, delete as many files as possible.[41] Morris did not do this, and the overwhelming majority of viruses that followed in the 1990s reflected similar authorial forbearance. In fact, the most well-known viruses of the '90s had completely innocuous payloads. For example, 2004's Mydoom spread like wildfire and affected connectivity for millions of computers around the world. Though it reputedly cost billions of dollars in lost productivity, the worm did not tamper with data, and it was programmed to stop spreading at a set time.[42]

The bad code of the '90s merely performed attacks for the circular purpose of spreading further, and its damage was measured by the effort required to eliminate it at each site of infection and by the burden placed upon network traffic as it spread, rather than by the number of files it destroyed or by the amount of sensitive information it compromised. There are only a few exceptions. The infamous Lovebug worm, released in May 2000, caused the largest outages and damage to Internet-connected PCs to date.[43] It affected more than just connectivity: it overwrote documents, music, and multimedia files with copies of itself on users' hard drives. In the panic that followed, software engineers and antivirus vendors mobilized to defeat the worm, and it was ultimately eradicated.[44] Lovebug was an anomaly. The few highly malicious viruses of the time were otherwise so poorly coded that they failed to spread very far. The Michelangelo virus created sharp anxiety in 1992, when antivirus companies warned that millions of hard drives could be erased by the virus's dangerous payload. It was designed to trigger itself on March 6, the artist's birthday. The number of computers actually affected was only in the tens of thousands—it spread only through the pre-Internet exchange of infected floppy diskettes— and it was soon forgotten.[45] Had Michelangelo's birthday been a little later in the year—giving the virus more time to spread before springing—it could have had a much greater impact. More generally, malicious viruses can be coded to avoid the problems of real-world viruses whose virulence helps stop their spread. Some biological viruses that incapacitate people too quickly can burn themselves out, destroying their hosts before their hosts can help them spread further.[46] Human-devised viruses can be intelligently designed—finetuned to spread before biting, or to destroy data within their hosts while still using the host to continue spreading.

Another reason for the delay of truly destructive malware is that network operations centers at universities and other institutions became more professionalized between the time of the Morris worm and the advent of the mainstream consumer Internet. For a while, most of the Internet's computers were staffed by professional administrators who generally heeded admonitions to patch regularly and scout for security breaches. They carried beepers and were prepared to intervene quickly in the case of an intrusion. Less adept mainstream consumers began connecting unsecured PCs to the Internet in earnest only in the mid-1990s. At first their machines were hooked up only through transient dial-up connections. This greatly limited both the amount of time per day during which they were exposed to security threats, and the amount of time that, if compromised and hijacked, they would themselves contribute to the problem.[47]

Finally, there was no business model backing bad code. Programs to trick users into installing them, or to bypass users entirely and just sneak onto the machine, were written only for fun or curiosity, just like the Morris worm. There was no reason for substantial financial resources to be invested in their creation, or in their virulence once created. Bad code was more like graffiti than illegal drugs. Graffiti is comparatively easier to combat because there are no economic incentives for its creation.[48] The demand for illegal drugs creates markets that attract sophisticated criminal syndicates.

Today each of these factors has substantially diminished. The idea of a Net-wide set of ethics has evaporated as the network has become so ubiquitous. Anyone is allowed online if he or she can find a way to a computer and a connection, and mainstream users are transitioning to always-on broadband. In July 2004 there were more U.S. consumers on broadband than on dial-up,[49] and two years later, nearly twice as many U.S. adults had broadband connections in their homes than had dial-up.[50] PC user awareness of security issues, however, has not kept pace with broadband growth. A December 2005 online safety study found 81 percent of home computers to be lacking first-order protection measures such as current antivirus software, spyware protection, and effective firewalls.[51] The Internet's users are no longer skilled computer scientists, yet the PCs they own are more powerful than the fastest machines of the 1980s. Because modern computers are so much more powerful, they can spread malware with greater efficiency than ever.

Perhaps most significantly, there is now a business model for bad code—one that gives many viruses and worms payloads for purposes other than simple reproduction.[52] What seemed truly remarkable when it was first discovered is now commonplace: viruses that compromise PCs to create large "botnets" open to later instructions. Such instructions have included directing the PC to become its own e-mail server, sending spam by the thousands or millions to e-mail addresses harvested from the hard disk of the machine itself or gleaned from Internet searches, with the entire process typically unnoticeable to the PC's owner. At one point, a single botnet occupied 15 percent of Yahoo's entire search capacity, running random searches on Yahoo to find text that could be inserted into spam e-mails to throw off spam filters.[53] One estimate pegs the number of PCs involved in such botnets at 100 to 150 million, or a quarter of all the computers on the Internet as of early 2007,[54] and the field is expanding: a study monitoring botnet activity in 2006 detected, on average, the emergence of 1 million new bots per month.[55] But as one account pulling together various guesses explains, the science is inexact:

> MessageLabs, a company that counts spam, recently stopped counting bot-infected computers because it literally could not keep up. It says it quit when the figure passed about 10 million a year ago. Symantec Corp. recently said it counted 6.7 million active bots during an Internet scan. Since all bots are not active at any given time, the number of infected computers is likely much higher. And Dave Dagon, who recently left Georgia Tech University to start a bot-fighting company named Damballa, pegs the number at closer to 30 million. The firm uses a "capture, mark, and release," strategy borrowed from environmental science to study the movement of bot armies and estimate their size.

> "It's like asking how many people are on the planet, you are wrong the second you give the answer. . . . But the number is in the tens of millions," Dagon said. "Had you told me five years ago that organized crime would control 1 out of every 10 home machines on the Internet, I would have not have believed that. And yet we are in an era where this is something that is happening."[56]

In one notable experiment conducted in the fall of 2003, a researcher connected a PC to the Internet that simulated running an "open proxy"—a condition in which many PC users unintentionally find themselves.[57] Within nine hours, spammers' worms located the computer and began attempting to commandeer it. Sixty-six hours later the researcher had recorded attempts to send 229,468 distinct messages to 3,360,181 would-be recipients.[58] (The researcher's computer pretended to deliver on the spam, but in fact threw it away.) Such zombie computers were responsible for more than 80 percent of the world's spam in June 2006, and spam in turn accounted for an estimated 80 percent of the world's total e-mail.[59] North American PCs led the world in December 2006, producing approximately 46 percent of the world's spam.[60] That spam produces profit, as a large enough number of people actually buy the items advertised or invest in the stocks touted.[61]

Botnets can also be used to launch coordinated attacks on a particular Internet endpoint. For example, a criminal can attack an Internet gambling Web site and then extort payment to make the attacks stop. The going rate for a botnet to launch such an attack is reputed to be about $50,000 per day.[62] Virus makers compete against each other to compromise PCs exclusively, some even using their access to install hacked versions of antivirus software on victim computers so that they cannot be poached away by other viruses.[63] The growth of virtual worlds and massively multiplayer online games provides another economic incentive for virus creators. As more and more users log in, create value, and buy and sell virtual goods, some are figuring out ways to turn such virtual goods into real-world dollars. Viruses and phishing e-mails target the acquisition of gaming passwords, leading to virtual theft measured in real money.[64]

The economics is implacable: viruses are now valuable properties, and that makes for a burgeoning industry in virus making where volume matters. Well-crafted worms and viruses routinely infect vast swaths of Internet-connected personal computers. In 2004, for example, the Sasser worm infected more than half a million computers in three days. The Sapphire/Slammer worm in January 2003 went after a particular kind of Microsoft server and infected 90 percent of those servers, about 120,000 of them, within *ten minutes*. Its hijacked machines together were performing fifty-five million searches per second for new targets just three minutes after the first computer fell victim to it. The sobig.f virus was released in August 2003 and within two days accounted for approximately 70 percent of all e-mail in the world, causing 23.2 million virus-laden e-mails to arrive on AOL's doorstep alone. Sobig was designed by its author to expire a few weeks later.[65] In May 2006 a virus exploiting a vulnerability in Microsoft Word propagated through the computers of the U.S. Department of State in eastern Asia, forcing the machines to be taken offline during critical weeks prior to North Korea's missile tests.[66]

Antivirus companies receive about two reports a minute of possible new viruses in the wild, and have abandoned individual review by staff in favor of automated sorting of viruses to investigate only the most pressing threats.[67] Antivirus vendor Eugene Kaspersky of Kaspersky Labs told an industry conference that antivirus vendors "may not be able to withstand the onslaught."[68] Another vendor executive said more directly: "I think we've failed."[69]

CERT/CC's malware growth statistics confirm the anecdotes. The organization began documenting the number of attacks—called "incidents"—against Internet-connected systems from its founding in 1988, as reproduced in Figure 3.1.

The increase in incidents since 1997 has been roughly geometric, doubling each year through 2003. In 2004, CERT/CC announced that it would no longer keep track of the figure, since attacks had become so commonplace and widespread as to be indistinguishable from one another.[70] IBM's Internet Se-

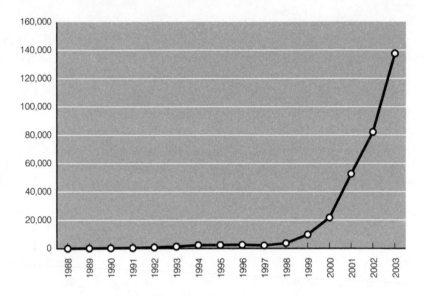

Figure 3.1 Number of security incidents reported to CERT/CC, 1988–2003. *Source:* CERT Coordination Center, CERT/CC Statistics 1988–2005, http://www.cert.org/stats#incidents.

curity Systems reported a 40 percent increase in Internet vulnerabilities—situations in which a machine was compromised, allowing access or control by attackers—between 2005 and 2006.[71] Nearly all of those vulnerabilities could be exploited remotely, and over half allowed attackers to gain full access to the machine and its contents.[72] Recall that at the time of the Morris worm there were estimated to be 60,000 distinct computers on the Internet. In July 2006 the same metrics placed the count at over 439 million.[73] Worldwide there were approximately 1.1 billion e-mail users in 2006.[74] By one credible estimate, there will be over 290 million PCs in use in the United States by 2010 and 2 billion PCs in use worldwide by 2011.[75] In part because the U.S. accounts for 18 percent of the world's computer users, it leads the world in almost every type of commonly measured security incident (Table 3.1, Figure 3.2).[76]

These numbers show that viruses are not simply the province of computing backwaters, away from the major networks where there has been time to develop effective countermeasures and best practices. Rather, the war is being lost across the board. Operating system developers struggle to keep up with providing patches for newly discovered computer vulnerabilities. Patch development time increased throughout 2006 for all of the top operating system providers (Figure 3.3).[77]

Table 3.1. Rankings of malicious activity by country

Country	Malicious Code	Spam Hosts	Command and Control Services	Phishing Hosts	Bots	Attacks
United States	1	1	1	1	2	1
China	3	2	4	8	1	2
Germany	7	3	3	2	4	3
France	9	4	14	4	3	4
United Kingdom	4	13	9	3	6	6
South Korea	12	9	2	9	11	9
Canada	5	23	5	7	10	5
Spain	13	5	15	16	5	7
Taiwan	8	11	6	6	7	11
Italy	2	8	10	14	12	10

Source: SYMANTEC CORP., SYMANTEC INTERNET SECURITY THREAT REPORT: TRENDS FOR JULY–DECEMBER 06, at 9 (2007) [hereinafter SYMANTEC INTERNET SECURITY THREAT REPORT], http://eval.symantec.com/mktginfo/enterprise/white_papers/ent-whitepaper_internet_security_threat_report_xi_03_2007.en-us.pdf.

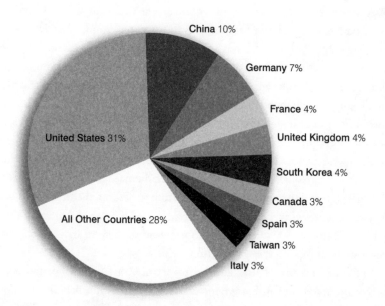

Figure 3.2 Countries as a percentage of all detected malicious activity. *Source:* SYMANTEC INTERNET SECURITY THREAT REPORT at 26.

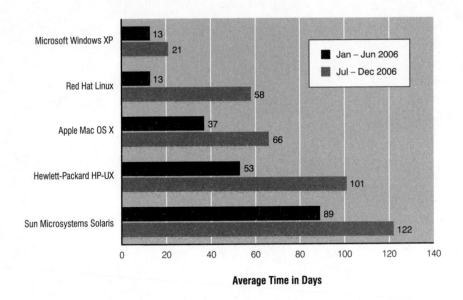

Figure 3.3 Patch development time by operating system. *Source:* SYMANTEC INTERNET SECURITY THREAT REPORT at 39–40.

Antivirus researchers and firms require extensive coordination efforts just to agree on a naming scheme for viruses as they emerge—much less a strategy for battling them.[78] Today, the idea of casually cleaning a virus off of a PC once it has been infected has been abandoned. When computers are compromised, users are now typically advised to completely reinstall everything on them—either losing all their data or laboriously figuring out what to save and what to exorcise. For example, in 2007, some PCs at the U.S. National Defense University fell victim to a virus. The institution shut down its network servers for two weeks and distributed new laptops to instructors, because "the only way to ensure the security of the systems was to replace them."[79]

One Microsoft program manager colorfully described the situation: "When you are dealing with rootkits and some advanced spyware programs, the only solution is to rebuild from scratch. In some cases, there really is no way to recover without nuking the systems from orbit."[80]

In the absence of such drastic measures, a truly "mal" piece of malware could be programmed to, say, erase hard drives, transpose numbers inside spreadsheets randomly, or intersperse nonsense text at random intervals in Word documents found on infected computers—and nothing would stand in the way.

A massive number of always-on powerful PCs with high-bandwidth connections to the Internet and run by unskilled users is a phenomenon new to the twenty-first century.[81] This unprecedented set of circumstances leaves the PC and the Internet vulnerable to across-the-board compromise. If one carries forward the metaphor of "virus" from its original public health context,[82] today's viruses are highly and near-instantly communicable, capable of causing worldwide epidemics in a matter of hours.[83] The symptoms may reveal themselves to users upon infection or they may lie in remission, at the whim of the virus author, while the virus continues to spread. Even fastidiously protected systems can suffer from a widespread infection, since the spread of a virus can disrupt network connectivity. And, as mentioned earlier, sometimes viruses are programmed to attack a particular network host by sending it a barrage of requests. Summed across all infected machines, such a distributed denial of service attack can ruin even the most well-connected and well-defended server, even if the server itself is not infected.

The compounded threat to the system of generative PCs on a generative network that arises from the system's misuse hinges on both the ability of a few malicious experts to bring down the system and this presence of a large field of always-connected, easily exploited computers. Scholars like Paul Ohm caution that the fear inspired by anecdotes of a small number of dangerous hackers should not provide cause for overbroad policy, noting that security breaches come from many sources, including laptop theft and poor business practices.[84] Ohm's concern about regulatory overreaction is not misplaced. Nonetheless, what empirical data we have substantiate the gravity of the problem, and the variety of ways in which modern mainstream information technology can be subverted does not lessen the concern about any given vector of compromise. Both the problem and the likely solutions are cause for concern.

Recognition of the basic security problem has been slowly growing in Internet research communities. Nearly two-thirds of academics, social analysts, and industry leaders surveyed by the Pew Internet & American Life Project in 2004 predicted serious attacks on network infrastructure or the power grid in the coming decade.[85] Though few appear to employ former U.S. cybersecurity czar Richard Clarke's evocative language of a "digital Pearl Harbor,"[86] experts are increasingly aware of the vulnerability of Internet infrastructure to attack.[87]

When will we know that something truly has to give? There are at least two possible models for a fundamental shift in our tolerance of the status quo: a collective watershed security moment, or a more glacial death of a thousand cuts. Both are equally threatening to the generativity of the Internet.

A WATERSHED SCENARIO

Suppose that a worm is released that exploits security flaws both in a commonly used Web server and in a Web browser found on both Mac and Windows platforms. The worm quickly spreads through two mechanisms. First, it randomly knocks on the doors of Internet-connected machines, immediately infecting vulnerable Web servers that answer the knock. Unwitting consumers, using vulnerable Internet browsers, visit the infected servers, which infect users' computers. Compromised machines become zombies, awaiting direction from the worm's author. The worm asks its zombies to look for other nearby machines to infect for a day or two and then tells the machines to erase their own hard drives at the stroke of midnight, adjusting for time zones to make sure the collective crash takes place at the same time around the globe.

This is not science fiction. It is merely another form of the Morris episode, a template that has been replicated countless times since, so often that those who run Web servers are often unconcerned about exploits that might have crept into their sites. Google and StopBadware.org, which collaborate on tracking and eliminating Web server exploits, report hundredfold increases in exploits between August 2006 and March 2007. In February 2007, Google found 11,125 infected servers on a web crawl.[88] A study conducted in March 2006 by Google researchers found that out of 4.5 million URLs analyzed as potentially hosting malicious code, 1.15 million URLs were indeed distributing malware.[89] Combine one well-written worm of the sort that can penetrate firewalls and evade antivirus software with one truly malicious worm-writer, and we have the prospect of a panic-generating event that could spill over to the real world: no check-in at some airline counters using Internet-connected PCs; no overnight deliveries or other forms of package and letter distribution; no payroll software producing paychecks for millions of workers; the elimination, release, or nefarious alteration of vital personal records hosted at medical offices, schools, town halls, and other data repositories that cannot afford a full-time IT staff to perform backups and ward off technological demons. Writing and distributing such a worm could be a tempting act of information warfare by any of the many enemies of modernity—asymmetric warfare at that, since the very beliefs that place some enemies at odds with the developed world may lead them to rely less heavily on modern IT themselves.

A GLACIAL SHIFT

The watershed scenario is plausible, but a major malware catastrophe depends on just the right combination of incentives, timing, and luck. Truly malicious foes like terrorists may see Internet-distributed viruses as damaging but refrain from pursuing them because they are not terror-inducing: such events simply do not create fear the way that lurid physical attacks do. Hackers who hack for fun still abide by the ethic of doing no or little harm by their exploits. And those who hack for profit gain little if their exploits are noticed and disabled, much less if they should recklessly destroy the hosts they infect.

Hacking a machine to steal and exploit any personal data within is currently labor-intensive; credit card numbers can be found more easily through passive network monitoring or through the distribution of phishing e-mails designed to lure people voluntarily to share sensitive information.[90] (To be sure, as banks and other sensitive destinations increase security on their Web sites through such tools as two-factor authentication, hackers may be more attracted to PC vulnerabilities as a means of compromise.[91] A few notable instances of bad code directed to this purpose could make storing data on one's PC seem tantamount to posting it on a public Web site.)

Finally, even without major security innovations, there are incremental improvements made to the growing arsenals of antivirus software, updated more quickly thanks to always-on broadband and boasting ever more comprehensive databases of viruses. Antivirus software is increasingly being bundled with new PCs or built into their operating systems.

These factors defending us against a watershed event are less effective against the death of a thousand cuts. The watershed scenario, indeed any threat following the Morris worm model, is only the most dramatic rather than most likely manifestation of the problem. Good antivirus software can still stop obvious security threats, but much malware is no longer so manifestly bad. Consider the realm of "badware" beyond viruses and worms. Most spyware, for example, purports to perform some useful function for the user, however halfheartedly it delivers. The nefarious Jessica Simpson screensaver does in fact show images of Jessica Simpson—and it also modifies the operation of other programs to redirect Web searches and installs spyware programs that cannot be uninstalled.[92] The popular file-sharing program KaZaA, though advertised as "spyware-free," contains code that users likely do not want. It adds icons to the desktop, modifies Microsoft Internet Explorer, and installs a program that cannot be closed by clicking "Quit." Uninstalling the program does not uninstall all these extras along with it, and the average user does not have the know-how to get rid of the code itself. FunCade, a downloadable arcade program, automatically installs spyware, adware, and remote control software designed to turn the PC into a zombie when signaled from afar. The program is installed while Web surfing. It deceives the user by opening a pop-up ad that looks like a Windows warning notice, telling the user to beware. Click "cancel" and the download starts.[93]

What makes such badware bad is often subjective rather than objective, having to do with the level of disclosure made to a consumer before he or she installs it. That means it is harder to intercept with automatic antivirus tools. For example, VNC is a free program designed to let people access other computers from afar—a VNC server is placed on the target machine, and a VNC client on the remote machine. Whether this is or is not malware depends entirely on the knowledge and intentions of the people on each end of a VNC connection. I have used VNC to access several of my own computers in the United States and United Kingdom simultaneously. I could also imagine someone installing VNC in under a minute after borrowing someone else's computer to check e-mail, and then using it later to steal personal information or to take over the machine. A flaw in a recent version of VNC's password processor allowed it to be accessed by anyone[94]—as I discovered one day when my computer's mouse started moving itself all over the screen and rapid-fire instructions appeared in the computer's command window. I fought with an unseen enemy for control of my own mouse, finally unplugging the machine the way some Morris worm victims had done twenty years earlier. (After disconnecting the machine from the network, I followed best practices and reinstalled everything on the machine from scratch to ensure that it was no longer compromised.)

BEYOND BUGS: THE GENERATIVE DILEMMA

The burgeoning gray zone of software explains why the most common responses to the security problem cannot solve it. Many technologically savvy people think that bad code is simply a Microsoft Windows issue. They believe that the Windows OS and the Internet Explorer browser are particularly poorly designed, and that "better" counterparts (Linux and Mac OS, or the Firefox and Opera browsers) can help protect a user. This is not much added protection. Not only do these alternative OSes and browsers have their own vulnerabilities, but the fundamental problem is that the point of a PC—regardless of its OS—is that its users can easily reconfigure it to run new software from anywhere.

When users make poor decisions about what new software to run, the results can be devastating to their machines and, if they are connected to the Internet, to countless others' machines as well. To be sure, Microsoft Windows has been the target of malware infections for years, but this in part reflects Microsoft's dominant market share. Recall Willie Sutton's explanation for robbing banks: that's where the money is.[95] As more users switch to other platforms, those platforms will become more appealing targets. And the most enduring way to subvert them may be through the front door, asking a user's permission to add some new functionality that is actually a bad deal, rather than trying to steal in through the back, silently exploiting some particular OS flaw that allows new code to run without the user or her antivirus software noticing.

The Microsoft Security Response Center offers "10 Immutable Laws of Security."[96] The first assumes that the PC is operating exactly as it is meant to, with the user as the weak link in the chain: "If a bad guy can persuade you to run his program on your computer, it's not your computer anymore."[97] This boils down to an admonition to the user to be careful, to try to apply judgment in areas where the user is often at sea:

> That's why it's important to never run, or even download, a program from an untrusted source—and by "source," I mean the person who wrote it, not the person who gave it to you. There's a nice analogy between running a program and eating a sandwich. If a stranger walked up to you and handed you a sandwich, would you eat it? Probably not. How about if your best friend gave you a sandwich? Maybe you would, maybe you wouldn't—it depends on whether she made it or found it lying in the street. Apply the same critical thought to a program that you would to a sandwich, and you'll usually be safe.[98]

The analogy of software to sandwiches is not ideal. The ways in which we pick up code while surfing the Internet is more akin to accepting a few nibbles of food from hundreds of different people over the course of the day, some established vendors, some street peddlers. Further, we have certain evolutionary gifts that allow us to directly judge whether food has spoiled by its sight and smell. There is no parallel way for us to judge programming code which arrives as an opaque ".exe." A closer analogy would be if many people we encountered over the course of a day handed us pills to swallow and often conditioned entrance to certain places on our accepting them. In a world in which we routinely benefit from software produced by unknown authors, it is impractical to apply the "know your source" rule.

Worse, surfing the World Wide Web often entails accepting and running new code. The Web was designed to seamlessly integrate material from disparate sources: a single Web page can draw from hundreds of different sources on the fly, not only through hyperlinks that direct users to other locations on the Web, but through placeholders that incorporate data and code from elsewhere into the original page. These Web protocols have spawned the massive advertising industry that powers companies like Google. For example, if a user visits the home page of the *New York Times,* he or she will see banner ads and other spaces that are filled on the fly from third-party advertising aggregators like Google and DoubleClick. These ads are not hosted at nytimes.com—they are hosted elsewhere and rushed directly to the user's browser as the nytimes .com page is rendered. To extend Microsoft's sandwich metaphor: Web pages are like fast food hamburgers, where a single patty might contain the blended meat of hundreds of cows spanning four countries.[99] In the fast food context, one contaminated carcass is reported to be able to pollute eight tons of ground meat.[100] For the Web, a single advertisement contaminated with bad code can instantly be circulated to those browsing tens of thousands of mainstream Web sites operated entirely in good faith. To visit a Web site is not only to be asked to trust the Web site operator. It is also to trust every third party—such as an ad syndicator—whose content is automatically incorporated into the Web site owner's pages, and every *fourth* party—such as an advertiser—who in turn provides content to that third party. Apart from advertising, generative technologies like RSS ("really simple syndication") have facilitated the automated repackaging of information from one Web site to another, creating tightly coupled networks of data flows that can pass both the latest world news and the latest PC attacks in adjoining data packets.

Bad code through the back door of a bug exploit and the front door of a poor user choice can intersect. At the Black Hat Europe hacker convention in 2006, two computer scientists gave a presentation on Skype, the wildly popular PC Internet telephony software created by the same duo that invented the KaZaA file-sharing program.[101] Skype is, like most proprietary software, a black box. It is not easy to know how it works or what it does except by watching it in action. Skype is installed on millions of computers, and so far works well if not flawlessly. It generates all sorts of network traffic, much of which is unidentifiable even to the user of the machine, and much of which happens even when Skype is not being used to place a call. How does one know that Skype is not doing something untoward, or that its next update might not contain a zombie-creating Trojan horse, placed by either its makers or someone who compromised the update server? The Black Hat presenters reverse engineered Skype enough to find a few flaws. What would happen if they were exploited? Their PowerPoint slide title may only slightly exaggerate: "Biggest Botnet Ever."[102] Skype is likely fine. I use it myself. Of course, I use VNC, too, and look where that ended up. The most salient feature of a PC is its openness to new functionality with minimal gatekeeping. This is also its greatest danger.

PC VS. INFORMATION APPLIANCE

PC users have increasingly found themselves the victims of bad code. In addition to overtly malicious programs like viruses and worms, their PCs are plagued with software that they have nominally asked for that creates pop-up windows, causes crashes, and damages useful applications. With increasing pressure from these experiences, consumers will be pushed in one of two unfortunate directions: toward independent information appliances that optimize a particular application and that naturally reject user or third-party modifications, or toward a form of PC lockdown that resembles the centralized control that IBM exerted over its rented mainframes in the 1960s, or that CompuServe and AOL exerted over their information services in the 1980s. In other words, consumers find themselves frustrated by PCs at a time when a variety of information appliances are arising as substitutes for the activities they value most. Digital video recorders, mobile phones, BlackBerries, and video game consoles will offer safer and more consistent experiences. Consumers will increasingly abandon the PC for these alternatives, or they will demand that the PC itself be appliancized.

That appliancization might come from the same firms that produced some of the most popular generative platforms. Microsoft's business model for PC operating systems has remained unchanged from the founding days of DOS through the Windows of today: the company sells each copy of the operating system at a profit, usually to PC makers rather than to end users. The PC makers then bundle Windows on the machine before it arrives at the customer's doorstep. As is typical for products that benefit from network externalities, having others write useful code associated with Windows, whether a new game, business application, or utility, makes Windows more valuable. Microsoft's interest in selling Windows is more or less aligned with an interest in making the platform open to third-party development.

The business models of the new generation of Internet-enabled appliances are different. Microsoft's Xbox 360 is a video game console that has as much computing power as a PC.[103] It is networked, so users can play games against other players around the world, at least if they are using Xboxes, too. The business model differs from that of the PC: it is Gillette's "give them the razor, sell them the blades." Microsoft loses money on every Xbox it sells. It makes that money back through the sale of games and other software to run on the Xbox. Third-party developers can write Xbox games, but they must obtain a license from Microsoft before they can distribute them—a license that includes giving Microsoft a share of profits.[104] This reflects the model the video game console market has used since the 1970s. But the Xbox is not just a video game console. It can access the Internet and perform other PC-like functions. It is occupying many of the roles of the gamer PC without being generative. Microsoft retains a privileged position with respect to reprogramming the machine, even after it is in users' hands: all changes must be certified by Microsoft. While this action would be considered an antitrust violation if applied to a PC operating system that enjoyed overwhelming market share,[105] it is the norm when applied to video game consoles.

To the extent that consoles like the Xbox take on some of the functions of the PC, consumers will naturally find themselves choosing between the two. The PC will offer a wider range of software, thanks to its generativity, but the Xbox might look like a better deal in the absence of a solution to the problem of bad code. It is reasonable for a consumer to factor security and stability into such a choice, but it is a poor choice to have to make. As explained in Chapter Five, the drawbacks of migration to non-generative alternatives go beyond the factors driving individual users' decisions.

Next-generation video game consoles are not the only appliances vying for a chunk of the PC's domain. With a handful of exceptions, mobile phones are in the same category: they are smart, and many can access the Internet, but the access is channeled through browsers provided and controlled by the phone service vendor. The vendor can determine what bookmarks to preinstall or update, what sites to allow or disallow, and, more generally, what additional software, if any, can run on the phone.[106] Many personal digital assistants come with software provided through special arrangements between device and software vendors, as Sony's Mylo does with Skype. Software makers without deals cannot have their code run on the devices, even if the user desires it. In 2006, AMD introduced the "Telmex Internet Box," which looks just like a PC but cannot run any new software without AMD's permission. It will run any software AMD chooses to install on it, even after the unit has been purchased.[107] Devices like these may be safer to use, and they may seem capacious in features so long as they offer a simple Web browser, but by limiting the damage that users can do through their own ignorance or carelessness, the appliance also limits the beneficial activities that users can create or receive from others— activities they may not even realize are important to them when they are purchasing the device.

Problems with generative PC platforms can thus propel people away from PCs and toward information appliances controlled by their makers. Eliminate the PC from many dens or living rooms, and we eliminate the test bed and distribution point of new, useful software from any corner of the globe. We also eliminate the safety valve that keeps those information appliances honest. If TiVo makes a digital video recorder that has too many limits on what people can do with the video they record, people will discover DVR software like MythTV that records and plays TV shows on their PCs.[108] If mobile phones are too expensive, people will use Skype. But people do not buy PCs as insurance policies against appliances that limit their freedoms, even though PCs serve exactly this vital function. People buy them to perform certain tasks at the moment of acquisition. If PCs cannot reliably perform these tasks, most consumers will not see their merit, and the safety valve will be lost. If the PC ceases to be at the center of the information technology ecosystem, the most restrictive aspects of information appliances will come to the fore.

PC AS INFORMATION APPLIANCE

PCs need not entirely disappear as people buy information appliances in their stead. They can themselves be made less generative. Recall the fundamental difference between a PC and an information appliance: the PC can run code from anywhere, written by anyone, while the information appliance remains tethered to its maker's desires, offering a more consistent and focused user experience at the expense of flexibility and innovation. Users tired of making the wrong choices about installing code on their PCs might choose to let someone else decide what code should be run. Firewalls can protect against some bad code, but they also complicate the installation of new good code.[109] As antivirus, antispyware, and antibadware barriers proliferate, they create new challenges to the deployment of new good code from unprivileged sources. And in order to guarantee effectiveness, these barriers are becoming increasingly paternalistic, refusing to allow users easily to overrule them. Especially in environments where the user of the PC does not own it—offices, schools, libraries, and cyber cafés—barriers are being put in place to prevent the running of any code not specifically approved by the relevant gatekeeper.

Short of completely banning unfamiliar software, code might be divided into first- and second-class status, with second-class, unapproved software allowed to perform only certain minimal tasks on the machine, operating within a digital sandbox. This technical solution is safer than the status quo but, in a now-familiar tradeoff, noticeably limiting. Skype works best when it can also be used to transfer users' files, which means it needs access to those files. Worse, such boundaries would have to be built into the operating system—placing the operating system developer or installer in the position of deciding what software will and will not run. If the user is allowed to make exceptions, the user can and will make the *wrong* exceptions, and the security restrictions will too often serve only to limit the deployment of legitimate software that has not been approved by the right gatekeepers. The PC will have become an information appliance, not easily reconfigured or extended by its users.

*   *   *

The Internet Engineering Task Force's RFC 1135 on the Morris worm closed with a section titled "Security Considerations." This section is the place in a standards document for a digital environmental impact statement—a survey of possible security problems that could arise from deployment of the standard. RFC 1135's security considerations section was one sentence: "If security considerations had not been so widely ignored in the Internet, this memo would not have been possible."[110]

What does that sentence mean? One reading is straightforward: if people had patched their systems and chosen good passwords, Morris's worm would not have been able to propagate, and there would have been no need to write the memo. Another is more profound: if the Internet had been designed with security as its centerpiece, it would never have achieved the kind of success it was enjoying, even as early as 1988. The basic assumption of Internet protocol design and implementation was that people would be reasonable; to assume otherwise runs the risk of hobbling it in just the way the proprietary networks were hobbled. The cybersecurity problem defies easy solution, because any of the most obvious solutions to it will cauterize the essence of the Internet and the generative PC.[111] That is the generative dilemma. The next chapter explains more systematically the benefits of generativity, and Chapter Five explores what the digital ecosystem will look like should our devices become more thoroughly applianCized. The vision is not a pleasant one, even though it may come about naturally through market demand. The key to avoiding such a future is to give that market a reason not to abandon or lock down the PCs that have served it so well—also giving most governments reason to refrain from major intervention into Internet architecture. The solutions to the generative dilemma will rest on social and legal innovation as much as on technical innovation, and the best guideposts can be found in other generative successes in those arenas. Those successes have faced similar challenges resulting from too much openness, and many have overcome them without abandoning generativity through solutions that inventively combine technical and social elements.

II

After the Stall

In Part I of this book I showed how generativity—both at the PC and network layers—was critical to the explosion of the Net, and how it will soon be critical to the explosion of the Net in a very different sense. In Part II I drill down a bit more into this concept of generativity. What is it? What does it mean? Where do we see it? Why is it good?

This part of the book offers an analytic definition of generativity and describes its benefits and drawbacks. It then explores the implications of a technological ecosystem in which non-generative devices and services—sterile "tethered appliances"—come to dominate. This trend threatens to curtail future innovation and to facilitate invasive forms of surveillance and control. A non-generative information ecosystem advances the regulability of the Internet to a stage that goes beyond addressing discrete regulatory problems, instead allowing regulators to alter basic freedoms that previously needed no theoretical or practical defense. I then turn to ways in which some systems—such as

Wikipedia—have managed to retain their essential generative character while confronting the internal limits and external scrutiny that have arisen because of their initial successes.

Some principles jump out:

Our information technology ecosystem functions best with generative technology at its core. A mainstream dominated by non-generative systems will harm innovation as well as some important individual freedoms and opportunities for self-expression. However, generative and non-generative models are not mutually exclusive. They can compete and intertwine within a single system. For example, a free operating system such as GNU/Linux can be locked within an information appliance like the TiVo, and classical, profit-maximizing firms like Red Hat and IBM can find it worthwhile to contribute to generative technologies like GNU/Linux.[1] Neither model is necessarily superior to the other for all purposes. Moreover, even if they occupy a more minor role in the mainstream, non-generative technologies still have valuable roles to serve. But they develop best when they can draw on the advances of generative systems.

Generativity instigates a pattern both within and beyond the technological layers of the information technology ecosystem. This book has so far described a trajectory for the generative Internet and PC, which begins in a backwater, accepts contribution from many quarters, experiences extraordinary success and unexpected mainstream adoption, and then encounters new and serious problems precisely because of that success. These problems can pose a lethal threat to generative systems by causing people to transform them into, or abandon them for, sterile alternatives. The forces that can stall the progress of the open Internet and return us to the days of proprietary networks can affect opportunities for generative enterprises like Wikipedia; such ventures are much more difficult to start without an open PC on a neutral Net. Moreover, the generative pattern of boom, bust, and possible renewal is not unique to technologies. It can also be found in generative expressive and social systems built with the help of those technologies. Recognizing the generative pattern can help us to understand phenomena across all the Internet's layers, and solutions at one layer—such as those offered by Wikipedians in the face of new pressures at the content layer— can offer insight into solutions at others, such as the problems of viruses and spam at the technical layer.

Proponents of generative systems ignore the drawbacks attendant to generativity's success at their peril. Generative systems are threatened by their mainstream success because new participants misunderstand or flout the ethos that makes the systems function well, and those not involved with the system find their legally protected interests challenged by it. Generative systems are not inherently self-sustaining when confronted with these challenges. We should draw lessons from instances in which such systems have survived and apply these lessons to problems arising within generative systems in other layers.

4

The Generative Pattern

Anyone can design new applications to operate over the Internet. Good applications can then be adopted widely while bad ones are ignored. The phenomenon is part of the Internet's "hourglass architecture" (Figure 4.1).

The hourglass portrays two important design insights. First is the notion that the network can be carved into conceptual layers. The exact number of layers varies depending on who is drawing the hourglass and why,[1] and even by chapter of this book.[2] On one basic view the network can be understood as having three layers. At the bottom is the "physical layer," the actual wires or airwaves over which data will flow. At the top is the "application layer," representing the tasks people might want to perform on the network. (Sometimes, above that, we might think of the "content layer," containing actual information exchanged among the network's users, and above that the "social layer," where new behaviors and interactions among people are enabled by the technologies underneath.) In the middle is the "protocol layer," which establishes consistent ways for data to flow so that the

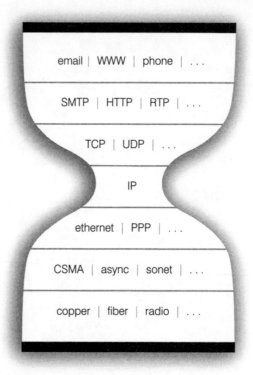

Figure 4.1 Hourglass architecture of the Internet

sender, the receiver, and anyone necessary in the middle can know the basics of who the data is from and where the data is going.

By dividing the network into layers and envisioning some boundaries among them, the path is clear to a division of labor among people working to improve the overall network. Tinkerers can work on one layer without having to understand much about the others, and there need not be any coordination or relationship between those working at one layer and those at another. For example, someone can write a new application like an instant messenger without having to know anything about whether its users will be connected to the network by modem or broadband. And an ISP can upgrade the speed of its Internet service without having to expect the authors of instant messenger programs to rewrite them to account for the new speed: the adjustment happens naturally. On the proprietary networks of the 1980s, in contrast, such divisions among layers were not as important because the networks sought to offer a one-stop solution to their customers, at the cost of having to design everything themselves. Layers facilitate polyarchies, and the proprietary networks were hierarchies.[3]

The second design insight of the hourglass is represented by its shape. The framers of Internet Protocol did not undertake to predict what would fill the upper or lower layers of the hourglass. As a technical matter, anyone could become part of the network by bringing a data-carrying wire or radio wave to the party. One needed only to find someone already on the network willing to share access, and to obtain a unique IP address, an artifact not intended to be hoarded. Thus, wireless Internet access points could be developed by outsiders without any changes required to Internet Protocol: the Protocol embodied so few assumptions about the nature of the medium used that going wireless did not violate any of them. The large variety of ways of physically connecting is represented by the broad base to the hourglass. Similarly, the framers of Internet Protocol made few assumptions about the ultimate uses of the network. They merely provided a scheme for packaging and moving data, whatever its purpose. This scheme allowed a proliferation of applications from any interested and talented source—from the Web to e-mail to instant messenger to file transfer to video streaming. Thus, the top of the hourglass is also broad. It is only the middle that is narrow, containing Internet Protocol, because it is meant to be as feature-free as possible. It simply describes how to move data, and its basic parameters have evolved slowly over the years. Innovation and problem-solving are pushed up or down, and to others: Chapter Two's procrastination principle at work.

This same quality is found within traditional PC architecture. It greatly facilitates the way that the overall network operates, although those joining the debate on Internet openness have largely ignored this quality. Operating system designers like Microsoft and Apple have embraced the procrastination principle of their counterparts in Internet network design. Their operating systems, as well as Unix and its variants, are intentionally incomplete; they were built to allow users to install new code written by third parties. Such code could entirely revise the way a computer operates, which gives individuals other than the original designers the capacity to solve new problems and redirect the purposes of PCs.[4] We could even sketch a parallel hourglass of PC architecture (Figure 4.2).

The PC can run code from a broad number of sources, and it can be physically placed into any number and style of physical chassis from many sources, at least as a technical matter. (Sometimes the operating system maker may object as a strategic and legal matter: Apple, for example, has with few exceptions

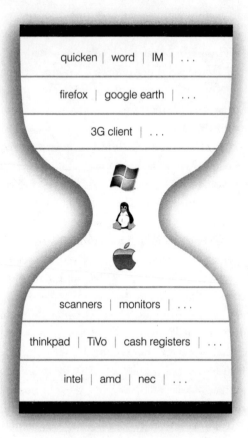

Figure 4.2 Hourglass architecture of the PC

notoriously insisted on bundling its operating system with Apple hardware, perhaps a factor in its mere 5 percent market share for PCs.[5])

I have termed this quality of the Internet and of traditional PC architecture "generativity." *Generativity is a system's capacity to produce unanticipated change through unfiltered contributions from broad and varied audiences.* Terms like "openness" and "free" and "commons" evoke elements of it, but they do not fully capture its meaning, and they sometimes obscure it.

Generativity pairs an input consisting of unfiltered contributions from diverse people and groups, who may or may not be working in concert, with the output of unanticipated change. For the inputs, how much the system facilitates audience contribution is a function of both technological design and social behavior. A system's generativity describes not only its objective characteristics, but also the ways the system relates to its users and the ways users relate to one another. In turn, these relationships reflect how much the users identify as contributors or participants, rather than as mere consumers.

FEATURES OF A GENERATIVE SYSTEM

What makes something generative? There are five principal factors at work: (1) how extensively a system or technology leverages a set of possible tasks; (2) how well it can be adapted to a range of tasks; (3) how easily new contributors can master it; (4) how accessible it is to those ready and able to build on it; and (5) how transferable any changes are to others—including (and perhaps especially) nonexperts.

Leverage: Leverage makes a difficult job easier. Leverage is not exclusively a feature of generative systems; non-generative, specialized technologies can provide leverage for their designated tasks.[6] But as a baseline, the more a system can do, the more capable it is of producing change. Examples of leverage abound: consider a lever itself (with respect to lifting physical objects), a band saw (cutting them), an airplane (transporting them from one place to another), a piece of paper (hosting written language, wrapping fish), or an alphabet (constructing words). Our world teems with useful objects and processes, both natural and artificial, tangible and intangible. Both PCs and network technologies have proven very leveraging. A typical PC operating system handles many of the chores that the author of an application would otherwise have to worry about, and properly implemented Internet Protocol sees to it that bits of data move from one place to another without application authors having to worry on either end. A little effort can thus produce a very powerful computer program, whether a file-sharing program or a virus comprising just a few lines of code.

Adaptability: Adaptability refers to how easily the system can be built on or modified to broaden its range of uses. A given instrumentality may be highly leveraging yet suited only to a limited range of applications. For example, TiVo is greatly leveraging—television viewers describe its impact on their lives as revolutionary—but it is not very adaptable. A plowshare enables one to plant a variety of seeds; however, its comparative leverage quickly vanishes when devoted to other tasks such as holding doors open. The same goes for swords (they really make poor plowshares), guns, chairs, band saws, and even airplanes. Adaptability is clearly a spectrum. Airplanes can transport people and things, or they can be configured to dust or bomb what lies below. But one can still probably count the *kinds* of uses for an airplane on two hands. A technology that affords hundreds of different, additional kinds of uses beyond its essential application is more adaptable and, all else being equal, more generative than a technology that offers fewer kinds of uses. The emphasis here is on uses not anticipated at the time the technology was developed. A thick Swiss Army knife may have plenty of built-in tools compared with a simple pocket knife, but many of those are highly specialized.[7]

By this reckoning, electricity is an amazingly adaptable technology, as is plastic (hence the historical use of "plastic" to refer to notions of sculptability).[8] And so are the PC and the Internet: they can be endlessly diverted to new tasks not counted on by their original makers.

Ease of mastery: A technology's ease of mastery reflects how easy it is for broad audiences to understand how to adopt and adapt it. The airplane is not readily mastered, being neither easy to fly nor easy to learn how to modify for new purposes. The risk of physical injury if the modifications are poorly designed or executed is a further barrier to such tinkering. Paper, on the other hand, is readily mastered: we teach our children how to use it, draw on it, and even fold it into paper airplanes (which are much easier to fly and modify than real ones), often before they enter preschool. The skills required to understand many otherwise generative technologies are often not very readily absorbed. Many technologies require apprenticeships, formal training, or many hours of practice if one is to become conversant in them. The small electronic components used to build radios and doorbells fall into this category—one must learn both how each piece functions and how to solder—as do antique car engines that the enthusiast wants to customize. Of course, the skills necessary to operate certain technologies, rather than modify them, are often more quickly acquired. For example, many quickly understand how to drive a car, an understanding probably assisted by user-friendly inventions such as the automatic transmission.

Ease of mastery also refers to the ease with which various types of people might deploy and adapt a given technology, even if their skills fall short of full mastery. A pencil is easily mastered: it takes a moment to understand and put to many uses, even though it might require a lifetime of practice and innate artistic talent to achieve Da Vincian levels of leverage from it. The more useful a technology is both to the neophyte and to the expert, the more generative it is. PCs and network technologies are not easy for everyone to master, yet many people are able to learn how to code, often (or especially) without formal training.

Accessibility: The easier it is to obtain access to a technology, along with the tools and information necessary to achieve mastery of it, the more generative it is. Barriers to accessibility can include the sheer expense of producing (and therefore consuming) the technology, taxes, regulations associated with its adoption or use, and the secrecy its producers adopt to maintain scarcity or control.

Measured by accessibility, paper, plowshares, and guns are highly accessible, planes hardly at all, and cars somewhere in between. It might be easy to learn how to drive a car, but cars are expensive, and the government can always revoke a user's driving privileges, even after the privileges have been earned through a demonstration of driving skill. Moreover, revocation is not an abstract threat because effective enforcement is not prohibitively expensive. Measured by the same factors, scooters and bicycles are more accessible, while snowplows are less so. Standard PCs are very accessible; they come in a wide range of prices, and in a few keystrokes or mouse-clicks one can be ready to write new code for them. On the other hand, specialized PC modes—like those found in "kiosk mode" at a store cycling through slides—cannot have their given task interrupted or changed, and they are not accessible.

Transferability: Transferability indicates how easily changes in the technology can be conveyed to others. With fully transferable technology, the fruits of skilled users' adaptations can be easily conveyed to less-skilled others. The PC and the Internet together possess very strong transferability: a program written in one place can be shared with, and replicated by, tens of millions of other machines in a matter of moments. By contrast, a new appliance made out of a 75-in-1 Electronic Project Kit is not easily transferable because the modifier's changes cannot be easily conveyed to another kit. Achieving the same result requires manually wiring a new kit to look like the old one, which makes the project kit less generative.

GENERATIVE AND NON-GENERATIVE SYSTEMS COMPARED

Generative tools are not inherently better than their non-generative ("sterile") counterparts. Appliances are often easier to master for particular uses, and because their design often anticipates uses and abuses, they can be safer and more effective. For example, on camping trips, Swiss Army knives are ideal. Luggage space is often at a premium, and such a tool will be useful in a range of expected and even unexpected situations. In situations when versatility and space constraints are less important, however, a Swiss Army knife is comparatively a fairly poor knife—and an equally awkward magnifying glass, saw, and scissors.

As the examples and terms suggest, the five qualities of leverage, adaptability, ease of mastery, accessibility, and transferability often reinforce one another. And the absence of one of these factors may prevent a technology from being generative. A system that is accessible but difficult to master may still be generative if a small but varied group of skilled users make their work available to less-sophisticated users. Usually, however, a major deficiency in any one factor greatly reduces overall generativity. This is the case with many tools that are leveraging and adaptable but difficult to master. For example, while some enjoy tinkering in home workshops, making small birdhouses using wood and a saw, most cannot build their own boats or decks, much less pass those creations on to others. Similarly, there are plenty of examples of technology that is easy to master and is quite adaptable, but lacks leverage. Lego building blocks are easy to master and can produce a great range of shapes, but regardless of the skill behind their arrangement they remain small piles of plastic, which largely confines their uses to that of toys.

The more that the five qualities are maximized, the easier it is for a system or platform to welcome contributions from outsiders as well as insiders. Maximizing these qualities facilitates the technology's deployment in unanticipated ways. Table 4.1 lists examples of generative tools. For comparison, the table also includes some of these tools' less generative counterparts. Views on these categories or particular examples will undoubtedly vary, but some themes emerge. In general, generative tools are more basic and less specialized for accomplishing a particular purpose; these qualities make such tools more usable for many tasks. Generative technologies may require the user to possess some skill in order for the tool to be even minimally useful—compare a piano with a music box—but once the user has acquired some skill, the tools support a wider range of applications.

Generative *tools* are individually useful. Generative *systems* are sets of tools and practices that develop among large groups of people. These systems provide an environment for new and best—or at least most popular—practices to spread and diversify further within them. Generative systems can be built on non-generative platforms—no technical reason prevented CompuServe from developing wiki-like features and inviting its subscribers to contribute to something resembling Wikipedia—but frequently generativity at one layer is the best recipe for generativity at the layer above.

Table 4.1. Examples of generative tools

	Generative	Less Generative	
Tools/ Construction	Duct tape[a] Hammer	Anchor bolts Jackhammer	Jackhammers, while highly leveraging for demolition, have few other uses. Hammers can be used for a greater variety of activities. They are more adaptable and accessible, and they are easier to master.
	Square tiles	Patterned tiles	Square tiles of different colors can be laid out in a variety of different patterns. Particularly shaped and colored tiles aesthetically fit together in only a certain way.
	Paint	Decals	
Games/Toys	Dice, playing cards	Board games	Dice and playing cards are building blocks for any number of games. Board games are generally specialized for playing only one particular game. All, however are accessible: just as with dice and playing cards, one could make up entirely new rules for Monopoly using its board, game pieces, and money.
	Lego bricks, plastic girder and panel construction sets, erector sets	Prefabricated dollhouse	Lego bricks can be assembled into houses or reconfigured for various other uses. A dollhouse facilitates variety in play by its users. While less reconfigurable than Legos, it can be a platform for other outputs. Compared with a board game, a dollhouse is thus a more generative toy.
	Chess, checkers	Connect Four	Many variants on traditional games involve chess and checkers. The pieces can also be generalized to create different games.
	Etch-a-Sketch, crayons, paper	Coloring book, paint-by-numbers	

(continued)

[a]Duct tape has been celebrated as having thousands of uses. *See, e.g.,* Duck Prods., Creative Uses http://www.duckproducts.com/creative (last visited May 16, 2007). Interestingly, one of them is decidedly not patching ducts. *See* Paul Preuss, Sealing HVAC Ducts: Use Anything but Duct Tape (1998), http://www.lbl.gov/Science-Articles/Archive/duct-tape-HVAC.html.

Table 4.1. Continued

	Generative	Less Generative	
Kitchen Devices	Knife	Potato peeler	Peelers can be used only on particular foods. Knives have greater versatility to tasks besides peeling, as well as greater adaptability for uses outside cooking.
	Stove	Slot toaster	Generally, toasters are dedicated to heating bread. An electric stove can be adapted for that task as well as for many other meals.
	Kettle	Coffeemaker	A "pod" coffee system restricts the user to making coffee from supplies provided by that vendor. Even a traditional coffeemaker is limited to making coffee. A kettle, however, can be used to heat water for use in any number of hot drinks or meals, such as oatmeal or soup.
Sports	Dumbbells	Exercise machine	An exercise machine's accessibility is often limited by its cost. The possible workouts using the machine are also limited by its configuration. Dumbbells can be combined for a variety of regimens. An exercise machine is safer, however, and perhaps less intimidating to new users.
Cooking/ Food	Vodka	Flavored wine cooler	
	Rice, salt	Prepared sushi	Prepared sushi may be less accessible due to its price. Rice and salt are staple foods that are easier to add and use in a variety of dishes.
	Corn	Microwave popcorn	

GENERATIVITY AND ITS COUSINS

The notion of generativity is itself an adaptation. It is related to other conceptions of information technology and, to some degree, draws upon their meanings.

The Free Software Philosophy

The normative ideals of the free software movement and the descriptive attributes of generativity have much in common. According to this philosophy, any software functionality enjoyed by one person should be understandable and modifiable by everyone. The free software philosophy emphasizes the value of sharing not only a tool's functionality, but also knowledge about how the tool works so as to help others become builders themselves. Put into our terms, accessibility is a core value. When the free software approach works, it helps to expand the audiences capable of building software, and it increases the range of outputs the system generates.

While generativity has some things in common with the free software approach, it is not the same. Free software satisfies Richard Stallman's benchmark "four freedoms": freedom to run the program, freedom to study how it works, freedom to change it, and freedom to share the results with the public at large.[9] These freedoms overlap with generativity's four factors, but they depart in several important respects. First, some highly generative platforms may not meet all of free software's four freedoms. While proprietary operating systems like Windows may not be directly changeable—the Windows source code is not regularly available to outside programmers—the flexibility that software authors have to build on top of the Windows OS allows a programmer to revise nearly any behavior of a Windows PC to suit specific tastes. Indeed, one could implement GNU/Linux on top of Windows, or Windows on top of GNU/Linux.[10] So, even though Windows is proprietary and does not meet the definition of free software, it is generative.

Free software can also lack the accessibility associated with generativity. Consider "trapped" PCs like the one inside the TiVo. TiVo is built on Linux, which is licensed as free software, but, while the code is publicly published, it is nearly impossible for the Linux PC inside a TiVo to run anything but the code that TiVo designates for it. The method of deploying a generative technology can have a non-generative result: the free software satisfies the leveraging quality of generativity, but it lacks accessibility.[11]

Affordance Theory

Fields such as psychology, industrial design, and human-computer interaction use the concept of "affordances."[12] Originally the term was used to refer to the possible actions that existed in a given environment. If an action were objectively possible, the environment was said to "afford" that action. The concept has since been adapted to focus on "perceived affordances," the actions or uses that an individual is subjectively likely to make, rather than on actions or uses that are objectively possible. As a design tool, affordances can help the creator of an environment ensure that the available options are as obvious and inviting as possible to the intended users.

A theory of affordances can also be used to predict what various people might do when presented with an object by asking what that object invites users to do. A ball might be thrown; a chair might be sat on. A hyperlink that is not underlined may be "poorly afforded" because it may impede users from realizing that they can click on it, suggesting that a better design would visually demarcate the link.

Generativity shares some of this outlook. If poorly afforded, some forms of technical user empowerment, such as the ability to run software written by others, can harm users who mistakenly run code that hurts their machines. This leads to the unfortunate result that the unqualified freedom to run any code can result in restrictions on what code is or can be run: adverse experiences cause less-skilled users to become distrustful of all new code, and they ask for environments that limit the damage that they can inadvertently do.

Yet unlike generativity, affordance theory does not focus much on systemic output. Instead, it takes one object at a time and delineates its possible or likely uses. More recent incarnations of the theory suggest that the object's designer ought to anticipate its uses and tailor the object's appearance and functionality accordingly. Such tailoring is more consistent with the development of applicanced systems than with generative ones. Generativity considers how a system might grow or change over time as the uses of a technology by one group are shared with other individuals, thereby extending the generative platform.

Theories of the Commons

Generativity also draws from recent scholarship about the commons. Some commentators, observing the decentralized and largely unregulated infrastructure of the Internet, have noted how these qualities have enabled the development of an innovation commons where creativity can flourish.[13] Projects like

Creative Commons have designed intellectual property licenses so that authors can clearly declare the conditions under which they will permit their technical or expressive work to be copied and repurposed. Such licensing occurs against the backdrop of copyright law, which generally protects all original work upon fixation, even work for which the author has been silent as to how it may be used. By providing a vehicle for understanding that authors are willing to share their work, Creative Commons licenses are a boon for content-level generativity because the licenses allow users to build on their colleagues' work.

Other scholars have undertaken an economic analysis of the commons. They claim that the Internet's economic value as a commons is often significantly underestimated, and that there are strong economic arguments for managing and sustaining an infrastructure without gatekeepers.[14] In particular, they argue that nonmonopolized Internet access is necessary to ensure meritocratic competition among content providers.[15]

These arguments about infrastructure tend to end where the network cable does. A network on which anyone can set up a node and exchange bits with anyone else on the network is necessary but not sufficient to establish competition, to produce innovative new services, to promote the free flow of information to societies in which the local media is censored, or to make the most efficient use of network resources. As the next chapter explains, the endpoints have at least as much of a role to play. Focusing on the generativity of a system without confining that system to a particular technical locus can help us evaluate what values the system embodies—and what it truly affords.

Values, of course, vary from one person and stakeholder to the next. Generative systems can encourage creativity and spur innovation, and they can also make it comparatively more difficult for institutions and regulators to assert control over the systems' uses. If we are to draw conclusions about whether a field balanced between generative and non-generative systems ought to be preserved, we need to know the benefits and drawbacks of each in greater detail.

THE STRENGTHS OF GENERATIVE SYSTEMS

Generative systems facilitate change. The first part of this book introduced positive and negative faces of generativity: it told an optimistic tale of Internet development, followed by pessimistic predictions of trouble due to deep-rooted vulnerabilities in that network.

A generative system can be judged from both within the system and outside of it. A set of PCs being destroyed by a virus from afar is a change brought about by a generative system that is internally bad because it harms the system's generativity. The development and distribution of a generic installer program for a PC, which makes it easy for other software authors to bundle their work so that users can easily install and use it, is an example of a generative system producing an internally good change, because it makes the system more generative.

Generative outputs can also be judged as good or bad by reference to external values. If people use a generative system to produce software that allows its users to copy music and video without the publishers' permissions, those supportive of publishers will rationally see generativity's disruptive potential as bad. When a generative system produces the means to circumvent Internet filtering in authoritarian states, people in favor of citizen empowerment will approve.

Generativity's benefits can be grouped more formally as at least two distinct goods, one deriving from unanticipated change, and the other from inclusion of large and varied audiences. The first good is its innovative output: new things that improve people's lives. The second good is its participatory input, based on a belief that a life well lived is one in which there is opportunity to connect to other people, to work with them, and to express one's own individuality through creative endeavors.

GENERATIVITY'S OUTPUT: INNOVATION

To those for whom innovation is important, generative systems can provide for a kind of organic innovation that might not take place without them.

The Limits of Non-generative Innovation

Non-generative systems can grow and evolve, but their growth is channeled through their makers: a new toaster is released by Amana and reflects anticipated customer demand or preferences, or an old proprietary network like CompuServe adds a new form of instant messaging by programming it itself. When users pay for products or services in one way or another, those who control the products or services amid competition are responsive to their desires through market pressure. This is an indirect means of innovation, and there is a growing set of literature about its limitation: a persistent bottleneck that prevents certain new uses from being developed and cultivated by large incumbent firms, despite the benefits they could enjoy with a breakthrough.[16]

We have already seen this phenomenon by anecdote in the first part of this book. Recall the monopoly telephone system in the United States, where AT&T attempted to extend its control through the network and into the endpoint devices hooked up to the network, at first barring the Hush-A-Phone and the Carterfone. The telephone system was stable and predictable; its uses evolved slowly if at all from its inception in the late nineteenth century. It was designed to facilitate conversations between two people at a distance, and with some important exceptions, that is all it has done. The change it has wrought for society is, of course, enormous, but the contours of that change were known and set once there was a critical mass of telephones distributed among the general public. Indeed, given how revolutionary a telephone system is to a society without one, it is striking that the underlying technology and its uses have seen only a handful of variations since its introduction. This phenomenon is an artifact of the system's rejection of outside contributions. In the United States, after the law compelled AT&T to permit third-party hardware to connect, we saw a number of new endpoint devices: new telephone units in various shapes, colors, and sizes; answering machines; and, most important, the telephone modem, which allows the non-generative network itself to be repurposed for widespread data communication.

We saw a similar pattern as the Internet overtook proprietary networks that did not even realize it was a competitor. The generative Internet is a basic, flexible network, which began with no innate content. The content was to appear as people and institutions were moved to offer it. By contrast, the proprietary networks of CompuServe, AOL, Prodigy, and Minitel were out beating the bushes for content, arranging to provide it through the straightforward economic model of being paid by people who would spend connect time browsing it. If anything, we would expect the proprietary networks to offer more, and for a while they did. But they also had a natural desire to act as gatekeepers—to validate anything appearing on their network, to cut individual deals for revenue sharing with their content providers, and to keep their customers from affecting the network's technology. These tendencies meant that their rates of growth and differentiation were slow. A few areas that these networks consigned to individual contribution experienced strong activity and subscriber loyalty, such as their topical bulletin boards run by hired systems operators (called "sysops") and boasting content provided by subscribers in public conversations with each other. These forums were generative at the content layer because people could post comments to each other without prescreening and could choose to take up whatever topics they chose, irrespective of the designated labels for the forums themselves ("Pets" vs. "Showbiz").[17] But they were not generative at the technical layer. The software driving these communities was stagnant: subscribers who were both interested in the communities' content and technically minded had few outlets through which to contribute technical improvements to the way the communities were built. Instead, any improvements were orchestrated centrally. As the initial offerings of the proprietary networks plateaued, the Internet saw developments in technology that in turn led to developments in content and ultimately in social and economic interaction: the Web and Web sites, online shopping, peer-to-peer networking, wikis, and blogs.

The hostility of AT&T toward companies like Hush-A-Phone and of the proprietary networks to the innovations of enterprising subscribers is not unusual, and it is not driven solely by their status as monopolists. Just as behavioral economics shows how individuals can consistently behave irrationally under particular circumstances,[18] and how decision-making within groups can fall prey to error and bias,[19] so too can the incumbent firms in a given market fail to seize opportunities that they rationally ought to exploit. Much of the academic work in this area draws from further case studies and interviews with decision-makers at significant firms. It describes circumstances that echo the reluctance of CompuServe, AOL, and other proprietary online services to allow third-party innovation—or to innovate much themselves.

For example, Tim Wu has shown that when wireless telephone carriers exercise control over the endpoint mobile phones that their subscribers may use, those phones will have undesirable features—and they are not easy for third parties to improve.[20] In design terms, there is no hourglass. Carriers have forced telephone providers to limit the mobile phones' Web browsers to certain carrier-approved sites. They have eliminated call timers on the phones, even though they would be trivial to implement—and are in much demand by users, who would like to monitor whether their use of a phone has gone beyond allotted minutes for a monthly plan.[21] Phones' ability to transfer photos and recorded sounds is often limited to using the carriers' preferred channels and fees. For those who wish to code new applications to run on the increasingly powerful computers embedded within the phones, the barriers to contribution are high. The phones' application programming interfaces are poorly disclosed, or are at best selectively disclosed, making the programming platform difficult to master. Often, the coding must be written for a "virtual machine" that bars access to many of the phone's features, reducing accessibility. And the virtual machines run slowly, eliminating leverage. These factors persist despite competition among several carriers.

Oxford's Andrew Currah has noted a similar reluctance to extend business models beyond the tried-and-true in a completely different setting. He has studied innovation within the publishing industries, and has found cultural barriers to it across studios and record companies. As one studio president summarized:

> The fiscal expectations are enormous. We have to act in a rational and cautious fashion, no matter how much potential new markets like the Internet have. Our core mission is to protect the library of films, and earn as much as possible from that library over time. . . . So that means focusing our efforts on what's proven—i.e. the DVD—and only dipping our toes into new consumer technologies. We simply aren't programmed to move quickly.[22]

And the studio's vice-chairman said:

> You have to understand [studio] strategy in relation to the lifestyle here. . . . Once you reach the top of the hierarchy, you acquire status and benefits that can soon be lost—the nice cars, the home in Brentwood, the private schools. . . . It doesn't make sense to jeopardize any of that by adopting a reckless attitude towards new technologies, new markets. Moving slow, and making clear, safe progress is the mantra.[23]

The puzzle of why big firms exhibit such innovative inertia was placed into a theoretical framework by Clayton Christensen in his pioneering book *The Innovator's Dilemma*.[24] Christensen found the hard disk drive industry representative. In it, market leaders tended to be very good at quickly and successfully adopting some technological advancements, yet were entirely left behind by upstarts. To explain the discrepancy, he created a taxonomy of "sustaining" and "disruptive" innovations. When technological innovations are consistent with the performance trajectory of established market leaders—that is, when they are a more efficient way of doing what they already do—alert leaders will be quick to develop and utilize such "sustaining" innovations.

It is with disruptive innovations that the market leaders will lag behind. These innovations are not in the path of what the company is already doing well. Indeed, Christensen found that the innovations which market leaders were the worst at exploiting were "technologically straightforward, consisting of off-the-shelf components put together in a product architecture that was often simpler than prior approaches. They offered less of what customers in established markets wanted and so could rarely be initially employed there. They offered a different package of attributes valued only in emerging markets remote from, and unimportant to, the mainstream."[25]

It is not the case, Christensen argues, that these large companies lack the technological competence to deploy a new technology, but rather that their managements choose to focus on their largest and most profitable customers, resulting in an unwillingness to show "*downward* vision and mobility."[26]

Subsequent authors have built on this theory, arguing that a failure to innovate disruptively is not simply an issue of management, but the organizational inability of large firms to respond to changes in consumer preferences caused by such disruptive innovations. Established firms are structurally reluctant to investigate whether an innovative product would be marketable to a sector outside what they perceive to be their traditional market.[27] They want to ride a wave, and they fail to establish alternatives or plumb new markets even as competitors begin to do so.

This observation has led others to conclude that in order for large organizations to become more innovative, they must adopt a more "ambidextrous organizational form" to provide a buffer between exploitation and exploration.[28] This advice might be reflected in choices made by companies like Google, whose engineers are encouraged to spend one day a week on a project of their own choosing—with Google able to exploit whatever they come up with.[29]

But large firms struggling to learn lessons from academics about becoming more creative need not be the only sources of innovation. In fact, the competitive market that appears to be the way to spur innovation—a market in which barriers to entry are low enough for smaller firms to innovate disruptively where larger firms are reluctant to tread—can be made much more competitive, since generative systems reduce barriers to entry and allow contributions from those who do not even intend to compete.

THE GENERATIVE DIFFERENCE

Generative systems allow users at large to try their hands at implementing and distributing new uses, and to fill a crucial gap that is created when innovation is undertaken only in a profit-making model, much less one in which large firms dominate. Generatively-enabled activity by amateurs can lead to results that would not have been produced in a firm-mediated market model.

The brief history of the Internet and PC illustrates how often the large and even small firm market model of innovation missed the boat on a swath of significant advances in information technology while non-market-motivated and amateur actors led the charge. Recall that Tasmanian amateur coder Peter Tattam saw the value of integrating Internet support into Windows before Microsoft did, and that the low cost of replicating his work meant that millions of users could adopt it even if they did not know how to program computers themselves.[30] Hundreds of millions of dollars were invested in proprietary information services that failed, while Internet domain names representing firms' identities were not even reserved by those firms.[31] (McDonald's might be forgiven for allowing someone else to register mcdonalds.com before it occurred to the company to do so; even telecommunications giant MCI failed to notice the burgeoning consumer Internet before Sprint, which was the first to register mci.com—at a time when such registrations were given away first-come, first-served, to anyone who filled out the electronic paperwork.)[32]

The communally minded ethos of the Internet was an umbrella for more activity, creativity, and economic value than the capitalistic ethos of the proprietary networks, and the openness of the consumer PC to outside code resulted in a vibrant, expanding set of tools that ensured the end of the information appliances and proprietary services of the 1980s.

Consider new forms of commercial and social interaction made possible by new software that in turn could easily run on PCs or be offered over the Internet. Online auctions might have been ripe for the plucking by Christie's or Sotheby's, but upstart eBay got there first and stayed. Craigslist, initiated as a ".org" by a single person, dominates the market for classified advertising online.[33] Ideas like free Web-based e-mail, hosting services for personal Web pages, instant messenger software, social networking sites, and well-designed search engines emerged more from individuals or small groups of people wanting to solve their own problems or try something neat than from firms realizing there were profits to be gleaned. This is a sampling of major Internet applications founded and groomed by outsiders; start sliding down what *Wired* editor Chris Anderson calls the Long Tail—niche applications for obscure interests—and we see a dominance of user-written software.[34] Venture capital money and the other artifacts of the firm-based industrial information economy can kick in after an idea has been proven, and user innovation plays a crucial role as an initial spark.

GENERATIVITY AND A BLENDING OF MODELS FOR INNOVATION

Eric von Hippel has written extensively about how rarely firms welcome improvements to their products by outsiders, including their customers, even when they could stand to benefit from them.[35] His work tries to persuade otherwise rational firms that the users of their products often can and do create new adaptations and uses for them—and that these users are commonly delighted to see their improvements shared. Echoing Christensen and others, he points out that firms too often think that their own internal marketing and R&D departments know best, and that users cannot easily improve on what they manufacture.

Von Hippel then goes further, offering a model that integrates user innovation with manufacturer innovation (Figure 4.3).

Von Hippel's analysis says that users can play a critical role in adapting technologies to entirely new purposes—a source of disruptive innovation. They come up with ideas before there is widespread demand, and they vindicate their ideas sufficiently to get others interested. When interest gets big enough, companies can then step in to smooth out the rough edges and fully commercialize the innovation.

Von Hippel has compiled an extensive catalog of user innovation. He points to examples like farmers who roped a bicycle-like contraption to some PVC

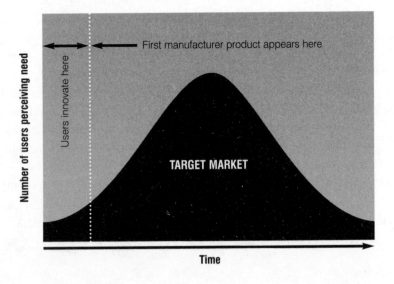

Figure 4.3 Eric von Hippel's zones of innovation

pipes to create a portable center-pivot irrigation system, which, now perfected by professional manufacturers, is a leading way to water crops.[36] Or a paramedic who placed IV bags filled with water into his knapsack and ran the outlet tubes from behind so he could drink from them while bicycling, akin to the way some fans at football games drink beer out of baseball caps that have cup holders that hang on either side of the head. The IV bag system has since been adopted by large manufacturers and is now produced for hikers and soldiers.[37] Von Hippel's studies show that 20 percent of mountain bikers modify their bikes in some way, and an equal number of surgeons tinker with their surgical implements. Lego introduced a set of programmable blocks for kids—traditional Lego toys with little engines inside—and the toys became a runaway hit with adults, who accounted for 70 percent of the market. The adults quickly hacked the Lego engines and made them better. Silicon Valley firms then banned Legos as a drain on employee productivity. Lego was stumped for over a year about how to react—this market was not part of the original business plan—before concluding that it was good.

The building blocks for most of von Hippel's examples are not even particularly generative ones. They represent tinkering done by that one person in a hundred or a thousand who is so immersed in an activity or pursuit that improving it would make a big difference—a person who is prepared to experiment with a level of persistence that calls to mind the Roadrunner's nemesis, Wile E. Coyote. Generative systems and technologies are more inviting to disruptive innovation thanks to their leverage, adaptability, ease of mastery, and accessibility, and they make it easier for their fruits to spread.

Most firms cannot sift through the thousands of helpful and not-so-helpful suggestions sent in by their customers, and they might not even dare look at them institutionally, lest a sender claim later on that his or her idea was stolen. Offers of partnership or affiliation from small businesses may not fare much better, just as deals between proprietary networks and individual technology and content providers numbered only in the tens rather than in the thousands. Yet when people and institutions other than the incumbents have an opportunity to create and distribute new uses as is possible in a generative system, the results can outclass what is produced through traditional channels.

If one values innovation, it might be useful to try to figure out how much disruptive innovation remains in a particular field or technology. For mature technologies, perhaps generativity is not as important: the remaining leaps, such as that which allows transistors to be placed closer and closer together on a chip over time without fundamentally changing the things the chip can do, will come from exploitative innovation or will necessitate well-funded research through institutional channels.

For the Internet, then, some might think that outside innovation is a transitory phenomenon, one that was at its apogee when the field of opportunity was new and still unnoticed by more traditional firms, and when hardware programming capacity was small, as in the early days of the PC.[38] If so, the recent melding of the PC and the Internet has largely reset the innovative clock. Many of the online tools that have taken off in recent years, such as wikis and blogs, are quite rudimentary both in their features and in the sophistication of their underlying code. The power of wikis and blogs comes from the fact that nothing quite like them existed before, and that they are so readily adopted by Internet users intrigued by their use. The genius behind such innovations is truly inspiration rather than perspiration, a bit of tinkering with a crazy idea rather than a carefully planned and executed invention responding to clear market demand.

Due to the limitations of the unconnected PC, one could credibly claim that its uses were more or less known by 1990: word processing, spreadsheets, databases, games. The rest was merely refinement. The reinvigorated PC/Internet grid makes such applications seem like a small corner of the landscape, even as those applications remain important to the people who continue to use them.

We have thus settled into a landscape in which both amateurs and professionals as well as small- and large-scale ventures contribute to major innovations. Much like the way that millions of dollars can go into production and marketing for a new musical recording[39] while a gifted unknown musician hums an original tune in the shower that proves the basis for a hit album, the Internet and PC today run a fascinating juxtaposition of sweepingly ambitious software designed and built like a modern aircraft carrier by a large contractor, alongside "killer applets" that can fit on a single floppy diskette.[40] OS/2, an operating system created as a joint venture between IBM and Microsoft,[41] absorbed billions of dollars of research and development investment before its plug was pulled,[42] while Mosaic, the first graphical PC Internet browser, was written by a pair of students in three months.[43]

A look at sites that aggregate various software projects and their executable results reveals thousands of projects under way.[44] Such projects might be tempting to write off as the indulgences of hobbyists, if not for the roll call of pivotal software that has emerged from such environments:[45] software to enable encryption of data, both stored on a hard drive and transmitted across a network,[46] peer-to-peer file-sharing software,[47] e-mail clients,[48] Web browsers,[49] and sound and image editors.[50] Indeed, it is difficult to find software *not* initiated by amateurs, even as later versions are produced through more formal corporate means to be more robust, to include consumer help files and otherwise attempt to improve upon others' versions or provide additional services for which users are willing to pay a premium.[51] Many companies are now releasing their software under a free or open source license to enable users to tinker with the code, identify bugs, and develop improvements.[52]

It may well be that, in the absence of broad-based technological accessibility, there would eventually have been the level of invention currently witnessed in the PC and on the Internet. Maybe AT&T would have invented the answering machine on its own, and maybe AOL or CompuServe would have agreed to hyperlink to one another's walled gardens. But the hints we have suggest otherwise: less-generative counterparts to the PC and the Internet—such as stand-alone word processors and proprietary information services—had far fewer technological offerings, and they stagnated and then failed as generative counterparts emerged. Those proprietary information services that remain, such as Lexis/Nexis and Westlaw, sustain themselves because they are the only way to access useful proprietary content, such as archived news and some scholarly journal articles.[53]

Of course, there need not be a zero-sum game in models of software creation, and generative growth can blend well with traditional market models. Consumers can become enraptured by an expensive, sophisticated shooting game designed by a large firm in one moment and by a simple animation featuring a dancing hamster in the next.[54] Big firms can produce software when market structure and demand call for such enterprise; smaller firms can fill niches; and amateurs, working alone and in groups, can design both inspirational "applets" and more labor-intensive software that increase the volume and diversity of the technological ecosystem.[55] Once an eccentric and unlikely invention from outsiders has gained notoriety, traditional means of raising and spending capital to improve a technology can shore it up and ensure its exposure to as wide an audience as possible. An information technology ecosystem comprising only the products of the free software movement would be much less usable by the public at large than one in which big firms help sand off rough edges.[56] GNU/Linux has become user-friendly thanks to firms that package and sell copies, even if they cannot claim proprietary ownership in the software itself, and tedious tasks that improve ease of mastery for the uninitiated might best be done through corporate models: creating smooth installation engines, extensive help guides, and other handholding for what otherwise might be an off-putting technical piece of PC software or Web service.[57]

As the Internet and the PC merge into a grid, people can increasingly lend or barter computing cycles or bandwidth for causes they care about by simply installing a small piece of software.[58] This could be something like SETI@home, through which astronomers can distribute voluminous data from radio telescopes to individual PCs,[59] which then look for patterns that might indicate the presence of intelligent life, or it could be a simple sharing of bandwidth through mechanisms such as amateur-coded (and conceived, and designed) BitTorrent,[60] by which large files are shared among individuals as they download them, making it possible for users to achieve very rapid downloads by accumulating bits of files from multiple sources, all while serving as sources themselves. Generativity, then, is a parent of invention, and an open network connecting generative devices makes the fruits of invention easy to share if the inventor is so inclined.

GENERATIVITY'S INPUT: PARTICIPATION

A second good of generativity is its invitation to outside contribution on its own terms. This invitation occurs at two levels: the individual act of contribution itself, and the ways in which that contribution becomes part of a self-reinforcing community. On the first level, there is a unique joy to be had in building something, even if one is not the best craftsperson. This is a value best appreciated by experiencing it; those who demand proof may not be easy to persuade. Fortunately, there are many ways in which people have a chance to build and contribute. Many jobs demand intellectual engagement, which can be fun for its own sake. People take joy in rearing children: teaching, interacting, guiding. They can also immerse themselves in artistic invention or software coding.

Famed utilitarian John Stuart Mill may have believed in the greatest happiness for the greatest number, but he was also a champion of the individual and a hater of custom. He first linked idiosyncrasy to innovation when he argued that society should "give the freest scope possible to uncustomary things, in order that it may in time appear which of these are fit to be converted into customs."[61] He then noted the innate value of being able to express oneself idiosyncratically:

But independence of action, and disregard of custom, are not solely deserving of en-couragement for the chance they afford that better modes of action, and customs more worthy of general adoption, may be struck out; nor is it only persons of de-cided mental superiority who have a just claim to carry on their lives in their own way. . . . The same things which are helps to one person towards the cultivation of his higher nature are hindrances to another. The same mode of life is a healthy ex-citement to one, keeping all his faculties of action and enjoyment in their best order, while to another it is a distracting burthen, which suspends or crushes all internal life.[62]

The generative Internet and PC allow more than technical innovation and participation as new services and software are designed and deployed. In addi-tion, much of that software is geared toward making political and artistic ex-pression easier. Yochai Benkler has examined the opportunities for the democ-ratization of cultural participation offered by the Internet through the lens of liberal political theory:

The networked information economy makes it possible to reshape both the "who" and the "how" of cultural production relative to cultural production in the twentieth century. It adds to the centralized, market-oriented production system a new frame-work of radically decentralized individual and cooperative nonmarket production. It thereby affects the ability of individuals and groups to participate in the production of the cultural tools and frameworks of human understanding and discourse. It affects the way we, as individuals and members of social and political clusters, inter-act with culture, and through it with each other. It makes culture more transparent to its inhabitants. It makes the process of cultural production more participatory, in the sense that more of those who live within a culture can actively participate in its creation. We are seeing the possibility of an emergence of a new popular culture, pro-duced on the folk-culture model and inhabited actively, rather than passively con-sumed by the masses. Through these twin characteristics—transparency and partic-ipation—the networked information economy also creates greater space for critical evaluation of cultural materials and tools. The practice of producing culture makes us all more sophisticated readers, viewers, and listeners, as well as more engaged makers.[63]

Benkler sees market-based models of cultural production as at odds with the folk-culture model, and he much prefers the latter: from "the perspective of lib-eral political theory, the kind of open, participatory, transparent folk culture that is emerging in the networked environment is normatively more attractive than was the industrial cultural production system typified by Hollywood and the recording industry."[64] Here, the lines between entertainment and more profound civic communication are understood to be thin, if they exist at all. An ability to participate in the making of culture is seen to be as paramount to full citizenship as the traditionally narrower activities of engaging in direct political debate or discussion of pressing policy issues.

Benkler points out the merits of systems that do what he calls "sharing nicely," systems in which people help each other without demanding the formalities and corresponding frictions of economic exchange.[65] He argues that much wealth has been created by an economy parallel to the corporate one, an economy of people helping out others without direct expectation of recompense, and that the network revolution makes it easier for that informal engine to generate much more—more participation, and more innovation.

The joy of being able to be helpful to someone—to answer a question simply because it is asked and one knows a useful answer, to be part of a team driving toward a worthwhile goal—is one of the best aspects of being human, and our information technology architecture has stumbled into a zone where those qualities can be elicited and affirmed for tens of millions of people.[66] It is captured fleetingly when strangers are thrown together in adverse situations and unite to overcome them—an elevator that breaks down, or a blizzard or blackout that temporarily paralyzes the normal cadences of life in a city but that leads to wonder and camaraderie along with some fear. Part of the Net of the early twenty-first century has distilled some of these values, promoting them without the kind of adversity or physical danger that could make a blizzard fun for the first day but divisive and lawless after the first week without structured relief.

William Fisher has noted a similar potential in his discussion of semiotic democracy, a media studies concept drawn from the work of John Fiske.[67] Fisher argues that "[i]n an attractive society all persons would be able to participate in the process of making cultural meaning. Instead of being merely passive consumers of images and artifacts produced by others, they would help shape the world of ideas and symbols in which they live."[68]

Technology is not inherently helpful in achieving these ends. At its core, it is a way of taking useful practices and automating them—offering at least greater leverage. Laundry that took a day to do can now be done in an hour or two. But leverage alone, if packaged in a way that does not allow adaptation, is not generative. It threatens conformity. The more there are prescribed ways to do something, the more readily people fall into identical patterns. Such prescriptions can come about through rules (as in the fractally thorough guidebooks on how to operate a McDonald's franchise) or technology (as in the linearity of a

PowerPoint slide show and the straitjacket of some of its most favored templates).[69] These rules might ensure a certain minimum competence in the preparation of a hamburger or of a business presentation precisely because they discourage what might be unhelpful or unskilled freelancing by the people implementing them. However, the regularity needed to produce consistent sandwiches and talks can actively discourage or prevent creativity. That drives critics of technology like Neil Postman, author of such evocatively titled books as *Building a Bridge to the 18th Century*[70] and *Technopoly: The Surrender of Culture to Technology*,[71] to argue that the ascendance of engineering and information technology is making sheep of us.

However, this understanding of technology stops at those systems that are built once, originating elsewhere, and then imposed (or even eagerly snapped up) by everyone else, who then cannot change them and thus become prisoners to them. It need not be that way. Technologies that are adaptable and accessible—not just leveraging—allow people to go a step further once they have mastered the basics. The Lego company offers suggestions of what to build on the boxes containing Lego blocks, and they even parcel out a certain number of each type of block in a package so the user can easily produce exactly those suggestions. But they are combinable into any number of new forms as soon as the user feels ready to do more than what the box instructs. The PC and the Internet have been just the same in that way. The divide is not between technology and nontechnology, but between hierarchy and polyarchy.[72] In hierarchies, gatekeepers control the allocation of attention and resources to an idea. In polyarchies, many ideas can be pursued independently. Hierarchical systems appear better at nipping dead-end ideas in the bud, but they do so at the expense of crazy ideas that just might work. Polyarchies can result in wasted energy and effort, but they are better at ferreting out and developing obscure, transformative ideas. More importantly, they allow many more people to have a hand at contributing to the system, regardless of the quality of the contribution.

Is this only a benefit for those among us who are technically inclined? Most of Mill's passion for individuality was channeled into a spirited defense of free speech and free thinking, not free building—and certainly not free programming.

However, as Benkler's linkage of the Internet to cultural expression suggests, the current incarnation of cyberspace offers a generative path that is not simply an avenue of self-expression for individual nerds. Generativity at the technical layer can lead to new forms of expression for other layers to which nonprogrammers contribute—culture, political, social, economic, and literary. We can call this recursive generativity, repeated up through the layers of the hourglass. Generativity at the technical layer can also enable new forms of group interaction, refuting Mill's dichotomy of the mediocre masses versus the lone eccentric.

GROUPS AND GENERATIVITY: FROM GENERATIVE TOOLS TO GENERATIVE SYSTEMS

Creative talent differs greatly from one person to the next, not only in degree but in preferred outlet. Mozart might have turned to painting if there were no musical instruments for which to compose, but there is no particular reason to believe that his paintings would be as good among the work of painters as his music is judged to be among that of musicians. Generativity solicits invention, which in turn can be an important expression of the inventor—a fulfillment of a human urge that is thought to represent some of the highest endeavor and purpose of which we are capable. New technologies welcome new groups of people who may excel at manipulating them.

People can work alone or in groups. Working in groups has practical limitations. It is typically not easy to collaborate from far away. The combination of networks and PCs, however, has made it particularly easy to arrange such collaborations. Open source projects too ambitious for a single programmer or localized group of programmers to achieve alone have been made possible by cheap networking,[73] and the free software movement has developed tools that greatly ease collaboration over a distance, such as CVS, the "concurrent versions system."[74] CVS automates many of the difficult tasks inherent in having many people work on the same body of code at the same time. Itself an open source project, CVS permits users to establish a virtual library of the code they are working on, checking out various pieces to work on and then checking them back in for others to use.[75] Successive versions are maintained so that changes by one person that are regretted by another can be readily unmade. People with complementary talents who otherwise would not have known or met each other, much less found a way to collaborate without much logistical friction, can be brought together to work on a project. Creativity, then, is enhanced not only for individuals, but also for groups as distinct entities, thanks to the linkage of the PC and the Internet.

RECURSION FROM TECHNOLOGY TO CONTENT TO SOCIETY

The emergence of a vibrant public Internet and a powerful PC affects many traditional forms of creative and artistic expression because the accessibility of the PC and the Internet to coding by a variety of technically capable groups has translated to a number of platforms for use by *artistically* capable groups.

For example, thanks to the hypertext standards first developed by researcher Tim Berners-Lee,[76] the Web came into existence, and because Berners-Lee's html hypertext markup language was easy to master, people without much technical know-how could build Web sites showcasing their creative work,[77] or Web sites that were themselves creative works. Once html took off, others wrote html processors and converters so that one did not even have to know the basics of html to produce and edit Web pages.[78]

Similarly, simple but powerful software written by amateurs and running on Internet servers has enabled amateur journalists and writers to prepare and customize chronological accounts of their work—"blogs"[79]—and the pervasiveness of online search software has made these blogs accessible to millions of people who do not seek them out by name but rather by a topical search of a subject covered by a blog entry.[80] The blog's underlying software may be changeable itself, as Wordpress is, for example, and therefore generative at the technical layer. But even if it were not so readily reprogrammed, as Microsoft's proprietary MSN Spaces is not, the opportunity to configure a blog for nearly any purpose—group commentary, seeking help finding a lost camera,[81] expressing and then sorting and highlighting various political opinions—makes it generative at the content layer.

A signal example of both recursive and group generativity can be found in the wiki. Software consultant Ward Cunningham was intrigued by the ways in which strangers might collaborate online.[82] He wrote some basic tools that would allow people to create Web pages even if they didn't know anything about Web page creation, and that would allow others to modify those pages, keeping track of revisions along the way—a sort of CVS for nonprogramming content.[83] He opened a Web site using these tools in 1995 to host an ongoing conversation about computer programming, and called it a "wiki" after a trip to Hawaii had exposed him to airport shuttle buses called "wiki-wikis" (*wiki* is the Hawaiian word for "quick").[84]

Cunningham's own wiki was successful among a group of several hundred people—to be sure, he did not appear to be aiming for mass adoption—and it inspired the founding of Wikipedia in 2001.[85] Wikipedia built on Cunningham's concepts with the ambition to create an online encyclopedia written and edited by the world at large. With few exceptions anyone can edit a Wikipedia entry at any time. As discussed at length later in this book, the possibility for inaccuracy or outright falsehood is thus legion, and Wikipedia's users have both created new technology and solicited commitments from people who share Wikipedia's ethos to maintain its accuracy without significantly denting its generativity. Wikipedia stands at the apex of amateur endeavor: an undertaking done out of sheer interest in or love of a topic, built on collaborative software that enables a breathtakingly comprehensive result that is the sum of individual contributions, and one that is extraordinarily trusting of them.[86] Wikipedia's character will no doubt evolve as, say, companies discover its existence and begin editing (and policing) entries that mention or describe them,[87] just as ownership of domain names evolved from an informal and free first-come, first-served system to a hotly contested battlefield once their true value was recognized.[88] Today, Wikipedia's success showcases the interactions that can take place among the layers of a technical system, with the Internet's absence of gatekeepers allowing wiki software to be developed, shared, and then taken up for educational and social purposes with contributions from people who have little to no technical expertise.

The ubiquity of PCs and networks—and the integration of the two—have thus bridged the interests of technical audiences and artistic and expressive ones, making the grid's generativity relevant not only to creativity in code-writing as an end, but to creativity in other artistic ventures as well, including those that benefit from the ability of near-strangers to encounter each other on the basis of mutual interest, form groups, and then collaborate smoothly enough that actual works can be generated. If one measures the value of generativity through the amount of creativity it unleashes,[89] then the generativity of the PC and Internet grid should be measured not solely by the creativity it enables among coders, but also by the creativity it enables among artists—and among groups of each.[90]

THE GENERATIVE PATTERN

Generative technologies need not produce forward progress, if by progress one means something like increasing social welfare. Rather, they foment change. They solicit the distributed intellectual power of humanity to harness the leveraging power of the product or system for new applications, and, if they are adaptable enough, such applications may be quite unexpected. To use an evolutionary metaphor, they encourage mutations, branchings away from the status quo—some that are curious dead ends, others that spread like wildfire. They invite disruption—along with the good things and bad things that can come with such disruption.

The harm from disruption might differ by field. Consider a hypothetical highly generative children's chemistry set, adaptable and exceptionally leveraging. It would contain chemicals that could accomplish a variety of tasks, with small quantities adding up to big results if the user so desired. It would also be easy to master: children would be able to learn how to use it. But such generativity would have a manifest downside risk: a chemical accident could be dangerous to the child or even to the entire neighborhood.[91] A malicious child—or adult, for that matter—could wreak greater havoc as the set's generativity grew. The same principle applies to gene splicing kits, atom smashers, and many of the power tools at a local hardware store. The more experimentation allowed, the more harm the tool invites. One might want to allow more room for experimentation in information technology than for physics because the risks of harm—particularly physical harm—are likely to be lower as a structural matter from misuse or abuse of information technology. The law of negligence echoes this divide: it is ready to intervene in cases of physical harm but usually refuses to do so when someone's misdeed results in "only" economic harm.[92]

Nonetheless, economic harm is real, whether caused to the Internet itself or to interests external to it. Disruption benefits some while others lose, and the power of the generative Internet, available to anyone with a modicum of knowledge and a broadband connection, can be turned to network-destroying ends. As the previous chapter illustrated, the Internet's very generativity—combined with that of the PCs attached—sows the seeds for a "digital Pearl Harbor."[93] If we do not address this problem, the most likely first-order solutions in reaction to the problem will be at least as bad as the problem itself, because they will increase security by reducing generativity.

The Internet security problem is only one item within a basket of conflicts whose balance is greatly affected by the rise of the generative Internet. Some entrepreneurs who have benefited from the disruption of the late 1990s naturally wish to close the door behind them—enjoying the fruits of the generative grid while denying them to the next round of innovators. First among the injured are the publishing industries whose intellectual property's value is premised on maintaining scarcity, if not fine-grained control, over the creative works in which they have been granted some exclusive rights.

Von Hippel's work emphasizes the ways in which established firms and non-market-acting individuals can innovate in their respective spheres and benefit from one another's activities. Benkler, on the other hand, sees war between the amateur authors empowered by generative systems and the industries whose work they will affect:

> If the transformation I describe as possible occurs, it will lead to substantial redistri-
> bution of power and money from the twentieth-century industrial producers of in-
> formation, culture, and communications—like Hollywood, the recording industry,
> and perhaps the broadcasters and some of the telecommunications services giants—
> to a combination of widely diffuse populations around the globe, and the market ac-
> tors that will build the tools that make this population better able to produce its own
> information environment rather than buying it ready-made. None of the industrial
> giants of yore are taking this reallocation lying down. The technology will not over-
> come their resistance through an insurmountable progressive impulse.[94]

For others, the impact of a generative system may be not just a fight between upstarts and incumbents, but a struggle between control and anarchy. Mill in part reconciled his embrace of individual rights with his utilitarian recognition of the need for limits to freedom by conceding that there are times where regulation is called for. However, he saw his own era as one that was too regulated:

> Whoever thinks that individuality of desires and impulses should not be encouraged
> to unfold itself, must maintain that society has no need of strong natures—is not the
> better for containing many persons who have much character—and that a high gen-
> eral average of energy is not desirable.
>
> In some early states of society, these forces might be, and were, too much ahead of
> the power which society then possessed of disciplining and controlling them. There
> has been a time when the element of spontaneity and individuality was in excess, and
> the social principle had a hard struggle with it. The difficulty then was, to induce
> men of strong bodies or minds to pay obedience to any rules which required them to
> control their impulses. To overcome this difficulty, law and discipline, like the Popes
> struggling against the Emperors, asserted a power over the whole man, claiming to
> control all his life in order to control his character—which society had not found
> any other sufficient means of binding. But society has now fairly got the better of in-
> dividuality; and the danger which threatens human nature is not the excess, but the
> deficiency, of personal impulses and preferences. Things are vastly changed, since the
> passions of those who were strong by station or by personal endowment were in a
> state of habitual rebellion against laws and ordinances, and required to be rigorously

chained up to enable the persons within their reach to enjoy any particle of security. In our times, from the highest class of society down to the lowest every one lives as under the eye of a hostile and dreaded censorship.[95]

A necessary reaction to the lawlessness of early societies had become an over-reaction and, worse, self-perpetuating regulation. The generative Internet and PC were at first perhaps more akin to new societies; as people were connected, they may not have had firm expectations about the basics of the interaction. Who pays for what? Who shares what? The time during which the Internet remained an academic backwater, and the PC was a hobbyist's tool, helped situate each within the norms of Benkler's parallel economy of sharing nicely, of greater control in the hands of users and commensurate trust that they would not abuse it. Some might see this configuration as spontaneity and individuality in excess. One holder of a mobile phone camera can irrevocably compromise someone else's privacy;[96] one bootleg of a concert can make the rounds of the whole world. And one well-crafted virus can take down millions of machines.

This is the generative pattern, and we can find examples of it at every layer of the network hourglass:

1. An idea originates in a backwater.
2. It is ambitious but incomplete. It is partially implemented and released anyway, embracing the ethos of the procrastination principle.
3. Contribution is welcomed from all corners, resulting in an influx of usage.
4. Success is achieved beyond any expectation, and a higher profile draws even more usage.
5. Success is cut short: "There goes the neighborhood" as newer users are not conversant with the idea of experimentation and contribution, and other users are prepared to exploit the openness of the system to undesirable ends.
6. There is movement toward enclosure to prevent the problems that arise from the system's very popularity.

The paradox of generativity is that with an openness to unanticipated change, we can end up in bad—and non-generative—waters. Perhaps the forces of spam and malware, of phishing and fraud and exploitation of others, are indeed "too much ahead of the power which society then possessed of disciplining and controlling them."[97] For too long the framers of the Internet have figured that ISPs can simply add bandwidth to solve the spam problem; if so, who cares that 90 percent of e-mail is spam?[98] Or vendors can add PC computing cycles to solve the malware problem, at least from the PC owner's point of view—a PC can function just fine while it is infected because, with the latest processor, it can spew spam while still giving its user plenty of attention for game playing or word processing or Web surfing.

This complacency is not sustainable in the long term because it ignores the harm that accrues to those who cannot defend themselves against network mischief the way that technologically sophisticated users can. It fails to appreciate that the success of the Internet and PC has created a set of valid interests beyond that of experimentation. In the next chapter, we will see how the most natural reactions to the generative problem of excess spontaneity and individuality will be overreactions, threatening the entire generative basis of the Net and laying the groundwork for the hostile and dreaded censorship that Mill decried. In particular, a failure to solve generative problems at the technical layer will result in outcomes that allow for unwanted control at the content and social layers.

Then we will turn to solutions: ways in which, as the vibrant information society matures, we can keep problems in check while retaining the vital spark that drives it, and us, to new heights.

5

Tethered Appliances, Software as Service, and Perfect Enforcement

As Part I of this book explained, the generative nature of the PC and Internet—a certain incompleteness in design, and corresponding openness to outside innovation—is both the cause of their success and the instrument of their forthcoming failure.

The most likely reactions to PC and Internet failures brought on by the proliferation of bad code, if they are not forestalled, will be at least as unfortunate as the problems themselves. People now have the opportunity to respond to these problems by moving away from the PC and toward more centrally controlled—"tethered"—information appliances like mobile phones, video game consoles, TiVos, iPods, iPhones, and BlackBerries. The ongoing communication between this new generation of devices and their vendors assures users that functionality and security improvements can be made as new problems are found. To further facilitate glitch-free operation, devices are built to allow no one but the vendor to change them. Users are also now able to ask for the appliancization of their own PCs, in the process forfeiting the ability to easily install new code themselves. In a development reminiscent of the old days of AOL and CompuServe, it is increasingly possible to use a PC as a mere dumb terminal to access Web sites with interactivity but with little room for tinkering. ("Web 2.0" is a new buzz-word that celebrates this migration of applications traditionally found on the PC onto the Internet. Confusingly, the term also refers to the separate phenom-enon of increased user-generated content and indices on the Web—such as re-lying on user-provided tags to label photographs.) New information appliances that are tethered to their makers, including PCs and Web sites refashioned in this mold, are tempting solutions for frustrated consumers and businesses.

None of these solutions, standing alone, is bad, but the aggregate loss will be enormous if their emergence represents a wholesale shift of our information ecosystem away from generativity. Some are skeptical that a shift so large can take place.[1] But confidence in the generative Internet's inertia is misplaced. It discounts the power of fear should the existing system falter under the force of particularly well-written malware. People might argue about the merits of one platform compared to another ("Linux never needs to be rebooted"),[2] but the fact is that no operating system is perfect, and, more importantly, any PC open to running third-party code at the user's behest can fail when poor code is adopted. The fundamental problem arises from too much functionality in the hands of users who may not exercise it wisely: even the safest Volvo can be driven into a wall.

People are frustrated by PC kinks and the erratic behavior they produce. Such unexpected variations in performance have long been smoothed out in refrigerators, televisions, mobile phones, and automobiles. As for PCs, telling users that their own surfing or program installation choices are to blame un-derstandably makes them no less frustrated, even if they realize that a more re-liable system would inevitably be less functional—a trade-off seemingly not re-quired by refrigerator improvements. Worse, the increasing reliance on the PC and Internet that suggests momentum in their use means that more is at risk when something goes wrong. Skype users who have abandoned their old-fash-ioned telephone lines may regret their decision if an emergency arises and they need to dial an emergency number like 911, only to find that they cannot get through, let alone be located automatically.[3] When one's finances, contacts, and appointments are managed using a PC, it is no longer merely frustrating if the computer comes down with a virus. It is enough to search for alternative ar-chitectures.

A shift to tethered appliances and locked-down PCs will have a ripple effect on long-standing cyberlaw problems, many of which are tugs-of-war between individuals with a real or perceived injury from online activity and those who wish to operate as freely as possible in cyberspace. The capacity for the types of disruptive innovation discussed in the previous chapter will not be the only casualty. A shift to tethered appliances also entails a sea change in the *regulability* of the Internet. With tethered appliances, the dangers of excess come not from rogue third-party code, but from the much more predictable interventions by regulators into the devices themselves, and in turn into the ways that people can use the appliances.

The most obvious evolution of the computer and network—toward tethered appliancization—is on balance a bad one. It invites regulatory intervention that disrupts a wise equilibrium that depends upon regulators acting with a light touch, as they traditionally have done within liberal societies.

THE LONG ARM OF MARSHALL, TEXAS

TiVo introduced the first digital video recorder (DVR) in 1998.[4] It allowed consumers to record and time-shift TV shows. After withstanding several claims that the TiVo DVR infringed other companies' patents because it offered its users on-screen programming guides,[5] the hunted became the hunter. In 2004, TiVo sued satellite TV distributor EchoStar for infringing TiVo's own patents[6] by building DVR functionality into some of EchoStar's dish systems.[7]

A Texas jury found for TiVo. TiVo was awarded $90 million in damages and interest. In briefs filed under seal, TiVo apparently asked for more. In August 2006, the court issued the following ruling:

> Defendants are hereby . . . ORDERED to, within thirty (30) days of the issuance of this order, disable the DVR functionality (i.e., disable all storage to and playback from a hard disk drive of television data) in all but 192,708 units of the Infringing Products that have been placed with an end user or subscriber.[8]

That is, the court ordered EchoStar to kill the DVR functionality in products already owned by "end users": millions of boxes which were already sitting in living rooms around the world[9] with owners who might be using them at that very instant.[10] Imagine sitting down to watch television on an EchoStar box, and instead finding that all your recorded shows had been zapped, along with the DVR functionality itself—killed by remote signal traceable to the stroke of a judge's quill in Marshall, Texas.

The judicial logic for such an order is drawn from fundamental contraband rules: under certain circumstances, if an article infringes on intellectual property rights, it can be impounded and destroyed.[11] Impoundment remedies are usually encountered only in the form of Prohibition-era-style raids on warehouses and distribution centers, which seize large amounts of contraband before it is sold to consumers.[12] There are no house-to-house raids to, say, seize bootleg concert recordings or reclaim knockoff Rolexes and Louis Vuitton handbags from the people who purchased the goods.

TiVo saw a new opportunity in its patent case, recognizing that EchoStar's dish system is one of an increasing number of modern tethered appliances. The system periodically phones home to EchoStar, asking for updated programming for its internal software.[13] This tethered functionality also means EchoStar can remotely destroy the units. To do so requires EchoStar only to load its central server with an update that kills EchoStar DVRs when they check in for new features.

As of this writing, *TiVo v. EchoStar* is pending appeal on other grounds.[14] The order has been stayed, and no DVRs have yet been remotely destroyed.[15] But such remote remedies are not wholly unprecedented. In 2001, a U.S. federal court heard a claim from a company called PlayMedia that AOL had included PlayMedia's AMP MP3 playback software in version 6.0 of AOL's software in violation of a settlement agreement between PlayMedia and a company that AOL had acquired. The court agreed with PlayMedia and ordered AOL to prevent "any user of the AOL service from completing an online 'session' . . . without AMP being removed from the user's copy of AOL 6.0 by means of an AOL online 'live update.'"[16]

TiVo v. EchoStar and *PlayMedia v. AOL* broach the strange and troubling issues that arise from the curious technological hybrids that increasingly populate the digital world. These hybrids mate the simplicity and reliability of television-like appliances with the privileged power of the vendor to reprogram those appliances over a network.

REGULABILITY AND THE TETHERED APPLIANCE

As legal systems experienced the first wave of suits arising from use of the Internet, scholars such as Lawrence Lessig and Joel Reidenberg emphasized that code could be law.[17] In this view, the software we use shapes and channels our online behavior as surely as—or even more surely and subtly than—law itself. Restrictions can be enforced by the way a piece of software operates. Our ways of thinking about such "west coast code"[18] are still maturing, and our instincts for when we object to such code are not well formed. Just as technology's functionality defines the universe in which people can operate, it also defines the range of regulatory options reasonably available to a sovereign. A change in technology can change the power dynamic between those who promulgate the law and those who are subject to it.[19]

If regulators can induce certain alterations in the nature of Internet technologies that others could not undo or widely circumvent, then many of the regulatory limitations occasioned by the Internet would evaporate. Lessig and others have worried greatly about such potential changes, fearing that blunderbuss technology regulation by overeager regulators will intrude on the creative freedom of technology makers and the civic freedoms of those who use the technology.[20]

So far Lessig's worries have not come to pass. A system's level of generativity can change the direction of the power flow between sovereign and subject in favor of the subject, and generative Internet technology has not been easy to alter. There have been private attempts to use code to build so-called trusted systems, software that outsiders can trust to limit users' behavior—for example, by allowing a song to be played only three times before it "expires," or by preventing an e-book from being printed.[21] (Code-based enforcement mechanisms are also variously called digital rights management systems or technological protection measures.)[22] Most trusted systems have failed, often because either savvy users have cracked them early on or the market has simply rejected them. The few that have achieved some measure of adoption—like Apple iTunes's FairPlay, which allows purchased songs to exist on only five registered devices at once[23]—are either readily circumvented, or tailored so they do not prevent most users' desired behavior.

Even the governments most determined to regulate certain flows of information—such as China—have found it difficult to suppress the flow of data on the Internet.[24] To be sure, with enough effort, censorship can have some effect, especially because most citizens prefer to slow down for speed bumps rather than invent ways around them.[25] When a Web site fails to load, for example, users generally visit a substitute site rather than wait. Taking advantage of this reality, Chinese regulators have used their extensive control over ISPs' routing of data packets to steer users away from undesirable Web sites by simply causing the Web pages to fail to load in the course of normal surfing.

But so long as the *endpoints* remain generative and any sort of basic Internet access remains available, subversively minded techies can make applications that offer a way around network blocks.[26] Such applications can be distributed through the network, and unsavvy users can then partake simply by double-clicking on an icon. Comprehensive regulatory crackdowns require a non-generative endpoint or influence over the individual using it to ensure that the endpoint is not repurposed.

For example, non-generative endpoints like radios and telephones can be constrained by filtering the networks they use. Even if someone is unafraid to turn a radio tuning knob or dial a telephone number to the outside world, radio broadcasts can be jammed, and phone connections can be disabled or monitored. Because radios and telephones are not generative, such jamming cannot be circumvented. North Korea has gone even further with endpoint lockdown. There, by law, the radios themselves are built so that they cannot be tuned to frequencies other than those with official broadcasts.[27]

With generative devices like PCs, the regulator must settle for either much leakier enforcement or much more resource-intensive measures that target the individual—such as compelling citizens to perform their Internet surfing in cyber cafés or public libraries, where they might limit their activities for fear that others are watching.

The shift toward non-generative endpoint technology driven by consumer security worries of the sort described in this book changes the equation.[28] The traditional appliance, or nearly any object, for that matter, once placed with an individual, belongs to that person. Tethered appliances belong to a new class of technology. They are *appliances* in that they are easy to use, while not easy to tinker with. They are *tethered* because it is easy for their vendors to change them from afar, long after the devices have left warehouses and showrooms. Consider how useful it was in 2003 that Apple could introduce the iTunes Store directly into iTunes software found on PCs running Mac OS.[29] Similarly, consumers can turn on a TiVo—or EchoStar—box to find that, thanks to a remote update, it can do new things, such as share programs with other televisions in the house.[30]

These tethered appliances receive remote updates from the manufacturer, but they generally are not configured to allow anyone else to tinker with them—to invent new features and distribute them to other owners who would not know how to program the boxes themselves. Updates come from only one source, with a model of product development limited to non-user innovation. Indeed, recall that some recent devices, like the iPhone, are updated in ways that actively seek out and erase any user modifications. These boxes thus resemble the early proprietary information services like CompuServe and AOL, for which only the service providers could add new features. Any user inventiveness was cabined by delays in chartering and understanding consumer focus groups, the hassles of forging deals with partners to invent and implement suggested features, and the burdens of performing technical R&D.

Yet tethered appliances are much more powerful than traditional appliances. Under the old regime, a toaster, once purchased, remains a toaster. An upgraded model might offer a third slot, but no manufacturer's representative visits consumers and retrofits old toasters. Buy a record and it can be played as many times as the owner wants. If the original musician wishes to rerecord a certain track, she will have to feature it in a successive release—the older work has been released to the four winds and cannot be recalled.[31] A shift to smarter appliances, ones that can be updated by—and only by—their makers, is fundamentally changing the way in which we experience our technologies. Appliances become *contingent:* rented instead of owned, even if one pays up front for them, since they are subject to instantaneous revision.

A continuing connection to a producer paves the way for easier postacquisition improvements: the modern equivalent of third slots for old toasters. That sounds good: more features, instantly distributed. So what is the drawback? Those who believe that markets reflect demand will rightly ask why a producer would make post hoc changes to technology that customers may not want.

One answer is that they may be compelled to do so. Consider EchoStar's losing verdict in Marshall, Texas. If producers can alter their products long after the products have been bought and installed in homes and offices, it occasions a sea change in the *regulability* of those products and their users. With products tethered to the network, regulators—perhaps on their own initiative to advance broadly defined public policy, or perhaps acting on behalf of parties like TiVo claiming private harms—finally have a toolkit for exercising meaningful control over the famously anarchic Internet.

TYPES OF PERFECT ENFORCEMENT

The law as we have known it has had flexible borders. This flexibility derives from prosecutorial and police discretion and from the artifice of the outlaw. When code is law, however, execution is exquisite, and law can be self-enforcing. The flexibility recedes. Those who control the tethered appliance can control the behavior undertaken with the device in a number of ways: preemption, specific injunction, and surveillance.

Preemption

Preemption entails anticipating and designing against undesirable conduct before it happens. Many of the examples of code as law (or, more generally, architecture as law) fit into this category. Lessig points out that speeding can be regulated quite effectively through the previously mentioned use of speed bumps.[32] Put a speed bump in the road and people slow down rather than risk damaging their cars. Likewise, most DVD players have Macrovision copy protection that causes a signal to be embedded in the playback of DVDs, stymieing most attempts to record DVDs onto a VCR.[33] Owners of Microsoft's Zune music player can beam music to other Zune owners, but music so transferred can be played only three times or within three days of the transfer.[34] This kind of limitation arguably preempts much of the damage that might otherwise be thought to arise if music subject to copyright could be shared freely. With TiVo, a broadcaster can flag a program as "premium" and assign it an expiration date.[35] A little red flag then appears next to it in the viewer's list of recorded programs, and the TiVo will refuse to play the program after its expiration date. The box's makers (or regulators of the makers) could further decide to automatically reprogram the TiVo to limit its fast-forwarding functionality or to restrict its hours of operability. (In China, makers of multiplayer games have been compelled to limit the number of hours a day that subscribers can play in an effort to curb gaming addiction.)[36] Preemption does not require constant updates so long as the device cannot easily be modified once it is in the user's possession; the idea is to design the product with broadly defined limits that do not require further intervention to serve the regulator's or designer's purposes.

Specific Injunction

Specific injunction takes advantage of the communication that routinely occurs between a particular tethered appliance and its manufacturer, *after* it is in consumer hands, to reflect changed circumstances. The *TiVo v. EchoStar* remedy belongs in this category, as it mandates modification of the EchoStar units after they have already been designed and distributed. This remote remedy was practicable because the tethering allowed the devices to be completely reprogrammed, even though the initial design of the EchoStar device had not anticipated a patent infringement judgment.

Specific injunction also allows for much more tailored remedies, like the PlayMedia-specific court order discussed earlier. Such tailoring can be content-specific, user-specific, or even time-specific. These remedies can apply to some units and not others, allowing regulators to winnow out bad uses from good ones on the basis of individual adjudication, rather than rely on the generalities of *ex ante* legislative-style drafting. For example, suppose a particular television broadcast were found to infringe a copyright or to damage someone's reputation. In a world of old-fashioned televisions and VCRs, or PCs and peer-to-peer networks, the broadcaster or creator could be sued, but anyone who recorded the broadcast could, as a practical matter, retain a copy. Today, it is possible to require DVR makers to delete the offending broadcast from any DVRs that have recorded it or, perhaps acting with more precision, to retroactively edit out the slice of defamatory content from the recorded program. This control extends beyond any particular content medium: as e-book devices become popular, the same excisions could be performed for print materials. Tailoring also could be user-specific, requiring, say, the prevention or elimination of prurient material from the devices of registered sex offenders but not from others' devices.

Surveillance

Tethered appliances have the capacity to relay information about their uses back to the manufacturer. We have become accustomed to the idea that Web sites track our behavior when we access them—an online bookseller, for example, knows what books we have browsed and bought at its site. Tethered appliances take this knowledge a step further, recording what we do with the appliances even in transactions that have nothing to do with the vendor. A TiVo knows whether its owner watches FOX News or PBS. It knows when someone replays some scenes and skips others. This information is routinely sent to the TiVo mothership;[37] for example, in the case of Janet Jackson's "wardrobe malfunction" during the 2004 Super Bowl halftime show, TiVo was able to calculate that this moment was replayed three times more frequently than any other during the broadcast.[38]

TiVo promises not to release such surveillance information in personally identifiable form, but the company tempers the promise with an industry-standard exception for regulators who request it through legal process.[39] Automakers General Motors and BMW offer similar privacy policies for the computer systems, such as OnStar, built into their automobiles. OnStar's uses range from providing turn-by-turn driving directions with the aid of Global Positioning System (GPS) satellites, to monitoring tire pressure, providing emergency assistance, and facilitating hands-free calling with embedded microphones and speakers. The FBI realized that it could eavesdrop on conversations occurring inside an OnStar-equipped vehicle by remotely reprogramming the system to activate its microphones for use as a "roving bug," and it has secretly ordered an anonymous carmaker to do just that on at least one occasion.[40]

A similar dynamic is possible with nearly all mobile phones. Mobile phones can be reprogrammed at a distance, allowing their microphones to be secretly turned on even when the phone is powered down. All ambient noise and conversation can then be continuously picked up and relayed back to law enforcement authorities, regardless of whether the phone is being used for a call.[41] On modern PCs equipped with an automatic update feature, there is no technical barrier that prevents the implementation of any similar form of surveillance on the machine, whether it involves turning on the PC's microphone and video camera, or searching and sharing any documents stored on the machine. Such surveillance could be introduced through a targeted update from the OS maker or from any other provider of software running on the machine.

Surveillance need not be limited to targeted eavesdropping that is part of a criminal or civil investigation. It can also be effected more generally. In 1996, law student Michael Adler offered the hypothetical of an Internet-wide search for contraband.[42] He pointed out that some digital items might be illegal to possess or be indicative of other illegal activity—for example, child pornography, leaked classified documents, or stores of material copied without permission of the copyright holder. A Net-wide search could be instigated that would inventory connected machines and report back when smoking guns were found.

Tethering makes these approaches practicable and inexpensive for regulators. A government need only regulate certain critical private intermediaries—those who control the tethered appliances—to change the way individuals experience the world. When a doctrine's scope has been limited by prudential enforcement costs, its reach can be increased as the costs diminish.

EVALUATING PERFECT ENFORCEMENT

The prospect of more thorough or "perfect" law enforcement may seem appealing. If one could wave a wand and make it impossible for people to kill each other, there might seem little reason to hesitate. Although the common law has only rarely sought to outright prohibit the continued distribution of defamatory materials by booksellers and newsstands, much less continued possession by purchasers, ease of enforcement through tethered appliances could make it so that all such material—wherever it might be found—could vanish into the memory hole. Even when it comes to waving the regulator's wand for the purpose of eradicating online evils like harassment, invasion of privacy, and copyright infringement, there are important reasons to hesitate.[43]

Objections to the Underlying Substantive Law

Some people are consistently diffident about the presence of law in the online space. Those with undiluted libertarian values might oppose easier enforcement of laws as a general matter, because they believe that self-defense is the best solution to harm by others, especially within a medium that carries bits, not bullets.[44] By these lights, the most common online harms simply are not as harmful as those in the physical world, and therefore they call for lesser intrusions. For example, defamatory speech might be met not by a lawsuit for money damages or an injunction requiring deletion of the lies, but rather by more speech that corrects the record. A well-configured e-mail client can adequately block spam, making it unnecessary to resort to intervention by a public authority. Material harmful to minors can be defanged by using parental filters, or by providing better education to children about what to expect when they go online and how to deal with images of violence and hate.

Such "just deal with it" arguments are deployed less often against the online circulation of images of child abuse. The creation and distribution of child pornography is nearly universally understood as a significant harm. In this context, those arguing in favor of an anarchic environment shift to claims that the activity is not very common or that existing tools and remedies are sufficiently effective—or they rely on some of the other objections described below.

One can also argue against stronger enforcement regimes by objecting to the laws that will be enforced. For example, many of those who argue against increased copyright enforcement—undertaken through laws that broaden infringement penalties[45] or through trusted systems that preempt infringement[46]—argue that copyright law itself is too expansive.[47] For those who believe that intellectual property rights have gone too far, it is natural to argue against regimes that make such rights easier to enforce, independent of seeking to reform the copyright law itself. Similarly, those who believe in lower taxes might object to a plan that makes it easier for intermediaries to collect and remit use and sales taxes for online transactions.[48] Likewise, the large contingent of people who routinely engage in illegal online file sharing may naturally disfavor anything that interferes with these activities.[49] To be sure, some of those people may download even though they believe it to be wrong—in which case they might welcome a system that better prevents them from yielding to temptation.

Law professor William Stuntz notes the use of legal procedure—evolving doctrines of Fourth and Fifth Amendment protection—as a way of limiting the substantive application of unpopular laws in eighteenth- and nineteenth-century America such as those involving first heresy and sedition, and later railroad and antitrust regulation.[50] In that context, he argues, judges interpreted the Fourth and Fifth Amendments in ways designed to increase the costs to law enforcement of collecting evidence from private parties. When the judiciary began defining and enforcing a right to privacy that limited the sorts of searches police could undertake, it became more difficult to successfully prosecute objectionable crimes like heresy, sedition, or trade offenses: "It is as if privacy protection were a proxy for something else, a tool with which courts or juries could limit the government's substantive power."[51] Challenging the rise of tethered appliances helps maintain certain costs on the exercise of government power—costs that reduce the enforcement of objectionable laws.

The drawback to arguing generally against perfect enforcement because one objects to the laws likely to be enforced is that it preaches to the choir. Certainly, those who oppose copyright laws will also oppose changes to code that facilitate the law's online enforcement. To persuade those who are more favorably disposed to enforcement of substantive laws using tethered appliances, we must look to other objections.

Portability and Enforceability Without the Rule of Law

While it might be understandable that those opposed to a substantive law would also favor continued barriers to its enforcement, others might say that the price of living under the rule of law is that law ought to be respected, even if one disagrees with it. In this view, the way to protest an undesirable law is to pursue its modification or repeal, rather than to celebrate the difficulty of its enforcement.[52] The rise of procedural privacy limits described by Stuntz was itself an artifact of the law—the decisions of judges with license to interpret the Constitution. This legally sanctioned mandate is distinct from one allowing individuals to flout the law when they feel like it, simply because they cannot be easily prevented from engaging in the illicit act or caught.

But not every society operates according to a framework of laws that are democratically promulgated and then enforced by an independent judiciary.

Governments like those of China or Saudi Arabia might particularly benefit from technological configurations that allow for inexpensive surveillance or the removal of material authored by political dissidents. In a world where tethered appliances dominate, the cat-and-mouse game tilts toward the cat. Recall that the FBI can secretly eavesdrop on any automobile with an OnStar navigation system by obtaining a judge's order and ensuring that the surveillance does not otherwise disrupt the system's functioning. In a place without the rule of law, the prospect of cars rolling off the assembly line surveillance-ready is particularly unsettling. China's government has already begun experimenting with these sorts of approaches. For example, the PC telephone program Skype is not amenable to third-party changes and is tethered to Skype for its updates. Skype's distribution partner in China has agreed to censor words like "Falun Gong" and "Dalai Lama" in its text messaging for the Chinese version of the program.[53] Other services that are not generative at the technical layer have been similarly modified: Google.cn is censored by Google at the behest of the Chinese government, and Microsoft's MSN Spaces Chinese blog service automatically filters out sensitive words from blog titles.[54]

There is an ongoing debate about the degree to which firms chartered in freer societies should assist in censorship or surveillance taking place in less free societies.[55] The argument considered here is one layer deeper than that debate: if the information ecosystem at the cutting edge evolves into one that is not generative at its core, then authoritarian governments will naturally inherit an ability to enforce their wills more easily, without needing to change technologies and services or to curtail the breadth of their influence. Because it is often less obvious to users and the wider world, the ability to enforce quietly using qualities of the technology itself is worrisome. Technologies that lend themselves to an easy and tightly coupled expression of governmental power simply will be portable from one society to the next. It will make irrelevant the question about how firms like Google and Skype should operate outside their home countries.

This conclusion suggests that although some social gain may result from better enforcement of existing laws in free societies, the gain might be more than offset by better enforcement in societies that are less free—under repressive governments today, or anywhere in the future. If the gains and losses remain coupled, it might make sense to favor retention of generative technologies to put what law professor James Boyle has called the "Libertarian gotcha" to authoritarian regimes: if one wants technological progress and the associated economic benefits, one must be prepared to accept some measure of social liberalization made possible with that technology.[56] Like many regimes that want to harness the benefits of the market while forgoing political liberalization, China is wrestling with this tension today.[57] In an attempt to save money and establish independence from an overseas software vendor like Microsoft, China has encouraged the adoption of GNU/Linux,[58] an operating system least amenable in its current form to appliancization because anyone can modify it and install it on a non-locked-down endpoint PC. China's attempt, therefore, represents either a misunderstanding of the key role that endpoints can play in regulation or a calculated judgment that the benefits of international technological independence outweigh the costs of less regulability.

If one objects to censorship in societies that have not developed the rule of law, one can support the maintenance of a generative core in information technology, minimizing the opportunities for some societies that wish to exploit the information revolution to discover new tools for control.

Amplification and the Lock-in of Mistakes

When a regulator makes mistakes in the way it construes or applies a law, a stronger ability to compel compliance implies a stronger ability to compel compliance with all mandates, even those that are the results of mistaken interpretations. Gaps in translation may also arise between a legal mandate and its technological manifestation. This is especially true when technological design is used as a preemptive measure. Under U.S. First Amendment doctrine, prior restraints on speech—preventing speech from occurring in the first place, rather than punishing it after the fact if indeed it is unlawful—are greatly disfavored.[59] Design features mandated to prevent speech-related behaviors, on the premise that such behaviors might turn out to be unlawful, could be thought to belong in just that category.[60] Consider the Australian Web hosting company that automatically deletes all of its clients' multimedia files every night unless it receives specific assurances up front that the files in a given directory are placed with the permission of the copyright owner or are uncopyrighted.[61]

Preemptive design may have a hard time tailoring the technical algorithms to the legal rules. Even with some ongoing human oversight, the blacklists of objectionable Web sites maintained by commercial filtering programs are consistently overbroad, erroneously placing Web sites into categories to which they do not belong.[62] For example, when the U.S. government sponsored a service to assist Iranians in overcoming Internet filtering imposed by the Iranian government, the U.S.-sponsored service in turn sought to filter out pornographic sites so that Iranians would not use the circumvention service to obtain pornography. The service filtered any site with "ass" in its domain name—including usembassy.state.gov, the U.S. Department of State's online portal for its own overseas missions.[63]

In the realm of copyright, whether a particular kind of copying qualifies for a fair use defense is in many instances notoriously difficult to determine ahead of time.[64] Some argue that broad attempts to embed copyright protections in technology fall short because the technology cannot easily take into account possible fair use defenses.[65] The law prohibiting the circumvention of trusted systems disregards possibilities for fair use—which might make sense, since such an exception could swallow the rule.[66] Such judgments appear to rely on the fact that the materials within a trusted system can still be found and copied in non-trusted analog formats, thus digital prohibitions are never complete.[67] The worry that a particular speech-related activity will be precluded by design is blunted when the technology merely makes the activity less convenient rather than preventing it altogether. However, if we migrate to an information ecosystem in which tethered appliances predominate, that analog safety valve will wane.

For specific injunctions, the worries about mistakes may appear weaker. A specific injunction to halt an activity or destroy its fruits issues only after an adjudication. If we move to a regime in which individuals, and not just distributors, are susceptible to impoundment remedies for digital contraband, these remedies might be applied only after the status of the contraband has been officially determined.[68] Indeed, one might think that an ability to easily recall infringing materials after the fact might make it possible to be more generous about allowing distribution in the first place—cases could proceed to final judgments rather than being functionally decided in earlier stages on the claim that continued distribution of the objectionable material would cause irreparable harm. If cats can easily be put back into bags, there can be less worry about letting them out to begin with.

However, the ability to perfectly (in the sense of thoroughly) scrub everyone's digital repositories of unlawful content may compromise the values that belie fear of prior restraints, even though the scrub would not be "prior" in fact. Preventing the copying of a work of copyrighted music stops a behavior without removing the work from the public sphere, since presumably the work is still available through authorized channels. It is a different matter to eliminate entirely a piece of digital contraband. Such elimination can make it difficult to understand, reevaluate, or even discuss what happened and why. In ruling against a gag order at a trial, the U.S. Supreme Court worried that the order was an "immediate and irreversible sanction."[69] "If it can be said that a threat of criminal or civil sanctions after publication 'chills' speech, prior restraint 'freezes' it at least for the time."[70] Post hoc scrubs are not immediate, but they have the prospect of being permanent and irreversible—a freezing of speech that takes place after it has been uttered, and no longer just "for the time." That the speech had an initial opportunity to be broadcast may make a scrub less worrisome than if it were blocked from the start, but removing this information from the public discourse means that those who come after us will have to rely on secondary sources to make sense of its removal.

To be sure, we can think of cases where complete elimination would be ideal. These are cases in which the public interest is not implicated, and for which continued harm is thought to accrue so long as the material circulates: leaked medical records, child abuse images, and nuclear weapon designs.[71] But the number of instances in which legal judgments effecting censorship are overturned or revised—years later—counsels that an ability to thoroughly enforce bans on content makes the law too powerful and its judgments too permanent, since the material covered by the judgment would be permanently blocked from the public view. Imagine a world in which all copies of once-censored books like *Candide, The Call of the Wild,* and *Ulysses* had been permanently destroyed at the time of the censoring and could not be studied or enjoyed after subsequent decision-makers lifted the ban.[72] In a world of tethered appliances, the primary backstop against perfectly enforced mistakes would have to come from the fact that there would be different views about what to ban found among multiple sovereigns—so a particular piece of samizdat might live on in one jurisdiction even as it was made difficult to find in another.

The use of tethered appliances for surveillance may be least susceptible to an objection of mistake, since surveillance can be used to start a case rather than close it. For example, the use of cameras at traffic lights has met with some objection because of the level of thoroughness they provide—a sense of snooping simply not possible with police alone doing the watching.[73] And there are instances where the cameras report false positives.[74] However, those accused can have their day in court to explain or deny the charges inspired by the cameras' initial reviews. Moreover, since running a red light might cause an accident and result in physical harm, the cameras seem well-tailored to dealing with a true hazard, and thus less objectionable. And the mechanization of identifying violators might even make the system more fair, because the occupant of the vehicle cannot earn special treatment based on individual characteristics like race, wealth, or gender. The prospects for abuse are greater when the cameras in mobile phones or the microphones of OnStar can be serendipitously repurposed for surveillance. These sensors are much more invasive and general purpose.

Bulwarks Against Government

There has been a simmering debate about the meaning of the Second Amendment to the U.S. Constitution, which concerns "the right of the people to keep and bear Arms."[75] It is not clear whether the constitutional language refers to a collective right that has to do with militias, or an individual one that could more readily be interpreted to preclude gun control legislation. At present, most reported decisions and scholarly authority favor the former interpretation, but the momentum may be shifting.[76] For our purposes, we can extract one strand from this debate without having to join it: one reason to prohibit the government's dispossession of individual firearms is to maintain the prospect that individuals could revolt against a tyrannical regime, or provide a disincentive to a regime considering going down such a path.[77] These check-on-government notions are echoed by some members of technical communities, such as those who place more faith in their own encryption to prevent secrets from being compromised than in any government guarantees of self-restraint. Such a description may unnecessarily demean the techies' worries as a form of paranoia. Translated into a more formal and precise claim, one might worry that the boundless but unnoticeable searches permitted by digital advances can be as disruptive to the equilibrium between citizen and law enforcement as any enforcement-thwarting tools such as encryption.

The equilibrium between citizens and law enforcement has crucially relied on some measure of citizen cooperation. Abuse of surveillance has traditionally been limited not simply by the conscience of those searching or by procedural rules prohibiting the introduction of illegally obtained evidence, but also by the public's own objections. If occasioned through tethered appliances, such surveillance can be undertaken almost entirely in secret, both as a general matter and for any specific search. Stuntz has explained the value of a renewed focus on physical "data mining" via group sweeps—for example, the searching of all cars near the site of a terrorist threat—and pointed out that such searches are naturally (and healthily) limited because large swaths of the public are noticeably burdened by them.[78] The public, in turn, can effectively check such government action by objecting through judicial or political processes, should the sweeps become too onerous. No such check is present in the controlled digital environment; extensive searching can be done with no noticeable burden—indeed, without notice of any kind—on the parties searched. For example, the previously mentioned FBI use of an OnStar-like system to listen in on the occupants of a car is public knowledge only because the manufacturer chose to formally object.[79]

The rise of tethered appliances significantly reduces the number and variety of people and institutions required to apply the state's power on a mass scale. It removes a practical check on the use of that power. It diminishes a rule's ability to attain legitimacy as people choose to participate in its enforcement, or at least not stand in its way.

A government able to pressure the provider of BlackBerries could insist on surveillance of e-mails sent to and from each device.[80] And such surveillance would require few people doing the enforcement work. Traditionally, ongoing mass surveillance or control would require a large investment of resources and, in particular, people. Eavesdropping has required police willing to plant and monitor bugs; seizure of contraband has required agents willing to perform raids. Further, a great deal of routine law enforcement activity has required the cooperation of private parties, such as landlords, banks, and employers. The potential for abuse of governmental power is limited not only by whatever procedural protections are afforded in a jurisdiction that recognizes the rule of law, but also more implicitly by the decisions made by parties asked to assist. Sometimes the police refuse to fire on a crowd even if a dictator orders it, and, less dramatically, whistleblowers among a group of participating enforcers can slow down, disrupt, leak, or report on anything they perceive as abusive in a law enforcement action.[81]

Compare a citywide smoking ban that enters into effect as each proprietor acts to enforce it—under penalty for failing to do so, to be sure—with an alternative ordinance implemented by installing highly sensitive smoke detectors in every public place, wired directly to a central enforcement office. Some in favor of the ordinance may still wish to see it implemented by people rather than mechanical fiat. The latter encourages the proliferation of simple punishment-avoiding behavior that is anathema to open, participatory societies. As law professor Lior Strahilevitz points out, most laws are not self-enforcing, and a measure of the law's value and importance may be found in just how much those affected by it (including as victims) urge law enforcement to take a stand, or invoke what private rights of action they may have.[82] Strahilevitz points to laws against vice and gambling, but the idea can apply to the problems arising from technology as well. Law ought to be understood not simply by its meaning as a text, but by the ways in which it is or is not internalized by the people it affects—whether as targets of the law, victims to be helped by it, or those charged with enforcing it.[83]

The Benefits of Tolerated Uses

A particular activity might be illegal, but in some cases those with standing to complain about it sometimes hold back on trying to stop it while they determine whether they really object. If they decide they do object, they can sue. Tim Wu calls this phenomenon "tolerated uses,"[84] and copyright infringement shows how it can work.

When Congress passed the Digital Millennium Copyright Act of 1998 (DMCA),[85] it sought to enlist certain online service providers to help stop the unauthorized spread of copyrighted material. ISPs that just routed packets for others were declared not responsible for copyright infringement taking place over their communication channels.[86] Intermediaries that hosted content—such as the CompuServe and Prodigy forums, or Internet hosting sites such as Geocities.com—had more responsibility. They would be unambiguously clear of liability for copyright infringement only if they acted expeditiously to take down infringing material once they were specifically notified of that infringement.[87]

Although many scholars have pointed out deficiencies and opportunities for abuse in this notice-and-takedown regime,[88] the scheme reflects a balance. Under the DMCA safe harbors, intermediaries have been able to provide flexible platforms that allow for a broad variety of amateur expression. For example, Geocities and others have been able to host personal home pages, precursors to the blogs of today, without fear of copyright liability should any of the home page owners post infringing material—at least so long as they act after specific notification of an infringement. Had these intermediaries stopped offering these services for fear of crushing liability under a different legal configuration, people would have had far fewer options to broadcast online: they could have either hosted content through their own personal PCs, with several incumbent shortcomings,[89] or forgone broadcasting altogether. Thanks to the incentives of notice-and-takedown, copyright holders gained a ready means of redress for the most egregious instances of copyright infringement, without chilling individual expression across the board in the process.

The DMCA legal regime supports the procrastination principle, allowing for experimentation of all sorts and later reining in excesses and abuses as they happen, rather than preventing them from the outset. Compelling copyright holders to specifically demand takedown may seem like an unnecessary burden, but it may be helpful to them because it allows them to tolerate some facially infringing uses without forcing copyright holders to make a blanket choice between enforcement and no enforcement. Several media companies and publishers simply have not figured out whether YouTube's and others' excerpts of their material are friend or foe. Companies are not monolithic, and there can be dissenting views within a company on the matter. A company with such diverse internal voices cannot come right out and give an even temporary blessing to apparent copyright infringement. Such a blessing would cure the material in question of its unlawful character, because the infringement would then be authorized. Yet at the same time, a copyright holder may be loath to issue DMCA notices to try to get material removed each time it appears, because clips can serve a valuable promotional function.

The DMCA regime maintains a loose coupling between the law's violation and its remedy, asking publishers to step forward and affirmatively declare that they want specific material wiped out as it arises and giving publishers the luxury to accede to some uses without forcing intermediaries to assume that the copyright holder would have wanted the material to be taken down. People might make videos that include copyrighted background music or television show clips and upload them to centralized video sharing services like YouTube. But YouTube does not have to seek these clips out and take them down unless it receives a specific complaint from the copyright holder.

While requiring unprompted attempts at copyright enforcement by a firm like YouTube may not end up being unduly burdensome to the intermediary—it all depends on how its business model and technology are structured—requiring unprompted enforcement may end up precluding uses of copyrighted material to which the author or publisher actually does not object, or on which it has not yet come to a final view.[90]

Thus there may be some cases when preemptive regimes can be undesirable to the entities they are designed to help. A preemptive intervention to preclude some particular behavior actually disempowers the people who might complain about it to decide that they are willing, after all, to tolerate it. Few would choose to tolerate a murder, making it a good candidate for preemption through design, were that possible,[91] but the intricacies of the markets and business models involved in the distribution of intellectual works means that reasonable copyright holders could disagree on whether it would be a good thing to prevent certain unauthorized distributions of their works.

The generative history of the Internet shows that allowing openness to third-party innovation from multiple corners and through multiple business models (or no business model at all) ends up producing widely adopted, socially useful applications not readily anticipated or initiated through the standard corporate production cycle.[92]

For example, in retrospect, permitting the manufacture of VCRs was a great boon to the publishers who were initially opposed to it. The entire video rental industry was not anticipated by publishers, yet it became a substantial source of revenue for them.[93] Had the Hush-A-Phones, Carterfones, and modems of Chapter Two required preapproval, or been erasable at the touch of a button the way that an EchoStar DVR of today can be killed, the decisions to permit them might have gone the other way, and AT&T would not have benefited as people found new and varied uses for their phone lines.

Some in the music, television, and movie industries are embracing cheap networks and the free flow of bits, experimenting with advertising models similar to those pioneered for free television, in which the more people who watch, the more money the publishers can make. For instance, the BBC has made a deal with the technology firm Azureus, makers of a peer-to-peer BitTorrent client that has been viewed as contraband on many university campuses and corporate networks.[94] Users of Azureus's software will now be able to download BBC television programs for free, and with authorization, reflecting both a shift in business model for the BBC and a conversion of Azureus from devil's tool to helpful distribution vehicle. BitTorrent software ensures that people upload to others as they download, which means that the BBC will be able to release its programs online without incurring the costs of a big bandwidth bill because many viewers will be downloading from fellow viewers rather than from the BBC. EMI is releasing music on iTunes without digital rights management—initially charging more for such unfettered versions.[95]

The tools that we now take as so central to the modern Internet, including the Web browser, also began and often remain on uncertain legal ground. As one surfs the Internet, it is easy to peek behind the curtain of most Web sites by asking the browser to "view source," thereby uncovering the code that generates the viewed pages. Users can click on nearly any text or graphic they see and promptly copy it to their own Web sites or save it permanently on their own PCs. The legal theories that make these activities possible are tenuous. Is it an implied license from the Web site owner? Perhaps, but what if the Web site owner has introductory text that demands that no copies like that be made?[96] Is it fair use? Perhaps. In the United States, fair use is determined by a fuzzy four-factor test that in practice rests in part on habit and custom, on people's expectations.[97] When a technology is deployed early, those expectations are unsettled, or perhaps settled in the wrong direction, especially among judges who might be called upon to apply the law without themselves having fully experienced the technologies in question. A gap between deployment and regulatory reaction gives the economic and legal systems time to adapt, helping to ensure that doctrines like fair use are applied appropriately.

The Undesirable Collapse of Conduct and Decision Rules

Law professor Meir Dan-Cohen describes law as separately telling people how to behave and telling judges what penalties to impose should people break the law. In more general terms, he has observed that law comprises both conduct rules and decision rules.[98] There is some disconnect between the two: people may know what the law requires without fully understanding the ramifications for breaking it.[99] This division—what he calls an "acoustic separation"—can be helpful: a law can threaten a tough penalty in order to ensure that people obey it, but then later show unadvertised mercy to those who break it.[100] If the mercy is not telegraphed ahead of time, people will be more likely to follow the law, while still benefiting from a lesser penalty if they break it and have an excuse to offer, such as duress.

Perfect enforcement collapses the public understanding of the law with its application, eliminating a useful interface between the law's terms and its application. Part of what makes us human are the choices that we make every day about what counts as right and wrong, and whether to give in to temptations that we believe to be wrong. In a completely monitored and controlled environment, those choices vanish. One cannot tell whether one's behavior is an expression of character or is merely compelled by immediate circumstance.

Of course, it may be difficult to embrace one's right to flout the law if the flouting entails a gross violation of the rights of another. Few would uphold the freedom of someone to murder as "part of what makes us human." So we might try to categorize the most common lawbreaking behaviors online and see how often they relate to "merely" speech-related wrongs rather than worse transgressions. This is just the sort of calculus by which prior restraints are disfavored especially when they attach to speech, rather than when they are used to prevent lawbreaking behaviors such as those that lead to physical harm. If most of the abuses sought to be prevented are well addressed through post hoc remedies, and if they might be adequately discovered through existing law enforcement mechanisms, one should disfavor perfect enforcement to preempt them. At the very least, the prospect of abuse of powerful, asymmetric law enforcement tools reminds us that there is a balance to be struck rather than an unmitigated good in perfect enforcement.

WEB 2.0 AND THE END OF GENERATIVITY

The situation for online copyright illustrates that for perfect enforcement to work, generative alternatives must not be widely available.[101] In 2007, the movie industry and technology makers unveiled a copy protection scheme for new high-definition DVDs to correct the flaws in the technical protection measures applied to regular DVDs over a decade earlier. The new system was compromised just as quickly; instructions quickly circulated describing how PC users could disable the copy protection on HD-DVDs.[102] So long as the generative PC remains at the center of the modern information ecosystem, the ability to deploy trusted systems with restrictions that interfere with user expectations is severely limited: tighten a screw too much, and it will become stripped.

So could the generative PC ever really disappear? As David Post wrote in response to a law review article that was a precursor to this book, "a grid of 400 million open PCs is not less generative than a grid of 400 million open PCs and 500 million locked-down TiVos."[103] Users might shift some of their activities to tethered appliances in response to the security threats described in Chapter Three, and they might even find themselves using locked-down PCs at work or in libraries and Internet cafés. But why would they abandon the generative PC at home? The prospect may be found in "Web 2.0." As mentioned earlier, in part this label refers to generativity at the content layer, on sites like Wikipedia and Flickr, where content is driven by users.[104] But it also refers to something far more technical—a way of building Web sites so that users feel less like they are looking at Web pages and more like they are using applications on their very own PCs.[105] New online map services let users click to grasp a map section and move it around; new Internet mail services let users treat their online e-mail repositories as if they were located on their PCs. Many of these technologies might be thought of as technologically generative because they provide hooks for developers from one Web site to draw upon the content and functionality of another—at least if the one lending the material consents.[106]

Yet the features that make tethered appliances worrisome—that they are less generative and that they can be so quickly and effectively regulated—apply with equal force to the software that migrates to become a service offered over the Internet. Consider Google's popular map service. It is not only highly useful to end users; it also has an open API (application programming interface) to its map data,[107] which means that a third-party Web site creator can start with a mere list of street addresses and immediately produce on her site a Google Map with a digital push-pin at each address.[108] This allows any number of "mash-ups" to be made, combining Google Maps with third-party geographic datasets. Internet developers are using the Google Maps API to create Web sites that find and map the nearest Starbucks, create and measure running routes, pinpoint the locations of traffic light cameras, and collate candidates on dating sites to produce instant displays of where one's best matches can be found.[109]

Because it allows coders access to its map data and functionality, Google's mapping service is generative. But it is also contingent: Google assigns each Web developer a key and reserves the right to revoke that key at any time, for any reason—or to terminate the whole Google Maps service.[110] It is certainly understandable that Google, in choosing to make a generative service out of something in which it has invested heavily, would want to control it. But this puts within the control of Google, and anyone who can regulate Google, all downstream uses of Google Maps—and maps in general, to the extent that Google Maps' popularity means other mapping services will fail or never be built.

Software built on open APIs that can be withdrawn is much more precarious than software built under the old PC model, where users with Windows could be expected to have Windows for months or years at a time, whether or not Microsoft wanted them to keep it. To the extent that we find ourselves primarily using a particular online service, whether to store our documents, photos, or buddy lists, we may find switching to a new service more difficult, as the data is no longer on our PCs in a format that other software can read. This disconnect can make it more difficult for third parties to write software that interacts with other software, such as desktop search engines that can currently paw through everything on a PC in order to give us a unified search across a hard drive. Sites may also limit functionality that the user expects or assumes will be available. In 2007, for example, MySpace asked one of its most popular users to remove from her page a piece of music promotion software that was developed by an outside company. She was using it instead of MySpace's own code.[111] Google unexpectedly closed its unsuccessful Google Video purchasing service and remotely disabled users' access to content they had purchased; after an outcry, Google offered limited refunds instead of restoring access to the videos.[112]

Continuous Internet access thus is not only facilitating the rise of appliances and PCs that can phone home and be reconfigured by their vendors at any moment. It is also allowing a wholesale shift in code and activities from endpoint PCs to the Web. There are many functional advantages to this, at least so long as one's Internet connection does not fail. When users can read and compose e-mail online, their inboxes and outboxes await no matter whose machines they borrow—or what operating system the machines have—so long as they have a standard browser. It is just a matter of getting to the right Web site and logging in. We are beginning to be able to use the Web to do word processing, spreadsheet analyses, indeed, nearly anything we might want to do.

Once the endpoint is consigned to hosting only a browser, with new features limited to those added on the other end of the browser's window, consumer demand for generative PCs can yield to demand for boxes that look like PCs but instead offer only that browser. Then, as with tethered appliances, when Web 2.0 services change their offerings, the user may have no ability to keep using an older version, as one might do with software that stops being actively made available.

This is an unfortunate transformation. It is a mistake to think of the Web browser as the apex of the PC's evolution, especially as new peer-to-peer applications show that PCs can be used to ease network traffic congestion and to allow people directly to interact in new ways.[113] Just as those applications are beginning to show promise—whether as ad hoc networks that PCs can create among each other in the absence of connectivity to an ISP, or as distributed processing and storage devices that could apply wasted computing cycles to faraway computational problems[114]—there is less reason for those shopping for a PC to factor generative capacity into a short-term purchasing decision. As a 2007 *Wall Street Journal* headline put it: "'Dumb terminals can be a smart move': Computing devices lack extras but offer security, cost savings."[115]

*   *   *

Generative networks like the Internet can be partially controlled, and there is important work to be done to enumerate the ways in which governments try to censor the Net.[116] But the key move to watch is a sea change in control over the endpoint: lock down the device, and network censorship and control can be extraordinarily reinforced. The prospect of tethered appliances and software as service permits major regulatory intrusions to be implemented as minor technical adjustments to code or requests to service providers. Generative technologies ought to be given wide latitude to find a variety of uses—including ones that encroach upon other interests. These encroachments may be undesirable, but they may also create opportunities to reconceptualize the rights underlying the threatened traditional markets and business models. An information technology environment capable of recursive innovation[117] in the realms of business, art, and culture will best thrive with continued regulatory forbearance, recognizing that the disruption occasioned by generative information technology often amounts to a long-term gain even as it causes a short-term threat to some powerful and legitimate interests.

The generative spirit allows for all sorts of software to be built, and all sorts of content to be exchanged, without anticipating what markets want—or what level of harm can arise. The development of much software today, and thus of the generative services facilitated at the content layer of the Internet, is undertaken by disparate groups, often not acting in concert, whose work can become greater than the sum of its parts because it is not funneled through a single vendor's development cycle.[118]

The keys to maintaining a generative system are to ensure its internal security without resorting to lockdown, and to find ways to enable enough enforcement against its undesirable uses without requiring a system of perfect enforcement. The next chapters explore how some enterprises that are generative at the content level have managed to remain productive without requiring extensive lockdown or external regulation, and apply those lessons to the future of the Internet.

6

The Lessons of Wikipedia

The Dutch city of Drachten has undertaken an unusual experiment in traffic management. The roads serving forty-five thousand people are "verkeersbordvrij": free of nearly all road signs. Drachten is one of several European test sites for a traffic planning approach called "unsafe is safe."[1] The city has removed its traffic signs, parking meters, and even parking spaces. The only rules are that drivers should yield to those on their right at an intersection, and that parked cars blocking others will be towed.

The result so far is counterintuitive: a dramatic improvement in vehicular safety. Without signs to obey mechanically (or, as studies have shown, disobey seventy percent of the time[2]), people are forced to drive more mindfully—operating their cars with more care and attention to the surrounding circumstances. They communicate more with pedestrians, bicyclists, and other drivers using hand signals and eye contact. They see other drivers rather than other cars. In an article describing the expansion of the experiment to a number of other European cities, including London's Kensington neighborhood, traffic expert Hans Monderman told Germany's *Der Spiegel*, "The many rules strip us of the most important thing: the ability to be considerate. We're losing our capacity for socially responsible behavior. The greater the number of prescriptions, the more people's sense of personal responsibility dwindles."[3]

Law has long recognized the difference between rules and standards—between very precise boundaries like a speed limit and the much vaguer admonishment characteristic of negligence law that warns individuals simply to "act reasonably." There are well-known tradeoffs between these approaches.[4] Rules are less subject to ambiguity and, if crafted well, inform people exactly what they can do, even if individual situations may render the rule impractical or, worse, dangerous. Standards allow people to tailor their actions to a particular situation. Yet they also rely on the good judgment of often self-interested actors—or on little-constrained second-guessing of a jury or judge that later decrees whether someone's actions were unreasonable.

A small lesson of the verkeersbordvrij experiment is that standards can work better than rules in unexpected contexts. A larger lesson has to do with the traffic expert's claim about law and human behavior: the more we are regulated, the more we may choose to hew only and exactly to the regulation or, more precisely, to what we can get away with when the regulation is not perfectly enforced. When we face heavy regulation, we see and shape our behavior more in relation to reward and punishment by an arbitrary external authority, than because of a commitment to the kind of world our actions can help bring about.[5] This observation is less about the difference between rules and standards than it is about the *source* of mandates: some may come from a process that a person views as alien, while others arise from a process in which the person takes an active part.

When the certainty of authority-sourced reward and punishment is lessened, we might predict two opposing results. The first is chaos: remove security guards and stores will be looted. The second is basic order maintained, as people choose to respect particular limits in the absence of enforcement. Such acting to reinforce a social fabric may still be due to a form of self-interest—game and norm theorists offer reasons why people help one another in terms that draw on longer-term mutual self-interest[6]—but it may also be because people have genuinely decided to treat others' interests as their own.[7] This might be because people feel a part of the process that brought about a shared mandate—even if compliance is not rigorously monitored. Honor codes, or students' pledges not to engage in academically dishonest behavior, can apparently result in lower rates of self-reported cheating.[8] Thus, without the traffic sign equivalent of pages of rules and regulations, students who apprentice to generalized codes of honor may be prone to higher levels of honesty in academic work—and benefit from a greater sense of camaraderie grounded in shared values.

More generally, order may remain when people see themselves as a part of a social system, a group of people—more than utter strangers but less than friends—with some overlap in outlook and goals. Whatever counts as a satisfying explanation, we see that sometimes the absence of law has not resulted in the absence of order.[9] Under the right circumstances, people will behave charitably toward one another in the comparative absence or enforcement of rules that would otherwise compel that charity.

In modern cyberspace, an absence of rules (or at least enforcement) has led both to a generative blossoming and to a new round of challenges at multiple layers. If the Internet and its users experience a crisis of abuse—behaviors that artfully exploit the twin premises of trust and procrastination—it will be tempting to approach such challenges as ones of law and jurisdiction. This rule-and-sanction approach frames the project of cyberlaw by asking how public authorities can find and restrain those it deems to be bad actors online. Answers then look to entry points within networks and endpoints that can facilitate control. As the previous chapter explained, those points will be tethered appliances and software-as-service—functional, fashionable, but non-generative or only contingently generative.[10]

The "unsafe is safe" experiment highlights a different approach, one potentially as powerful as traditional rule and sanction, without the sacrifice of generativity entailed by the usual means of regulation effected through points of control, such as the appliancization described earlier in this book. When people can come to take the welfare of one another seriously and possess the tools to readily assist and limit each other, even the most precise and well-enforced rule from a traditional public source may be less effective than that uncompelled goodwill. Such an approach reframes the project of cyberlaw to ask: What are the technical tools and social structures that inspire people to act humanely online? How might they be available to help restrain the damage that malevolent outliers can wreak? How can we arrive at credible judgments about what counts as humane and what counts as malevolent? These questions may be particularly helpful to answer while cyberspace is still in its social infancy, its tools for group cohesion immature, and the attitudes of many of its users still in an early phase which treats Internet usage as either a tool to augment existing relationships or as a gateway to an undifferentiated library of information from indifferent sources. Such an atomistic conception of cyberspace naturally produces an environment without the social signaling, cues, and relationships that tend toward moderation in the absence of law.[11] This is an outcome at odds with the original architecture of the Internet described in this book, an architecture built on neighborliness and cooperation among strangers occupying disparate network nodes.

The problem raised in the first part of this book underscores this dissonance between origins and current reality at the technical layer: PCs running wild, infected by and contributing to spyware, spam, and viruses because their users either do not know or do not care what they should be installing on their computers. The ubiquity of the PC among mainstream Internet users, and its flexibility that allows it to be reprogrammed at any instant, are both signal benefits and major flaws, just as the genius of the Web—allowing the on-the-fly composition of coherent pages of information from a staggering variety of unvetted sources—is also proving a serious vulnerability. In looking for ways to mitigate these flaws while preserving the benefits of such an open system, we can look to the other layers of the generative Internet which have been plagued with comparable problems, and the progress of their solutions. Some of these resemble verkeersbordvrij: curious experiments with unexpected success that suggest a set of solutions well suited to generative environments, so long as the people otherwise subject to more centralized regulation are willing to help contribute to order without it.

Recall that the Internet exists in layers—physical, protocol, application, content, social. Thanks to the modularity of the Internet's design, network and software developers can become experts in one layer without having to know much about the others. Some legal academics have even proposed that regulation might be most efficiently tailored to respect the borders of these layers.[12]

For our purposes, we can examine the layers and analyze the solutions from one layer to provide insight into the problems of another. The pattern of generative success and vulnerability present in the PC and Internet at the technical layer is also visible in one of the more recent and high profile content-layer endeavors on the Internet: Wikipedia, the free online encyclopedia that anyone can edit. It is currently among the top ten most popular Web sites in the world,[13] and the story of Wikipedia's success and subsequent problems—and evolving answers to them—provide clues to solutions for other layers. We need some new approaches. Without them, we face a Hobson's choice between fear and lockdown.

THE RISE OF WIKIPEDIA

Evangelists of proprietary networks and the Internet alike have touted access to knowledge and ideas. People have anticipated digital "libraries of Alexandria," providing the world's information within a few clicks.[14] Because the Internet began with no particular content, this was at first an empty promise. Most knowledge was understood to reside in forms that were packaged and distributed piece by piece, profitable because of a scarcity made possible by physical limitations and the restrictions of copyright. Producers of educational materials, including dictionaries and encyclopedias, were slow to put their wares into digital form. They worried about cannibalizing their existing paper sales—for *Encyclopaedia Britannica,* $650 million in 1990.[15] There was no good way of charging for the small transactions that a lookup of a single word or encyclopedia entry would require, and there were few ways to avoid users' copying, pasting, and sharing what they found. Eventually Microsoft released the *Encarta* encyclopedia on CD-ROM in 1993 for just under $1,000, pressuring *Britannica* to experiment both with a CD-ROM and a subscription-only Web site in 1994.[16]

As the Internet exploded, the slow-to-change walled garden content of formal encyclopedias was bypassed by a generative proliferation of topical Web pages, and search engines that could pinpoint them. There was no gestalt, though: the top ten results for "Hitler" on Google could include a biography written by amateur historian Philip Gavin as part of his History Place Web site,[17] a variety of texts from Holocaust remembrance organizations, and a site about "kitlers," cats bearing uncanny resemblances to the tyrant.[18] This scenario exhibits generativity along the classic Libertarian model: allow individuals the freedom to express themselves and they will as they choose. We are then free to read the results. The spirit of blogging also falls within this model. If any of the posted material is objectionable or inaccurate, people can either ignore it, request for it to be taken down, or find a theory on which to sue over it, perhaps imploring gatekeepers like site hosting companies to remove material that individual authors refuse to revise.

More self-consciously encyclopedic models emerged nearly simultaneously from two rather different sources—one the founder of the dot-org Free Software Foundation, and the other an entrepreneur who had achieved dot-com success in part from the operation of a search engine focused on salacious images.[19]

Richard Stallman is the first. He believes in a world where software is shared, with its benefits freely available to all, where those who understand the code can modify and adapt it to new purposes, and then share it further. This was the natural environment for Stallman in the 1980s as he worked among graduate students at the Massachusetts Institute of Technology, and it parallels the environment in which the Internet and Web were invented. Stallman holds the same views on sharing other forms of intellectual expression, applying his philosophy across all of the Internet's layers, and in 1999 he floated the idea of a free encyclopedia drawing from anyone who wanted to submit content, one article at a time. By 2001, some people were ready to give it a shot. Just as Stallman had sought to replace the proprietary Unix operating system with a similarly functioning but free alternative called GNU ("GNU's Not Unix"), the project was first named "GNUpedia," then GNE ("GNE's Not an Encyclopedia"). There would be few restrictions on what those submissions would look like, lest bias be introduced:

Articles are submitted on the following provisions:

- The article contains no previously copyrighted material (and if an article is consequently found to have offending material, it will then be removed).
- The article contains no code that will damage the GNE systems or the systems from which users view GNE.
- The article is not an advert, and has some informative content (persoengl [*sic*] information pages are not informative!).
- The article is comprehensible (can be read and understood).[20]

These provisions made GNE little more than a collective blog sans comments: people would submit articles, and that would be that. Any attempt to enforce quality standards—beyond a skim to see if the article was "informative"—was eschewed. The GNE FAQ explained:

Why don't you have editors?

There should be no level of "acceptable thought". This means you have to tolerate being confronted by ideas and opinions different to your own, and for this we offer no apologies. GNE is a resource for spe [*sic*] speech, and we will strive to keep it that way. Unless some insane country with crazy libel laws tries to stop something, we will always try and fight for your spe [*sic*] speech, even if we perhaps don't agree with your article. As such we will not allow any individuals to "edit" articles, thus opening GNE to the possibility of bias.[21]

As one might predict from its philosophy, at best GNE would be an accumulation of views rather than an encyclopedia—perhaps accounting for the "not" part of "GNE's Not an Encyclopedia." Today the GNE Web site is a digital ghost town. GNE was a generative experiment that failed, a place free of all digital traffic signs that never attracted any cars. It was eclipsed by another project that unequivocally aimed to be an encyclopedia, emanating from an unusual source.

Jimbo Wales founded the Bomis search engine and Web site at the onset of the dot-com boom in 1996.[22] Bomis helped people find "erotic photography,"[23] and earned money through advertising as well as subscription fees for premium content. In 2000, Wales took some of the money from Bomis to support a new idea: a quality encyclopedia free for everyone to access, copy, and alter for other purposes. He called it Nupedia, and it was to be built like other encyclopedias: through the commissioning of articles by experts. Wales hired philosopher Larry Sanger as editor in chief, and about twenty-five articles were completed over the course of three years.[24]

As the dot-com bubble burst and Bomis's revenues dropped, Wales sought a way to produce the encyclopedia that involved neither paying people nor enduring a lengthy review process before articles were released to the public. He and his team had been intrigued at the prospect of involving the public at large, at first to draft some articles which could then be subject to Nupedia's formal editing process, and then to offer "open review" comments to parallel a more elite peer review.[25] Recollections are conflicted, but at some point software consultant Ward Cunningham's wiki software was introduced to create a simple platform for contributing and making edits to others' contributions. In January 2001, Wikipedia was announced to run alongside Nupedia and perhaps feed articles into it after review. Yet Nupedia was quickly eclipsed by its easily modifiable counterpart. Fragments of Nupedia exist online as of this writing, a fascinating time capsule.[26] Wikipedia became an entity unto itself.[27]

Wikipedia began with three key attributes. The first was verkeersbordvrij. Not only were there few rules at first—the earliest ones merely emphasized the idea of maintaining a "neutral point of view" in Wikipedia's contents, along with a commitment to eliminate materials that infringe copyright and an injunction to ignore any rules if they got in the way of building a great encyclopedia—but there were also no gatekeepers. The way the wiki software worked, anyone, registered or unregistered, could author or edit a page at any time, and those edits appeared *instantaneously*. This of course means that disaster could strike at any moment—someone could mistakenly or maliciously edit a page to say something wrong, offensive, or nonsensical. However, the wiki software made the price of a mistake low, because it automatically kept track of every single edit made to a page in sequence, and one could look back at the page in time-lapse to see how it appeared before each successive edit. If someone should take a carefully crafted article about Hitler and replace it with "Kilroy was here," anyone else could come along later and revert the page with a few clicks to the way it was before the vandalism, reinstating the previous version. This is a far cry from the elements of perfect enforcement: there are few lines between enforcers and citizens; reaction to abuse is not instantaneous; and missteps generally remain recorded in a page history for later visitors to see if they are curious.

The second distinguishing attribute of Wikipedia was the provision of a discussion page alongside every main page. This allowed people to explain and justify their changes, and anyone disagreeing and changing something back could explain as well. Controversial changes made without any corresponding explanation on the discussion page could be reverted by others without having to rely on a judgment on the merits—instead, the absence of explanation for something non-self-explanatory could be reason enough to be skeptical of it. Debate was sure to arise on a system that accumulated everyone's ideas on a subject in one article (rather than, say, having multiple articles written on the same subject, each from a different point of view, as GNE would have done). The discussion page provided a channel for such debate and helped new users of Wikipedia make a transition from simply reading its entries to making changes and to understanding that there was a group of people interested in the page on which changes were made and whom could be engaged in conversation before, during, and after editing the page.

The third crucial attribute of Wikipedia was a core of initial editors, many drawn from Nupedia, who shared a common ethos and some substantive expertise. In these early days, Wikipedia was a backwater; few knew of it, and rarely would a Wikipedia entry be among the top hits of a Google search.

Like the development of the Internet's architecture, then, Wikipedia's original design was simultaneously ambitious in scope but modest in execution, devoted to making something work without worrying about every problem that could come up if its extraordinary flexibility were abused. It embodied principles of trust-your-neighbor and procrastination, as well as "Postel's Law," a rule of thumb written by one of the Internet's founders to describe a philosophy of Internet protocol development: "[B]e conservative in what you do; be liberal in what you accept from others."[28]

Wikipedia's initial developers shared the same goals and attitudes about the project, and they focused on getting articles written and developed instead of deciding who was or was not qualified or authorized to build on the wiki. These norms of behavior were learned by new users from the old ones through informal apprenticeships as they edited articles together.

The absence of rules was not nonnegotiable; this was not GNE. The procrastination principle suggests waiting for problems to arise before solving them. It does not eschew solutions entirely. There would be maximum openness until there was a problem, and then the problem would be tackled. Wikipedia's rules would be developed on the wiki like a student-written and student-edited honor code. They were made publicly accessible and editable, in a separate area from that of the substantive encyclopedia.[29] Try suddenly to edit an existing rule or add a new one and it will be reverted to its original state unless enough people are convinced that a change is called for. Most of the rules are substance-independent: they can be appealed to and argued about wholly apart from whatever argument might be going on about, say, how to characterize Hitler's childhood in his biographical article.

From these beginnings there have been some tweaks to the wiki software behind Wikipedia, and a number of new rules as the enterprise has expanded and problems have arisen in part because of Wikipedia's notoriety. For example, as Wikipedia grew it began to attract editors who had never crossed paths before, and who disagreed on the articles that they were simultaneously editing. One person would say that Scientology was a "cult," the other would change that to "religion," and the first would revert it back again. Should such an "edit war" be settled by whoever has the stamina to make the last edit? Wikipedia's culture says no, and its users have developed the "three-revert rule."[30] An editor should not undo someone else's edits to an article more than three times in one day. Disagreements can then be put to informal or formal mediation, where another Wikipedian, or other editors working on that particular article, can offer their views as to which version is more accurate—or whether the article, in the interest of maintaining a neutral point of view, should acknowledge that there is controversy about the issue.

For articles prone to vandalism—the entry for President George W. Bush, for example, or the front page of Wikipedia—administrators can create locks to ensure that unregistered or recently registered users may not make changes. Such locks are seen as necessary and temporary evils, and any administrator can choose to lift a lock at his or her discretion.[31]

How does an editor become an administrator with such powers? By making lots of edits and then applying for an administratorship. Wikipedians called "bureaucrats" have authority to promote editors to administrator status—or demote them. And to whom do the bureaucrats answer? Ultimately, to an elected arbitration committee, the board of Wikipedia's parent Wikimedia Foundation, or to Jimbo Wales himself. (There are currently only a handful of bureaucrats, and they are appointed by other bureaucrats.)

Administrators can also prevent particular users from editing Wikipedia. Such blocks are rare and usually temporary. Persistent vandals usually get four warnings before any action is taken. The warnings are couched in a way that presumes—often against the weight of the evidence—that the vandals are acting in good faith, experimenting with editing capabilities on live pages when they should be practicing on test articles created for that purpose. Other transgressions include deleting others' comments on the discussion page—since the discussion page is a wiki page, it can be edited in free form, making it possible to eliminate rather than answer someone else's argument. Threatening legal action against a fellow Wikipedian is also grounds for a block.[32]

Blocks can be placed against individual user accounts, if people have registered, or against a particular IP address, for those who have not registered. IP addresses associated with anonymizing networks such as Tor are not allowed to edit Wikipedia at all.[33]

Along with sticks there are carrots, offered bottom-up rather than top-down. Each registered Wikipedia user is automatically granted a space for an individual user page, and a corresponding page for discussion with other Wikipedians, a free form drop box for comments or questions. If a user is deemed helpful, a practice has evolved of awarding "barnstars"—literally an image of a star. To award a barnstar, named after the metal stars used to decorate German barns,[34] is simply to edit that user's page to include a picture of the star and a note of thanks.[35] Could a user simply award herself a pile of barnstars the way a megalomaniacal dictator can adorn himself with military ribbons? Yes, but that would defeat the point—and would require a bit of prohibited "sock puppetry," as the user would need to create alter identities so the page's edit history would show that the stars came from someone appearing to be other than the user herself.

*   *   *

Wikipedia has charted a path from crazy idea to stunning worldwide success. There are versions of Wikipedia in every major language—including one in simplified English for those who do not speak English fluently—and Wikipedia articles are now often among the top search engine hits for the topics they cover. The English language version surpassed one million articles in March of 2006, and it reached the 2 million mark the following September.[36]

Quality varies greatly. Articles on familiar topics can be highly informative, while more obscure ones are often uneven. Controversial topics like abortion and the Arab-Israeli conflict often boast thorough and highly developed articles. Perhaps this reflects Eric Raymond's observation about the collaborative development of free software: "[g]iven enough eyeballs, all bugs are shallow."[37] To be sure, Raymond himself does not claim that the maxim he coined works beyond software, where code either objectively runs or it doesn't. He has said that he thinks Wikipedia is "infested with moonbats": "The more you look at what some of the Wikipedia contributors have done, the better *Britannica* looks."[38] Still, a controversial study by *Nature* in 2005 systematically compared a set of scientific entries from Wikipedia and *Britannica* (including some from the *Britannica* Web edition), and found a similar rate of error between them.[39] For timeliness, Wikipedia wins hands-down: articles near-instantly appear about breaking events of note. For any given error that is pointed out, it can be corrected on Wikipedia in a heartbeat. Indeed, Wikipedia's toughest critics can become Wikipedians simply by correcting errors as they find them, at least if they maintain the belief, not yet proven unreasonable, that successive changes to an article tend to improve it, so fixing an error will not be futile as others edit it later.

THE PRICE OF SUCCESS

As we have seen, when the Internet and PC moved from backwater to mainstream, their success set the stage for a new round of problems. E-mail is no longer a curiosity but a necessity for most,[40] and the prospect of cheaply reaching so many recipients has led to the scourge of spam, now said to account for over 90 percent of all e-mail.[41] The value of the idle processing power of millions of Internet-connected PCs makes it worthwhile to hijack them, providing a new, powerful rationale for the creation of viruses and worms.[42]

Wikipedia's generativity at the content level—soliciting uncoordinated contribution from tens of thousands of people—provides the basis for similar vulnerabilities now that it is so successful. It has weathered the most obvious perils well. Vandals might be annoying, but they are kept in check with a critical mass of Wikipedians who keep an eye on articles and quickly revert those that are mangled. Some Wikipedians even appear to enjoy this duty, declaring membership in the informal Counter-Vandalism Unit and, if dealing with vandalism tied to fraud, perhaps earning the Defender of the Wiki Barnstar.[43] Still others have written scripts that detect the most obvious cases of vandalism and automatically fix them.[44] And there remains the option of locking those pages that consistently attract trouble from edits by new or anonymous users.

But just as there is a clearer means of dealing with the threat of outright malicious viruses to PCs than there is to more gray-zone "badware," vandals are the easy case for Wikipedia. The well-known controversy surrounding John Seigenthaler, Sr., a retired newspaper publisher and aide to Robert F. Kennedy, scratches the surface of the problem. There, a prankster had made an edit to the Wikipedia article about Seigenthaler suggesting that it had once been thought that he had been involved in the assassinations of John F. Kennedy and RFK.[45] The statement was false but not manifestly obvious vandalism. The article sat unchanged for four months until a friend alerted Seigenthaler to it, replacing the entry with his official biography, which was then replaced with a short paraphrase as part of a policy to avoid copyright infringement claims.[46] When Seigenthaler contacted Jimbo Wales about the issue, Wales ordered an administrator to delete Wikipedia's record of the original edit.[47] Seigenthaler then wrote an op-ed in *USA Today* decrying the libelous nature of the previous version of his Wikipedia article and the idea that the law would not require Wikipedia to take responsibility for what an anonymous editor wrote.[48]

Wikipedians have since agreed that biographies of living persons are especially sensitive, and they are encouraged to highlight unsourced or potentially libelous statements for quick review by other Wikipedians. Jimbo and a handful of other Wikipedia officials reserve the right not only to have an article edited—something anyone can do—but to change its edit history so the fact that it *ever* said a particular thing about someone will no longer be known to the general public, as was done with the libelous portion of the Seigenthaler article. Such practice is carried out not under legal requirements—in the United States, federal law protects information aggregators from liability for defamatory statements made by independent information providers from which they draw[49]—but as an ethical commitment.

Still, the reason that Seigenthaler's entry went uncorrected for so long is likely that few people took notice of it. Until his op-ed appeared, he was not a national public figure, and Jimbo himself attributed the oversight to an increasing pace of article creation and edits—overwhelming the Wikipedians who have made a habit of keeping an eye on changes to articles. In response to the Seigenthaler incident, Wikipedia has altered its wiki software so that unregistered users cannot create new articles, but can only edit existing ones.[50] (Of course, anyone can still register.)

This change takes care of casual or heat-of-the-moment vandalism, but it does little to address a new category of Wikipedian somewhere between committed community member and momentarily vandalizing teenager, one that creates tougher problems. This Wikipedian is someone who cares little about the social act of working with others to create an encyclopedia, but instead cares about the content of a particular Wikipedia entry. Now that a significant number of people consult Wikipedia as a resource, many of whom come to the site from search engine queries, Wikipedia's contents have effects far beyond the site's own community of user-editors.

One of Wikipedia's community-developed standards is that individuals should not create or edit articles about themselves, nor prompt friends to do so. Instead they are to lobby on the article's discussion page for other editors to make corrections or amplifications. (Jimbo himself has expressed regret for editing his own entry in Wikipedia in violation of this policy.)[51] What about companies, or political aides? When a number of edits were made to politicians' Wikipedia entries by Internet Protocol addresses traceable to Capitol Hill, Wikipedians publicized the incidents and tried to shame the politicians in question into denouncing the grooming of their entries.[52] In some cases it has worked. After Congressman Marty Meehan's chief of staff edited his entry to omit mention of a broken campaign promise to serve a limited number of terms, and subsequently replaced the text of the entire article with his official biography, Meehan repudiated the changes. He published a statement saying that it was a waste of time and energy for his staff to have made the edits ("[t]hough the actual time spent on this issue amounted to 11 minutes") because "part of being an elected official is to be regularly commented on, praised, and criticized on the Web."[53] Meehan's response sidestepped the issue of whether and how politicians ought to respond to material about them that they believe to be false or misleading. Surely, if the *New York Times* published a story that he thought was damaging, he would want to write a letter to the editor to set the record straight.

If the Wikipedia entry on Wal-Mart is one of the first hits in a search for the store, it will be important to Wal-Mart to make sure the entry is fair—or even more than fair, omitting true and relevant facts that nonetheless reflect poorly on the company. What can a group of volunteers do if a company or politician is implacably committed to editing an entry? The answer so far has been to muddle along, assuming the best intentions of all editors and hoping that there is epistemic strength in numbers.[54] If disinterested but competent editors outnumber shills, the shills will find their edits reverted or honed, and if the shills persist, they can be halted by the three-revert rule.

In August 2006, a company called MyWikiBiz was launched to help people and companies promote themselves and shape their reputations on Wikipedia. "If your company or organization already has a well-designed, accurately-written article on Wikipedia, then congratulations—our services are not for you. However, if your business is lacking a well-written article on Wikipedia, read on—we're here to help you!"[55] MyWikiBiz offers to create a basic Wikipedia stub of three to five sentences about a company, with some links, for $49. A "standard article" fetches $79, with a premium service ($99) that includes checking the client's Wikipedia article after a year to see "if further changes are needed."[56]

Wikipedia's reaction to MyWikiBiz was swift. Jimbo himself blocked the firm's Wikipedia account on the basis of "paid editing on behalf of customers."[57] The indefinite block was one of only a handful recorded by Jimbo in Wikipedia's history. Wales talked to the firm on the phone the same day and reported that they had come to an accommodation. Identifying the problem as a conflict of interest and appearance of impropriety arising from editors being paid to write by the subjects of the articles, Wales said that MyWikiBiz had agreed to post well-sourced "neutral point of view" articles about its clients on its own Web site, which regular Wikipedians could then choose to incorporate or not as they pleased into Wikipedia.[58] Other Wikipedians disagreed with such a conservative outcome, believing that good content was good content, regardless of source, and that it should be judged on its merits, without a per se rule prohibiting direct entry by a for-profit firm like MyWikiBiz.

The accommodation was short-lived. Articles submitted or sourced by MyWikiBiz were nominated for deletion—itself a process that entails a discussion among any interested Wikipedians and then a judgment by any administrator about whether that discussion reached consensus on a deletion. MyWikiBiz participated wholeheartedly in those discussions and appealed to the earlier "Jimbo Concordat," persuading some Wikipedians to remove their per se objections to an article because of its source. Wales himself participated in one of the discussions, saying that his prior agreement had been misrepresented and, after telling MyWikiBiz that it was on thin ice, once again banned it for what he viewed as spamming Wikipedia with corporate advertisements rather than "neutral point of view" articles.

As a result, MyWikiBiz has gone into "hibernation," according to its founder, who maintains that all sources, even commercial ones, should be able to play a role in contributing to Wikipedia, especially since the sources for most articles and edits are not personally identifiable, even if they are submitted under the persistent pseudonyms that are Wikipedia user identities. Rules have evolved concerning those identities, too. In 2007, Wikipedia user Essjay, the administrator who cleaned Seigenthaler's defamatory edit logs, was found to have misrepresented his credentials. Essjay had claimed to hold various graduate degrees along with a professorship in theology, and had contributed to many Wikipedia articles on the subject. When Jimbo Wales contacted him to discuss a job opportunity at Wales's for-profit company Wikia, Essjay's real identity was revealed. In fact, he was a twenty-four-year-old editor with no graduate degrees. His previous edits—and corresponding discussions in which he invoked his credentials—were called into question. In response to the controversy, and after a request for comments from the Wikipedia community,[59] Jimbo proposed a rule whereby the credentials of those Wikipedia administrators who chose to assert them would be verified.[60] Essjay retired from Wikipedia.[61]

*   *   *

A constitutional lawyer might review these tales of Wikipedia and see a mess of process that leads to a mess of substance: anonymous and ever-shifting users; a God-king who may or may not be able to act unilaterally;[62] a set of rules now large enough to be confusing and ambiguous but small enough to fail to reach most challenges. And Wikipedia is decidedly not a democracy: consensus is favored over voting and its head counts. Much the same could be said about the development process for the Internet's fundamental technical protocols, which is equally porous.[63] The Internet Engineering Task Force (IETF) has no "members"; anyone can participate. But it also has had a proliferation of standards and norms designed to channel arguments to productive resolution, along with venerated people in unelected positions of respect and authority who could, within broad boundaries, affect the path of Internet standards.[64] As the Internet succeeded, the IETF's standards and norms were tested by outsiders who did not share them. Corporate interests became keenly interested in protocol development, and they generally respond to their own particular pecuniary incentives rather than to arguments based on engineering efficiency. The IETF avoided the brunt of these problems because its standards are not self-enforcing; firms that build network hardware, or for-profit Internet Service Providers, ultimately decide how to make their routers behave. IETF endorsement of one standard or another, while helpful, is no longer crucial. With Wikipedia, decisions made by editors and administrators can affect real-world reputations since the articles are live and highly visible via search engines; firms do not individually choose to "adopt" Wikipedia the way they adopt Internet standards.

Yet Wikipedia's awkward and clumsy growth in articles, and the rules governing their creation and editing, is so far a success story. It is in its essence a work in progress, one whose success is defined by the survival—even growth— of a core of editors who subscribe to and enforce its ethos, amid an influx of users who know nothing of that ethos. Wikipedia's success, such as it is, is attributable to a messy combination of constantly updated technical tools and social conventions that elicit and reflect personal commitments from a critical mass of editors to engage in argument and debate about topics they care about. Together these tools and conventions facilitate a notion of "netizenship": belonging to an Internet project that includes other people, rather than relating to the Internet as a deterministic information location and transmission tool or as a cash-and-carry service offered by a separate vendor responsible for its content.

THE VALUE OF NETIZENSHIP

We live under the rule of law when people are treated equally, without regard to their power or station; when the rules that apply to them arise legitimately from the consent of the governed; when those rules are clearly stated; and when there is a source of dispassionate, independent application of those rules.[65]

Despite the apparent mess of process and users, by these standards Wikipedia has charted a remarkable course. Although different users have different levels of capabilities, anyone can register, and anyone, if dedicated enough, can rise to the status of administrator. And while Jimbo Wales may have extraordinary influence, his power on Wikipedia depends in large measure on the consent of the governed—on the individual decisions of hundreds of administrators, any of whom can gainsay each other or him, but who tend to work together because of a shared vision for Wikipedia. The effective implementation of policy in turn rests on the thousands of active editors who may exert power in the shape of the tens of thousands of decisions they make as Wikipedia's articles are edited and reedited. Behaviors that rise to the level of consistent practice are ultimately described and codified as potential policies, and some are then affirmed as operative ones, in a process that is itself constantly subject to revision.

In one extraordinary chat room conversation of Wikipedians recorded online, Wales himself laments that Larry Sanger is billed in several Wikipedia articles about Wikipedia as a "co-founder" of the encyclopedia. But apart from a few instances that he has since publicly regretted, Wales has not edited the articles himself, nor does he directly instruct others to change them with specific text, since that would violate the rule against editing articles about oneself. Instead, he makes a case that an unremarked use of the co-founder label is inaccurate, and implores people to consider how to improve it.[66] At times—they are constantly in flux—Wikipedia's articles about Wikipedia note that there is controversy over the "co-founder" label for Sanger. In another example of the limits of direct power, then-Wikimedia Foundation board member Angela Beesley fought to have the Wikipedia entry about her deleted. She was rebuffed, with administrators concluding that she was newsworthy enough to warrant one.[67] (She tried again after resigning from the Foundation board, to no avail.)[68]

*   *   *

Wikipedia—with the cooperation of many Wikipedians—has developed a system of self-governance that has many indicia of the rule of law without heavy reliance on outside authority or boundary. To be sure, while outside regulation is not courted, Wikipedia's policy on copyright infringement exhibits a desire to integrate with the law rather than reject it. Indeed, its copyright policy is much stricter than the laws of major jurisdictions require. In the United States, Wikipedia could wait for formal notifications of specific infringement before taking action to remove copyrighted material.[69] And despite the fact that Wales himself is a fan of Ayn Rand[70]—whose philosophy of "objectivism" closely aligns with libertarian ideals, a triumph of the individual over the group—Wikipedia is a consummately communitarian enterprise.[71] The activity of building and editing the encyclopedia is done in groups, though the structure of the wiki allows for large groups to naturally break up into manageable units most of the time: a nano-community coalesces around each article, often from five to twenty people at a time, augmented by non-subject-specific roving editors who enjoy generic tasks like line editing or categorizing articles. (Sometimes articles on roughly the same subject can develop independently, at which point there is a negotiation between the two sets of editors on whether and how to merge them.)

This structure is a natural form of what constitutionalists would call subsidiarity: centralized, "higher" forms of dispute resolution are reserved for special cases, while day-to-day work and decisions are undertaken in small, "local" groups.[72] Decisions are made by those closest to the issues, preventing the lengthy, top-down processes of hierarchical systems. This subsidiarity is also expressed through the major groupings drawn according to language. Each different language version of Wikipedia forms its own policies, enforcement schemes, and norms. Sometimes these can track national or cultural standards—as a matter of course people from Poland primarily edit the Polish version of Wikipedia—but at other times they cross such boundaries. The Chinese language Wikipedia serves mainland China (when it is not being blocked by the government, which it frequently is),[73] Hong Kong, Taiwan, and the many Chinese speakers scattered around the world.[74]

When disputes come up, consensus is sought before formality, and the lines between subject and regulator are thin. While not everyone has the powers of an administrator, the use of those special powers is reserved for persistent abuse rather than daily enforcement. It is the editors—that is, those who choose to participate—whose decisions and work collectively add up to an encyclopedia—or not. And most—at least prior to an invasion of political aides, PR firms, and other true cultural foreigners—subscribe to the notion that there is a divide between substance and process, and that there can be an appeal to content-independent rules on which meta-agreement can be reached, even as editors continue to dispute a fact or portrayal in a given article.

This is the essence of law: something larger than an arbitrary exercise of force, and something with meaning apart from a pretext for that force, one couched in neutral terms only for the purpose of social acceptability. It has been rediscovered among people who often profess little respect for their own sovereigns' "real" law, following it not out of civic agreement or pride but because of a cynical balance of the penalties for being caught against the benefits of breaking it. Indeed, the idea that a "neutral point of view" even exists, and that it can be determined among people who disagree, is an amazingly quaint, perhaps even naïve, notion. Yet it is invoked earnestly and often productively on Wikipedia. Recall the traffic engineer's observation about road signs and human behavior: "The greater the number of prescriptions, the more people's sense of personal responsibility dwindles."[75] Wikipedia shows, if perhaps only for a fleeting moment under particularly fortuitous circumstances, that the inverse is also true: the fewer the number of prescriptions, the more people's sense of personal responsibility escalates.

Wikipedia shows us that the naïveté of the Internet's engineers in building generative network technology can be justified not just at the technical layer of the Internet, but at the content layer as well. The idiosyncratic system that has produced running code among talented (and some not-so-talented) engineers has been replicated among writers and artists.

There is a final safety valve to Wikipedia that encourages good-faith contribution and serves as a check on abuses of power that accretes among administrators and bureaucrats there: Wikipedia's content is licensed so that anyone may copy and edit it, so long as attribution of its source is given and it is further shared under the same terms.[76] This permits Wikipedia's content to be sold or used in a commercial manner, so long as it is not proprietized—those who make use of Wikipedia's content cannot claim copyright over works that follow from it. Thus dot-com Web sites like Answers.com mirror all of Wikipedia's content and also display banner ads to make money, something Jimbo Wales has vowed never to do with Wikipedia.[77] (A list maintained on Wikipedia shows dozens of such mirrors.)[78] Mirrors can lead to problems for people like John Seigenthaler, who not only have to strive to correct misrepresentations in the original article on Wikipedia, but in any mirrors as well. But Wikipedia's free content license has the benefit of allowing members of the Wikipedia community an option to exit—and to take a copy of the encyclopedia with them. It also allows for generative experimentation and growth. For example, third parties can come up with ways of identifying accurate articles on Wikipedia and then compile them as a more authoritative or vetted subset of the constant work-in-progress that the site represents.

Larry Sanger, the original editor of Nupedia and organizer (and, according to some, co-founder) of Wikipedia, has done just that. He has started "Citizendium," an attempt to combine some of Nupedia's original use of experts with Wikipedia's appeal to the public at large. Citizendium seeks to fork Wikipedia, and solicit volunteers who agree not to be anonymous, so that their edits may be credited more readily, and their behavior made more accountable. If Citizendium draws enough people and content, links to it from other Web sites will follow, and, given enough links, its entries could appear as highly ranked search results. Wikipedia's dominance has a certain measure of inertia to it, but the generative possibilities of its content, guaranteed by its choice of a permissive license, allow a further check on its prominence.

Wikipedia shows us a model for interpersonal interaction that goes beyond the scripts of customer and business. The discussions that take place adjunct to editing can be brusque, but the behavior that earns the most barnstars is directness, intelligence, and good faith. An owner of a company can be completely bemused that, in order to correct (and have stay corrected) what he sees as inaccuracies in an article about his firm, he will have to discuss the issues with random members of the public. Steve Scherf, co-founder of dot-com Gracenote, ended up engaged in an earnest, lengthy exchange with someone known as "Fatandhappy" about the way his company's history was portrayed.[79] The exchange was heated and clearly frustrating for Scherf, but after another

Wikipedian intervened to make edits, Scherf pronounced himself happy if not thrilled with the revised text. These conversations are possible, and they are still the norm at Wikipedia.

The elements of Wikipedia that have led to its success can help us come to solutions for problems besetting generative successes at other layers of the Internet. They are verkeersbordvrij, a light regulatory touch coupled with an openness to flexible public involvement, including a way for members of the public to make changes, good or bad, with immediate effect; a focus on earnest discussion, including reference to neutral dispute resolution policies, as a means of being strengthened rather than driven by disagreements; and a core of people prepared to model an ethos that others can follow. With any of these pieces missing Wikipedia would likely not have worked. Dot-coms that have rushed in to adopt wikis as the latest cool technology have found mixed results. Microsoft's Encarta Web site, in a naked concession to the popularity of Wikipedia, now has an empty box at the bottom of each article where users are asked to enter comments or corrections, which will be forwarded to the Encarta staff for review. Users receive no further feedback.

Makers of cars and soap have run contests[80] for the public to make advertisements based on stock footage found in their respective commercials, complete with online editing tools so that amateurs can easily put their commercials together. Dove ran the winner of its contest during the Super Bowl.[81] Many commercial Web sites like Amazon solicit customer reviews of products as a way to earn credibility with other customers—and some, like epinions.com, have business models premised entirely on the reviews themselves. Yelp.com asks for such ratings while also organizing its users into geographically based groups and giving them the basic tools of social networking: an ability to praise each other for good reviews, to name fellow reviewers as friends, and to discuss and comment on each others' views. As one Yelp participant put it in reviewing the very Yelp "elite status" that she had just earned for contributing so many well-regarded reviews, "[It m]akes you feel special for about two weeks. Then you either realize you're working for someone else without getting paid, you totally lose interest, or you get really into it."[82]

Such "user-generated content," whether cultivated through fully grassroots-motivated dot-org enterprises or well-constructed dot-com ones, forms part of a new hybrid economy now studied by Lessig, Benkler, von Hippel, and others. These public solicitations to manipulate corporate and cultural symbols, pitched at varying levels of expertise, may prove to be further building blocks of "semiotic democracy," where we can participate in the making and remaking of cultural meanings instead of having them foisted upon us.[83]

But Wikipedia stands for more than the ability of people to craft their own knowledge and culture. It stands for the idea that people of diverse backgrounds can work together on a common project with, whatever its other weaknesses, a noble aim—bringing such knowledge to the world. Jimbo Wales has said that the open development model of Wikipedia is only a means to that end—recall that he started with the far more restrictive Nupedia development model. And we see that Wikipedia rejects straightforward democracy, favoring discussion and consensus over outright voting, thereby sidestepping the kinds of ballot-stuffing that can take place in a digital environment, whether because one person adopts multiple identities or because a person can simply ask friends to stack a sparsely attended vote.

Instead, Wikipedia has since come to stand for the idea that involvement of people in the information they read—whether to fix a typographical error or to join a debate over its veracity or completeness—is an important end itself, one made possible by the recursive generativity of a network that welcomes new outposts without gatekeepers; of software that can be created and deployed at those outposts; and of an ethos that welcomes new ideas without gatekeepers, one that asks the people bearing those ideas to argue for and substantiate them to those who question.

There are plenty of online services whose choices can affect our lives. For example, Google's choices about how to rank and calculate its search results can determine which ideas have prominence and which do not. That is one reason why Google's agreement to censor its own search results for the Chinese version of Google has attracted so much disapprobation.[84] But even those who are most critical of Google's actions appear to wish to pressure the company through standard channels: moral suasion, shareholder resolutions, government regulation compelling noncensorship, or a boycott to inflict financial pressure. Unlike Wikipedia, no one thinks that Google ought to be "governed" by its users in some democratic or communitarian way, even as it draws upon the wisdom of the crowds in deciding upon its rankings,[85] basing them in part on the ways in which millions of individual Web sites have decided about to whom to link. Amazon and Yelp welcome user reviews (and reviews of those reviews), but the public at large does not "govern" these institutions.

People instinctively expect more of Wikipedia. They see it as a shared resource and a public one, even though it is not an arm of any territorial sovereign. The same could be said of the Internet Engineering Task Force and the Internet itself, but Wikipedia appears to have further found a way to involve nontechnical people in its governance. Every time someone reads a Wikipedia article and knowingly chooses not to vandalize it, he or she has an opportunity to identify with and reinforce its ethos. Wales is setting his sights next on a search engine built and governed on this model, "free and transparent" about its rankings, with a "huge degree of human community oversight."[86] The next chapters explore how that ethos may be replicable: vertically to solve generative problems found at other layers of the Internet, and horizontally to other applications within the content and social layers.

If Wikipedia did not exist there would still be reason to cheer the generative possibilities of the Internet, its capacity to bring people together in meaningful conversations, commerce, or action. There are leading examples of each—the community of commentary and critique that has evolved around blogging, the user-driven reputation system within eBay, the "civil society" type of gatherings fostered by Meetup, or the social pressure–induced promises via Pledgebank, each drawing on the power of individuals contributing to community-driven goals. But Wikipedia is the canonical bee that flies despite scientists' skepticism that the aerodynamics add up.[87] These examples will grow, transform, or fade over time, and their futures may depend not just on the public's appetites and attention, but on the technical substrate that holds them all: the powerful but delicate generative Internet and PC, themselves vaulted unexpectedly into the mainstream because of amateur contribution and cooperation. We now explore how the lessons of Wikipedia, both its successes and shortcomings, shed light on how to maintain our technologies' generativity in the face of the problems arising from their widespread adoption.

III

Solutions

This book has explained how the Internet's generative characteristics primed it for extraordinary success—and now position it for failure. The response to the failure will most likely be sterile tethered appliances and Web services that are contingently generative, if generative at all. The trajectory is part of a larger pattern. If we can understand the pattern and what drives it, we can try to avoid an end that eliminates most disruptive innovation while facilitating invasive and all-too-inexpensive control by regulators.

The pattern begins with a technology groomed in a backwater, as much for fun as for profit. The technology is incomplete even as it is shared. It is designed to welcome contribution and improvement from many corners. New adopters refine it as it spreads, and it spreads more as it improves, a virtuous circle that vaults the technology into the mainstream, where commercial firms help to package and refine it for even more people. This is the story of the PC against information appliances, and it is the story of the Internet against the proprietary networks.

Developments then take a turn for the worse: mainstream success brings in people with no particular talent or tolerance for the nuts and bolts of the technology, and no connection with the open ethos that facilitates the sharing of improvements. It also attracts those who gain by abusing or subverting the technology and the people who use it. Users find themselves confused and hurt by the abuse, and they look for alternatives.

The most obvious solution to abuse of an open system is to tighten or altogether close it. A bank robbery calls for more guards; a plane hijacking suggests narrowing the list of those permitted to fly and what they are permitted to take with them. For the Internet and PC, it seems natural that a system beset by viruses ought not to propagate and run new code so easily. The same goes for that which is built on top of the Internet: when Wikipedia is plagued by vandals the obvious response is to disallow editing by anonymous users. Such solutions carry their own steep price within information technology: a reduction in the generativity of the system, clamping its innovative capacity while enhancing the prospects of control by the parties left in charge, such as in the likely shift by users away from generative PCs toward tethered appliances and Web services. What works in the short or medium term for banks and airlines has crucial drawbacks for consumer information technology, even as consumers themselves might bring such solutions about precisely where regulators would have had difficulty intervening, consigning generative technologies to the backwaters from which they came.

So what to do to stop this future? We need a strategy that blunts the worst aspects of today's popular generative Internet and PC without killing these platforms' openness to innovation. Give users a reason to stick with the technology and the applications that have worked so surprisingly well—or at least reduce the pressures to abandon it—and we may halt the movement toward a nongenerative digital world. This is easier said than done, because our familiar toolkits for handling problems are not particularly attuned to maintaining generativity. Solely regulatory interventions—such as banning the creation or distribution of deceptive or harmful code—are both under- and overinclusive. They are underinclusive for the usual reasons that regulation is difficult on today's Net, and that it is hard to track the identities of sophisticated wrongdoers. Even if found, many wrongdoers may not be in cooperative jurisdictions. They are overinclusive because so much of the good code we have seen has come from unaccredited people sharing what they have made for fun, collaborating in ways that would make businesslike regulation of their activities burdensome for them—quite possibly convincing them not to share to begin with. If we make it more difficult for new software to spread, good software from obscure sources can be fenced out along with the bad.

The key to threading the needle between needed change and undue closure can be forged from understanding the portability of both problems and solutions among the Internet's layers. We have seen that generativity from one layer can recur to the next. The open architecture of the Internet and Web allowed Ward Cunningham to invent the wiki, generic software that offers a way of editing or organizing information within an article, and spreading this information to other articles. Wikis were then used by unrelated nontechies to form a Web site at the content layer like Wikipedia. Wikipedia is in turn generative because people are free to take all of its contents and experiment with different ways of presenting or changing the material, perhaps by placing the information on otherwise unrelated Web sites in different formats.[1]

If generativity and its problems flow from one layer to another, so too can its solutions. There are useful guidelines to be drawn from the success stories of generative models at each layer, transcending the layer where they originate, revealing solutions for other layers. For example, when the Morris worm abused the openness of the 1987 Internet, the first line of defense was the community of computer scientists who populated the Internet at that time: they cooperated on diagnosing the problem and finding a solution. Recall that the Internet Engineering Task Force's (IETF's) report acknowledged the incident's seriousness and sought to forestall future viruses not through better engineering but by recommending better community ethics and policing.[2] This is exactly Wikipedia's trump card. When abuses of openness beset Wikipedia, it turned to its community—aided by some important technical tools—as the primary line of defense. Most recently, this effort has been aided by the introduction of Virgil Griffith's Wikiscanner, a simple tool that uses Wikipedia's page histories to expose past instances of article whitewashing by organizations.[3] So what distinguishes the IETF recommendation, which seems like a naïve way to approach Internet and PC-based problems, from the Wikipedian response, which so far appears to have held many of Wikipedia's problems at bay?

The answer lies in two crucial differences between generative solutions at the content layer and those at the technical layer. The first is that much content-layer participation—editing Wikipedia, blogging, or even engaging in transactions on eBay and Amazon that ask for reviews and ratings to establish reputations—is understood to be an innately social activity.[4] These services solicit and depend upon participation from the public at large, and their participation mechanisms are easy for the public to master. But when the same generative opportunity exists at the technical layer, mainstream users balk—they are eager to have someone else solve the underlying problem, which they perceive as technical rather than social.

The second difference is that many content-layer enterprises have developed technical tools to support collective participation, augmenting an individualistic ethos with community mechanisms.[5] In the Internet and PC security space, on the other hand, there have been few tools available to tap the power of groups to, say, distinguish good code from bad. Instead, dealing with bad code has been left either to individual users who are ill-positioned to, say, decipher whether a Web site's digital certificate is properly signed and validated, or to Internet security firms that try to sort out good code from bad according to a one-size-fits-all standard. Such a defense still cannot easily sift bad gray-zone software that is not a virus but still causes user regret—spyware, for instance—from unusual but beneficial code. As with the most direct forms of regulation, this solution is both under- and overinclusive.

These two differences point to two approaches that might save the generative spirit of the Net, or at least keep it alive for another interval. The first is to reconfigure and strengthen the Net's experimentalist architecture to make it fit better with its now-mainstream home. The second is to create and demonstrate the tools and practices by which relevant people and institutions can help secure the Net themselves instead of waiting for someone else to do it.

Befitting the conception of generative systems as works in progress that muddle through on the procrastination principle, the concrete ideas spawned by these solutions are a bit of a grab bag. They are evocative suggestions that show the kinds of processes that can work rather than a simple, elegant patch. Silver bullets belong to the realm of the appliance. Yet as with many of the Internet's advances, some of these hodge-podge solutions can be developed and deployed to make a difference without major investment—and with luck, they will be. The most significant barriers to adoption are, first, a wide failure to realize the extent of the problem and the costs of inaction; second, a collective action problem, exacerbated by the Internet's modular design, thanks to which no single existing group of actors who appreciates the problem sees it as its own responsibility; and third, a too-easily cultivated sense among Internet users that the system is supposed to work like any other consumer device.

7

Stopping the Future of the Internet: Stability on a Generative Net

There is a phrase from the days when television was central: "Not ready for prime time." Prime time refers to the precious time between dinner and bedtime when families would gather around the TV set looking to be informed or entertained. Viewership would be at its apex, both in numbers and in quality of viewers, defined as how much money they had and how ready they were to spend it on the things advertised during commercial breaks. During prime time, the average viewer was, comparatively speaking, a rich drunken sailor. Prime time programming saw the most expensive and elaborate shows, made with the highest production values.

Shows on channels other than those part of networks with big audiences, or at times of the day when most people were not watching TV, had less investment and lower production values. Their actors or presenters were not A-list. Flaws in the shows would prove them not ready for prime time—now a metaphor to mean anything that has not been buffed and polished to a fine, predictable shine. "Not ready" has the virtue of suggesting that someday a B-list program *could* be ready, vaulting from the backwaters to the center stage. And prime time concedes that there are other times beside it: there are backwaters that are accessible to masses of people so long as they are willing to surf to an unfamiliar channel or stay up a little later than usual.

To be sure, while the barriers to getting a show on an obscure network were less than those to landing a show on a major one, they were still high. And with only a handful of networks that people watched in prime time, the definitions of what was worthy of prime time ended up a devastatingly rough aggregation of preferences. There was not much room for programs finely honed to niche markets. TV's metaphor is powerful in the Internet space. As we have seen, the generative Internet allows experimentation from all corners, and it used to be all backwater and no prime time.

Now that the generative PC is so ubiquitous and its functions so central to both leisure and commerce, much of what it offers happens in prime time: a set of core applications and services that people are anxious to maintain. Links between backwater and prime time are legion; today's obscure but useful backwater application can find itself wildly popular and relied upon overnight. No intervention is needed from network executives running some prime time portion of the Internet, and realizing that there is something good going on among the farm teams that deserves promotion to the major league. The Net was built without programming executives, and its users have wide latitude to decide for themselves where they would like to go that day.

The first major challenge in preserving the generative Net, then, is to reconcile its role as a boisterous laboratory with its role as a purveyor of prime time, ensuring that inventions can continue to move easily from one to the other. Today our prime time applications and data share space with new, probationary ones, and they do not always sit well together. There are some technical inspirations we can take from successes like Wikipedia that, with enough alert users, can help.

THE RED AND THE GREEN

Wikis are designed so that anyone can edit them. This entails a risk that people will make bad edits, through either incompetence or malice. The damage that can be done, however, is minimized by the wiki technology, because it allows bad changes to be quickly reverted. All previous versions of a page are kept, and a few clicks by another user can restore a page to the way it was before later changes were made. Our PCs can be similarly equipped. For years Windows XP (and now Vista) has had a system restore feature, where snapshots are taken of the machine at a moment in time, allowing later bad changes to be rolled back. The process of restoring is tedious, restoration choices can be frustratingly all-or-nothing, and the system restore files themselves can become corrupted, but it represents progress. Even better would be the introduction of features that are commonplace on wikis: a quick chart of the history of each document, with an ability to see date-stamped sets of changes going back to its creation. Because our standard PC applications assume a safer environment than really exists, these features have never been demanded or implemented. Because wikis are deployed in environments prone to vandalism, their contents are designed to be easily recovered after a problem.

The next stage of this technology lies in new virtual machines, which would obviate the need for cyber cafés and corporate IT departments to lock down their PCs. Without virtual machine technology, many corporate IT departments relegate most employees to the status of guests on their own PCs, unable to install any new software, lest it turn out to be bad. Such lockdown reduces the number of calls to the helpdesk, as well as the risk that a user might corrupt or compromise a firm's data. (Perhaps more precisely, calls for help become calls for permission.) Similarly, cyber cafés and libraries want to prevent one user's ill-advised actions from cascading to future users. But lockdown eliminates the good aspects of the generative environment.

In an effort to satisfy the desire for safety without full lockdown, PCs could be designed to pretend to be more than one machine, capable of cycling from one split personality to the next. In its simplest implementation, we could divide a PC into two virtual machines: "Red" and "Green."[1] The Green PC would house reliable software and important data—a stable, mature OS platform and tax returns, term papers, and business documents. The Red PC would have everything else. In this setup, nothing that happens on one PC could easily affect the other, and the Red PC could have a simple reset button that sends it back to a predetermined safe state. Someone could confidently store important data on the Green PC and still use the Red PC for experimentation. Knowing which virtual PC to use would be akin to knowing when a sport utility vehicle should be placed into four-wheel drive mode instead of two-wheel drive, a decision that mainstream users could learn to make responsibly and knowledgeably.

A technology that splits the difference between lockdown and openness means that intermediaries could afford to give their end users more flexibility—which is to say, more opportunity to run others' code. Indeed, the miniaturization of storage means that users could bring their own system on a keychain (or download it from a remote site) to plug into a library or café's processing unit, screen, and network connection—a rediscovery of the hobbyist PC and its own modularization that made it better and cheaper than its appliancized counterparts.

There could be a spectrum of virtual PCs on one unit, one for each member of the family. Already, most consumer operating systems enable separate login names with customized desktop wallpaper and e-mail accounts for each user.[2] If the divide were developed further, a parent could confidently give her twelve-year-old access to the machine under her own account and know that nothing that the child could do—short of hurling the machine out the window—would hurt the data found within the other virtual PCs.[3] (To be sure, this does not solve problems at the social layer—of what activities children may undertake to their detriment once online.)

Easy reversion, coupled with virtual PCs, seeks to balance the experimentalist spirit of the early Internet with the fact that there are now important uses for those PCs that we do not want to disrupt. Still, this is not a complete solution. The Red PC, despite its experimental purpose, might end up accumulating data that the user wants to keep, occasioning the need for what Internet architect David Clark calls a "checkpoint Charlie" to move sensitive data from Red to Green without also carrying a virus or anything else undesirable that could hurt the Green PC.[4] There is also the question of what software can be deemed safe for Green—which is just another version of the question of what software to run on today's single-identity PCs. If users could competently decide what should go on Red and what on Green, then they could competently decide what to run on today's simpler machines, partially obviating the need for the virtual PC solution in the first place.

Worse, an infected Red PC still might be capable of hurting other PCs across the network, by sending spam or viruses, or by becoming a zombie PC controlled from afar for any number of other bad purposes. Virtualization technology eases some of the sting to users of an experimental platform whose experiments sometimes go awry, but it does not do much to reduce the burdens—negative externalities—that such failures can place on everyone else.

Most fundamentally, many of the benefits of generativity come precisely thanks to an absence of walls. We want our e-mail programs to have access to any document on our hard drive, so that we can attach it to an e-mail and send it to a friend. We want to edit music downloaded from a Web site with an audio mixing program and then incorporate it into a presentation. We want to export data from one desktop calendar application to a new one that we might like better. The list goes on, and each of these operations requires the ability to cross the boundaries from one application to another, or one virtual PC to another. For similar reasons, we may be hesitant to adopt complex access control and privilege lists to designate what software can and cannot do.[5]

It is not easy to anticipate what combinations of applications and data we will want in one place, and the benefits of using virtual machines will not always outweigh the confusion and limitations of having them. It is worth trying them out to buy us some more time—but they will not be panaceas. A guiding principle emerges from the Net's history at the technical layer and Wikipedia's history at the content layer: an experimentalist spirit is best maintained when failures can be contained as learning experiences rather than catastrophes.

BETTER INFORMED EXPERIMENTS

The Internet's original design relied on few mechanisms of central control. This lack of control has the added generative benefit of allowing new services to be introduced, and new destinations to come online, without any up-front vetting or blocking, by either private incumbents or public authorities.

With this absence of central control comes an absence of measurement. CompuServe or Prodigy could have reported exactly how many members they had at any moment, because they were centralized. Wikipedia can report the number of registered editors it has, because it is a centralized service run at wikipedia.org. But the Internet itself cannot say how many users it has, because it does not maintain user information. There is no "it" to query. Counting the number of IP addresses delegated is of little help, because many addresses are allocated but not used, while other addresses are shared. For example, QTel is the only ISP in Qatar, and it routes all users' traffic through a handful of IP addresses. Not only does this make it difficult to know the number of users hailing from Qatar, but it also means that when a site like Wikipedia has banned access from the IP address of a single misbehaving user from Qatar, it inadvertently has banned nearly every other Internet user in Qatar.[6]

Such absence of measurement extends to a lack of awareness at the network level of how much bandwidth is being used by whom. This has been beneficial for the adoption of new material on the Web by keeping the Internet in an "all you can eat" mode of data transmission, which happens when large ISPs peering with one another decide to simply swap data rather than trying to figure out how to charge one another per unit of information exchanged. This absence of measurement is good from a generative point of view because it allows initially whimsical but data-intensive uses of the network to thrive—and perhaps to turn out to be vital. For example, the first online webcams were set up within office cubicles and were about as interesting as watching paint dry. But people could tinker with them because they (and their employers, who might be paying for the network connection) did not have to be mindful of their data consumption. From an economic point of view this might appear wasteful, since non-value-producing but high-bandwidth activities—goldfish bowl cams—will not be constrained. But the economic point of view is at its strongest when there is scarcity, and from nearly the beginning of the Internet's history there has been an abundance of bandwidth on the network backbones. It is the final link to a particular PC or cluster of PCs—still usually a jury-rigged link on twisted copper wires or coaxial cable originally intended for other purposes like telephone and cable television—that can become congested. And in places where ISPs enjoy little competition, they can further choose to segment their services with monthly caps—a particular price plan might allow only two gigabytes of data transfer per month, with users then compelled to carefully monitor their Internet usage, avoiding the fanciful surfing that could later prove central. In either case, the owner of the PC can choose what to do with that last slice of bandwidth, realizing that watching full screen video might, say, slow down a file transfer in the background. (To be sure, on many broadband networks this final link is shared among several unrelated subscribers, causing miniature tragedies of the commons as a file-sharing neighbor slows down the Internet performance for someone nearby trying to watch on-demand video.)

The ability to tinker and experiment without watching a meter provides an important impetus to innovate; yesterday's playful webcams on aquariums and cubicles have given rise to Internet-facilitated warehouse monitoring, citizen-journalist reporting from remote locations, and, as explained later in this book, even controversial experiments in a distributed neighborhood watch system where anyone can watch video streamed from a national border and report people who look like they are trying to cross it illegally.[7]

However, an absence of measurement is starting to have generative drawbacks. Because we cannot easily measure the network and the character of the activity on it, we are left incapable of easily assessing and dealing with threats from bad code without laborious and imperfect cooperation among a limited group of security software vendors. It is like a community in which only highly specialized private mercenaries can identify crimes in progress and the people who commit them, with the nearby public at large ignorant of the transgressions until they themselves are targeted.

Creating a system where the public can help requires work from technologists who have more than a set of paying customers in mind. It is a call to the academic environment that gave birth to the Net, and to the public authorities who funded it as an investment first in knowledge and later in general infrastructure. Experiments need measurement, and the future of the generative Net depends on a wider circle of users able to grasp the basics of what is going on within their machines and between their machines and the network.

What might this system look like? Roughly, it would take the form of toolkits to overcome the digital solipsism that each of our PCs experiences when it attaches to the Internet at large, unaware of the size and dimension of the network to which it connects. These toolkits would have the same building blocks as spyware, but with the opposite ethos: they would run unobtrusively on the PCs of participating users, reporting back—to a central source, or perhaps only to each other—information about the vital signs and running code of that PC that could help other PCs figure out the level of risk posed by new code. Unlike spyware, the code's purpose would be to use other PCs' anonymized experiences to empower the PC's user. At the moment someone is deciding whether to run some new software, the toolkit's connections to other machines could say how many other machines on the Internet were running the code, what proportion of machines of self-described experts were running it, whether those experts had vouched for it, and how long the code had been in the wild. It could also signal the amount of unattended network traffic, pop-up ads, or crashes the code appeared to generate. This sort of data could become part of a simple dashboard that lets the users of PCs make quick judgments about the nature and quality of the code they are about to run in light of their own risk preferences, just as motor vehicle drivers use their dashboards to view displays of their vehicle's speed and health and to tune their radios to get traffic updates.

Harvard University's Berkman Center and the Oxford Internet Institute— multidisciplinary academic enterprises dedicated to charting the future of the Net and improving it—have begun a project called StopBadware, designed to assist rank-and-file Internet users in identifying and avoiding bad code.[8] The idea is not to replicate the work of security vendors like Symantec and McAfee, which seek to bail new viruses out of our PCs faster than they pour in. Rather, it is to provide a common technical and institutional framework for users to devote some bandwidth and processing power for better measurement: to let us know what new code is having what effect amid the many machines taking it up. Not every PC owner is an expert, but each PC is a precious guinea pig— one that currently is experimented upon with no record of what works and what does not, or with the records hoarded by a single vendor. The first step in the toolkit is now available freely for download: "Herdict." Herdict is a small piece of software that assembles the vital signs described above, and places them in a dashboard usable by mainstream PC owners. These efforts will test the hypothesis that solutions to generative problems at the social layer might be applicable to the technical layer—where help is desperately needed. Herdict is an experiment to test the durability of experiments.[9] And it is not alone. For example, Internet researchers Jean Camp and Allan Friedman have developed the "good neighbors" system to allow people to volunteer their PCs to detect and patch vulnerabilities among their designated friends' PCs.[10]

The value of aggregating data from individual sources is well known. Yochai Benkler approvingly cites Google Pagerank algorithms over search engines whose results are auctioned, because Google draws on the individual linking decisions of millions of Web sites to calculate how to rank its search results.[11] If more people are linking to a Web site criticizing Barbie dolls than to one selling them, the critical site will, all else equal, appear higher in the rankings when a user searches for "Barbie." This concept is in its infancy at the application layer on the PC. When software crashes on many PC platforms, a box appears asking the user whether to send an error report to the operating system maker. If the user assents, and enough other users reported a similar problem, sometimes a solution to the problem is reported back from the vendor. But these implementations are only halfway there from a generative standpoint. The big institutions doing the gathering—Google because it has the machines to scrape the entire Web; Microsoft and Apple because they can embed error reporting in their OSes—make use of the data (if not the wisdom) of the crowds, but the data is not further shared, and others are therefore unable to make their own interpretations of it or build their own tools with it. It is analogous to Encarta partially adopting the spirit of Wikipedia, soliciting suggestions from readers for changes to its articles, but not giving any sense of where those suggestions go, how they are used, or how many other suggestions have been received, what they say, or why they say it.

A full adoption of the lessons of Wikipedia would be to give PC users the opportunity to have some ownership, some shared stake, in the process of evaluating code, especially because they have a stake in getting it right for their own machines. Sharing useful data from their PCs is one step, but this may work best when the data is going to an entity committed to the public interest of solving PC security problems, and willing to share that data with others who want to take a stab at solving them. The notion of a civic institution here does not necessarily mean cumbersome governance structures and formal lines of authority so much as it means a sense of shared responsibility and participation.[12] It is the opposite of the client service model in which one calls a helpline and for a fee expects to be helped—and those who do not pay receive no help. Instead, it is the volunteer fire department or neighborhood watch where, while not everyone is able to fight fires or is interested in watching, a critical mass of people are prepared to contribute, and such contributions are known to the community more broadly.[13] A necessary if not sufficient condition to fighting the propagation of bad code as a social problem is to allow people to enter into a social configuration in order to attack it.

These sorts of solutions are not as easily tried for tethered appliances, where people make a decision only about whether to acquire them, and the devices are otherwise controlled from afar. Of course, they may not be as necessary, since the appliances are not, by definition, as vulnerable to exploits performed by un- approved code. But tethered appliances raise the concern of perfect enforce- ment described earlier in this book: they can too readily, almost casually, be used to monitor and control the behavior of their users. When tools drawing on group generativity are deployed, the opposite is true. Their success is depen- dent on participation, and this helps establish the legitimacy of the project both to those participating and those not. It also means that the generative uses to which the tools are put may affect the number of people willing to assist. If it turned out that the data generated and shared from a PC vital signs tool went to help design viruses, word of this could induce people to abandon their com- mitment to help. Powerful norms that focus collaborators toward rather than against a commitment to the community are necessary. This is an emerging form of netizenship, where tools that embed particular norms grow more pow- erful with the public's belief in the norms' legitimacy.

It is easy for Internet users to see themselves only as consumers whose partic- ipation is limited to purchasing decisions that together add up to a market force pushing one way or another. But with the right tools, users can also see them- selves as participants in the shaping of generative space—as netizens. This is a crucial reconception of what it means to go online. The currency of cyberspace is, after all, ideas, and we shortchange ourselves if we think of ideas to be, in the words of Electronic Frontier Foundation co-founder John Perry Barlow, merely "another industrial product, no more noble than pig iron,"[14] broadcast to us for our consumption but not capable of also being shaped by us. If we insist on treating the Net as an invisible conduit, capable of greater or lesser bandwidth but otherwise meant to be invisible, we naturally turn to service providers with demands to keep it working, even when the problems arising are social in nature.

RECRUITING HELP AT THE BARRICADES: THE GENERATIVITY PRINCIPLE AND THE LIMITS OF END-TO-END NEUTRALITY

Some commentators believe that software authors and operating system makers have it easy.[15] They produce buggy code open to viruses and malware, but they are not held accountable the way that a carmaker would be for a car whose wheels fell off, or a toaster maker would be if its toasters set bread on fire.[16] Why should there be a difference? The security threats described in this book might be thought so pervasive and harmful that even if they do not physically hurt anyone, software makers ought to pay for the harm their bugs cause.

This is already somewhat true of information appliances. If a TiVo unit did not operate as promised—suppose it simply crashed and failed to record any television programs—the law of warranty would quickly come into play. If the TiVo unit were new enough, the company would make good on a repair or replacement.[17] Yet this simple exchange rarely takes place after the purchase of a standard generative PC. Suppose a new PC stops functioning: after a week of using it to surf the Internet and send e-mail, the consumer turns it on and sees only a blue error screen.[18] Unless smoke pours out of the PC to indicate a genuine hardware problem, the hardware manufacturer is likely to diagnose the problem as software-related. The operating system maker is not likely to be helpful. Because the user no doubt installed software after purchasing the machine, pinpointing the problem is not easy. In particularly difficult cases, the OS maker will simply suggest a laborious and complete reinstallation of the OS, wiping clean all the changes that the consumer has made. Finally, appealing to individual software makers results in the same problem: a software maker will blame the OS maker or a producer of other software found on the machine.

So why not place legal blame on each product maker and let them sort it out? If the consumer is not skilled enough to solve PC security problems or wealthy enough to pay for someone else to figure it out, a shifting of legal responsibility to others could cause them to create and maintain more secure software and hardware. Unfortunately, such liability would serve only to propel PC lockdown, reducing generativity. The more complex that software is, the more difficult it is to secure it, and allowing third parties to build upon it increases the complexity of the overall system even if the foundation is a simple one. If operating system makers were liable for downstream accidents, they would start screening who can run what on their platforms, resulting in exactly the non-generative state of affairs we want to avoid. Maintainers of technology platforms like traditional OS makers and Web services providers should be encouraged to keep their platforms open and generative, rather than closed to eliminate outside sources of malware or to facilitate regulatory control, just as platforms for content built on open technologies are wisely not asked to take responsibility for everything that third parties might put there.[19]

Hardware and OS makers are right that the mishmash of software found on even a two-week-old Internet-exposed PC precludes easily identifying the source of many problems. However, the less generative the platform already is, the less there is to lose by imposing legal responsibility on the technology provider to guarantee a functioning system. To the extent that PC OSes do control what programs can run on them, the law should hold OS developers responsible for problems that arise, just as TiVo and mobile phone manufacturers take responsibility for issues that arise with their controlled technologies.

If the OS remains open to new applications created by third parties, the maker's responsibility should be duly lessened. It might be limited to providing basic tools of transparency that empower users to understand exactly what their machines are doing. These need not be as sophisticated as Herdict aims to be. Rather, they could be such basic instrumentation as what sort of data is going in and out of the box and to whom. A machine turned into a zombie will be communicating with unexpected sources that a free machine will not, and insisting on better information to users could be as important as providing a speedometer on an automobile—even if users do not think they need one.

Such a regime permits technology vendors to produce closed platforms but encourages them to produce generative platforms by scaling liabilities accordingly. Generative platform makers would then be asked only to take certain basic steps to make their products less autistic: more aware of their digital surroundings and able to report what they see to their users. This tracks the intuition behind secondary theories of liability: technology makers may shape their technologies largely as they please, but the configurations they choose then inform their duties and liabilities.[20]

Apart from hardware and software makers, there is another set of technology providers that reasonably could be asked or required to help: Internet Service Providers. So far, like PC, OS, and software makers, ISPs have been on the sidelines regarding network security. The justification for this—apart from the mere explanation that ISPs are predictably and rationally lazy—is that the Internet was rightly designed to be a dumb network, with most of its features and complications pushed to the endpoints. The Internet's engineers embraced the simplicity of the end-to-end principle (and its companion, the procrastination principle) for good reasons. It makes the network more flexible, and it puts designers in a mindset of making the system work rather than anticipating every possible thing that could go wrong and trying to design around or for those things from the outset.[21] Since this early architectural decision, "keep the Internet free" advocates have advanced the notion of end-to-end neutrality as an ethical ideal, one that leaves the Internet without filtering by any of its intermediaries. This use of end-to-end says that packets should be routed between the sender and the recipient without anyone stopping them on the way to ask what they contain.[22] Cyberlaw scholars have taken up end-to-end as a battle cry for Internet freedom,[23] invoking it to buttress arguments about the ideological impropriety of filtering Internet traffic or favoring some types or sources of traffic over others.

These arguments are powerful, and end-to-end neutrality in both its technical and political incarnations has been a crucial touchstone for Internet development. But it has its limits. End-to-end does not fully capture the overall project of maintaining openness to contribution from unexpected and unaccredited sources. Generativity more fundamentally expresses the values that attracted cyberlaw scholars to end-to-end in the first place.

According to end-to-end theory, placing control and intelligence at the edges of a network maximizes not just network flexibility, but also user choice.[24] The political implication of this view—that end-to-end design preserves users' freedom, because the users can configure their own machines however they like—depends on an increasingly unreliable assumption: whoever runs a machine at a given network endpoint can readily choose how the machine will work. To see this presumption in action, consider that in response to a network teeming with viruses and spam, network engineers recommend more bandwidth (so the transmission of "deadweights" like viruses and spam does not slow down the much smaller proportion of legitimate mail being carried by the network) and better protection at user endpoints, rather than interventions by ISPs closer to the middle of the network.[25] But users are not well positioned to painstakingly maintain their machines against attack, leading them to prefer locked-down PCs, which carry far worse, if different, problems. Those who favor end-to-end principles because an open network enables generativity should realize that intentional inaction at the network level may be self-defeating, because consumers may demand locked-down endpoint environments that promise security and stability with minimum user upkeep. This is a problem for the power user and consumer alike.

The answer of end-to-end theory to threats to our endpoints is to have them be more discerning, transforming them into digital gated communities that must frisk traffic arriving from the outside. The frisking is accomplished either by letting next to nothing through—as is the case with highly controlled information appliances—or by having third-party antivirus firms perform monitoring, as is done with increasingly locked-down PCs. Gated communities offer a modicum of safety and stability to residents as well as a manager to complain to when something goes wrong. But from a generative standpoint, these moated paradises can become prisons. Their confinement is less than obvious, because what they block is not escape but generative possibility: the ability of outsiders to offer code and services to users, and the corresponding opportunity of users and producers to influence the future without a regulator's permission. When endpoints are locked down, and producers are unable to deliver innovative products directly to users, openness in the middle of the network becomes meaningless. Open highways do not mean freedom when they are so dangerous that one never ventures from the house.

Some may cling to a categorical end-to-end approach; doubtlessly, even in a world of locked-down PCs there will remain old-fashioned generative PCs for professional technical audiences to use. But this view is too narrow. We ought to see the possibilities and benefits of PC generativity made available to everyone, including the millions of people who give no thought to future uses when they obtain PCs, and end up delighted at the new uses to which they can put their machines. And without this ready market, those professional developers would have far more obstacles to reaching critical mass with their creations.

Strict loyalty to end-to-end neutrality should give way to a new generativity principle, a rule that asks that any modifications to the Internet's design or to the behavior of ISPs be made where they will do the least harm to generative possibilities. Under such a principle, for example, it may be preferable in the medium term to screen out viruses through ISP-operated network gateways rather than through constantly updated PCs.[26] Although such network screening theoretically opens the door to additional filtering that may be undesirable, this speculative risk should be balanced against the very real threats to generativity inherent in PCs operated as services rather than products. Moreover, if the endpoints remain free as the network becomes slightly more ordered, they remain as safety valves should network filtering begin to block more than bad code.

In the meantime, ISPs are in a good position to help in a way that falls short of undesirable perfect enforcement, and that provides a stopgap while we develop the kinds of community-based tools that can facilitate salutary endpoint screening. There are said to be tens of thousands of PCs converted to zombies daily,[27] and an ISP can sometimes readily detect the digital behavior of a zombie when it starts sending thousands of spam messages or rapidly probes a sequence of Internet addresses looking for yet more vulnerable PCs. Yet ISPs currently have little incentive to deal with this problem. To do so creates a two-stage customer service nightmare. If the ISP quarantines an infected machine until it has been recovered from zombie-hood—cutting it off from the network in the process—the user might claim that she is not getting the network access she paid for. And quarantined users will have to be instructed how to clean their machines, which is a complicated business.[28] This explains why ISPs generally do not care to act when they learn that they host badware-infected Web sites or consumer PCs that are part of a botnet.[29]

Whether through new industry best practices or through a rearrangement of liability motivating ISPs to take action in particularly flagrant and egregious zombie situations, we can buy another measure of time in the continuing security game of cat and mouse. Security in a generative system is something never fully put to rest—it is not as if the "right" design will forestall security problems forevermore. The only way for such a design to be foolproof is for it to be nongenerative, locking down a computer the same way that a bank would fully secure a vault by neither letting any customers in nor letting any money out. Security of a generative system requires the continuing ingenuity of a few experts who want it to work well, and the broader participation of others with the goodwill to outweigh the actions of a minority determined to abuse it.

A generativity principle suggests additional ways in which we might redraw the map of cyberspace. First, we must bridge the divide between those concerned with network connectivity and protocols and those concerned with PC design—a divide that end-to-end neutrality unfortunately encourages. Such modularity in stakeholder competence and purview was originally a useful and natural extension of the Internet's architecture. It meant that network experts did not have to be PC experts, and vice versa. But this division of responsibilities, which works so well for technical design, is crippling our ability to think through the trajectory of applied information technology. Now that the PC and the Internet are so inextricably intertwined, it is not enough for network engineers to worry only about network openness and assume that the endpoints can take care of themselves. It is abundantly clear that many endpoints cannot. The procrastination principle has its limits: once a problem has materialized, the question is how best to deal with it, with options ranging from further procrastination to effecting changes in the way the network or the endpoints behave. Changes to the network should not be categorically off the table.

Second, we need to rethink our vision of the network itself. "Middle" and "endpoint" are no longer subtle enough to capture the important emerging features of the Internet/PC landscape. It remains correct that, from a network standpoint, protocol designs and the ISPs that implement them are the "middle" of the network, as distinct from PCs that are "endpoints." But the true import of this vernacular of "middle" and "endpoint" for policy purposes has lost its usefulness in a climate in which computing environments are becoming services, either because individuals no longer have the power to exercise meaningful control over their PC endpoints, or because their computing activities are hosted elsewhere on the network, thanks to "Web services." By ceding decision-making control to government, to a Web 2.0 service, to a corporate authority such as an OS maker, or to a handful of security vendors, individuals permit their PCs to be driven by an entity in the middle of the network, causing their identities as endpoints to diminish. The resulting picture is one in which there is no longer such a clean separation between "middle" and "endpoint." In some places, the labels have begun to reverse.

Abandoning the end-to-end debate's divide between "middle" and "endpoint" will enable us to better identify and respond to threats to the Internet's generativity. In the first instance, this might mean asking that ISPs play a real role in halting the spread of viruses and the remote use of hijacked machines.

This reformulation of our vision of the network can help with other problems as well. For instance, even today consumers might not want or have the ability to fine-tune their PCs. We might say that such fine-tuning is not possible because PCs, though leveraged and adaptable, are not easy for a mass audience to master. Taking the generativity-informed view of what constitutes a network, though, we can conceptualize a variety of methods by which PCs might compensate for this difficulty of mastery, only some of which require centralized control and education. For example, users might be able to choose from an array of proxies—not just Microsoft, but also Ralph Nader, or a public interest organization, or a group of computer scientists, or StopBadware—for guidance on how best to configure their PCs. For the Herdict program described earlier, the ambition is for third parties to contribute their own dash-board gauges—allowing users of Herdict to draw from a market of advisers, each of whom can draw from some combination of the herd's data and their own expertise to give users advice. The idea is that by reformulating our vision of the network to extend beyond mere "endpoints" and "middles," we can keep our eyes on the real value at stake: individual freedom to experiment with new code and anything made possible by it, the touchstone of a generative system.

EXTRA-LEGAL INCENTIVES TO SOLVE THE GENERATIVE PROBLEM: FROM WIKIPEDIA TO MAPS AND STOPBADWARE

Some of the suggested solutions here include legal intervention, such as liability for technology producers in certain circumstances. Legal interventions face certain hurdles in the Internet space. One sovereign cannot reach every potentially responsible entity on a global network, and while commercial forces can respond well to legal incentives,[30] the amateur technology producers that are so important to a generative system are less likely to shape their behavior to conform to subtle legal standards.

The ongoing success of enterprises like Wikipedia suggests that social problems can be met first with social solutions—aided by powerful technical tools—rather than by resorting to law. As we have seen, vandalism, copyright infringement, and lies on Wikipedia are typically solved not by declaring that vandals are breaking laws against "exceeding authorized access" to Wikipedia or by suits for infringement or defamation, but rather through a community process that, astoundingly, has impact.

In the absence of consistent interventions by law, we also have seen some peer-produced-and-implemented responses to perceived security problems at the Internet's technical layer, and they demonstrate both the value and drawbacks of a grassroots system designed to facilitate choice by endpoints about with whom to communicate or what software to run.

One example is the early implementation of the Mail Abuse Prevention System (MAPS) as a way of dealing with spam. In the summer of 1997, Internet pioneer Paul Vixie decided he had had enough of spam. He started keeping a list of those IP addresses that he believed were involved in originating spam, discovered through either his own sleuthing or that of others whom he trusted. The first thing he did with the list was make sure the entities on it could not send him e-mail. Next he made his list instantly available over the network so anyone could free-ride off of his effort to distinguish between spammers and nonspammers. In 1999, leading Web-based e-mail provider Hotmail decided to do just that on behalf of its customers.[31] Thus if Paul Vixie believed a particular mail server to be accommodating a spammer, no one using that server could send e-mail to anyone with an account at hotmail.com. MAPS was also known as the "Realtime Blackhole List," referring to the black hole that one's e-mail would enter if one's outgoing e-mail provider were listed. The service was viewed as a deterrent as much as an incapacitation: it was designed to get people who e-mail (or who run e-mail servers) to behave in a certain way.[32]

Vixie was not the only social entrepreneur in this space. Others also offered tools for deciding what was spam and who was sending it, with varying tolerance for appeals from those incorrectly flagged. The Open Relay Behavior-modification System (ORBS) sent automated test e-mails through others' e-mail servers to figure out who maintained so-called open relays. If ORBS was able to send itself e-mail through another's server successfully, it concluded that the server could be used to send spam and would add it to its own blacklist. Vixie concluded that the operator of ORBS was therefore also a spammer—for sending the test e-mails. He blackholed them on MAPS, and they blackholed him on ORBS, spurring a brief digital war between these private security forces.[33]

Vixie's efforts were undertaken with what appear to be the best of intentions, and a sense of humility. Vixie expressed reservations about his system even as he continued to develop it. He worried about the heavy responsibilities attendant on private parties who amass the power to affect others' lives to exercise the power fairly.[34] The judgments of one private party about another—perhaps in turn informed by other private parties—can become as life-affecting as the judgments of public authorities, yet without the elements of due process that cabin the actions of public authorities in societies that recognize the rule of law. At the time, being listed on MAPS or other powerful real time blackhole lists could be tantamount to having one's Internet connection turned off.[35]

MAPS was made possible by the generative creation and spread of tools that would help interested network administrators combat spam without reliance on legal intervention against spammers. It was a predictable response by a system of users in which strong norms against spamming had lost effectiveness as the Internet became more impersonal and the profits to be gleaned from sending spam increased.[36] In the absence of legal solutions or changes at the center of the network, barriers like MAPS could be put in place closer to the endpoints, as end-to-end theory would counsel. But MAPS as a generative solution has drawbacks. The first is that people sending e-mail through blackholed servers could not easily figure out why their messages were not being received, and there were no easy avenues for appeal if a perceived spammer wanted to explain or reform. Further, the use of MAPS and other lists was most straightforward when the IP addresses sending spam were either those of avowed spammers or those of network operators with willful ignorance of the spammers' activities, in a position to stop them if only the operators would act. When spammers adjusted tactics in this game of cat and mouse and moved their spamming servers to fresh IP addresses, the old IP addresses would be reassigned to new, innocent parties—but they would remain blackholed without easy appeal. Some IP addresses could thus become sullied, with people signing on to the Internet having no knowledge that the theoretically interchangeable IP address that they were given had been deemed unwelcome by a range of loosely coordinated entities across the Net.[37] Finally, as spammers worked with virus makers to involuntarily and stealthily transform regular Internet users' machines into ad hoc mail servers spewing spam, users could find themselves blocked without realizing what was going on.

MAPS is just one example of individual decisions being aggregated, or single decisions sent back out to individuals or their proxies for implementation. In 2006, in cooperation with the Harvard and Oxford StopBadware initiative, Google began automatically identifying Web sites that had malicious code hidden in them, ready to infect users' browsers as soon as they visited the site.[38] Some of these sites were set up expressly for the purpose of spreading viruses, but many more were otherwise-legitimate Web sites that had been hacked. For example, the puzzlingly named chuckroast.com sells fleece jackets and other clothing just as thousands of other e-commerce sites do. Visitors can browse chuckroast's offerings and place and pay for orders. However, hackers had subtly changed the code in the chuckroast site, either by guessing the site owner's password or by exploiting an unpatched vulnerability in the site's Web server. The hackers left the site's basic functionalities untouched while injecting the smallest amount of code on the home page to spread an infection to visitors.

Thanks to the generative design of Web protocols, allowing a Web page to direct users' browsers seamlessly to pull together data and software from any number of Internet sites to compose a single Web page, the infecting code needed to be only one line long, directing a browser to visit the hacker's site quietly and deposit and run a virus on the user's machine.[39] Once Google found the waiting exploit on chuckroast's site, it tagged it every time it came up as a

Google search result: "Warning: This site may harm your computer."[40] Those who clicked on the link anyway would, instead of being taken to chuckroast .com, get an additional page from Google with a much larger warning and a suggestion to visit StopBadware or pick another page instead of chuckroast's.

Chuckroast's visits plummeted after the warning was given, and the site owner was understandably anxious to figure out what was wrong and how to get rid of the warning. But cleaning the site requires leaving the realm of the amateur Web designer and entering the zone of the specialist who knows how to diagnose and clean a virus. Requests for review—which included pleas for help in understanding the problem to begin with—inundated StopBadware researchers, who found themselves overwhelmed in a matter of days by appeals from thousands of Web sites listed.[41] Until StopBadware could check each site and verify it had been cleaned of bad code, the warning page stayed up. Difficult questions were pressed by site owners and users: does Google owe notice to webmasters before—or even after—it lists their sites as being infected and warns Google users away from them? Such notice is not easy to effect, because there is no centralized index of Web site owners, nor a standardized way to reach them. (Sometimes domain name records have a space for such data,[42] but the information domain name owners place there is often false to throw off spammers, and when true it often reaches the ISP hosting the Web site rather than the Web site owner. When the ISP is alerted, it either ignores the request or immediately pulls the plug on the site—a remedy more drastic than simply warning Google users away from it.) Ideally, such notice would be given after a potentially labor-intensive search for the Web owner, and the site owner would be helped in figuring out how to find and remove the offending code—and secure the site against future hacking. (Chuckroast eliminated the malicious code, and, not long afterward, Google removed the warning about the site.)

Prior to the Google/StopBadware project, no one took responsibility for this kind of security. Ad hoc alerts to webmasters—those running the hacked sites—and their ISPs garnered little reaction. The sites were working fine for their intended purposes even as they were spreading viruses, and site customers would likely not be able to trace infections back to (and thereby blame) the merchant. As one Web site owner said after conceding that his site was unintentionally distributing malware, "Someone had hacked us and then installed something that ran an 'Active X' something or rather [*sic*]. It would be caught with any standard security software like McAfee."[43] In other words, the site owner figured that security against malware was the primary responsibility of his visitors—if they were better defended, they would not have to worry about

malicious, and to be transparent about the judgments they make. It is even harder to apply to a collective power from something like Herdict, where there is not a Paul Vixie or Microsoft channeling it but, rather, a collective peer-to-peer consciousness generating judgments and the data on which they are based. How does one tell a decentralized network that it needs to be mindful of due process?

The first answer ought to be: through suasion. Particularly in efforts like the partnership between Google and StopBadware, public interest entities are involved with a mandate to try to do the right thing. They may not have enough money or people to handle what due process might be thought to require, and they might come to decisions about fairness where people disagree, but the first way to make peace in cyberspace is through genuine discussion and shaping of practices that can then catch on and end up generally regarded as fair. Failing that, law might intrude to regulate not the wrongdoers but those private parties who have stepped up first to help stop the wrongdoers. This is because accumulation of power in third parties to stop the problems arising from the generative pattern may be seen as both necessary and worrisome—it takes a network endpoint famously configurable by its owner and transforms it into a network middle point subject to only nominal control by its owner. The touchstone for judging such efforts should be according to the generative principle: do the solutions encourage a system of experimentation? Are the users of the system able, so far as they are interested, to find out how the resources they control—such as a PC—are participating in the environment? Done well, these interventions can lower the ease of mastery of the technology, encouraging even casual users to have some part in directing it, while reducing the accessibility of those users' machines to outsiders who have not been given explicit and informed permission by the users to make use of them. It is automatic accessibility by outsiders—whether by vendors, malware authors, or governments—that can end up depriving a system of its generative character as its own users are proportionately limited in their own control.

*   *   *

We need a latter-day Manhattan project, not to build a bomb but to design the tools and conventions by which to continually defuse one. We need a series of conversations, arguments, and experiments whose participants span the spectrum between network engineers and PC software designers, between expert users with time to spend tinkering and those who simply want the system to work—but who appreciate the dangers of lockdown. And we need constitutionalists: lawyers who can help translate the principles of fairness and due process that have been the subject of analysis for liberal democracies into a new space where private parties and groups come together with varying degrees of hierarchy to try to solve the problems they find in the digital space. Projects like the National Science Foundation's FIND initiative have tried to take on some of this work, fostering an interdisciplinary group of researchers to envision the future shape of the Internet.[48]

CompuServe and AOL, along with the IBM System 360 and the Friden Flexowriter, showed us the kind of technological ecosystem the market alone was ready to yield. It was one in which substantial investment and partnership with gatekeepers would be needed to expose large numbers of people to new code—and ultimately to new content. The generative Internet was crucially funded and cultivated by people and institutions acting outside traditional markets, and *then* carried to ubiquity by commercial forces. Its success requires an ongoing blend of expertise and contribution from multiple models and motivations—and ultimately, perhaps, a move by the law to allocate responsibility to commercial technology players in a position to help but without economic incentive to do so, and to those among us, commercial or not, who step forward to solve the pressing problems that elude simpler solutions.

8

Strategies for a Generative Future

Even if the generative Internet is preserved, those who stand to lose from the behaviors taking place over it will maintain pressure for change. Threats to the technical stability of the newly expanded network are not the only factors at work shaping the digital future. At the time of the founding of the Internet and the release of the PC, little attention was given to whether a system that allows bits to move freely would be an instrument of contributory copyright infringement, or whether it was necessary to build in mechanisms of government surveillance for the new medium. Now that the PC and Internet are in the mainstream, having trumped proprietary systems that would have been much tamer, there remain strong regulatory pressures. This chapter considers how the law ought to be shaped if one wants to reconcile generative experimentation with other policy goals beyond continued technical stability. For those who think that good code and content can come from amateur sources, there are some important ways for the law to help facilitate generativity—or at least not hurt it. And for those whose legitimate interests have been threatened or harmed by applications of the generative Internet, we can look for ways to give them some redress without eliminating that generative character.

The ideas here fall into several broad categories. First, we ought to take steps to make the tethered appliances and software-as-service described in Chapter Five more palatable, since they are here to stay, even if the PC and Internet are saved. Second, we can help ensure a balance between generative and non-generative segments of the IT ecosystem. Third, we can make generative systems less threatening to legally protected interests.

PROTECTIONS FOR A WORLD OF TETHERED APPLIANCES AND WEB 2.0

Maintaining Data Portability

A move to tethered appliances and Web services means that more and more of our experiences in the information space will be contingent. A service or product we use at one moment could act completely differently the next, since it can be so quickly reprogrammed without our assent. Each time we power up a mobile phone, video game console, or BlackBerry, it might have gained some features and lost others. Each time we visit a Web site offering an ongoing service like e-mail access or photo storage, the same is true. People are notoriously poor at planning ahead, and their decisions about whether to start hosting all the family's photos on one site or another may not take into account the prospect that the function and format of the site can change at any time.

Older models of software production are less problematic. Because traditional software has clearly demarcated updates, users can stick with an older version if they do not like the tradeoffs of a newer one. These applications usually feature file formats that are readable by other applications, so that data from one program can be used in another: WordPerfect users, for example, can switch to Microsoft Word and back again. The pull of interoperability compelled most software developers to allow data to be exportable in common formats, and if one particular piece of software were to reach market dominance—and thereby no longer need to be as interoperable—existing versions of that software would not retroactively lose that capability.

If the security issues on generative platforms are mitigated, it is likely that technology vendors can find value with both generative and non-generative business models. For example, it may be beneficial for a technology maker to sell below-cost hardware and to make up much of the loss by collecting licensing fees from any third-party contributions that build on that hardware. This is the business model for many video game console makers.[1] This business model offers cheap hardware to consumers while creating less generative systems. So long as generative consoles can compete with non-generative ones, it would seem that the market can sort out this tradeoff—at least if people can easily switch from one platform to another. Maintaining the prospect that users can switch ensures that changes to wildly popular platforms and services are made according to the interests of their users. There has been ongoing debate about just how much of a problem lock-in can be with a technology.[2] The tradeoff of, say, a long-term mobile phone contract in exchange for a heavy discount on a new handset is one that the consumer at least knows up front. Much less understood are the limits on extracting the information consumers deposit into a non-generative platform. Competition can be stymied when people find themselves compelled to retain one platform only because their data is trapped there.

As various services and applications become more self-contained within particular devices, there is a minor intervention the law could make to avoid undue lock-in. Online consumer protection law has included attention to privacy policies. A Web site without a privacy policy, or one that does not live up to whatever policy it posts, is open to charges of unfair or deceptive trade practices.[3] Makers of tethered appliances and Web sites keeping customer data similarly ought to be asked to offer portability policies. These policies would declare whether they will allow users to extract their own data should they wish to move their activities from one appliance or Web site to another.

In some cases, the law could create a right of data portability, in addition to merely insisting on a clear statement of a site's policies. Traditional software as product nearly always keeps its data files stored on the user's PC in formats that third parties can access.[4] Software as product therefore allows for the routine portability of data, including data that could be precious: one's trove of e-mail, or the only copy of family photos from a cherished vacation. Imagine cameras that effectively made those photos property of Kodak, usable only in certain ways that the company dictated from one moment to the next. These cameras likely would not sell so long as there were free alternatives and people knew the limitations up front. Yet as with those hypothetical cameras, when one uses tethered appliances the limitations are neither advertised nor known, and they may not at first even be on the minds of the service providers themselves. They are latent in the design of the service, able to be activated at any moment according to the shifting winds of a dot-com's business model and strategy. The law should provide some generous but firm borders.[5] The binding promise that

Wikipedia's content can be copied, modified, and put up elsewhere by anyone else at any time—expressly permitted by Wikipedia's content license[6]—is a backstop against any abuse that might arise from Wikipedia's operators, mitigating the dangers that Wikipedia is a service rather than a product and that the plug at wikipedia.org can be pulled or the editors shut out at any time.

As we enter an era in which a photograph moves ephemerally from a camera's shutter click straight to the photographer's account at a proprietary storage Web site with no stop in between, it will be helpful to ensure that the photos taken can be returned fully to the custody of the photographer. Portability of data is a generative insurance policy to apply to individual data wherever it might be stored. A requirement to ensure portability need not be onerous. It could apply only to uniquely provided personal data such as photos and documents, and mandate only that such data ought to readily be extractable by the user in some standardized form. Maintaining data portability will help people pass back and forth between the generative and the non-generative, and, by permitting third-party backup, it will also help prevent a situation in which a non-generative service suddenly goes offline, with no recourse for those who have used the service to store their data.[7]

Network Neutrality and Generativity

Those who provide content and services over the Internet have generally lined up in favor of "network neutrality," by which faraway ISPs would not be permitted to come between external content or service providers and their customers. The debate is nuanced and far ranging.[8] Proponents of various forms of network neutrality invoke the Internet's tradition of openness as prescriptive: they point out that ISPs usually route packets without regard for what they contain or where they are from, and they say that this should continue in order to allow maximum access by outsiders to an ISP's customers and vice versa. Reliable data is surprisingly sparse, but advocates make a good case that the level of competition for broadband provision is low: there are few alternatives for high-speed broadband at many locations at the moment, and they often entail long-term consumer contracts. Such conditions make it difficult for market competition to prevent undesirable behavior such as ISPs' favoring access to their own content or services, and even some measure of competition in the broadband market does not remove a provider's incentives to discriminate.[9] For example, an ISP might block Skype in order to compel the ISP's users to subscribe to its own Internet telephony offering.[10] Likewise, some argue that independent application and content providers might innovate less out of fear of discriminatory behavior. While proponents of net neutrality are primarily concerned about restrictions on application and content, their arguments also suggest that general restrictions on technical ways of using the network should be disfavored.

Skeptics maintain that competition has taken root for broadband, and they claim that any form of regulatory constraint on ISPs—including enforcing some concept of neutrality—risks limiting the ways in which the Internet can continue to evolve.[11] For example, market conditions might bring about a situation in which an ISP could charge Google for access to that ISP's customers: without payment from Google, those customers would not be allowed to get to Google. If Google elected to pay—a big "if," of course—then some of Google's profits would go to subsidizing Internet access. Indeed, one could imagine ISPs then offering free Internet access to their customers, with that access paid for by content providers like Google that want to reach those customers. Of course, there is no guarantee that extra profits from such an arrangement would be passed along to the subscribers, but, in the standard model of competition, that is exactly what would happen: surplus goes to the consumer. Even if this regime hampered some innovation by increasing costs for application providers, this effect might—and this is speculative—be outweighed by increased innovation resulting from increased broadband penetration.

Similarly, a situation whereby consumers share their Internet connections with their neighbors may be salutary for digital access goals. When wireless access points first came to market, which allowed people to share a single physical Internet point throughout their houses the way that cordless telephones could be added to their telephone jacks, most ISPs' contracts forbade them.[12] Some vendors marketed products for ISPs to ferret out such access points when they were in use.[13] However, the ISPs ended up taking a wait-and-see approach at variance with the unambiguous limits of their contracts, and wi-fi access points became tolerated uses of the sort described in Chapter Five. Eventually the flagstones were laid for paths where people were walking rather than the other way around, and nearly every ISP now permits sharing within a household.

However, most access points are also automatically built to share the Internet connection with anyone in range,[14] friend or stranger, primarily to reduce the complexity of installation and corresponding calls to the access point makers' customer service and return lines. This laziness by access point makers has made it a commonplace for users to be able to find "free" wi-fi to glom onto in densely populated areas, often without the knowledge of the subscribers who installed the wireless access points. Again ISPs have dithered about how to respond. Services like FON now provide a simple box that people can hook up to their broadband Internet connection, allowing other FON users to share the connection for free when within range, and nonmembers to pay for access to the FON network.[15] Those acquiring FON boxes can in turn use others' FON connections when they are on the road. Alternatively, FON users can elect to have their FON box request a small payment from strangers who want to share the connection, and the payment is split between FON and the box owner.

Most ISPs have not decided whether such uses are a threat and therefore have not taken action against them, even as the ISPs still have contractual terms that forbid such unauthorized use,[16] and some have lobbied for theft-of-service laws that would appear to criminalize both sharing Internet connections and accepting invitations to share.[17] For ISPs, customers' ability to share their service could increase the demand for it since customers could themselves profit from use by strangers. But this would also increase the amount of bandwidth used on the ill-measured "all you can eat" access plans that currently depend on far less than constant usage to break even.[18] Some advocates have tried to steer a middle course by advocating a "truth in advertising" approach to network neutrality: broadband providers can shape their services however they want, so long as they do not call it "Internet" if it does not meet some definition of neutrality.[19] This seems a toothless remedy if one believes there is a problem, for network providers inclined to shape their services could simply call it "broadband" instead.

The procrastination principle has left these issues open, and so far generativity is alive and well at the network level. So what can generativity contribute to this debate? One lesson is that the endpoints matter at least as much as the network. If network providers try to be more constraining about what traffic they allow on their networks, software can and will be written to evade such restrictions—so long as generative PCs remain common on which to install that software. We see exactly this trend in network environments whose users are not the network's paying customers. When employers, libraries, or schools provide network access and attempt to limit its uses, clever PC software can generally get around the limitations so long as general Web surfing is permitted, using exactly the tools available to someone in China or Saudi Arabia who wants to circumvent national filtering.[20] Even in some of the worst cases of network traffic shaping by ISPs, the generative PC provides a workaround. Just as Skype is designed to get around the unintended blockages put in place by some home network routers,[21] it would not be a far leap for Linksys or FON to produce home boxes designed expressly to get around unwanted violations of network neutrality. (Of course, such workarounds would be less effective if the network provider merely slowed down all traffic that was not expressly favored or authorized.) The harshest response by ISPs to this—to ban such boxes and then to try to find and punish those disobeying the ban—represents expensive and therefore undesirable territory for them. One answer, then, to the question of network neutrality is that wide-open competition is good and can help address the primary worries of network neutrality proponents. In the absence of broad competition some intervention could be helpful, but in a world of open PCs some users can more or less help themselves, routing around some blockages that seek to prevent them from doing what they want to do online.

From Network Neutrality to API Neutrality

The debate on network neutrality, when viewed through a generative overlay, suggests a parallel debate that is not taking place at all. That debate centers on the lack of pretense of neutrality to begin with for tethered appliances and the services offered through them. Reasonable people disagree on the value of defining and mandating network neutrality. If there is a present worldwide threat to neutrality in the movement of bits, it comes not from restrictions on traditional Internet access that can be evaded using generative PCs, but from enhancements to traditional and emerging appliancized services that are not open to third-party tinkering. For example, those with cable or satellite television have their TV experiences mediated through a set-top box provided or specified by the cable or satellite company. The box referees what standard and premium channels have been paid for, what pay-per-view content should be shown, and what other features are offered through the service.

The cable television experience is a walled garden. Should a cable or satellite company choose to offer a new feature in the lineup called the "Internet channel," it could decide which Web sites to allow and which to prohibit. It could offer a channel that remains permanently tuned to one Web site, or a channel that could be steered among a preselected set of sites, or a channel that can be tuned to any Internet destination the subscriber enters so long as it is not on a blacklist maintained by the cable or satellite provider. Indeed, some video game consoles are configured for broader Internet access in this manner.[22] Puzzlingly, parties to the network neutrality debate have yet to weigh in on this phenomenon.

The closest we have seen to mandated network neutrality in the appliancized space is in pre-Internet cable television and post-Internet mobile telephony.

Long before the mainstreaming of the Internet, the Cable Television Consumer Protection and Competition Act of 1992 allowed local broadcast television stations to demand that cable TV companies carry their signal, and established a limited regime of open-access cable channels.[23] This was understandably far from a free-for-all of actual "signal neutrality" because the number of channels a cable service could transmit was understood to be limited.[24] The must-carry policies—born out of political pressure by broadcasters and justified as a way of eliminating some bottleneck control by cable operators—have had little discernable effect on the future of cable television, except perhaps to a handful of home shopping and religious broadcasting stations that possess broadcast licenses but are of little interest to large television viewerships.[25] Because cable systems of 1992 had comparatively little bandwidth, and because the systems were designed almost solely to transmit television and nothing else, the Act had little impact on the parched generative landscape for cable.

Mobile telephony, often featuring a tight relationship between service providers and endpoint devices used by their subscribers, has also drawn calls for mandated neutrality. Recall the *Carterfone* case from Chapter Two, which compelled AT&T to open the endpoints of its monopoly telephone network—that is, mobile phones—to third-party hardware providers.[26] Tim Wu has called for a *Carterfone* rule for mobile phone service providers, allowing consumers to select whatever handset they want to work on the network, and Skype has petitioned the FCC for such a rule—at just the time that, like the old AT&T, Steve Jobs insists that the iPhone must be tethered to Apple and forced to use AT&T as its network provider "to protect carrier networks and to make sure the phone was not damaged."[27] The analogy between AT&T and telephones on the one hand and mobile phone providers and handsets on the other is strong, and it works because there is already an understood divide between network and device in both cases. But because a cable or satellite TV company's regular service is intertwined with a content offering—the channels—and a specialized appliance to recognize proprietary transmission encryption schemes—the set-top box—it has been significantly harder to implement the spirit of *Carterfone* for cable television.[28] A model that begins as sterile is much harder to open meaningfully to third-party contribution than one that is generative from the start.

We see a parallel discrepancy of attitudes between PCs and their counterpart information appliances. Microsoft was found to possess a monopoly in the market for PC operating systems.[29] Indeed, it was found to be abusing that monopoly to favor its own applications—such as its Internet Explorer browser—over third-party software, against the wishes of PC makers who wanted to sell their hardware with Windows preinstalled but adjusted to suit the makers' tastes.[30] By allowing third-party contribution from the start—an ability to run outside software—after achieving market dominance, Microsoft was forced to meet ongoing requirements to maintain a level playing field for third-party software and its own.[31]

Yet we have not seen the same requirements arising for appliances that do not allow, or that strictly control, the ability of third parties to contribute from the start. So long as the market favorite video game console maker never opens the door to generative third-party code, it is hard to see how the firm could be found to be violating the law. A manufacturer is entitled to make an appliance, and to try to bolt down its inner workings so that they cannot be modified by others.[32]

So when should we consider network neutrality-style mandates for appliancized systems? The answer lies in that subset of appliancized systems that seeks to gain the benefits of third-party contribution while reserving the right to exclude it later. Those in favor of network neutrality suggest, often implicitly, how foundational the Internet is for the services offered over it.[33] If downstream services cannot rely on the networks they use to provide roughly equal treatment of their bits, the playing field for Internet activities can shift drastically. If the AT&T telephone network had been permitted to treat data calls differently from voice calls—and to change originally generous policies in a heartbeat—the foundation to link consumer telecommunications with the existing Internet might have collapsed, or at least have been greatly constrained only to business models provable from the start and thus ripe for partnerships with AT&T. Network neutrality advocates might explain their lack of concern for nonneutral treatment of bits over cable television by pointing out that cable television never purported to offer a platform for downstream third-party development—and indeed has never served that purpose. It is bait and switch that ought to be regulated.

The common law recognizes vested expectations in other areas. For example, the law of adverse possession dictates that people who openly occupy another's private property without the owner's explicit objection (or, for that matter, permission) can, after a lengthy period of time, come to legitimately acquire it.[34] More commonly, property law can find prescriptive easements—rights-of-way across territory that develop by force of habit—if the owner of the territory fails to object in a timely fashion as people go back and forth across it.[35] The law of promissory estoppel identifies times when one person's behavior can give rise to an obligation to another without a contract or other agreement between them; acting in a way that might cause someone else to reasonably rely on those actions can create a "quasi-contract."[36] These doctrines point to a deeply held norm that certain consistent behaviors can give rise to obligations, sometimes despite fine print that tries to prevent those obligations from coming about.[37] Recall Bill Gates's insistence that the Xbox video game console is not just for games: "It is a general purpose computer. . . . [W]e wouldn't have done it if it was just a gaming device. We wouldn't have gotten into the category at all. It was about strategically being in the living room."[38] Network neutrality's spirit applied to the box would say: if Microsoft wants to make the Xbox a general-purpose device but still not open to third-party improvement, no regulation should prevent it. But if Microsoft does so by welcoming third-party contribution, it should not later be able to impose barriers to outside software continuing to work. Such behavior is a bait and switch that is not easy for the market to anticipate and that stands to allow a platform maker to harness generativity to reach a certain plateau, dominate the market, and then make the result proprietary—exactly what the Microsoft antitrust case rightly was brought to prevent.

The principles and factual assumptions that animate network neutrality—that the network has been operated in a particular socially beneficial way and that, especially in the absence of effective competition, it should stay that way—can also apply to Internet services that solicit mash-ups from third-party programmers described in Chapter Five, like Google Maps or Facebook, while makers of pure tethered appliances such as TiVo may do as they please. Those who offer open APIs on the Net in an attempt to harness the generative cycle ought to remain application-neutral after their efforts have succeeded, so all those who have built on top of their interfaces can continue to do so on equal terms. If Microsoft retroactively changed Windows to prevent WordPerfect or Firefox from running, it would answer under the antitrust laws and perhaps also in tort for intentional interference with the relationship between the independent software makers and their consumers.[39] Similarly, providers of open APIs to their services can be required to commit to neutral offerings of them, at least when they have reached a position of market dominance for that particular service. Skeptics may object that these relations can be governed by market forces, and if an open API is advertised as contingent, then those who build on it are on notice and can choose to ignore the invitation if they do not like the prospect that it can be withdrawn at any moment. The claim and counterclaim follow the essential pattern of the network neutrality debate. Just as our notions of network security ought to include the endpoints as well as the middle of the network—with a generative principle to determine whether and when it makes sense to violate the end-to-end principle—our far-ranging debates on network neutrality ought to be applied to the new platforms of Web services that in turn depend on Internet connectivity to function. At least Internet connectivity is roughly commoditized; one can move from one provider to another so long as there is sufficient competition, or—in an extreme case—one can even move to a new physical location to have better options for Internet access. With open APIs for Web services there is much less portability; services built for one input stream—such as for Google Maps—cannot easily be repurposed to another, and it may ultimately make sense to have only a handful of frequently updated mapping data providers for the world, at least as much as it can make sense only to invest in a handful of expensive physical network conduits to a particular geographic location.

Maintaining Privacy as Software Becomes Service

As Chapter Five explained, the use of our PCs is shrinking to that of mere workstations, with private data stored remotely in the hands of third parties. This section elaborates on that idea, showing that there is little reason to think that people have—or ought to have—any less of a reasonable expectation of privacy for e-mail stored on their behalf by Google and Microsoft than they would have if it were stored locally in PCs after being downloaded and deleted from their e-mail service providers.

The latest version of Google Desktop is a PC application that offers a "search across computers" feature. It is advertised as allowing users with multiple computers to use one computer to find documents that are stored on another.[40] The application accomplishes this by sending an index of the contents of users' documents to Google itself.[41] While networking one's own private computers would not appear to functionally change expectations of privacy in their contents, the placement or storage of the data in others' hands does not hew well to the doctrinal boundaries of privacy protection by the U.S. Constitution. These boundaries treat the things one has held onto more gingerly than things entrusted to others. For example, in *SEC v. Jerry T. O'Brien, Inc.*,[42] the Supreme Court explained: "It is established that, when a person communicates information to a third party even on the understanding that the communication is confidential, he cannot object if the third party conveys that information or records thereof to law enforcement authorities. . . . These rulings disable respondents from arguing that notice of subpoenas issued to third parties is necessary to allow a target to prevent an unconstitutional search or seizure of his papers."[43]

The movement of data from the PC means that warrants served upon personal computers and their hard drives will yield less and less information as the data migrates onto the Web, driving law enforcement to the networked third parties now hosting that information. When our diaries, e-mail, and documents are no longer stored at home but instead are business records held by a dot-com, nearly all formerly transient communication ends up permanently and accessibly stored in the hands of third parties, and subject to comparatively weak statutory and constitutional protections against surveillance.[44] A warrant is generally required for the government to access data on one's own PC, and warrants require law enforcement to show probable cause that evidence of a crime will be yielded by the search.[45] In other words, the government must surmount a higher hurdle to search one's PC than to eavesdrop on one's data communications, and it has the fewest barriers when obtaining data stored elsewhere.[46] Entrusting information to third parties changes the ease of surveillance because those third parties are often willing to give it up, and typically the first party is not even aware the transfer has occurred. Online data repositories of all stripes typically state in their terms of use that they may disclose any information upon the request of the government—at least after receiving assurances by the requesting party that the information is sought to enhance the public safety.[47] In the United States, should a custodian deny a mere request for cooperation, the records might further be sought under the Stored Communications Act, which does not erect substantial barriers to government access.[48]

The holders of private records also may be compelled to release them through any of a series of expanded information-gathering tools enacted by Congress in the wake of September 11. For example, a third party that stores networked, sensitive personal data could be sent a secretly obtained PATRIOT Act section 215 order, directing the production of "any tangible things (including books, records, papers, documents, and other items) for an investigation . . . to protect against international terrorism or clandestine intelligence activities."[49] The party upon whom a section 215 order is served can neither disclose nor appeal the order.[50] Moreover, since the party searched—whether a library, accountant, or ISP—is not itself the target of interest, the targeted individual will not readily know that the search is occurring. Probable cause is not required for the search to be ordered, and indeed the target of interest may be presumed innocent but still monitored so long as the target is still generating records of interest to the government in an international terrorism or counterintelligence investigation. Roughly 1,700 applications to the secret Foreign Intelligence Surveillance Act (FISA) court were lodged in each of 2003 and 2004 seeking records of some kind. Only four were rejected each year. In 2005, 2,074 applications were made, with 2 rejections, and in 2006, 2,181 were made, with 5 rejections.[51]

Any custodians might also be served a national security letter concerning the production of so-called envelope information. These letters are written and executed without judicial oversight, and those who receive such letters can be prohibited by law from telling anyone that they received them.[52] National security letters may be used to solicit information held by particular kinds of private parties, including the records of telephone companies, financial institutions (now including such entities as pawnshops and travel agencies), as well as ISPs.[53] For ISPs, the sorts of information that can be sought this way are "subscriber information and toll billing records information, or electronic communication transactional records."[54] This envelope information is not thought to extend to the contents of e-mail but includes such things as the "to" and "from" fields of e-mail—or perhaps even the search engine queries made by a subscriber, since such queries are usually embedded in the URLs visited by that subscriber.

If the government has questions about the identity of a user of a particular Internet Protocol address, a national security letter could be used to match that address to a subscriber name. Under section 505 of the PATRIOT Act, national security letters do not need to meet the probable cause standard associated with a traditional warrant: the FBI merely needs to assert to the private recipients of such letters that the records are sought in connection with an investigation into international terrorism.[55] Government officials have indicated that more than thirty thousand national security letters are issued per year.[56] A recent internal FBI audit of 10 percent of the national security letters obtained since 2002 discovered more than a thousand potential violations of surveillance laws and agency rules.[57]

Recipients of FISA orders or national security letters may press challenges to be permitted to disclose to the public that they have received such mandates—just as an anonymous car manufacturer sued to prevent its onboard navigation system from being used to eavesdrop on the car's occupants[58]—but there is no assurance that they will do so. Indeed, many may choose to remain silent about cooperating with the government under these circumstances, thereby keeping each of these searches secret from the target.

As we move our most comprehensive and intimate details online—yet intend them to be there only for our own use—it is important to export the values of privacy against government intrusion along with them. For remotely stored data, this suggests limiting the holdings like that of *SEC v. Jerry T. O'Brien, Inc.* to financial records held by brokers similar to the ones in that case, rather than extending the relaxation of Fourth Amendment protections to all cases of third-party custody of personal information. The balance of accessibility for financial transactions need not be the same as that for our most personal communications and data. This is a reasonable limit to draw when the physical borders of one's home no longer correlate well with the digital borders of one's private life. Indeed, it is simply extending the protections we already enjoy to fit a new technological configuration. That is the spirit of *Chapman v. United States*,[59] in which a police search of a rented house for a whiskey still was found to be a violation of the Fourth Amendment rights of the tenant, despite the fact that the landlord had consented to the search.[60] The Court properly refused to find that the right against intrusion was held only by the absentee owner of the place intruded—rather, it was held by the person who actually lived and kept his effects there. Similarly, the data we store for ourselves in servers that others own ought to be thought of as our own papers and effects in which we have a right to be secure.

There is some suggestion that the courts may be starting to move in this direction. In the 2007 case *Warshak v. United States*, the U.S. Court of Appeals for the Sixth Circuit held that the government's warrantless attempt to seize e-mail records through an ISP without notice to the account holder violated Fourth Amendment privacy rights.[61] At the time of writing, the ruling stands, though it faces further review.[62]

The ability to store nearly all one's data remotely is an important and helpful technological advance, all the more so because it can still be made to appear to the user as if the data were sitting on his or her own personal computer. But this suggests that the happenstance of where data are actually stored should not alone control the constitutional assessment of which standard the government must meet.

BALANCING GENERATIVE AND NON-GENERATIVE SYSTEMS

Code thickets

A number of scholars have written about the drawbacks to proprietary rights thickets: overlapping claims to intellectual property can make it difficult for those creating new but not completely original creative works to avoid infringing others' rights. This is a particular problem for code developed with the tools of group generativity. For the past twenty years, the modern landscape of information technology has accommodated competing spheres of software production. These spheres can be grouped roughly around two poles warring for dominance in the field. On one side is proprietary software, which typically provides cash-and-carry functionality for the user. Its source code "recipe" is nearly always hidden from view as a technical matter, and as a legal matter it cannot be used by independent programmers to develop new software without the rarely given permission of its unitary rights holder. On the other side is free software, referring not to the price paid for a copy, but to the fact that the source code of the software is open to public view and modification.

It is not easy for the law to maintain neutrality in the conflict between the two spheres, evenhandedly encouraging development in both models. For example, the free software movement has produced some great works, but under prevailing copyright law even a slight bit of poison, in the form of code from a proprietary source, could amount to legal liability for anyone who copies or potentially even uses the software. (Running software entails making at least a temporary copy of it.)

The collaborative nature of free software development makes it harder to determine where various contributions are coming from and whether contributions belong to those who purport to donate them. Indeed, in the case of an employee of a software company charitably moonlighting for a free software project, the employee's work may not even be the employee's to give. A barely remembered but still enforceable employment agreement may commit all software written by the employee to the employer's possession, which would set the stage for an infringement claim against those within the free software project for making use of the employee's contributions.

Major free software projects try to avoid these problems by soliciting declarations from participants that they are only contributing code that they wrote or to which they have free license. The Free Software Foundation even suggests that employees obtain a disclaimer from their employers of all interest in employee contributions.[63] But the danger of poisoned code remains, just as it is possible for someone to contribute copyrighted material to Wikipedia or a Geocities home page at any moment. The kind of law that shields Wikipedia and Geocities from liability for material contributed by outsiders, as long as the organization acts expeditiously to remove infringing material once it is notified, ought to be extended to the production of code itself.[64] Code that incorporates infringing material is not given a free pass, but those who have promulgated it without knowledge of the infringement would have a chance to repair the code or cease copying it before becoming liable.

The patent thicket is also worrisome. There is a large and growing literature devoted to figuring out whether and under what circumstances software patents contribute to innovation, since they can promise returns to those who innovate. Scholars James Bessen and Robert Hunt have observed that the number of software patents has grown substantially since the early 1980s, from one thousand per year to over twenty thousand per year.[65] These patents are obtained, on average, by larger firms than those acquiring patents in other fields, and non-software firms acquire over 90 percent of software patents.[66] Bessen and Hunt suggest that these patterns are consistent with a patent thicket—large firms obtaining patents to extract royalties from rivals and to defend themselves from their rivals' patents.[67]

While large firms can reach patent détente with each other through cross-licensing,[68] smaller firms and individuals may be left out. There are thousands of software patents, and patent infringement, unlike copyright, does not require a copying of the original material: so long as someone else already came up with the idea, the new work is infringing. With copyright, if someone miraculously managed independently to come up with the tune to a Beatles song, that tune would not be infringing the Beatles' copyright, since it did not copy the song—it was independently invented. It is this virtue of copyright law that allowed Richard Stallman to begin the free software movement's effort to reproduce Unix's functionality without infringing its copyright by simply creating new code from scratch that acts the same way that Unix's code does.

Not only does patent not have such a limitation, but it also applies to the abstract concepts expressed in code, rather than to a specific set of code.[69] Thus, someone can sit down to write some software in an empty room and, by that act, infringe multiple patents. Patent infringement can be asserted without having to claim appropriation of any code. For example, Microsoft has said that it believes that pieces of GNU/Linux infringe its patents, though it has not sued anyone over it.[70] Microsoft may well be right, given the number and breadth of patents it possesses. So far the best protection against copyright or patent infringement for a contributor to a free software project is that he or she is not worth suing; litigation can be expensive for the plaintiff, and any victory hollow if the defendant cannot pay. The principle of tolerated uses comes back into play, not necessarily because patent holders are uncertain whether others' uses are good or bad for them, but because the others are simply not worth suing. Certainly many amateur programmers seem undeterred by the prospect of patent infringement, and there is evidence that young commercial software firms plunge blithely ahead with innovations without being concerned about the risks of patent infringement.[71]

This is not an ideal state of affairs for anyone. If those who see value in software patents are correct, infringement is rampant. And to those who think patents are chilling innovation, the present regime needs reform. To be sure, amateurs who do not have houses to lose to litigation can still contribute to free software projects. Others can contribute anonymously, evading any claims of patent infringement since they simply cannot be found. But this turns coding into a gray market activity, eliminating what otherwise could be a thriving middle class of contributing firms should patent warfare ratchet into high gear. There may only be a working class of individual coders not worth suing and an upper class of IBMs—companies powerful enough to fight patent infringement cases without blinking.

The law can help level the playing field without major changes to the scopes of copyright or patent. Statutes of limitations define how quickly someone must come forward to claim that the law has been broken. For patent infringement in the United States, the limit is six years; for civil copyright infringement it is three.[72] Unfortunately, this limit has little meaning for computer code because the statute of limitations starts from the time of the last infringement. Every time someone copies (or perhaps even runs) the code, the clock starts ticking again on a claim of infringement. This should be changed. The statute of limitations could be clarified for software, requiring that anyone who suspects or should suspect his or her work is being infringed sue within, for instance, one year of becoming aware of the suspect code. For example, the acts of those who contribute to free software projects—namely, releasing their code into a publicly accessible database like SourceForge—could be found to be enough to start the clock ticking on that statute of limitations.[73] The somewhat obscure common-law defense of laches is available when plaintiffs sleep on their rights—sandbagging in order to let damages rack up—and it also might be adapted to this purpose.[74]

In the absence of such a rule, companies who think their proprietary interests have been compromised can wait to sue until a given piece of code has become wildly popular—essentially sandbagging the process. This proposed modification to the statute of limitations will still allow the vindication of proprietary rights, but users and developers of a particular version of code will know that lawsuits will be precluded after a specific interval of time. A system that requires those holding proprietary interests to advance them promptly will remove a significant source of instability and uncertainty from the freewheeling development processes that have given us—truly given, because no remuneration has been sought—everything from GNU/Linux to the Apache Web server to wikis. This approach would also create extra incentives for those holding proprietary code to release the source code so that the clock could start counting down on any infringement claims against it.[75]

The legal uncertainties in the process of writing and distributing new code currently express themselves most in the seams stitching together the worlds of amateur and commercial software production and use. With no change to copyright or patent, the amateur production of free software will likely continue; it is the adoption and refinement of the fruits of that production by commercial firms that is most vulnerable to claims of proprietary infringement. The uptake of generative outputs by commercial firms has been an important part of the generative cycle from backwater to mainstream. Interventions in the legal regimes to facilitate it—while offering redress for those whose proprietary rights have been infringed, so long as claims are made promptly—would help negotiate a better interface between generative and non-generative.

Content Thickets

Thickets similar to those found at the code layer also exist at the content layer. While patent does not significantly affect content, legal scholars Lawrence Lessig and Yochai Benkler, as well as others, have underscored that even the most rudimentary mixing of cultural icons and elements, including snippets of songs and video, can potentially result in thousands of dollars in legal liability for copyright infringement without causing any harm to the market for the original proprietary goods.[76] Benkler believes that the explosion of amateur creativity online has occurred despite the legal system, not thanks to it.[77] The high costs of copyright enforcement and the widespread availability of tools to produce and disseminate what he calls "creative cultural bricolage"[78]—something far more subtle and transformative than merely ripping a CD and sending its contents to a friend—currently allow for a variety of voices to be heard even when what they are saying is theoretically sanctionable by fines between $750 and $30,000 per copy made, $150,000 if the infringement contained within their expression is done "willfully."[79] As with code, this situation shoehorns otherwise laudable activity into a sub-rosa gray zone. The frequent unlawfulness of amateur creativity may be appealing to those who see it as a countercultural movement, like that of graffiti—part of the point of doing it is that it is edgy or illegal. It may even make the products of amateur cultural innovation less co-optable by the mainstream industrial information economy, since it is hard to clear rights for an anonymous film packing in images and sounds from hundreds of different sources, some proprietary.

But if prevention of commercial exploitation is the goal of some authors, it is best to let them simply structure their licenses to preclude it. Authors can opt to share their work under Creative Commons licenses that restrict commercial reuse of the work, while permitting limitless noncommercial use and modification by others.[80]

Finding ways through content thickets as Benkler and his cohort suggest is especially important if tethered appliances begin to take up more of the information space, making information that much more regulable. In a more regulable space the gap between prohibited uses and tolerated uses shrinks, creating the prospect that content produced by citizens who cannot easily clear permissions for all its ingredients will be squeezed out.

MAINTAINING REGULATORS' TOLERANCE OF GENERATIVE SYSTEMS

Individual Liability Instead of Technology Mandates

As the capacity to inflict damage on "real world" interests increases with the Internet's reach and with the number of valuable activities reliant upon it, the imperatives to take action will also increase. As both generative and non-generative devices maintain constant contact with various vendors and software providers, regulators may seek to require those manufacturers to shape the services they offer more precisely, causing a now-familiar wound to generativity.

One way to reduce pressure on institutional and technological gatekeepers is to ensure that individual wrongdoers can be held directly responsible. Some piecemeal solutions to problems such as spam take this approach. ISPs are working with makers of major PC e-mail applications to provide for forms of sender authentication.[81] A given domain can, using public key encryption tools, authenticate that it is indeed the source of e-mail it sends. With Sender ID, e-mail purporting—but not proved—to be from a user at yahoo.com can be so trivially filtered as spam that it will no longer be worthwhile to send. This regime will hold ISPs more accountable for the e-mail that originates on their networks because they will find themselves shunned by other ISPs if they permit excessive anonymous spam—a system similar to the MAPS and Google/StopBadware regimes discussed in the previous chapter. This opportunity for greater direct liability reduces the pressure on those processing incoming e-mail—both the designated recipients and their ISPs—to resort to spam filtration heuristics that may unintentionally block legitimate e-mail.[82]

The same principle can apply to individuals' uses of the Internet that are said to harm legally protected interests. Music industry lawsuits against individual file sharers may be bad policy if the underlying substantive law demarcating the protected interest is itself ill-advised—and there are many reasons to think that it is—but from the point of view of generativity, such lawsuits inflict little damage on the network and PCs themselves. The Internet's future may be brighter if technology permits easier identification of Internet users combined with legal processes, and perhaps technical limitations, to ensure that such identification occurs only when good cause exists. The mechanisms to make it less than impossible to find copyright infringers and defamers ought not to make it trivial for authoritarian states to single out subversives.

As the discussion of FON explained, a growing number of Internet users are acquiring wireless routers that default to sharing their connection with anyone nearby who has a PC configured with a wireless antenna. Consumers may not intend to open their networks, but doing so creates generative benefits for those nearby without their own Internet access.[83] Usage by others does not typically impede the original consumer's enjoyment of broadband, but should outsiders use that connection, say, to send viruses or to pirate copyrighted files, the original consumer could be blamed when the Internet connection is traced.[84] Current legal doctrine typically precludes such blame—nearly all secondary liability schemes require some form of knowledge or benefit before imposing responsibilities[85]—but a sea change in the ability of lawbreakers to act untraceably by using others' wi-fi could plausibly result in an adjustment to doctrine.

As such examples arise and become well known, consumers will seek to cut off others' access to their surplus network resources, and the manufacturers of wireless routers might change the default to closed. If, however, genuine individual identity can be affirmed in appropriate circumstances, wi-fi sharing need not be impeded: each user will be held responsible for his or her own actions and no more. Indeed, the FON system of sharing wireless access among members of the "FON club" maintains users' accounts for the purpose of identity tracing in limited circumstances—and to prevent additional pressure on regulators to ban FON itself. Such identification schemes need not be instant or perfect. Today's status quo requires a series of subpoenas to online service providers and ISPs to discern the identity of a wrongdoer. This provides balance between cat and mouse, a space for tolerated uses described in Chapter Five, that precludes both easy government abuse of personal privacy and outright anarchy.

Beyond the Law

Regimes of legal liability can be helpful when there is a problem and no one has taken ownership of it. When a manufacturing plant pollutes a stream, it ought to pay—to internalize the negative externality it is inflicting on others by polluting. No one fully owns today's problems of copyright infringement and defamation online, just as no one fully owns security problems on the Net. But the solution is not to conscript intermediaries to become the Net police. Under prevailing law Wikipedia could get away with much *less* stringent monitoring of its articles for plagiarized work, and it could leave plainly defamatory material in an article but be shielded in the United States by the Communications Decency Act provision exempting those hosting material from responsibility for what others have provided.[86]

Yet Wikipedia polices itself according to an ethical code—a set of community standards that encourages contributors to do the right thing rather than the required thing or the profitable thing. To harness Wikipedia's ethical instinct across the layers of the generative Internet, we must figure out how to inspire people to act humanely in digital environments that today do not facilitate the appreciative smiles and "thank yous" present in the physical world. This can be accomplished with tools—such those discussed in the previous chapter and those yet to be invented—to foster digital environments that inspire people to act humanely. For the generative Internet fully to come into its own, it must allow us to harness the connections we have with each other, to coordinate when we have the time, talent, and energy, and to benefit from others' coordination when we do not. Such tools allow us to express and live our civic instincts online, trusting that the expression of our collective character will be one at least as good as that imposed by outside sovereigns—sovereigns who, after all, are only people themselves.

To be sure, this expression of collective character will not always be just, even if participants seek to act in good faith. Some users have begun to deploy tools like Blossom, whereby individual PC users can agree to let their Internet connections be used so that others can see the Internet from their point of view.[87] As states increasingly lean on their domestic ISPs and overseas online service providers to filter particular content, a tool like Blossom can allow someone in China to see the Internet as if he or she were a New Yorker, and vice versa. But such a tool undermines individual state sovereignty worldwide, just as a tool to facilitate filtering can be deployed to encroach on fundamental freedoms when ported to regimes that do not observe the rule of law. A tool like Blossom not only makes it hard for China to filter politically sensitive content, but it prevents Germany and France from filtering images of Nazi swastikas, and it gets in the way of attempts by copyright holders to carve the world into geographic zones as they seek to release online content in one place but not another: the *New York Times* could not as easily provide an article with an update about a British criminal investigation everywhere but within Britain, as it recently did to respect what it took to be the law of the United Kingdom on pretrial publicity.[88]

Tools like Blossom, which succeed only as much as netizens are impelled to want to adopt them, ask the distributed users of the Internet to decide, one by one, how much they are willing to create a network to subvert the enforcement of central authorities around the world.[89] Each person can frame a view balancing the risks of misuse of a network against the risks of abuse of a sovereign's power to patrol it, and devote his or her processor cycles and network bandwidth accordingly. Lessig is chary of such power, thinking of these tools as "technological tricks" that short-circuit the process of making the case in the political arena for the substantive values they enable.[90] But this disregards a kind of acoustic separation found in a society that is not a police state, by which most laws, especially those pertaining to personal behavior, must not only be entered on to the books, but also reinforced by all sorts of people, public and private, in order to have effect.[91] Perhaps it is best to say that neither the governor nor the governed should be able to monopolize technological tricks. We are better off without flat-out trumps that make the world the way either regulator or target wants it to be without the need for the expenditure of some effort and cooperation from others to make it so. The danger of a trump is greater for a sterile system, where a user must accept the system as it is if he or she is to use it at all, than for the tools developed for a generative one, where there is a constant—perhaps healthy—back-and-forth between tools to circumvent regulation and tools to effect the regulation anyway.[92] The generative Internet upholds a precious if hidden dynamic where a regulator must be in a relationship with both those regulated and those who are needed to make the regulation effective. This dynamic is not found solely within the political maneuvers that transpire in a liberal democracy to put a law in place at the outset.

Today our conception of the Internet is still largely as a tool whose regulability is a function of its initial design, modified by the sum of vectors to rework it for control: as Lessig has put it, code is law, and commerce and government can work together to change the code. There is a hierarchy of dogs, cats, and mice: Governments might ask ISPs to retain more data or less about their users; individual users might go to greater or lesser lengths to cloak their online activities from observation by their ISPs.[93] Tethered appliances change the equation's results by making life far easier for the dogs and cats. Tools for group generativity can change the equation itself, but in unpredictable directions. They allow the level of regulability to be affected by conscious decisions by the mice about the kind of online world they want, not only for themselves but for others. If there is apathy about being able to experience the Internet as others do elsewhere, tools like Blossom will not be able to sustain much traffic, and the current level of regulability of the Internet will remain unchanged. If there is a wellspring of interest on this front, it can become easy to evade geographic restrictions.

One objection to the unfettered development of generative tools that can defy centralized authority in proportion to the number and passion of those willing to use them is that there are large groups of people who would be empowered to do ill with them. Criminal law typically penalizes conspiracy as a separate crime because it recognizes that the whole can be bigger than the sum of the parts—people working in concert can create more trouble than when they each act alone. Continued pressure on public file-sharing networks has led to fully realized "darknets," semi-private systems whose sole purpose is to enable the convenient sharing of music and other content irrespective of copyright.[94] For example, a network called Oink incorporates many of the community features of Wikipedia without being open to the public.[95] People may join only on invitation from an existing member. Oink imposes strict rules on the sharing of files to ensure maximum availability: users must maintain a certain ratio of uploaded-to-downloaded material. Those who fall short risk being cut off from the service—and the penalty may also be applied to the members who sponsored them. The Oink service has none of the difficulties of the public networks, where files are nominated for takedown as they are discovered by publishers' automated tools, and where publishers have inserted decoy files that do not contain what they promise.[96] Oink is easier and faster to use than the iTunes store. And, of course, it is cheaper because it is free. If there are enough people to see to the creation and maintenance of such a community—still one primarily of strangers—is it a testament to the dangers of group generativity or to the fact that the current application of copyright law finds very little legitimacy?

One's answer may differ to the extent that similar communities exist for people to share stolen credit card numbers or images of child abuse. If such communities do not exist it suggests that a change to copyright's policy and business model could eliminate the most substantial disjunct between laws common to free societies and the online behavior of their citizens.[97] Here there is no good empirical data to guide us. But the fact remains that so long as these communities are as semi-open as they must be in order to achieve a threatening scale—ready to accept new members who are not personally known to existing ones—they are in a position to be infiltrated by law enforcement. Private Yahoo! groups whose members trade in images of child abuse—a far less sophisticated counterpart to Oink's community of copyright infringers—are readily monitored.[98] This monitoring could take place by Yahoo! itself, or in a decentralized model, by even one or two members who have second thoughts—practically anyone is in a position to compromise the network. As theories multiply about the use of the Internet as a terrorist recruiting tool,[99] we can see the downside to criminals as well: open networks cannot keep secrets very well. (The use of the Internet for more specialized conspiracies that do not depend on semi-public participation for their success is likely here to stay; sophisticated criminals can see to it that they retain generative devices even if the mainstream public abandons them.)

Wikipedia, as a tool of group generativity, reflects the character of thousands of people. Benkler compares Wikipedia's entry on Barbie dolls to that of other encyclopedias developed in more traditional ways, and finds that most of the others fail to make mention of any of the controversies surrounding Barbie as a cultural icon.[100] Wikipedia has extensive discussion on the topic, and *Britannica* has a share, too. Benkler freely concedes that a tool of group generativity like Wikipedia is not the only way to include important points of view that might not accord with the more monolithic views of what he calls the "industrial information economy." More traditional institutions, such as universities, have established a measure of independence, too. And he also acknowledges that tools of group generativity can be abused by a group; there can be powerful norms that a majority enforces upon a minority to squelch some views. But he rightly suggests that the world is improved by a variety of models of production of culture, models that draw on different incentives, with different biases, allowing people to be exposed to a multiplicity of viewpoints, precluding a monopoly on truth. The same can be true of our technology, here the technology that undergirds our access to those viewpoints, and our ability to offer our own.

Can groups be trusted to behave well in the absence of formal government to rein in their excesses?[101] The story of the American Revolution is sometimes romantically told as one in which small communities of virtue united against a common foe, and then lost their way after the revolution succeeded. Virtue gave way to narrow self-interest and corruption. The mechanisms of due process and separation of powers adapted by Madison to help substitute the rule of law for plain virtue will have to be translated into those online communities empowered with generative tools to govern themselves and to affect the larger offline world. Using the case of privacy, the next chapter seeks to sketch out some of the puzzles raised by the use of the powerful tools that this book has advocated to bring the generative Net fully into its own. Privacy problems that have been stable for the past thirty-five years are being revolutionized by the generative Internet, and how they are handled will tell us much about the future of the Net and our freedoms within and from it.

9

Meeting the Risks of Generativity:
Privacy 2.0

So far this book has explored generative successes and the problems they cause at the technical and content layers of the Internet. This chapter takes up a case study of a problem at the social layer: privacy. Privacy showcases issues that can worry individuals who are not concerned about some of the other problems discussed in this book, like copyright infringement, and it demonstrates how generativity puts old problems into new and perhaps unexpected configurations, calling for creative solutions. Once again, we test the notion that solutions that might solve the generative problems at one layer—solutions that go light on law, and instead depend on the cooperative use of code to cultivate and express norms—might also work at another.

The heart of the next-generation privacy problem arises from the similar but uncoordinated actions of individuals that can be combined in new ways thanks to the generative Net. Indeed, the Net enables individuals in many cases to compromise privacy more thoroughly than the government and commercial institutions traditionally targeted for scrutiny and regulation. The standard approaches that have been developed to analyze and limit institutional actors do not work well for this new breed of problem, which goes far beyond the compromise of sensitive information.

PRIVACY 1.0

In 1973, a blue-ribbon panel reported to the U.S. Secretary of Health, Education, and Welfare (HEW) on computers and privacy. The report could have been written today:

> It is no wonder that people have come to distrust computer-based record-keeping operations. Even in non-governmental settings, an individual's control over the personal information that he gives to an organization, or that an organization obtains about him, is lessening as the relationship between the giver and receiver of personal data grows more attenuated, impersonal, and diffused. There was a time when information about an individual tended to be elicited in face-to-face contacts involving personal trust and a certain symmetry, or balance, between giver and receiver. Nowadays an individual must increasingly give information about himself to large and relatively faceless institutions, for handling and use by strangers—unknown, unseen and, all too frequently, unresponsive. Sometimes the individual does not even know that an organization maintains a record about him. Often he may not see it, much less contest its accuracy, control its dissemination, or challenge its use by others.[1]

The report pinpointed troubles arising not simply from powerful computing technology that could be used both for good and ill, but also from its impersonal quality: the sterile computer processed one's warm, three-dimensional life into data handled and maintained by faraway faceless institutions, viewed at will by strangers. The worries of that era are not obsolete. We are still concerned about databases with too much information that are too readily accessed; databases with inaccurate information; and having the data from databases built for reasonable purposes diverted to less noble if not outright immoral uses.[2]

Government databases remain of particular concern, because of the unique strength and power of the state to amass information and use it for life-altering purposes. The day-to-day workings of the government rely on numerous databases, including those used for the calculation and provision of government benefits, decisions about law enforcement, and inclusion in various licensing regimes.[3] Private institutional databases also continue to raise privacy issues, particularly in the realms of consumer credit reporting, health records, and financial data.

Due to political momentum generated by the HEW report and the growing controversy over President Richard Nixon's use of government power to inves-

tigate political enemies, the U.S. Congress enacted comprehensive privacy legislation shortly after the report's release. The Privacy Act of 1974 mandated a
set of fair information practices, including disclosure of private information
only with an individual's consent (with exceptions for law enforcement, archiv-
ing, and routine uses), and established the right of the subject to know what
was recorded about her and to offer corrections. While it was originally intended to apply to a broad range of public and private databases to parallel the
HEW report, the Act was amended before passage to apply only to government
agencies' records.[4] Congress never enacted a comparable comprehensive regulatory scheme for private databases. Instead, private databases are regulated
only in narrow areas of sensitivity such as credit reports (addressed by a complex scheme passed in 1970 affecting the handful of credit reporting agencies)[5]
and video rental data,[6] which has been protected since Supreme Court nomi-
nee Robert Bork's video rental history was leaked to a newspaper during his
confirmation process in 1987.[7]

The HEW report expresses a basic template for dealing with the informational privacy problem: first, a sensitivity is identified at some stage of the
information production process—the gathering, storage, or dissemination of
one's private information—and then a legal regime is proposed to restrict these
activities to legitimate ends. This template has informed analysis for the past
thirty years, guiding battles over privacy both between individuals and government and between individuals and "large and faceless" corporations. Of course,
a functional theory does not necessarily translate into successful practice. Pressures to gather and use personal data in commerce and law enforcement
have increased, and technological tools to facilitate such data processing have
matured without correspondingly aggressive privacy protections.[8] (Consider
Chapter Five's description of the novel uses of tethered appliances to conduct
surveillance.) In 1999, Scott McNealey, CEO of Sun Microsystems, was asked
whether a new Sun technology to link consumer devices had any built-in privacy protection. "You have zero privacy anyway," he replied. "Get over it."[9]

McNealey's words raised some ire at the time; one privacy advocate called
them "a declaration of war."[10] McNealey has since indicated that he believes his
answer was misunderstood.[11] But the plain meaning of "getting over it" seems
to have been heeded: while poll after poll indicates that the public is concerned
about privacy,[12] the public's actions frequently belie these claims. Apart from
momentary spikes in privacy concerns that typically arise in the wake of high-
profile scandals—such as Watergate or the disclosure of Judge Bork's video
rentals—we routinely part with personal information and at least passively

consent to its use, whether by surfing the Internet, entering sweepstakes, or using a supermarket discount card.

Current scholarly work on privacy tries to reconcile people's nonchalant behavior with their seemingly heartfelt concerns about privacy. It sometimes calls for industry self-regulation rather than direct governmental regulation as a way to vindicate privacy interests, perhaps because such regulation is seen as more efficient or just, or because direct governmental intervention is understood to be politically difficult to achieve. Privacy scholarship also looks to the latest advances in specific technologies that could further weaken day-to-day informational privacy.[13] One example is the increasing use of radio frequency identifiers (RFIDs) in consumer items, allowing goods to be scanned and tracked at a short distance. One promise of RFID is that a shopper could wheel her shopping cart under an arch at a grocery store and obtain an immediate tally of the price of its contents; one peril is that a stranger could drive by a house with an RFID scanner and instantly inventory its contents, from diapers to bacon to flat-screen TVs, immediately discerning the sort of people who live within.

This work on privacy generally hews to the original analytic template of 1973: both the analysis and suggested solutions talk in terms of institutions gathering data, and of developing ways to pressure institutions to better respect their customers' and clients' privacy. This approach is evident in discussions about electronic commerce on the Internet. Privacy advocates and scholars have sought ways to ensure that Web sites disclose to people what they are learning about consumers as they browse and buy. The notion of "privacy policies" has arisen from this debate. Through a combination of regulatory suasion and industry best practices, such policies are now found on many Web sites, comprising little-read boilerplate answering questions about what information a Web site gathers about a user and what it does with the information. Frequently the answers are, respectively, "as much as it can" and "whatever it wants"—but, to some, this is progress. It allows scholars and companies alike to say that the user has been put on notice of privacy practices.

Personal information security is another area of inquiry, and there have been some valuable policy innovations in this sphere. For example, a 2003 California law requires firms that unintentionally expose their customers' private data to others to alert the customers to the security breach.[14] This has led to a rash of well-known banks sending bashful letters to millions of their customers, gently telling them that, say, a package containing tapes with their credit card and social security numbers has been lost en route from one processing center to another.[15] Bank of America lost such a backup tape with 1.2 million customer records in 2005.[16] That same year, a MasterCard International security breach exposed information of more than 40 million credit card holders.[17] Boston College lost 120,000 alumni records to hackers as a result of a breach.[18] The number of incidents shows little sign of decreasing,[19] despite the incentives provided by the embarrassment of disclosure and the existence of obvious ways to improve security practices. For minimal cost, firms could minimize some types of privacy risks to consumers—for example, by encrypting their backup tapes before shipping them anywhere, making them worthless to anyone without a closely held digital key.

Addressing Web site privacy and security has led to elaborations on the traditional informational privacy framework. Some particularly fascinating issues in this framework are still unfolding: is it fair, for example, for an online retailer like Amazon to record the average number of nanoseconds each user spends contemplating an item before clicking to buy it? Such data could be used by Amazon to charge impulse buyers more, capitalizing on the likelihood that this group of consumers does not pause long enough to absorb the listed price of the item they just bought. A brief experiment by Amazon in differential pricing resulted in bad publicity and a hasty retreat as some buyers noticed that they could save as much as $10 on a DVD by deleting browser cookies that indicated to Amazon that they had visited the site before.[20] As this example suggests, forthrightly charging one price to one person and another price to someone else can generate resistance. Offering individualized discounts, however, can amount to the same thing for the vendor while appearing much more palatable to the buyer. Who would complain about receiving a coupon for $10 off the listed price of an item, even if the coupon were not transferable to any other Amazon user? (The answer may be "someone who did not get the coupon," but to most people the second scenario is less troubling than the one in which different prices were charged from the start.)[21]

If data mining could facilitate price discrimination for Amazon or other online retailers, it could operate in the tangible world as well. As a shopper uses a loyal-customer card, certain discounts are offered at the register personalized to that customer. Soon, the price of a loaf of bread at the store becomes indeterminate: there is a sticker price, but when the shopper takes the bread up front, the store can announce a special individualized discount based on her relationship with the store. The sticker price then becomes only that, providing little indication of the price that shoppers are actually paying. Merchants can also vary service. Customer cards augmented with RFID tags can serve to identify those undesirable customers who visit a home improvement store, monopolize the attention of the attendants, and exit without having bought so much as a single nail. With these kinds of cards, the store would be able to discern the "good" (profitable) customers from the "bad" (not profitable) ones and appropriately alert the staff to flee from bad customers and approach good ones.

PRIVACY 2.0

While privacy issues associated with government and corporate databases remain important, they are increasingly dwarfed by threats to privacy that do not fit the standard analytical template for addressing privacy threats. These new threats fit the generative pattern also found in the technical layers for Internet and PC security, and in the content layer for ventures such as Wikipedia. The emerging threats to privacy serve as an example of generativity's downsides on the social layer, where contributions from remote amateurs can enable vulnerability and abuse that calls for intervention. Ideally such intervention would not unduly dampen the underlying generativity. Effective solutions for the problems of Privacy 2.0 may have more in common with solutions to other generative problems than with the remedies associated with the decades-old analytic template for Privacy 1.0.

The Era of Cheap Sensors

We can identify three successive shifts in technology from the early 1970s: cheap processors, cheap networks, and cheap sensors.[22] The third shift has, with the help of the first two, opened the doors to new and formidable privacy invasions.

The first shift was cheap processors. Moore's Law tells us that processing power doubles every eighteen months or so.[23] A corollary is that existing processing power gets cheaper. The cheap processors available since the 1970s have allowed Bill Gates's vision of a "computer on every desk" to move forward. Cheap processors also underlie information appliances: thanks to Moore's Law, there is now sophisticated microprocessor circuitry in cars, coffeemakers, and singing greeting cards.

Cheap networks soon followed. The pay-per-minute proprietary dial-up networks gave way to an Internet of increasing bandwidth and dropping price. The all-you-can-eat models of measurement meant that, once established, idle network connections were no cheaper than well-used ones, and a Web page in New York cost no more to access from London than one in Paris. Lacking gatekeepers, these inexpensive processors and networks have been fertile soil for whimsical invention to take place and become mainstream. This generativity has occurred in part because the ancillary costs to experiment—both for software authors and software users—have been so low.

The most recent technological shift has been the availability of cheap sensors. Sensors that are small, accurate, and inexpensive are now found in cameras, microphones, scanners, and global positioning systems. These characteristics have made sensors much easier to deploy—and then network—in places where previously it would have been impractical to have them.

The proliferation of cheap surveillance cameras has empowered the central authorities found within the traditional privacy equation. A 2002 working paper estimated that the British government had spent several hundred million dollars on closed-circuit television systems, with many networked to central law enforcement stations for monitoring.[24] Such advances, and the analysis that follows them, fit the template of Privacy 1.0: governments have access to more information thanks to more widely deployed monitoring technologies, and rules and practices are suggested to prevent whatever our notions might be of abuse.[25] To see how cheap processors, networks, and sensors create an entirely new form of the problem, we must look to the excitement surrounding the participatory technologies suggested by one meaning of "Web 2.0." In academic circles, this meaning of Web 2.0 has become known as "peer production."

The Dynamics of Peer Production

The aggregation of small contributions of individual work can make once-difficult tasks seem easy. For example, Yochai Benkler has approvingly described the National Aeronautics and Space Administration's (NASA's) use of public volunteers, or "clickworkers."[26] NASA had a tedious job involving pictures of craters from the moon and Mars. These were standard bitmap images, and they wanted the craters to be vectorized: in other words, they wanted people to draw circles around the circles they saw in the photos. Writing some custom software and deploying it online, NASA asked Internet users at large to undertake the task. Much to NASA's pleasant surprise, the clickworkers accomplished in a week what a single graduate student would have needed a year to complete.[27] Cheap networks and PCs, coupled with the generative ability to costlessly offer new code for others to run, meant that those who wanted to pitch in to help NASA could do so.

The near-costless aggregation of far-flung work can be applied in contexts other than the drawing of circles around craters—or the production of a free encyclopedia like Wikipedia. Computer scientist Luis von Ahn, after noting that over nine billion person-hours were spent playing Windows Solitaire in a single year, devised the online "ESP" game, in which two remote players are randomly paired and shown an image. They are asked to guess the word that best describes the image, and when they each guess the same word they win points.[28] Their actions also provide input to a database that reliably labels images for use in graphical search engines—improving the ability of image search engines to identify images. In real time, then, people are building and participating in a collective, organic, worldwide computer to perform tasks that real computers cannot easily do themselves.[29]

These kinds of grid applications produce (or at least encourage) certain kinds of public activity by combining small, individual private actions. Benkler calls this phenomenon "coordinate coexistence producing information."[30] Benkler points out that the same idea helps us find what we are looking for on the Internet, even if we do not go out of our way to play the ESP game; search engines commonly aggregate the artifacts of individual Internet activity, such as webmasters' choices about where to link, to produce relevant search results. Search engines also track which links are most often clicked on in ordered search results in order, and then more prominently feature those links in future searches.[31] The value of this human-derived wisdom has been noted by spammers, who create "link farms" of fake Web sites containing fragments of text drawn at random from elsewhere on the Web ("word salad") that link back to the spammers' sites in an attempt to boost their search engine rankings. The most useful links are ones placed on genuinely popular Web sites, though, and the piles of word salad do not qualify.

As a result, spammers have turned to leaving comments on popular blogs that ignore the original entry to which they are attached and instead simply provide links back to their own Web sites. In response, the authors of blogging software have incorporated so-called captcha boxes that must be navigated before anyone can leave a comment on a blog. Captchas—now used on many mainstream Web sites including Ticketmaster.com—ask users to prove that they are human by typing in, say, a distorted nonsense word displayed in a small graphic.[32] Computers can start with a word and make a distorted image in a heartbeat, but they cannot easily reverse engineer the distorted image back to the word. This need for human intervention was intended to force spammers to abandon automated robots to place their blog comment spam. For a while they did, reportedly setting up captcha sweatshops that paid people to solve captchas from blog comment prompts all day long.[33] (In 2003, the going rate was $2.50/hour for such work.)[34] But spammers have continued to explore more efficient solutions. A spammer can write a program to fill in all the information but the captcha, and when it gets to the captcha it places it in front of a real person trying to get to a piece of information—say on a page a user might get after clicking a link that says, "You've just won $1000! Click here!"[35]—or perhaps a pornographic photo.[36] The captcha had been copied that instant from a blog where a spammer's robot was waiting to leave a comment, and then pasted into the prompt for the human wanting to see the next page. The human's answer to the captcha was then instantly ported back over to the blog site in order to solve the captcha and leave the spammed comment.[37] Predictably, companies have also sprung up to meet this demand, providing custom software to thwart captchas on a contract basis of $100 to $5,000 per project.[38] Generative indeed: the ability to remix different pieces of the Web, and to deploy new code without gatekeepers, is crucial to the spammers' work. Other uses of captchas are more benign but equally subtle: a project called reCAPTCHA provides an open API to substitute for regular captchas where a Web site might want to test to see if it is a human visiting.[39] reCAPTCHA creates an image that pairs a standard, automatically generated test word image with an image of a word from an old book that a computer has been unable to properly scan and translate. When the user solves the captcha by entering both words, the first word is used to validate that the user is indeed human, and the second is used to put the human's computing power to work to identify one more word of one more book that otherwise would be unscannable.

*   *   *

What do captchas have to do with privacy? New generative uses of the Internet have made the solutions proposed for Privacy 1.0 largely inapplicable. Fears about "mass dataveillance"[40] are not misplaced, but they recognize only part of the problem, and one that represents an increasingly smaller slice of the pie. Solutions such as disclosure[41] or encryption[42] still work for Privacy 1.0, but new approaches are needed to meet the challenge of Privacy 2.0, in which sensitive data is collected and exchanged peer-to-peer in configurations as unusual as that of the spammers' system for bypassing captchas.

The power of centralized databases feared in 1973 is now being replicated and amplified through generative uses of individual data and activity. For example, cheap sensors have allowed various gunshot-detecting technologies to operate through microphones in public spaces.[43] If a shot is fired, sensors associated with the microphones triangulate the shot's location and summon the police. To avoid false alarms, the system can be augmented with help from the public at large, minimizing the need for understaffed police to make the initial assessment about what is going on when a suspicious sound is heard. Interested citizens can review camera feeds near a reported shot and press a button if they see something strange happening on their computer monitors. Should a citizen do so, other citizens can be asked for verification. If the answer is yes, the police can be sent.

In November of 2006, the state of Texas spent $210,000 to set up eight web-cams along the Mexico border as part of a pilot program to solicit the public's help in reducing illegal immigration.[44] Webcam feeds were sent to a public Web site, and people were invited to alert the police if they thought they saw suspicious activity. During the month-long trial the Web site took in just under twenty-eight million hits. No doubt many were from the curious rather than the helpful, but those wanting to volunteer came forward, too. The site regis-tered over 220,000 users, and those users sent 13,000 e-mails to report suspi-cious activity. At three o'clock in the morning one woman at her PC saw some-one signal a pickup truck on the webcam. She alerted police, who seized over four hundred pounds of marijuana from the truck's occupants after a high-speed chase. In separate incidents, a stolen car was recovered, and twelve un-documented immigrants were stopped. To some—especially state officials—this was a success beyond any expectation;[45] to others it was a paltry result for so much investment.[46]

Beyond any first-order success of stopping crime, some observers welcome involvement by members of the public as a check on law enforcement surveil-lance.[47] Science fiction author David Brin foresaw increased use of cameras and other sensors by the government and adopted an if-you-can't-beat-them-join-them approach to dealing with the privacy threat. He suggested allowing ubiquitous surveillance so long as the watchers themselves were watched: live cameras could be installed in police cars, station houses, and jails. According to Brin, everyone watching everywhere would lessen the likelihood of unobserved government abuse. What the Rodney King video did for a single incident[48]— one that surely would have passed without major public notice but for the am-ateur video capturing what looked like excessive force by arresting officers— Brin's proposal could do for nearly all state activities. Of course, Brin's calculus does not adequately account for the invasions of privacy that would take place whenever random members of the public could watch—and perhaps record— every interaction between citizens and authorities, especially since many of those interactions take place at sensitive moments for the citizens. And ubiqui-tous surveillance can lead to other problems. The Sheriff's Office of Anderson

County, Tennessee, introduced one of the first live "jailcams" in the country, covering a little area in the jail where jailors sit and keep an eye on everything—the center of the panopticon.[49] The Anderson County webcam was very Web 2.0: the Web site included a chat room where visitors could meet other viewers, there was a guestbook to sign, and a link to syndicated advertising to help fund the webcam. However, some began using the webcam to make crank calls to jailors at key moments and even, it is claimed, to coordinate the delivery of contraband.[50] The webcam was shut down.

This example suggests a critical difference between Privacy 1.0 and 2.0. If the government is controlling the observation, then the government can pull the plug on such webcams if it thinks they are not helpful, balancing whatever policy factors it chooses.[51] Many scholars have considered the privacy problems posed by cheap sensors and networks, but they focus on the situations where the sensors serve only government or corporate masters. Daniel Solove, for instance, has written extensively on emergent privacy concerns, but he has focused on the danger of "digital dossiers" created by businesses and governments.[52] Likewise, Jerry Kang and Dana Cuff have written about how small sensors will lead to "pervasive computing," but they worry that the technology will be abused by coordinated entities like shopping malls, and their prescriptions thus follow the pattern established by Privacy 1.0.[53] Their concerns are not misplaced, but they represent an increasingly smaller part of the total picture. The essence of Privacy 2.0 is that government or corporations, or other intermediaries, need not be the source of the surveillance. Peer-to-peer technologies can eliminate points of control and gatekeeping from the transfer of personal data and information just as they can for movies and music. The intellectual property conflicts raised by the generative Internet, where people can still copy large amounts of copyrighted music without fear of repercussion, are rehearsals for the problems of Privacy 2.0.[54]

The Rodney King beating was filmed not by a public camera, but by a private one, and its novel use in 1991 is now commonplace. Many private cameras, including camera-equipped mobile phones, fit the generative mold as devices purchased for one purpose but frequently used for another. The Rodney King video, however, required news network attention to gain salience. Videos depicting similar events today gain attention without the prior approval of an intermediary.[55] With cheap sensors, processors, and networks, citizens can quickly distribute to anywhere in the world what they capture in their backyard. Therefore, any activity is subject to recording and broadcast. Perform a search on a video aggregation site like YouTube for "angry teacher" or "road rage" and hundreds of videos turn up. The presence of documentary evidence not only makes such incidents reviewable by the public at large, but for, say, angry teachers it also creates the possibility of getting fired or disciplined where there had not been one before. Perhaps this is good: teachers are on notice that they must account for their behavior the way that police officers must take responsibility for their own actions.

If so, it is not just officers and teachers: we are all on notice. The famed "Bus Uncle" of Hong Kong upbraided a fellow bus passenger who politely asked him to speak more quietly on his mobile phone.[56] The mobile phone user learned an important lesson in etiquette when a third person captured the argument and then uploaded it to the Internet, where 1.3 million people have viewed one version of the exchange.[57] (Others have since created derivative versions of the exchange, including karaoke and a ringtone.) Weeks after the video was posted, the Bus Uncle was beaten up in a targeted attack at the restaurant where he worked.[58] In a similar incident, a woman's dog defecated on the floor of a South Korean subway. She refused to clean it up, even when offered a tissue—though she cleaned the dog—and left the subway car at the next stop. The incident was captured on a mobile phone camera and posted to the Internet, where the poster issued an all points bulletin seeking information about the dog owner and her relatives, and about where she worked. She was identified by others who had previously seen her and the dog, and the resulting firestorm of criticism apparently caused her to quit her job.[59]

The summed outrage of many unrelated people viewing a disembodied video may be disproportionate to whatever social norm or law is violated within that video. Lives can be ruined after momentary wrongs, even if merely misdemeanors. Recall verkeersbordvrij theory from Chapter Six: it suggests that too many road signs and driving rules change people into automatons, causing them to trade in common sense and judgment for mere hewing to exactly what the rules provide, no more and no less. In the same way, too much scrutiny can also turn us into automatons. Teacher behavior in a classroom, for example, is largely a matter of standards and norms rather than rules and laws, but the presence of scrutiny, should anything unusual happen, can halt desirable pedagogical risks if there is a chance those risks could be taken out of context, misconstrued, or become the subject of pillory by those with perfect hindsight.

These phenomena affect students as well as teachers, regular citizens rather than just those in authority. And ridicule or mere celebrity can be as chilling as outright disapprobation. In November 2002 a Canadian teenager used his high school's video camera to record himself swinging a golf ball retriever as though it were a light saber from *Star Wars*.[60] By all accounts he was doing it for his own amusement. The tape was not erased, and it was found the following spring by someone else who shared it, first with friends and then with the Internet at large. Although individuals want privacy for themselves, they will line up to see the follies of others, and by 2006 the "Star Wars Kid" was estimated to be the most popular word-of-mouth video on the Internet, with over nine hundred million cumulative views.[61] It has spawned several parodies, including ones shown on prime time television. This is a consummately generative event: a repurposing of something made for completely different reasons, taking off beyond any expectation, and triggering further works, elaborations, and commentaries—both by other amateurs and by Hollywood.[62] It is also clearly a privacy story. The student who made the video has been reported to have been traumatized by its circulation, and in no way did he seek to capitalize on his celebrity.

In this hyperscrutinized reality, people may moderate themselves instead of expressing their true opinions. To be sure, people have always balanced between public and private expression. As Mark Twain observed: "We are discreet sheep; we wait to see how the drove is going, and then go with the drove. We have two opinions: one private, which we are afraid to express; and another one—the one we use—which we force ourselves to wear to please Mrs. Grundy, until habit makes us comfortable in it, and the custom of defending it presently makes us love it, adore it, and forget how pitifully we came by it. Look at it in politics."[63]

Today we are all becoming politicians. People in power, whether at parliamentary debates or press conferences, have learned to stick to carefully planned talking points, accepting the drawbacks of appearing stilted and saying little of substance in exchange for the benefits of predictability and stability.[64] Ubiquitous sensors threaten to push everyone toward treating each public encounter as if it were a press conference, creating fewer spaces in which citizens can express their private selves.

Even the use of "public" and "private" to describe our selves and spaces is not subtle enough to express the kind of privacy we might want. By one definition they mean who manages the space: a federal post office is public; a home is private. A typical restaurant or inn is thus also private, yet it is also a place where the public gathers and mingles: someone there is "in public." But while activities in private establishments open to the public are technically in the public eye,[65] what transpires there is usually limited to a handful of eyewitnesses—likely strangers—and the activity is ephemeral. No more, thanks to cheap sensors and cheap networks to disseminate what they glean. As our previously *private* public spaces, like classrooms and restaurants, turn into *public* public spaces, the pressure will rise for us to be on press conference behavior.

There are both significant costs and benefits inherent in expanding the use of our public selves into more facets of daily life. Our public face may be kinder, and the expansion may cause us to rethink our private prejudices and excesses as we publicly profess more mainstream standards and, as Twain says, "habit makes us comfortable in it." On the other hand, as law professors Eric Posner and Cass Sunstein point out, strong normative pressure can prevent outlying behavior of any kind, and group baselines can themselves be prejudiced. Outlying behavior is the generative spark found at the social layer, the cultural innovation out of left field that can later become mainstream. Just as our information technology environment has benefited immeasurably from experimentation by a variety of people with different aims, motives, and skills, so too is our cultural environment bettered when commonly held—and therefore sometimes rarely revisited—views can be challenged.[66]

The framers of the U.S. Constitution embraced anonymous speech in the political sphere as a way of being able to express unpopular opinions without having to experience personal disapprobation.[67] No defense of a similar principle was needed for keeping private conversations in public spaces from becoming public broadcasts—disapprobation that begins with small "test" groups but somehow becomes society-wide—since there were no means by which to perform that transformation. Now that the means are there, a defense is called for lest we run the risk of letting our social system become metaphorically more applianced: open to change only by those few radicals so disconnected from existing norms as to not fear their imposition at all.

Privacy 2.0 is about more than those who are famous or those who become involuntary "welebrities." For those who happen to be captured doing particularly fascinating or embarrassing things, like Star Wars Kid or an angry teacher, a utilitarian might say that nine hundred million views is first-order evidence of a public benefit far exceeding the cost to the student who made the video. It might even be pointed out that the Star Wars Kid failed to erase the tape, so he can be said to bear some responsibility for its circulation. But the next-generation privacy problem cannot be written off as affecting only a few unlucky victims. Neither can it be said to affect only genuine celebrities who must now face constant exposure not only to a handful of professional paparazzi but also to hordes of sensor-equipped amateurs. (Celebrities must now contend with the consequences of cell phone videos of their slightest aberrations—such as one in which a mildly testy exchange with a valet parker is quickly circulated and exaggerated online[68]—or more comprehensive peer-produced sites like Gawker Stalker,[69] where people send in local sightings of celebrities as they happen. Gawker strives to relay the sightings within fifteen minutes and place them on a Google map, so that if Jack Nicholson is at Starbucks, one can arrive in time to stand awkwardly near him before he finishes his latte.)

Cybervisionary David Weinberger's twist on Andy Warhol's famous quotation is the central issue for the rest of us: "On the Web, everyone will be famous to fifteen people."[70] Although Weinberger made his observation in the context of online expression, explaining that microaudiences are worthy audiences, it has further application. Just as cheap networks made it possible for businesses to satisfy the "long tail," serving the needs of obscure interests every bit as much as popular ones[71] (Amazon is able to stock a selection of books virtually far beyond the best sellers found in a physical bookstore), peer-produced databases can be configured to track the people who are of interest only to a few others.

How will the next-generation privacy problem affect average citizens? Early photo aggregation sites like Flickr were premised on a seemingly dubious assumption that turned out to be true: not only would people want an online repository for their photos, but they would often be pleased to share them with the public at large. Such sites now boast hundreds of millions of photos,[72] many of which are also sorted and categorized thanks to the same distributed energy that got Mars's craters promptly mapped. Proponents of Web 2.0 sing the praises of "folksonomies" rather than taxonomies—bottom-up tagging done by strangers rather than expert-designed and -applied canonical classifications like the Dewey Decimal System or the Library of Congress schemes for sorting books.[73] Metadata describing the contents of pictures makes images far more useful and searchable. Combining user-generated tags with automatically generated data makes pictures even more accessible. Camera makers now routinely build cameras that use global positioning systems to mark exactly where on the planet each picture it snaps was taken and, of course, to time- and date-stamp them. Web sites like Riya, Polar Rose, and MyHeritage are perfecting facial recognition technologies so that once photos of a particular person are tagged a few times with his or her name, their computers can then automatically label all future photos that include the person—even if their image appears in the background. In August 2006 Google announced the acquisition of Neven Vision, a company working on photo recognition, and in May 2007 Google added a feature to its image search so that only images of people could be returned (to be sure, still short of identifying which image is which).[74] Massachusetts officials have used such technology to compare mug shots in "Wanted" posters to driver's license photos, leading to arrests.[75] Mash together these technologies and functionalities through the kind of generative mixing allowed by their open APIs and it becomes trivial to receive answers to questions like: Where was Jonathan Zittrain last year on the fourteenth of February?, or, Who could be found near the entrance to the local Planned Parenthood clinic in the past six months? The answers need not come from government or corporate cameras, which are at least partially secured against abuse through well-considered privacy policies from Privacy 1.0. Instead, the answers come from a more powerful, generative source: an army of the world's photographers, including tourists sharing their photos online without firm (or legitimate) expectations of how they might next be used and reused.

As generativity would predict, those uses may be surprising or even offensive to those who create the new tools or provide the underlying data. The Christian Gallery News Service was started by antiabortion activist Neal Horsley in the mid 1990s. Part of its activities included the Nuremberg Files Web site, where the public was solicited for as much information as possible about the identities, lives, and families of physicians who performed abortions, as well as about clinic owners and workers.[76] When a provider was killed, a line would be drawn through his or her name. (The site was rarely updated with new information, and it became entangled in a larger lawsuit lodged under the U.S. Freedom of Access to Clinic Entrances Act.[77] The site remains accessible.) An associated venture solicits the public to take pictures of women arriving at clinics, including the cars in which they arrive (and corresponding license plates), and posts the pictures in order to deter people from nearing clinics.[78]

With image recognition technology mash-ups, photos taken as people enter clinics or participate in protests can be instantly cross-referenced with their names. One can easily pair this type of data with Google Maps to provide fine-grained satellite imagery of the homes and neighborhoods of these individuals, similar to the "subversive books" maps created by computer consultant and tinkerer Tom Owad, tracking wish lists on Amazon.[79]

This intrusion can reach places that the governments of liberal democracies refuse to go. In early 2007, a federal court overseeing the settlement of a class action lawsuit over New York City police surveillance of public activities held that routine police videotaping of public events was in violation of the settlement: "The authority . . . conferred upon the NYPD 'to visit any place and attend any event that is open to the public, on the same terms and conditions of the public generally,' cannot be stretched to authorize police officers to video-tape everyone at a public gathering just because a visiting little old lady from Dubuque . . . could do so. There is a quantum difference between a police offi-cer and the little old lady (or other tourist or private citizen) videotaping or photographing a public event."[80]

The court expressed concern about a chilling of speech and political activi-ties if authorities were videotaping public events. But police surveillance be-comes moot when an army of little old ladies from Dubuque is naturally video-taping and sharing nearly everything—protests, scenes inside a mall (such that amateur video exists of a random shootout in a Salt Lake City, Utah, mall),[81] or picnics in the park. Peer-leveraging technologies are overstepping the bound-aries that laws and norms have defined as public and private, even as they are also facilitating beneficial innovation. Cheap processors, networks, and sensors enable a new form of beneficial information flow as citizen reporters can pro-vide footage and frontline analysis of newsworthy events as they happen.[82] For example, OhmyNews is a wildly popular online newspaper in South Korea with citizen-written articles and reports. (Such writers provide editors with their names and national identity numbers so articles are not anonymous.) Similarly, those who might commit atrocities within war zones can now be sur-veilled and recorded by civilians so that their actions may be watched and ulti-mately punished, a potential sea change for the protection of human rights.[83]

For privacy, peer-leveraging technologies might make for a much more con-strained world rather than the more chaotic one that they have wrought for in-tellectual property. More precisely, a world where bits can be recorded, manip-ulated, and transmitted without limitation means, in copyright, a free-for-all for the public and constraint upon firms (and perhaps upstream artists) with content to protect. For privacy, the public is variously creator, beneficiary, and victim of the free-for-all. The constraints—in the form of privacy invasion that Jeffrey Rosen crystallizes as an "unwanted gaze"—now come not only from the well-organized governments or firms of Privacy 1.0, but from a few people gen-eratively drawing upon the labors of many to greatly impact rights otherwise guaranteed by a legal system.

Privacy and Reputation

At each layer where a generative pattern can be discerned, this book has asked whether there is a way to sift out what we might judge to be bad generative re-sults from the good ones without unduly damaging the system's overall genera-tivity. This is the question raised at the technical layer for network security, at

the content layer for falsehoods in Wikipedia and failures of intellectual property protection, and now at the social layer for privacy. Can we preserve generative innovations without giving up our core privacy values? Before turning to
answers, it is helpful to explore a final piece of the Privacy 2.0 mosaic: the impact of emerging reputation systems. This is both because such systems can
greatly impact our privacy and because this book has suggested reputational
tools as a way to solve the generative sifting problem at other layers.

Search is central to a functioning Web,[84] and reputation has become central
to search. If people already know exactly what they are looking for, a network
needs only a way of registering and indexing specific sites. Thus, IP addresses
are attached to computers, and domain names to IP addresses, so that we can
ask for www.drudgereport.com and go straight to Matt Drudge's site. But
much of the time we want help in finding something without knowing the exact online destination. Search engines help us navigate the petabytes of publicly
posted information online, and for them to work well they must do more than
simply identify all pages containing the search terms that we specify. They must
rank them in relevance. There are many ways to identify what sites are most relevant. A handful of search engines auction off the top-ranked slots in search results on given terms and determine relevance on the basis of how much the site
operators would pay to put their sites in front of searchers.[85] These search engines are not widely used. Most have instead turned to some proxy for reputation. As mentioned earlier, a site popular with others—with lots of inbound
links—is considered worthier of a high rank than an unpopular one, and thus
search engines can draw upon the behavior of millions of other Web sites as
they sort their search results.[86] Sites like Amazon deploy a different form of
ranking, using the "mouse droppings" of customer purchasing and browsing
behavior to make recommendations—so they can tell customers that "people
who like the Beatles also like the Rolling Stones." Search engines can also more
explicitly invite the public to express its views on the items it ranks, so that users
can decide what to view or buy on the basis of others' opinions. Amazon users
can rate and review the items for sale, and subsequent users then rate the first
users' reviews. Sites like Digg and Reddit invite users to vote for stories and articles they like, and tech news site Slashdot employs a rating system so complex
that it attracts much academic attention.[87]

eBay uses reputation to help shoppers find trustworthy sellers. eBay users
rate each others' transactions, and this trail of ratings then informs future buyers how much to trust repeat sellers. These rating systems are crude but powerful. Malicious sellers can abandon poorly rated eBay accounts and sign up for

new ones, but fresh accounts with little track record are often viewed skeptically by buyers, especially for proposed transactions involving expensive items. One study confirmed that established identities fare better than new ones, with buyers willing to pay, on average, over 8 percent more for items sold by highly regarded, established sellers.[88] Reputation systems have many pitfalls and can be gamed, but the scholarship seems to indicate that they work reasonably well.[89] There are many ways reputation systems might be improved, but at their core they rely on the number of people rating each other in good faith well exceeding the number of people seeking to game the system—and a way to exclude robots working for the latter. For example, eBay's rating system has been threatened by the rise of "1-cent eBooks" with no shipping charges; sellers can create alter egos to bid on these nonitems and then have the phantom users highly rate the transaction.[90] One such "feedback farm" earned a seller a thousand positive reviews over four days. eBay intervenes to some extent to eliminate such gaming, just as Google reserves the right to exact the "Google death penalty" by de-listing any Web site that it believes is unduly gaming its chances of a high search engine rating.[91]

These reputation systems now stand to expand beyond evaluating people's behavior in discrete transactions or making recommendations on products or content, into rating people more generally. This could happen as an extension of current services—as one's eBay rating is used to determine trustworthiness on, say, another peer-to-peer service. Or, it could come directly from social networking: Cyworld is a social networking site that has twenty million subscribers; it is one of the most popular Internet services in the world, largely thanks to interest in South Korea.[92] The site has its own economy, with $100 million worth of "acorns," the world's currency, sold in 2006.[93]

Not only does Cyworld have a financial market, but it also has a market for reputation. Cyworld includes behavior monitoring and rating systems that make it so that users can see a constantly updated score for "sexiness," "fame," "friendliness," "karma," and "kindness." As people interact with each other, they try to maximize the kinds of behaviors that augment their ratings in the same way that many Web sites try to figure out how best to optimize their presentation for a high Google ranking.[94] People's worth is defined and measured precisely, if not accurately, by the reactions of others. That trend is increasing as social networking takes off, partly due to the extension of online social networks beyond the people users already know personally as they "befriend" their friends' friends' friends.

The whole-person ratings of social networks like Cyworld will eventually be available in the real world. Similar real-world reputation systems already exist in embryonic form. Law professor Lior Strahilevitz has written a fascinating monograph on the effectiveness of "How's My Driving" programs, where commercial vehicles are emblazoned with bumper stickers encouraging other drivers to report poor driving.[95] He notes that such programs have resulted in significant accident reductions, and analyzes what might happen if the program were extended to all drivers. A technologically sophisticated version of the scheme dispenses with the need to note a phone number and file a report; one could instead install transponders in every vehicle and distribute TiVo-like remote controls to drivers, cyclists, and pedestrians. If someone acts politely, say by allowing you to switch lanes, you can acknowledge it with a digital thumbs-up that is recorded on that driver's record. Cutting someone off in traffic earns a thumbs-down from the victim and other witnesses. Strahilevitz is supportive of such a scheme, and he surmises it could be even more effective than eBay's ratings for online transactions since vehicles are registered by the government, making it far more difficult escape poor ratings tied to one's vehicle. He acknowledges some worries: people could give thumbs-down to each other for reasons unrelated to their driving—racism, for example. Perhaps a bumper sticker expressing support for Republicans would earn a thumbs-down in a blue state. Strahilevitz counters that the reputation system could be made to eliminate "outliers"—so presumably only well-ensconced racism across many drivers would end up affecting one's ratings. According to Strahilevitz, this system of peer judgment would pass constitutional muster if challenged, even if the program is run by the state, because driving does not implicate one's core rights. "How's My Driving?" systems are too minor to warrant extensive judicial review. But driving is only the tip of the iceberg.

Imagine entering a café in Paris with one's personal digital assistant or mobile phone, and being able to query: "Is there anyone on my buddy list within 100 yards? Are any of the ten closest friends of my ten closest friends within 100 yards?" Although this may sound fanciful, it could quickly become mainstream. With reputation systems already advising us on what to buy, why not have them also help us make the first cut on whom to meet, to date, to befriend? These are not difficult services to offer, and there are precursors today.[96] These systems can indicate who has not offered evidence that he or she is safe to meet—as is currently solicited by some online dating sites—or it may use Amazon-style matching to tell us which of the strangers who have just entered the café is a good match for people who have the kinds of friends we do. People can rate their interactions with each other (and change their votes later, so they can show their companion a thumbs-up at the time of the meeting and tell the truth later on), and those ratings will inform future suggested acquaintances. With enough people adopting the system, the act of entering a café can be different from one person to the next: for some, the patrons may shrink away, burying their heads deeper in their books and newspapers. For others, the entire café may perk up upon entrance, not knowing who it is but having a lead that this is someone worth knowing. Those who do not participate in the scheme at all will be as suspect as brand new buyers or sellers on eBay.

Increasingly, difficult-to-shed indicators of our identity will be recorded and captured as we go about our daily lives and enter into routine transactions—our fingerprints may be used to log in to our computers or verify our bank accounts, our photo may be snapped and tagged many times a day, or our license plate may be tracked as people judge our driving habits. The more our identity is associated with our daily actions, the greater opportunities others will have to offer judgments about those actions. A government-run system like the one Strahilevitz recommends for assessing driving is the easy case. If the state is the record keeper, it is possible to structure the system so that citizens can know the basis of their ratings—where (if not by whom) various thumbs-down clicks came from—and the state can give a chance for drivers to offer an explanation or excuse, or to follow up. The state's formula for meting out fines or other penalties to poor drivers would be known ("three strikes and you're out," for whatever other problems it has, is an eminently transparent scheme), and it could be adjusted through accountable processes, just as legislatures already determine what constitutes an illegal act, and what range of punishment it should earn.

Generatively grown but comprehensively popular unregulated systems are a much trickier case. The more that we rely upon the judgments offered by these private systems, the more harmful that mistakes can be.[97] Correcting or identifying mistakes can be difficult if the systems are operated entirely by private parties and their ratings formulas are closely held trade secrets. Search engines are notoriously resistant to discussing how their rankings work, in part to avoid gaming—a form of security through obscurity.[98] The most popular engines reserve the right to intervene in their automatic rankings processes—to administer the Google death penalty, for example—but otherwise suggest that they do not centrally adjust results. Hence a search in Google for "Jew" returns an anti-Semitic Web site as one of its top hits,[99] as well as a separate sponsored advertisement from Google itself explaining that its rankings are automatic.[100] But while the observance of such policies could limit worries of bias to search algo-

rithm design rather than to the case-by-case prejudices of search engine operators, it does not address user-specific bias that may emerge from personalized
judgments.

Amazon's automatic recommendations also make mistakes; for a period of
time the *Official Lego Creator Activity Book* was paired with a "perfect partner"
suggestion: *American Jihad: The Terrorists Living Among Us Today.* If such mis-
matched pairings happen when discussing people rather than products, rare
mismatches could have worse effects while being less noticeable since they are
not universal. The kinds of search systems that say which people are worth getting to know and which should be avoided, tailored to the users querying the
system, present a set of due process problems far more complicated than a state-
operated system or, for that matter, any system operated by a single party. The
generative capacity to share data and to create mash-ups means that ratings and
rankings can be far more emergent—and far more inscrutable.

SOLVING THE PROBLEMS OF PRIVACY 2.0

Cheap sensors generatively wired to cheap networks with cheap processors
are transforming the nature of privacy. How can we respond to the notion
that nearly anything we do outside our homes can be monitored and shared?
How do we deal with systems that offer judgments about what to read or
buy, and whom to meet, when they are not channeled through a public authority or through something as suable, and therefore as accountable, as
Google?

The central problem is that the organizations creating, maintaining, using,
and disseminating records of identifiable personal data are no longer just "organizations"—they are people who take pictures and stream them online, who
blog about their reactions to a lecture or a class or a meal, and who share on social sites rich descriptions of their friends and interactions. These databases are
becoming as powerful as the ones large institutions populate and centrally define. Yet the sorts of administrative burdens we can reasonably place on established firms exceed those we can place on individuals—at some point, the
burden of compliance becomes so great that the administrative burdens are
tantamount to an outright ban. That is one reason why so few radio stations are
operated by individuals: it need not be capital intensive to set up a radio broadcasting tower—a low-power neighborhood system could easily fit in someone's
attic—but the administrative burdens of complying with telecommunications
law are well beyond the abilities of a regular citizen. Similarly, we could create a

privacy regime so complicated as to frustrate generative developments by individual users.

The 1973 U.S. government report on privacy crystallized the template for Privacy 1.0, suggesting five elements of a code of fair information practice:

- There must be no personal data record-keeping systems whose very existence is secret.
- There must be a way for an individual to find out what information about him is in a record and how it is used.
- There must be a way for an individual to prevent information about him that was obtained for one purpose from being used or made available for other purposes without his consent.
- There must be a way for an individual to correct or amend a record of identifiable information about him.
- Any organization creating, maintaining, using, or disseminating records of identifiable personal data must assure the reliability of the data for their intended use and must take precautions to prevent misuse of the data.[101]

These recommendations present a tall order for distributed, generative systems. It may seem clear that the existence of personal data record-keeping systems ought not to be kept secret, but this issue was easier to address in 1973, when such systems were typically large consumer credit databases or government dossiers about citizens, which could more readily be disclosed and advertised by the relevant parties. It is harder to apply the antisecrecy maxim to distributed personal information databases. When many of us maintain records or record fragments on one another, and through peer-produced social networking services like Facebook or MySpace share these records with thousands of others, or allow them to be indexed to create powerful mosaics of personal data, then exactly what the database *is* changes from one moment to the next—not simply in terms of its contents, but its very structure and scope. Such databases may be generally unknown while not truly "secret."[102]

Further, these databases are ours. It is one thing to ask a corporation to disclose the personal data and records it maintains; it is far more intrusive to demand such a thing of private citizens. Such disclosure may itself constitute an intrusive search upon the citizen maintaining the records. Similarly, the idea of mandating that an individual be able to find out what an information gatherer knows—much less to correct or amend the information—is categorically more difficult to implement when what is known is distributed across millions of people's technological outposts. To be sure, we can Google ourselves, but this does not capture those databases open only to "friends of friends"—a category that may not include us but may include thousands of others. At the same time, we may have minimal recourse when the information we thought we were circulating within social networking sites merely for fun and, say, only among fellow college students, ends up leaking to the world at large.[103]

What to do? There is a combination of steps drawn from the solutions sketched in the previous two chapters that might ameliorate the worst of Privacy 2.0's problems, and even provide a framework in which to implement some of the Privacy 1.0 solutions without rejecting the generative framework that gives rise to Privacy 2.0 in the first place.

The Power of Code-Backed Norms

The Web is disaggregated. Its pieces are bound together into a single virtual database by private search engines like Google. Google and other search engines assign digital robots to crawl the Web as if they were peripatetic Web surfers, clicking on one link after another, recording the results, and placing them into a concordance that can then be used for search.[104]

Early on, some wanted to be able to publish material to the Web without it appearing in search engines. In the way a conversation at a pub is a private matter unfolding in a public (but not publicly owned) space, these people wanted their sites to be private but not secret. The law offers one approach to vindicate this desire for privacy but not secrecy. It could establish a framework delineating the scope and nature of a right in one's Web site being indexed, and providing for penalties for those who infringe that right. An approach of this sort has well-known pitfalls. For example, it would be difficult to harmonize such doctrine across various jurisdictions around the world,[105] and there would be technical questions as to how a Web site owner could signal his or her choice to would-be robot indexers visiting the site.

The Internet community, however, fixed most of the problem before it could become intractable or even noticeable to mainstream audiences. A software engineer named Martijn Koster was among those discussing the issue of robot signaling on a public mailing list in 1993 and 1994. Participants, including "a majority of robot authors and other people with an interest in robots," converged on a standard for "robots.txt," a file that Web site authors could create that would be inconspicuous to Web surfers but in plain sight to indexing robots.[106] Through robots.txt, site owners can indicate preferences about what parts of the site ought to be crawled and by whom. Consensus among some influential Web programmers on a mailing list was the only blessing this standard received: "It is not an official standard backed by a standards body, or owned by any commercial organisation. It is not enforced by anybody, and there [sic] no guarantee that all current and future robots will use it. Consider it a common facility the majority of robot authors offer the WWW community to protect WWW server [sic] against unwanted accesses by their robots."[107]

Today, nearly all Web programmers know robots.txt is the way in which sites can signal their intentions to robots, and these intentions are respected by every major search engine across differing cultures and legal jurisdictions.[108] On this potentially contentious topic—search engines might well be more valuable if they indexed everything, *especially* content marked as something to avoid—harmony was reached without any application of law. The robots.txt standard did not address the legalities of search engines and robots; it merely provided a way to defuse many conflicts before they could even begin. The apparent legal vulnerabilities of robots.txt—its lack of ownership or backing of a large private standards setting organization, and the absence of private enforcement devices—may in fact be essential to its success.[109] Law professor Jody Freeman and others have written about the increasingly important role played by private organizations in the formation of standards across a wide range of disciplines and the ways in which some organizations incorporate governmental notions of due process in their activities.[110] Many Internet standards have been forged much less legalistically but still cooperatively.[111]

The questions not preempted or settled by such cooperation tend to be clashes between firms with some income stream in dispute—and where the law has then partially weighed in. For example, eBay sued data aggregator Bidder's Edge for using robots to scrape its site even after eBay clearly objected both in person and through robots.txt. eBay won in a case that has made it singularly into most cyberlaw casebooks and even into a few general property casebooks—a testament to how rarely such disputes enter the legal system.[112]

Similarly, the safe harbors of the U.S. Digital Millennium Copyright Act of 1998 give some protection to search engines that point customers to material that infringes copyright,[113] but they do not shield the actions required to create the search database in the first place. The act of creating a search engine, like the act of surfing itself, is something so commonplace that it would be difficult to imagine deeming it illegal—but this is not to say that search engines rest on any stronger of a legal basis than the practice of using robots.txt to determine when it is and is not appropriate to copy and archive a Web site.[114] Only recently, with Google's book scanning project, have copyright holders really begun to test this kind of question.[115] That challenge has arisen over the scanning of paper books, not Web sites, as Google prepares to make them searchable in the same way Google has indexed the Web.[116] The long-standing practice of Web site copying, guided by robots.txt, made that kind of indexing uncontroversial even as it is, in theory, legally cloudy.

The lasting lesson from robots.txt is that a simple, basic standard created by people of good faith can go a long way toward resolving or forestalling a problem containing strong ethical or legal dimensions. The founders of Creative Commons created an analogous set of standards to allow content creators to indicate how they would like their works to be used or reused. Creative Commons licenses purport to have the force of law behind them—one ignores them at the peril of infringing copyright—but the main force of Creative Commons as a movement has not been in the courts, but in cultural mindshare: alerting authors to basic but heretofore hidden options they have for allowing use of the photos, songs, books, or blog entries they create, and alerting those who make use of the materials to the general orientation of the author.

Creative Commons is robots.txt generalized. Again, the legal underpinnings of this standard are not particularly strong. For example, one Creative Commons option is "noncommercial," which allows authors to indicate that their material can be reused without risk of infringement so long as the use is noncommercial. But the definition of noncommercial is a model of vagueness, the sort of definition that could easily launch a case like *eBay v. Bidder's Edge*.[117] If one aggregates others' blogs on a page that has banner ads, is that a commercial use? There have been only a handful of cases over Creative Commons licenses, and none testing the meaning of noncommercial.[118] Rather, people seem to know a commercial (or derivative) use when they see it: the real power of the license may have less to do with a threat of legal enforcement and more to do with the way it signals one's intentions and asks that they be respected. Reliable empirical data is absent, but the sense among many of those using Creative Commons licenses is that their wishes have been respected.[119]

Applying Code-Backed Norms to Privacy: Data Genealogy

As people put data on the Internet for others to use or reuse—data that might be about other people as well as themselves—there are no tools to allow those who provide the data to express their preferences about how the data ought to be indexed or used. There is no Privacy Commons license to request basic limits on how one's photographs ought to be reproduced from a social networking site. There ought to be. Intellectual property law professor Pamela Samuelson has proposed that in response to the technical simplicity of collecting substantial amounts of personal information in cyberspace, a person should have a protectable right to control this personal data. She notes that a property-based legal framework is more difficult to impose when one takes into account the multiple interests a person might have in her personal data, and suggests a move to a contractual approach to protecting information privacy based in part on enforcement of Web site privacy policies.[120] Before turning to law directly, we can develop tools to register and convey authors' privacy-related preferences unobtrusively.

On today's Internet, the copying and pasting of information takes place with no sense of metadata.[121] It is difficult enough to make sure that a Creative Commons license follows the photograph, sound, or text to which it is related as those items circulate on the Web. But there is no standard at all to pass along for a given work and who recorded it, with what devices,[122] and most important, what the subject is comfortable having others do with it. If there were, links could become two-way. Those who place information on the Web could more readily canvas the public uses to which that information had been put and by whom. In turn, those who wish to reuse information would have a way of getting in touch with its original source to request permission. Some Web 2.0 outposts have generated promising rudimentary methods for this. Facebook, for example, offers tools to label the photographs one submits and to indicate what groups of people can and cannot see them. Once a photo is copied beyond the Facebook environment, however, these attributes are lost.[123]

The Web is a complex social phenomenon with information contributed not only by institutional sources like *Britannica,* CNN, and others that place large amounts of structured information on it, but also by amateurs like Wikipedians, Flickr contributors, and bloggers. Yet a Google search intentionally smoothes over this complexity; each linked search result is placed into a standard format to give the act of searching structure and order. Search engines and other aggregators can and should do more to enrich users' understanding of where the information they see is coming from. This approach would shadow the way that Theodor Nelson, coiner of the word "hypertext," envisioned "transclusion"—a means not to simply copy text, but also to reference it to its original source.[124] Nelson's vision was drastic in its simplicity: information would repose primarily at its source, and any quotes to it would simply frame that source. If it were deleted from the original source, it would disappear from its subsequent uses. If it were changed at the source, downstream uses would change with it. This is a strong version of the genealogy idea, since the metadata about an item's origin would actually be the item itself. It is data as service, and insofar as it leaves too much control with the data's originator, it suffers from many of the drawbacks of software as service described in Chapter Five. For the purposes of privacy, we do not need such a radical reworking of the copy-and-paste culture of the Web. Rather, we need ways for people to signal whether they would like to remain associated with the data they place on the Web, and to be consulted about unusual uses.

This weaker signaling-based version of Nelson's vision does not answer the legal question of what would happen if the originator of the data could not come to an agreement with someone who wanted to use it. But as with robots .txt and Creative Commons licenses, it could forestall many of the conflicts that will arise in the absence of any standard at all.[125] Most importantly, it would help signal authorial intention not only to end users but also to the intermediaries whose indices provide the engines for invasions of privacy in the first place. One could indicate that photos were okay to index by tag but not by facial recognition, for example. If search engines of today are any indication, such restrictions could be respected even without a definitive answer as to the extent of their legal enforceability. Indeed, by attaching online identity—if not physical identity—to the various bits of data that are constantly mashed up as people copy and paste what they like around the Web, it becomes possible for people to get in touch with one another more readily to express thanks, suggest collaboration, or otherwise interact as people in communities do. Similarly, projects like reCAPTCHA could seek to alert people to the extra good their solving of captchas is doing—and even let them opt out of solving the second word in the image, the one that is not testing whether they are human but instead is being used to perform work for someone else. Just as *Moore v. Regents of the University of California* struggled with the issue of whether a patient whose tumor was removed should be consulted before the tumor is used for medical research,[126] we will face the question of when people ought to be informed when their online behaviors are used for ulterior purposes—including beneficial ones.

Respect for robots.txt, Creative Commons licenses, and privacy "tags," and an opportunity to alert people and allow them to opt in to helpful ventures with their routine online behavior like captcha-solving, both requires and promotes a sense of community. Harnessing some version of Nelson's vision is a self-reinforcing community-building exercise—bringing people closer together while engendering further respect for people's privacy choices. It should be no surprise that people tend to act less charitably in today's online environment than they would act in the physical world.[127] Recall the discussion of ver-keersbordvrij in Chapter Six, where the elimination of most traffic signs can counterintuitively reduce accidents. Today's online environment is only half of the verkeersbordvrij system: there are few perceived rules, but there are also few ways to receive, and therefore respect, cues from those whose content or data someone might be using.[128] Verkeersbordvrij depends not simply on eliminat-ing most legal rules and enforcement, but also, in the view of its proponents, crucially on motorists' ability to roll down their windows and make eye contact with other motorists and pedestrians, to signal each other, and to pull them-selves away from the many distractions like mobile phones and snacking that turn driving into a mechanical operation rather than a social act. By devising tools and practices to connect distant individuals already building upon one another's data, we can promote the feedback loops found within functioning communities and build a framework to allow the *nicely* part of Benkler's "shar-ing nicely" to blossom.[129]

Enabling Reputation Bankruptcy

As biometric readers become more commonplace in our endpoint machines, it will be possible for online destinations routinely to demand unsheddable iden-tity tokens rather than disposable pseudonyms from Internet users. Many sites could benefit from asking people to participate with real identities known at least to the site, if not to the public at large. eBay, for one, would certainly profit by making it harder for people to shift among various ghost accounts. One could even imagine Wikipedia establishing a "fast track" for contributions if they were done with biometric assurance, just as South Korean citizen journal-ist newspaper OhmyNews keeps citizen identity numbers on file for the articles it publishes.[130] These architectures protect one's identity from the world at large while still making it much more difficult to produce multiple false "sock puppet" identities. When we participate in other walks of life—school, work, PTA meetings, and so on—we do so as ourselves, not wearing Groucho mus-taches, and even if people do not know exactly who we are, they can recognize us from one meeting to the next. The same should be possible for our online selves.

As real identity grows in importance on the Net, the intermediaries de-manding it ought to consider making available a form of reputation bank-ruptcy. Like personal financial bankruptcy, or the way in which a state often seals a juvenile criminal record and gives a child a "fresh start" as an adult, we ought to consider how to implement the idea of a second or third chance into our digital spaces. People ought to be able to express a choice to deemphasize if not entirely delete older information that has been generated about them by and through various systems: political preferences, activities, youthful likes and dislikes. If every action ends up on one's "permanent record," the press conference effect can set in. Reputation bankruptcy has the potential to facilitate desirably experimental social behavior and break up the monotony of static communities online and offline.[131] As a safety valve against excess experimentation, perhaps the information in one's record could not be deleted selectively; if someone wants to declare reputation bankruptcy, we might want it to mean throwing out the good along with the bad. The blank spot in one's history indicates a bankruptcy has been declared—this would be the price one pays for eliminating unwanted details.

The key is to realize that we can make design choices now that work to capture the nuances of human relations far better than our current systems, and that online intermediaries might well embrace such new designs even in the absence of a legal mandate to do so.

More, Not Less, Information

Reputation bankruptcy provides for the possibility of a clean slate. It works best within informationally hermetic systems that generate their own data through the activities of their participants, such as a social networking site that records who is friends with whom, or one that accumulates the various thumbs-up and thumbs-down array that could be part of a "How's My Driving"–style judgment.

But the use of the Internet more generally to spread real-world information about people is not amenable to reputation bankruptcy. Once injected into the Net, an irresistible video of an angry teacher, or a drunk and/or racist celebrity, cannot be easily stamped out without the kinds of network or endpoint control that are both difficult to implement and, if implemented, unacceptably corrosive to the generative Internet. What happens if we accept this as fact, and also assume that legal proscriptions against disseminating sensitive but popular data will be highly ineffective?[132] We might turn to contextualization: the idea, akin to the tort of false light, that harm comes from information plucked out of the rich thread of a person's existence and expression.[133] We see this in political controversies—even the slightest misphrasing of something can be extracted and blown out of proportion. It is the reason that official press conferences are not the same as bland conversation; they are even blander.

Contextualization suggests that the aim of an informational system should be to allow those who are characterized within it to augment the picture provided by a single snippet with whatever information, explanation, or denial that they think helps frame what is portrayed. Civil libertarians have long suggested that the solution to bad speech is more speech while realizing the difficulties of linking the second round of speech to the first without infringing the rights of the first speaker.[134] Criticisms of the "more speech" approach have included the observation that a retraction or amendment of a salacious newspaper story usually appears much less prominently than the original. This is particularly true for newspapers, where those seeing one piece of information may not ever see the follow-up. There is also the worry that the fog of information generated by a free-for-all is no way to have people discern facts from lies. Generative networks invite us to find ways to reconcile these views. We can design protocols to privilege those who are featured or described online so that they can provide their own framing linked to their depictions. This may not accord with our pre-Web expectations: it may be useful for a private newspaper to provide a right of reply to its subjects, but such an entity would quickly invoke a First Amendment–style complaint of compelled speech if the law were to provide for routine rights of reply in any but the narrowest of circumstances.[135] And many of us might wish to discuss Holocaust deniers or racists without giving them a platform to even link to a reply. The path forward is likely not a formal legal right but a structure to allow those disseminating information to build connections to the subjects of their discussions. In many cases those of us disseminating may not object—and a properly designed system might turn what would have otherwise been one-sided exchanges into genuine dialogues.

We already see some movement in this direction. The Harvard Kennedy School's Joseph Nye has suggested that a site like urban legend debunker snopes.com be instituted for reputation, a place that people would know to check to get the full story when they see something scandalous but decontextualized online.[136] The subjects of the scandalous data would similarly know to place their answers there—perhaps somewhat mitigating the need to formally link it to each instance of the original data. Google invites people quoted or discussed within news stories to offer addenda and clarification directly to Google, which posts these responses prominently near its link to the story when it is a search result within Google News.[137] Services like reputationdefender.com will, for a fee, take on the task of trying to remove or, failing that, contextualize sensitive information about people online.[138] ReputationDefender uses a broad toolkit of tactics to try to clear up perceived invasions of privacy—mostly moral suasion rather than legal threat.

To be sure, contextualization addresses just one slice of the privacy problem, since it only adds information to a sensitive depiction. If the depiction is embarrassing or humiliating, the opportunity to express that one is indeed embarrassed or humiliated does not much help. It may be that values of privacy are implacably in tension with some of the fruits of generativity. Just as the digital copyright problem could be solved if publishers could find a way to profit from abundance rather than scarcity, the privacy problem could be solved if we could take Sun Microsystems CEO McNealey's advice and simply get over it. This is not a satisfying rejoinder to someone whose privacy has been invaded, but, amazingly, this may be precisely what is happening: people are getting over it.

THE GENERATIONAL DIVIDE: BEYOND INFORMATIONAL PRIVACY

The values animating our concern for privacy are themselves in transition. Many have noted an age-driven gap in attitudes about privacy perhaps rivaled only by the 1960s generation gap on rock and roll.[139] Surveys bear out some of this perception.[140] Fifty-five percent of online teens have created profiles on sites like MySpace, though 66 percent of those use tools that the sites offer to limit access in some way.[141] Twice as many teens as adults have a blog.[142] Interestingly, while young people appear eager to share information online, they are more worried than older people about government surveillance.[143] Some also see that their identities may be discovered online, even with privacy controls.[144]

A large part of the personal information available on the Web about those born after 1985 comes from the subjects themselves. People routinely set up pages on social networking sites—in the United States, more than 85 percent of university students are said to have an entry on Facebook—and they impart reams of photographs, views, and status reports about their lives, updated to the minute. Friends who tag other friends in photographs cause those photos to be automatically associated with everyone mentioned—a major step toward the world in which simply showing up to an event is enough to make one's photo and name permanently searchable online in connection with the event.

Worries about such a willingness to place personal information online can be split into two categories. The first is explicitly paternalistic: children may lack the judgment to know when they should and should not share their personal information. As with other decisions that could bear significantly on their lives—signing contracts, drinking, or seeing movies with violent or sexual content—perhaps younger people should be protected from rash decisions that facilitate infringements of their privacy. The second relies more on the generative mosaic concern expressed earlier: people might make rational decisions about sharing their personal information in the short term, but underestimate what might happen to that information as it is indexed, reused, and repurposed by strangers. Both worries have merit, and to the extent that they do we could deploy the tools of intermediary gatekeeping to try to protect people below a certain age until they wise up. This is just the approach of the U.S. Children's Online Privacy Protection Act of 1998 (COPPA).[145] COPPA fits comfortably but ineffectually within a Privacy 1.0 framework, as it places restrictions on operators of Web sites and services that knowingly gather identifiable information from children under the age of thirteen: they cannot do so without parental consent. The result is discernable in most mainstream Web sites that collect data; each now presents a checkbox for the user to affirm that he or she is over thirteen, or asks outright for a birthday or age. The result has been predictable; kids quickly learn simply to enter an age greater than thirteen in order to get to the services they want.[146] To achieve limits on the flow of information about kids requires levels of intervention that so far exceed the willingness of any jurisdiction.[147] The most common scheme to separate kids from adults online is to identify individual network endpoints as used primarily or frequently by kids and then limit what those endpoints can do: PCs in libraries and public schools are often locked down with filtering software, sometimes due to much-litigated legal requirements.[148]

A shift to tethered appliances could greatly lower the costs of discerning age online. Many appliances could be initialized at the time of acquisition with the birthdays of their users, or sold assuming use by children until unlocked by the vendor after receiving proof of age. This is exactly how many tethered mobile phones with Internet access are sold,[149] and because they do not allow third-party code they can be much more securely configured to only access certain approved Web sites. With the right standards in place, PCs could broadcast to every Web site visited that they have not been unlocked for adult browsing, and such Web sites could then be regulated through a template like COPPA to restrict the transmission of certain information that could harm the young users. This is a variant of Lessig's idea for a "kid enabled browser," made much more robust because a tethered appliance is difficult to hack.[150]

These paternalistic interventions assume that people will be more careful about what they put online once they grow up. And even those who are not more careful and regret it have exercised their autonomy in ways that ought to be respected. But the generational divide on privacy appears to be more than the higher carelessness or risk tolerance of kids. Many of those growing up with the Internet appear not only reconciled to a public dimension to their lives— famous for at least fifteen people—but eager to launch it. Their notions of privacy transcend the Privacy 1.0 plea to keep certain secrets or private facts under control. Instead, by digitally furnishing and nesting within publicly accessible online environments, they seek to make such environments their own. My-Space—currently the third most popular Web site in the United States and sixth most popular in the world[151]—is evocatively named: it implicitly promises its users that they can decorate and arrange their personal pages to be expressive of themselves. Nearly every feature of a MySpace home page can be reworked by its occupant, and that is exactly what occupants do, drawing on tools provided by MySpace and outside developers.[152] This is generativity at work: MySpace programmers creating platforms that can in turn be directed and reshaped by users with less technical talent but more individualized creative energy. The most salient feature of privacy for MySpace users is not secrecy so much as autonomy: a sense of control over their home bases, even if what they post can later escape their confines. Privacy is about establishing a locus which we can call our own without undue intervention or interruption—a place where we can vest our identities. That can happen most directly in a particular location—"your home is your castle"—and, as law professor Margaret Radin explains, it can also happen with objects.[153] She had in mind a ring or other heirloom, but an iPod containing one's carefully selected music and video can fit the bill as well. Losing such a thing hurts more than the mere pecuniary value of obtaining a fresh one. MySpace pages, blogs, and similar online outposts can be repositories for our identities for which personal control, not secrecy, is the touchstone.

The 1973 U.S. government privacy report observed:

> An agrarian, frontier society undoubtedly permitted much less personal privacy than a modern urban society, and a small rural town today still permits less than a big city. The poet, the novelist, and the social scientist tell us, each in his own way, that the life of a small-town man, woman, or family is an open book compared to the more anonymous existence of urban dwellers. Yet the individual in a small town can retain his confidence because he can be more sure of retaining control. He lives in a face-to-face world, in a social system where irresponsible behavior can be identified and called to account. By contrast, the impersonal data system, and faceless users of the information it contains, tend to be accountable only in the formal sense of the word.

In practice they are for the most part immune to whatever sanctions the individual can invoke.[154]

Enduring solutions to the new generation of privacy problems brought about by the generative Internet will have as their touchstone tools of connection and accountability among the people who produce, transform, and consume personal information and expression: tools to bring about social systems to match the power of the technical one. Today's Internet is an uncomfortable blend of the personal and the impersonal. It can be used to build and refine communities and to gather people around common ideas and projects.[155] In contrast, it can also be seen as an impersonal library of enormous scale: faceless users perform searches and then click and consume what they see. Many among the new generation of people growing up with the Internet are enthusiastic about its social possibilities. They are willing to put more of themselves into the network and are more willing to meet and converse with those they have never met in person. They may not experience the same divide that Twain observed between our public and private selves. Photos of their drunken exploits on Facebook might indeed hurt their job prospects[156]—but soon those making hiring decisions will themselves have had Facebook pages. The differential between our public and private selves might be largely resolved as we develop digital environments in which views can be expressed and then later revised. Our missteps and mistakes will not be cause to stop the digital presses; instead, the good along with the bad will form part of a dialogue with both the attributes of a small town and a "world where anyone, anywhere may express his or her beliefs, no matter how singular, without fear of being coerced into silence or conformity."[157] Such an environment will not be perfect: there will be Star Wars Kids who wish to retract their private embarrassing moments and who cannot. But it will be better than one without powerful generative instrumentalities, one where the tools of monitoring are held and monopolized by the faceless institutions anticipated and feared in 1973.

Conclusion

Nicholas Negroponte, former director of the MIT Media Lab, announced the One Laptop Per Child (OLPC) project at the beginning of 2005. The project aims to give one hundred million hardy, portable computers to children in the developing world. The laptops, called XOs, are priced around $100, and they are to be purchased by governments and given to children through their schools.[1] As of this writing Brazil, Libya, Mexico, Nigeria, Peru, Rwanda, and Uruguay have committed to a pilot run that will have the XO's assembly lines ramping up to five million machines per month and totaling approximately 20 percent of all laptop manufacturing in the world.[2]

The pitch to governments footing the bill emphasizes alignment with existing schoolhouse curricula and practices. A laptop can be a cost-effective way to distribute textbooks, because it can contain so much data in a small space and can be updated after it has been distributed. Says Negroponte: "The hundred-dollar laptop is an education project. It's not a laptop project."[3]

Yet OLPC is about revolution rather than evolution, and it embodies both the promise and challenge of generativity. The project's intellectual pedigree and structure reveal an enterprise of breathtaking theoretical and logistical ambition. The education Negroponte refers to is not the rote learning represented by the typical textbook and the three R's that form the basis of most developing and developed country curricula. Rather, the XO is shaped to reflect the theories of fellow Media Lab visionary Seymour Papert. Alternately known as constructionism or constructivism, Papert's vision of education downplays drills in hard facts and abstract skills in favor of a model that teaches students how to learn by asking them to undertake projects that they find relevant to their everyday lives.[4]

A modest incarnation of the OLPC project would distribute PCs as electronic workbooks. The PCs would run the consumer operating systems and applications prevailing in the industrialized world—the better to groom students for work in call centers and other outsourced IT-based industries. Microsoft, under competition from free operating systems, has shown a willingness to greatly reduce the prices for its products in areas where wallets are smaller, so such a strategy is not necessarily out of reach, and in any case the XO machine could run one of the more consumer-friendly versions of free Linux without much modification.[5]

But the XO completely redesigns today's user interfaces from the ground up. Current PC users who encounter an XO have a lot to unlearn. For example, the arrow pointer serves a different purpose: moving the XO's arrow toward the center of the screen indicates options that apply only to that computer; moving the pointer toward any edge indicates interaction with nearby computers or the community at large.

The XO envisions students who are able to hack their own machines: to reprogram them even as they are learning to read and write—and to do so largely on their own initiative. The XO dissemination plan is remarkably light on both student and teacher training. There are a handful of trainers to cover the thousands of schools that will serve as distribution points, and the training function is more to ensure installation and functioning of the servers rather than true mastery of the machines. Students are expected to rely on each other and on trial-and-error to acquire most of the skills needed to use and reprogram the machines.

Content also seems a calculated afterthought. The XO project wiki—haphazardly organized, as wikis tend to be—featured a "call for content" in late 2006, mere months before millions of machines were to be placed in children's hands, for "content creators, collectors, and archivists, to suggest educational content for inclusion with the laptops, to be made available to millions of children in the developing the world, most of whom do not have access to learning materials."[6] Determining exactly what would be bundled on the machines, what would repose on servers at schools, and what would be available on the XO Web site for remote access was very much a work in progress even as deployment dates neared.

In other words, XO has embraced the procrastination principle that is woven through generative technologies. To the chagrin and discomfort of most educational academics following the project, there is little focus on specific educational outcomes or metrics.[7] There are no firm plans to measure usage of the laptops, or to correlate changes in test scores with their deployment and use. Instead, the idea is to create an infrastructure that is both simple and generative, stand back, and see what happens, fixing most major substantive problems only as they arise, rather than anticipating them from the start.

Thus as much as Negroponte insists that the project is not a technology play, the lion's share of the effort has gone into just that, and is calculated to promote a very special agenda of experimentation. Central to the XO's philosophy is that each machine should belong to a single child, rather than being found in a typical computer lab or children's cyber café. That partially explains the XO's radical design, both in physical form and in software. It features especially small keys so that adults cannot easily use it if they should steal it from a child, and it has no moving parts within. There is no hard drive to suffer from a fall; the screen is designed to be viewable in direct sunlight; and it consumes little enough power that it can be recharged with a crank or other physical motion in the absence of a source of electricity. The machines automatically form mesh networks with one another so that children can share programs and data with each other or connect to a school's data repository in the absence of any ISPs. It is a rediscovery of the principles behind FIDOnet, the ad hoc network of bulletin boards programmed on PCs that called each other using modems before PC users could connect to the Internet.

One bundled application, TamTam, lets a child use the machine to generate music and drumbeats, and nearby machines can be coordinated through their mesh networks so that each one represents a different instrument in a symphony the group can compose and play. Just as some students might develop and express talents at the technical layer, reprogramming the machines, others might be inspired to develop musical talents through the rough tools of Tam-Tam at the content layer.

Constructionism counts on curiosity and intellectual passion of self- or informally taught individuals as its primary engine, exactly the wellspring tapped by generative systems. From XO's founders we see an attempt to reprise the spirit that illuminated the original personal computer, Internet, and Web. They believe that it is less important to provide content than to provide a means of making it and passing it along, just as an Internet without any plan for content ended up offering far more than the proprietary walled gardens that had so carefully sponsored and groomed their offerings. There is a leap of faith that a machine given entirely to a child's custody, twenty-four hours a day, will not promptly be lost, stolen, or broken. Instead, children are predicted to treat these boxes as dear possessions, and some among them will learn to program, designing and then sharing new applications that in turn support new kinds of content and interaction that may not have been invented in the developed world.

Yet the makers of the XO are aware that it is not the dawn of the networked era. We have experienced market boom and wildly successful applications, but also bust, viruses, and spam. The sheer scale and public profile of the XO project make it difficult fully to embrace an experimentalist spirit, whether at the technical, content, or social layers. The sui generis modified Linux-based operating systems within the XO machines give them an initial immunity to the worms and viruses that plague the machines of the developed world, so that should they choose to surf the world's Web they will not be immediately overcome by the malware that otherwise requires constantly updated firewalls. They can breathe the digital air directly, without the need for the expensive antivirus "clean suits" that other PCs must have. XO's director of security has further implemented a security architecture for the machines that keeps programs from being able to communicate with each other, in order to preemptively quarantine any attack in one part of the machine.[8] This means that a word processor cannot talk directly to a music program, and an Internet program cannot talk to a drawing program. This protects the machine from hypothetical viruses, but it also adds a layer of inflexibility and complexity to an operating system that children are supposed to be able to understand and modify.

The XO thus combines its generative foundation with elements of a tethered appliance. XO staff have vowed never to accede to requests for content filtering[9]—yet they have built a kill switch into the machines so that stolen models can be selectively disabled,[10] and such a switch opens the door to later remote control. Thus, XOs are both independent as they can form mesh networks, and tethered as they can be updated, monitored, and turned off from afar, so long as they are connected to the Internet. They are generative in spirit and architecture, and they are also appliances, painstakingly designed to be reliable to and usable by someone who cannot read or write. They combine the hope of the early Internet era with the hard lessons of its second phase. They represent the confusion of the interregnum between the unbridled explosion of cheap and flexible processors, networks, and sensors, and the tightening up that comes as their true power is appreciated—and abused.

Perhaps the audience of schoolchildren in developing countries is remote and uninteresting enough to those who want to control or compromise today's information technology that it will be helpfully overlooked during the critical time period in which backwater status helps to foster generative development. Just as domain names were originally first-come, first-served, and no major companies reserved their own names or foresaw a trademark problem, poor schoolchildren may not be deemed enough of an economic market to be worth vying for—either in attracting their eyeballs to show them advertising, or in preventing them from exchanging bits that could be copyrighted. There are no preexisting CD sales among them to dent.

XO is but the most prominent and well-funded of a series of enterprises to attempt to bridge the digital divide. Other efforts, such as the Volkscomputer in Brazil, the VillagePDA, and the Ink have fared poorly, stuck at some phase of development or production.[11] Negroponte's impatience with tentative initial steps, and with the kind of planning and study that firm-based ventures usually require, has worried many in the international development community. They fear that a prominent failure of the project could unduly tarnish other attempts to deploy technology in the developing world. The Indian government announced in 2006 that it would not sign up to buy any XO machines, in part due to difficulties encountered with the Simputer, a for-profit project begun in 1998 to deliver handheld technology to India's rural population, which is made up mostly of farmers and laborers—many of whom are illiterate and speak regional dialects. In 2001, Bruce Sterling lionized the Simputer as "computing as it would have looked if Gandhi had invented it, then used Steve Jobs for his ad campaign."[12] It never took off. Instead India appears to be placing its bets on the Novantium Nova or a similar device, non-generative machines fully tethered to a subscription server for both software and content.[13]

Will XO fail like the others? Development experts view it as skeptically as education experts do, seeing XO as yet another risky heaving of hardware at problems that are actually political, social, and economic in nature. Debates on the XO wiki wonder whether teching-up an entire generation of millions of children will be good or bad for those already online. Some worry that the already-formidable sources of Nigerian "419" spam soliciting business deals will grow and diversify. There is even musing that guerrilla fighters could use the laptops' mesh networking capabilities to communicate secretly on the battlefield.[14] (Depending on which side one supports in that battle, that could be good, although it is a far cry from the notion of laptops as educational gateways for children.)

As computer scientist Gene Spafford wrote:

> We can't defend against the threats we are facing now. If these mass computer giveaways succeed, shortly we will have another billion users online who are being raised in environments of poverty, with little or no education about proper IT use, and often in countries where there is little history of tolerance (and considerable history of religious, ethnic and tribal strife). Access to eBay and YouTube isn't going to give them clean water and freedom from disease. But it may help breed resentment and discontent where it hasn't been before.
>
> Gee, I can barely wait. The metaphor that comes to mind is that if we were in the ramp-up to the Black Plague in the middle ages, these groups would be trying to find ways to subsidize the purchase of pet rats.[15]

Spafford appears to recognize the delicate condition of today's Net, and he believes that a pause in expansion is needed—a bit of time to digest the problems that beset it. The easier and more risk-averse path is to distribute mobile phones and other basic Net appliances to the developing world just as those devices are becoming more central in the developed one, bridging the digital divide in one sense—providing useful technology—while leaving out the generative elements most important to the digital space's success: the integration of people as participants in it rather than only consumers of it.

But a project like OLPC offers an opportunity to demonstrate fixes to the Net's problems among audiences that have yet to encounter it. Its XO represents a new path of continued if cautious generativity as the developed world's technology is beginning to ossify under the weight of its own success. It represents a faith not only that students can learn to reprogram their computers, but that what they direct them to do will be, on balance, good if disruptive.

The story of the XO is the story of the generative pattern. The pattern begins with the ambitious planting of a flag for a new enterprise in an overlooked backwater. The procrastination principle gives license for the idea's technical and social blueprints to be incomplete. Contribution is welcome from outsiders, and if the project takes off, the results may prove completely unexpected.

The XO's skeptics have much in common with generativity's skeptics. They can convincingly put forward the very real risks attendant to a project only partially planned, without extensive layers of measurement, control, and accountability. These risks are most obviously grouped under the rubric of security, but the label is far too narrow either to capture the problem or to point us to the most promising solutions—just as the story of badware on PCs is not simply a story about security worries on the Internet, narrowly defined.

Rather, the limits of an open PC and Net, and the fears for the XO, are much more general case studies of what happens within systems that are built with a peculiar and extraordinary openness to contribution and innovation and that succeed because of it. They challenge us to understand and meet the problems arising from success in a way that does not neuter what made the original success possible.

The puzzle of PC security is fundamentally the same as the puzzle of keeping Wikipedia honest and true—and perhaps giving birth to its version 2.0 successor—now that Wikipedia has entered the prime-time glare, attracting participants who are ignorant or scornful of its ideals. It is the puzzle of empowering people to share and trade stories, photos, and recommendations without losing their identities as they become not only the creators of distributed scrutiny and judgment, but also their subjects.

It is the puzzle of Herdict, the application designed to run on netizens' PCs to generate and share a collective map of vital signs, that can produce distributed judgments about good code and bad. One of the first questions asked about Herdict is whether makers of badware will simply hijack lots of PCs and compel them to report to Herdict that they are happy, when in fact they are not. One answer acknowledges the problem and then seeks, from day one, to forestall it while it is still on the drawing board, with attendant complication, investment, and elaboration. An alternative answer says: The point at which Herdict is worth the effort of bad people to game it is a milestone of *success*. It is a token of movement from the primordial soup that begins the generative pattern to the mainstream impact that attracts the next round of problems.

Imagine planning but not yet executing Wikipedia: "Won't people come along and vandalize it?" One response to that question, and to the others like it that arise for an idea as crazy as Wikipedia, would be to abandon the idea—to transform it so much in anticipation of the problems that it is unrecognizable from its original generative blueprint. The response instead was to deem the question reasonable but premature. The generativity that makes it vulnerable also facilitates the tools and relationships through which people can meet the problems when first-round success causes them to materialize.

The animating spirit: "Ready, fire, aim." This ethos is a major ingredient of Google's secret sauce as a company, a willingness to deploy big ideas that remain labeled "beta" for months even as they become wildly popular, as Google News was. It lies behind the scanning of all the world's books, despite the logistical burdens and legal uncertainties. To the amazement of those of us who work for universities and could not possibly persuade our general counsels to risk their clients' endowments on such a venture, Google simply started doing it. The litigation continues as this book goes to press, and so does the scanning of the books and the indexing of their contents, available to hundreds of millions of people who would otherwise never know of them, at books.google.com.

How we choose to approach generative puzzles animates the struggle between the models of the Net and of television, of the insurgent and the incumbent. Traditional cyberlaw frameworks tend to see the Net as an intriguing force for chaos that might as well have popped out of nowhere. It is too easy to then shift attention to the "issues raised" by the Net, usually by those threatened by it—whether incumbent technical-layer competitors like traditional telephony providers, or content-layer firms like record companies whose business models (and, to be sure, legally protected interests) are disrupted by it. Then the name of the game is seen to be coming up with the right law or policy by a government actor to address the issues. Such approaches can lead to useful, hard-nosed insights and suggestions, but they are structured to overlook the fact that the Net is quite literally what we make it.

The traditional approaches lead us in the direction of intergovernmental organizations and diplomatically styled talk-shop initiatives like the World Summit on the Information Society and its successor, the Internet Governance Forum, where "stakeholders" gather to express their views about Internet governance, which is now more fashionably known as "the creation of multi-stakeholder regimes." Such efforts import from professional diplomacy the notion of process and unanimity above all. Their solution for the difficulties of individual state enforcement on the Net is a kind of negotiated intellectual harmony among participants at a self-conscious summit—complex regimes to be mapped out in a dialogue taking place at an endlessly long table, with a role for all to play. Such dialogues end either in bland consensus pronouncements or in final documents that are agreed upon only because the range of participants has been narrowed.

It is no surprise that this approach rarely gets to the nuts and bolts of designing new tools or grassroots initiatives to take on the problems it identifies. The Net and its issues sail blithely on regardless of the carefully worded communiqués that emerge from a parade of meetings and consultations. Stylized gatherings of concerned stakeholders are not inherently bad—much can come of dialogue among parties whose interests interconnect. Indeed, earlier in this book I called for a latter-day Manhattan Project to take on the most pressing problems facing the generative Internet. But the types of people that such a project requires are missing from the current round of "stakeholder governance" structures. Missing are the computer scientists and geeks who would rather be coding than attending receptions in Geneva and Tunis. Without them we too easily neglect the prospect that we could code new tools and protocols to facilitate social solutions—the way that the robots.txt of Chapter Nine has so far headed off what otherwise would have been yet another cyberlaw issue.

To be sure, from the earliest days of the Internet the people who designed its protocols acceded to some formality and diplomacy. Recall that they published "RFCs," requests for comments designed to write up their ideas, creating institutional structure and memory as the project became bigger than just a few researchers in a room. The author of the first one—RFC 1—recalls: "We parceled out the work and wrote the initial batch of memos. In addition to participating in the technical design, I took on the administrative function of setting up a simple scheme for numbering and distributing the notes. Mindful that our group was informal, junior and unchartered, I wanted to emphasize these notes were the beginning of a dialog and not an assertion of control."[16]

Informal, junior, and unchartered, yet collaborative and at least partially structured: this includes people who are eager to take on a parcel of work and build. It represents the ingredients found in the generative soil of Wikipedia, Pledgebank, Meetup, CouchSurfing.com, and other countless innovations that abound on the Net, themselves made possible because the Net's soil is made of the same stuff. The way to secure it and the innovations built upon it is to empower rank-and-file users to contribute, rather than to impose security models that count on a handful of trusted people for control. We need tools that cure the autistic nature of today's Net experience: PC users unaware of their digital environments and therefore unable to act on social cues, whether of danger or of encouragement.

If history is a guide, these tools can just as likely come from one or two researchers as from hackers, and the properly executed Manhattan Project to bolster the Net for another round of success will not be marked by centralization so much as by focus: the application of money and encouragement to those who step forward to help fix the most important and endemic problems that can no longer tolerate any procrastination.

Just as the XO's technology platform seeks to cultivate such contributions as routine rather than as obscure or special, by placing generative technologies into as many children's hands as possible, the educational systems in the developed world could be geared to encourage and reward such behavior, whether at the technical, content, or social layers.

Unfortunately, the initial reaction by many educators to digital participatory enterprises—ones that indeed may be subverted by their users—is fear. Many teachers are decrying the ways in which the Net has made it easy to plagiarize outright or to draw from dubious sources.[17] Some schools and universities have banned the citation of Wikipedia in student papers,[18] while signing up for plagiarism detection services like TurnitIn.com and automatic essay-grading tools like SAGrader.com, which "uses computational intelligence strategies to grade students [*sic*] essays in seconds and respond with detailed, topic-specific feedback."[19]

Instead of being subject to technology that automates and reinforces the worst aspects of contemporary education—emphasizing regurgitation and summarization of content from an oracular source, followed by impersonal grading within a conceptual echo chamber—our children ought to be encouraged to accept the participatory invitation of the Net and that which has recursively emerged at its upper layers from its open technologies below. Wikipedia's conceded weakness as a source is an invitation to improve it, and the act of improving it can be as meaningful to the contributor as to those who come after. Our students can be given assignments that matter—reading with a critical eye the sources that the rest of the online world consults, and improving them as best they know how, using tools of research and argument and intellectual honesty that our schools can teach. Instead of turning in a report for a single teacher to read, they can put their skills into work that everyone can read. The millions of students doing make-work around the world can come to learn instead that what they do can have consequences—and that if they do not contribute, it is not necessarily true that others will. In other words, we can use our generative technologies to teach our children to take responsibility for the way the world works rather than to be merely borne along by its currents. This will work best if our teachers are on board. Without people to whom others can apprentice, to learn technical skills and social practice, generative technologies can flounder. This is the XO's vulnerability, too—if it fails, it may in large part be because the technology was too difficult to master and share, and its possibilities not hinted at enough to entice learners to persist in their attention to it.

Like the XO, generativity itself is, at its core, not a technology project. It is an education project, an exercise in intellect and community, the founding concepts of the university. Our universities are in a position to take a leadership role in the Net's future. They were the Net's original cradle, along with the self-taught hobbyists who advanced the PC from its earliest days. Business and commerce followed in their wake, refining and expanding the opportunities developed through largely nonmarket process and ethos. The Internet and attached generative platforms are invitations to code and to build. Universities—and not just their computer science departments—should see those invitations as central to their missions of teaching their students and bringing knowledge to the world.

As countries and groups in the developing world incline to brand new generative technologies, those in the developed world must fight to retain theirs. There is not a simple pendulum swinging from generative to non-generative and back again; we cannot count on the fact that screws tightened too far can become stripped. Any comprehensive redesign of the Internet at this late stage would draw the attention of regulators and other parties who will push for ways to prevent abuse before it can even happen. Instead, we must piecemeal refine and temper the PC and the Net so that they can continue to serve as engines of innovation and contribution while mitigating the most pressing concerns of those harmed by them. We must appreciate the connection between generative technology and generative content.

Today's consumer information technology is careening at breakneck pace, and most see no need to begin steering it. Our technologists are complacent because the ongoing success of the generative Net has taken place without central tending—the payoffs of the procrastination principle. Rank-and-file Internet users enjoy its benefits while seeing its operation as a mystery, something they could not possibly hope to affect. They boot their PCs each day and expect them more or less to work, and they access Wikipedia and expect it more or less to be accurate.

But our Net technologies are experiencing the first true shock waves from their generative successes. The state of the hacking arts is advancing. Web sites can be compromised in an instant, and many visitors will then come away with an infected PC simply for having surfed there. Without a new cadre of good hackers unafraid to take ownership of the challenges posed by their malicious siblings and create the tools needed to help nonhackers keep the Net on a constructive trajectory, the most direct solutions will be lockdown that cuts short the Net experiment, deprives us of its fruits, and facilitates a form of governmental control that upends a balance between citizen and sovereign. These ripples can be followed recursively up the Net's layers. Our generative technologies need technically skilled people of goodwill to keep them going, and the fledgling generative activities above—blogging, wikis, social networks—need artistically and intellectually skilled people of goodwill to serve as true alternatives to a centralized, industrialized information economy that asks us to identify only as consumers of meaning rather than as makers of it. Peer production alone does not guarantee collaborative meaning making. Services like InnoCentive place five-figure bounties on difficult but modular scientific problems, and ask the public at large to offer solutions.[20] But the solutions tendered then become the full property of the institutional bounty hunter.[21] Amazon's Mechanical Turk has created a marketplace for the solving of so-called human intelligence tasks on the other side of the scale: trivial, repetitive tasks like tracing lines around the faces in photographs for a firm that has some reason to need them traced.[22] If five years from now children with XOs were using them for hours each day primarily to trace lines at half a penny per trace, it could be a useful economic engine to some and a sweatshop to others—but either way it would not be an activity that is generative at the content layer.

The deciding factor in whether our current infrastructure can endure will be the sum of the perceptions and actions of its users. There are roles for traditional state sovereigns, pan-state organizations, and formal multistakeholder regimes to play. They can help reinforce the conditions necessary for generative blossoming, and they can also step in—with all the confusion and difficulty that notoriously attends regulation of a generative space—when mere generosity of spirit among people of goodwill cannot resolve conflict. But such generosity of spirit is a society's powerful first line of moderation.

Our fortuitous starting point is a generative device in tens of millions of hands on a neutral Net. To maintain it, the users of those devices must experience the Net as something with which they identify and belong. We must use the generativity of the Net to engage a constituency that will protect and nurture it. That constituency may be drawn from the ranks of a new generation able to see that technology is not simply a video game designed by someone else, and that content is not simply what is provided through a TiVo or iPhone.

Acknowledgments

Many people helped bring about this book. I am fortunate to have brainstormed, taught, and argued with Terry Fisher, Lawrence Lessig, Charlie Nesson, and John Palfrey. They helped me discover, shape, and refine the underlying ideas and themes. They are natural, effortless teachers—and the most helpful and generous colleagues anyone could hope for. David D. Clark was an unforgettable guest ten years ago in my first cyberlaw seminar. His breathless and brilliant synthesis of engineering and policy was an inspiration to my students and me—and the beginning of a series of regular visits between ZIP codes 02139 and 02138 that, in the span of an hour or two, opened up new avenues of thinking for me about the way the Internet does and does not work.

The students in my cyberlaw classes have been extraordinary. Many have continued as formal research assistants; others as fellow travelers willing to stay in touch and read a draft. Over the course of this work's development from a paper without a title, to a law review article, to a book, cyberlaw alumni and other students at Harvard, Oxford, and Stanford, graduate and undergraduate, have provided invaluable research and editing assistance. They include Erin Ashwell, Megan Ristau Baca, Malcolm Birdling, Nick Bramble, Geoff Brounell, Bryan Choi, Chloe Cockburn, Heather Connor, Charles Frentz, Steve Horowitz, Doug Kochelek, Adam Lawton, Dominique Lazanski, Sara Mayeux, Jacob Mermelstein, Max Mishkin, Christina Mulligan, Jason Neal, Joon Oh, Christina Olson, Leah Plunkett, Greg Price, Sangamitra Ramachander, Cynthia Robertson, Joshua Salzman, Matt Sanchez, Steve Schultze, Joe Shear, Greg Skidmore, Brett Thomas, Ryan Trinkle, Kathy Wong, and Andrew Zee. Many, many thanks.

I owe a debt to many who gave time and thought as sounding boards, whether in conversation or in reacting to drafts. They include David Allen, Alison Aubry, David Barron, Yochai Benkler, danah boyd, John Bracken, Sergey Brin, Sarah Brown, Bob Carp, Federica Casarova, Julie Cohen, Paul David, Rex du Pont, Einer Elhauge, Zelda Fischer, Sarah Garvey, Heather Gerken, Tarleton Gillespie, Mark Gordon, Wendy Gordon, Philip Greenspun, Eva Holtz, Molly Shaffer Van Houweling, Rebecca Hulse, Ramesh Johari, Russell Johnson, Elena Kagan, Ken Kahn, Samuel Klein, Alex MacGillivray, John Martin, Betsy Masiello, Lew McCreary, Andrew McLaughlin, Juliette Melton, Daniel Meltzer, Frank Michelman, Jo Miller, Martha Minow, Melissa Morris, Roberta Morris, Rebecca Nesson, Craig Newmark, Jackie Newmyer, Andy Oram, Frank Pasquale, David Post, Jan Radler, Lecia Rosenthal, Katie Schaaf, Ralph Schroeder, Doc Searls, Wendy Seltzer, Irwin Shapiro, Sonja Starr, Bill Stuntz, John Sutula, Zephyr Teachout, Beth Tovey, Barbara van Schewick, Adrian Vermuele, Eric von Hippel, Fred von Lohmann, Jimbo Wales, Ginny Walters, David Weinberger, Yorick Wilks, Ruth Zittrain, and Ethan Zuckerman.

The ideas here have also benefited greatly from a workshopping process, including seminars in the Harvard Law School summer workshop series, the Oxford Internet Institute, the Ditchley Foundation, and the Penn-Temple-Wharton Colloquium, as well as a vehement free-for-all on Groklaw.

Publishing mavens Will Goodlad, Michael O'Malley, Caroline Michel, and Jeff Schier helped to find the book a cover and a home.

And for the corps that helped bring the book to fruition—nearly always available on e-mail or IM, able to research a question or send along a promising link—I share my awe and gratitude. They are Ryan Budish, Tim Hwang, Blair Kaminsky, Sarah Kimball, Jon Novotny, Elisabeth Oppenheimer, Elizabeth Stark, Sarah Tierney, and Sally Walkerman.

Notes

INTRODUCTION

1. Steve Jobs, CEO, Apple, Macworld San Francisco 2007 Keynote Address, Jan. 9, 2007, *available at* http://www.apple.com/quicktime/qtv/mwsf07/.

2. David H. Ahl, *The First West Coast Computer Faire, in* 3 THE BEST OF CREATIVE COMPUTING 98 (David Ahl & Burchenal Green eds., 1980), *available at* http://www.atariarchives.org/bcc3/showpage.php?page=98.

3. *See* Tom Hormby, *VisiCalc and the Rise of the Apple II,* ORCHARD, Sept. 26, 2006, http://lowendmac.com/orchard/06/0922.html.

4. *See, e.g.,* ModMyiFone, *Main Page,* http://www.modmyifone.com/wiki/index .php/ (as of Sept. 30, 2007, 16:17 GMT) (containing code and instructions for modifications).

5. *See* Posting of Saul Hansell to N.Y. Times Bits Blog, Saul Hansell, *Steve Jobs Girds for the Long iPhone War,* http://bits.blogs.nytimes.com/2007/09/27/ steve-jobs-girds-for-the-long-iphone-war/ (Sept. 27, 2007, 19:01); Jane Wakefield, *Apple iPhone Warning Proves True,* BBC NEWS, Sept. 28, 2007, http://news .bbc.co.uk/2/hi/technology/7017660 .stm.

6. *See* John Markoff, *Steve Jobs Walks the Tightrope Again,* N.Y. TIMES, Jan. 12, 2007, *available at* http://www.nytimes.com/2007/01/12/technology/12apple .html.

7. Posting of Ryan Block to Engadget, *A Lunchtime Chat with Bill Gates,* http: //www
.engadget.com/2007/01/08/a-lunchtime-chat-with-bill-gates-at-ces/ (Jan. 8, 2007,
14:01).

PART I. THE RISE AND STALL OF THE GENERATIVE NET

1. For a discussion of the consolidation of the telephone industry at the turn of the twentieth century, see JASON A. HOIDA, AMERICAN TELEPHONY (1997); ROBERT W. GARNET,
THE TELEPHONE ENTERPRISE (1985).
2. For articles noting the centrality of end-to-end to the debate, see Marjory S. Blumenthal,
End-to-End and Subsequent Paradigms, 2002 LAW REV. MICH. ST. U.-DETROIT C. L.
709, 717 (describing end-to-end as the current paradigm for understanding the Internet); Lawrence Lessig, *The Architecture of Innovation,* 51 DUKE L. J. 1783 (2002) (arguing that end-to-end establishes the Internet as a commons). For an overview of the debate about the perceived values at stake in end-to-end arguments, see Yochai Benkler, e2e
Map (Dec. 1, 2000) (unpublished paper from the Policy Implications of End-to-End
workshop at Stanford Law School), http://cyberlaw.stanford.edu/e2e/e2e_map.html.
For arguments in favor of the preservation of end-to-end neutrality in network imple-
mentation, see Written Ex Parte of Professor Mark A. Lemley and Professor Lawrence
Lessig, In re Application for Consent to the Transfer of Control of Licenses MediaOne
Group, Inc. to AT&T Corp., No. 99–251 (F.C.C. 1999), *available at* http://cyber
.law.harvard.edu/works/lessig/cable/fcc/fcc.html; Mark A. Lemley & Lawrence Lessig,
The End of End-to-End: Preserving the Architecture of the Internet in the Broadband Era, 48
UCLA L. REV. 925 (2001); David D. Clark & Marjory S. Blumenthal, *Rethinking the
Design of the Internet: The End to End Arguments vs. the Brave New World,* 1 ACM TRANS-
ACTIONS ON INTERNET TECH. 70 (2001), *available at* http:// cyberlaw.stanford.edu/e2e/
papers/TPRC-Clark-Blumenthal.pdf (describing the benefits of end-to-end and how
those benefits are in tension with security concerns); Paul A. David, The Beginnings and
Prospective Ending of "End-to-End": An Evolutionary Perspective on the Internet's Architecture 26 (Stanford Econ. Dept., Working Paper, No. 01–012, 2001), *available at*
http://www-econ.stanford.edu/faculty/workp/swp01012.html (arguing that end-to-
end openness is a public good, the cost to society of its potential loss must be included
when considering more extensive security solutions); David P. Reed et al., Active Networking and End-to-End Arguments (Dec. 1, 2000) (unpublished paper from the Policy Implications of End-to-End workshop at Stanford Law School), http://cyberlaw
.stanford.edu/e2e/papers/Saltzer_Clark_Reed_ActiveNetworkinge2e.html (arguing for
the preservation of end-to-end and using end-to-end openness as an organizing principle against which to measure programmability and active networking).
3. For more about the value of amateur content creation, see YOCHAI BENKLER, WEALTH OF
NETWORKS 190–96 (2006); DAN GILLMOR, WE THE MEDIA (2006). For further discussion of amateur technological innovation, see *infra* Ch. 3.

CHAPTER 1. BATTLE OF THE BOXES

1. *See* Emerson W. Pugh, *Origins of Software Bundling,* IEEE ANNALS OF THE HISTORY OF COMPUTING, Jan.–Mar. 2002, at 57, 57–58; *see also* SIMSON GARFINKEL, DATABASE NATION: THE DEATH OF PRIVACY IN THE 21ST CENTURY 17–18 (2000).

2. GEOFFERY AUSTRIAN, HERMAN HOLLERITH: FORGOTTEN GIANT OF INFORMATION PROCESSING 52–53 (1982) ("Hollerith agreed to keep the machines in good condition and complete working order at his own expense. This mean[t] that he would also have to keep them proper[l]y connected. For, to tabulate different combinations of data, the wires leading from the press, where the holes on the cards were sensed, to the counters had to be resoldered between jobs. What was more, Hollerith was required to keep extra machines in readiness for 'instant connection.'").

3. *Id.* at 67. Hollerith's invention made the 1890 Census notable not only for the time saved in processing the data, but also for the huge financial savings that resulted from its implementation. "Before the Census, the Commission conducting the competitive test had projected that the tabulating machines would save $597,125 over previous methods. . . . In actual use, the strange-looking statistical pianos would save more than two years' time over the previous census and $5 million in taxpayers' money." *Id.* at 69.

4. *See* KEVIN MANEY, THE MAVERICK AND HIS MACHINE (2003) (discussing the transformation of Hollerith's Tabulating Machine Company into IBM); Burton Grad, *A Personal Recollection: IBM's Unbundling of Software and Services,* IEEE ANNALS OF THE HISTORY OF COMPUTING, Jan.–Mar. 2002, at 64, 64–71.

5. *See* Watts S. Humphrey, *Software Unbundling: A Personal Perspective,* IEEE ANNALS OF THE HISTORY OF COMPUTING, Jan.–Mar. 2002, at 59, 59–63 ("At the time of IBM's unbundling decision, IBM management worried that the Justice Department would view bundling as an anticompetitive practice. . . . [Bundling] made it more difficult for small firms to compete with IBM in almost any part of the rapidly growing computer business."); William D. Smith, *I.B.M. Readjusts Pricing Formula,* N.Y. TIMES, June 24, 1969, at 55.

6. *See* Lawrence O'Kane, *Computer a Help to 'Friendly Doc,'* N.Y. TIMES, May 22, 1966, at 348 (discussing the use of the Flexowriter for generating form letters for doctors' offices); Friden Flexowriter, http://www.blinkenlights.com/classiccmp/friden/ (last visited Apr. 1, 2007) (showing images of the Flexowriter and discussing its history).

7. *See* PAUL E. CERUZZI, A HISTORY OF MODERN COMPUTING 263–66, 268–69 (2d ed. 2003) (outlining the development of the modern personal computer for the period between 1977 and 1985); *see also* Mary Bellis, The History of the IBM PC—International Business Machines, http://inventors.about.com/library/weekly/aa031599.htm (last visited Apr. 20, 2007) (describing the development of IBM's first PC, which was released in 1981).

8. *See* Atari 8-Bit Computers: Frequently Asked Questions, http://www.faqs.org/faqs/atari-8-bit/faq/ (last visited Apr. 23, 2007); Computer History Museum, Timeline of Computer History: 1977, http://www.computerhistory.org/timeline/?year=1977 (last visited Apr. 20, 2007); Timex Sinclair 1000 Computer, http://oldcomputers.net/ts1000.html (last visited Apr. 20, 2007). *But see* Texas Instruments TI-99/4 Computer,

http://oldcomputers.net/ti994.html (last visited Apr. 20, 2007) (describing how a user had to purchase a monitor with the computer because no legal RF modulator allowing connection to a television set existed).

9. *See, e.g.,* Old-Computers.com, IBM PC-Model 5150, http://www.old-computers.com/museum/computer.asp?c=274 (last visited Apr. 20, 2007).

10. *See* WINN L. ROSCH, THE WINN L. ROSCH HARDWARE BIBLE 35–38 (6th ed. 2003).

11. While Radio Shack's project kits don't follow Moore's Law, they have been growing in size. The latest kit is 1000-in-1. The number of possibilities has seen punctuated equilibriums. A 100-in-1 kit was available in 1971, a 65-in-1 in 1972, a 160-in-1 in 1982, and a 200-in-1 in 1981. A gallery of some of the kits can be found online. *See* Science Fair Electronic Project Kit, http://musepat.club.fr/sfair.htm (last visited Apr. 20, 2007).

12. Such a device works on the principle that liars sweat, sweat changes skin resistance, and the kit's meter could measure it. *See* ALDERT VRIJ, DETECTING LIES AND DECEIT: THE PSYCHOLOGY OF LYING AND THE IMPLICATIONS FOR PROFESSIONAL PRACTICE 175–92 (2000); Posting of Phillip Torrone to MAKE Blog, *Lie Detector Electronic Kit and Circuit Explanation,* http://www.makezine.com/blog/archive/2006/01/lie_detector_electronic_kit_an.html (Jan. 19, 2006, 04:14); Wikipedia, *Galvanic Skin Response,* http://en.wikipedia.org/wiki/Galvanic_skin_response (as of Apr. 21, 2007, 00:00 GMT).

13. *See* PAUL FREIBERGER & MICHAEL SWAINE, FIRE IN THE VALLEY: THE MAKING OF THE PERSONAL COMPUTER 204 (2d ed. 2000).

14. *Id.* at 207.

15. *Id.* at 203, 214–15.

16. *Id.* at 164–65, 181–85.

17. *See* MARTIN CAMPBELL-KELLY, FROM AIRLINE RESERVATIONS TO SONIC THE HEDGEHOG: A HISTORY OF THE SOFTWARE INDUSTRY 276–79 (2003).

18. Brent Schlender & Henry Goldblatt, *Bill Gates and Paul Allen Talk,* FORTUNE, Oct. 2, 1995, at 68–86; *see also* MICROSOFT CORPORATION, INSIDE OUT: MICROSOFT—IN OUR OWN WORDS (2000).

19. *See, e.g.,* Microsoft Corp. v. United States, 530 U.S. 1301 (2000); Commission Decision No. Comp/C-3/37.792/ECC (2004); *see also* Steve Lohr, *Antitrust Suit Turns into a Partnership for Microsoft,* N.Y. TIMES, Oct. 12, 2005, at C2, *available at* http://www.nytimes.com/2005/10/12/technology/12soft.html?ex=1286769600&en=849f2175480efc0f&ei=5090&partner=rssuserland&emc=rss; Choe Sang-Hun, *Microsoft Settles Antitrust Suit over Windows in South Korea,* N.Y. TIMES, Nov. 12, 2005, at C3; News Release, No. 45/04, European Union, EU Commission Concludes Microsoft Investigation, Imposes Conduct Remedies and a Fine (Mar. 24, 2004), *available at* http://www.eurunion.org/News/press/2004/20040045.htm; Keith Regan, *Microsoft Says EU Overreached in Antitrust Case,* E-COMMERCE TIMES, Apr. 23, 2006, http://technewsworld.com/story/49878.html.

20. *See* John Hagel & Marc Singer, *Unbundling the Corporation,* HARV. BUS. REV., Mar.–Apr. 1999, at 133 (suggesting that the open architecture of the PC lowered costs of interaction between firms to the point where an "unbundled" market structure mutually benefited specialized producers of both hardware and software).

21. For documents related to the United States case, see U.S. Department of Justice, United

States v. Microsoft: Current Case, http://www.usdoj.gov/atr/cases/ms_index.htm. For information on the European Commission case, see Paul Meller, *EC Still Objects to Microsoft: Antitrust Case Says Monopoly Abuses Are Continuing,* S. F. CHRON., Aug. 7, 2003, at B1, *available at* http://www.sfgate.com/cgi-bin/article.cgi?file=/chronicle/archive/2003/08/07/BU27986.DTL&type=business.

22. Grad, *supra* note 4.

CHAPTER 2. BATTLE OF THE NETWORKS

1. In October 1984, 73 percent of home computers had been purchased in the previous two years. ROBERT KOMINSKI, U.S. DEP'T OF COMMERCE, COMPUTER AND INTERNET USE IN THE UNITED STATES: 1984, at 9 tbl.1 (1988), *available at* http://www.census.gov/population/www/socdemo/computer/p23–155.html. But over 50 percent of adults with a home computer, which were present in nearly seven million households, did not even use the machine; instead, their children were the primary users. *Id.* at 4. Among those who did brave the waters, "learning to use" was the most popular activity, followed by video games, household records, and word processing. *Id.* at 16 tbl.5.

By 1989, the number of computer-owning households had doubled. ROBERT KOMINSKI, U.S. DEP'T OF COMMERCE, COMPUTER AND INTERNET USE IN THE UNITED STATES: 1989, at 1 (1991), *available at* http://www.census.gov/population/www/socdemo/computer/p23-.html. And although children were still the proportionately dominant users (and in many cases the reason why the machine was purchased), adults had begun to use bulletin board services (5.7 percent) and e-mail (5.3 percent) on their PCs. *Id.* at 10, 16 tbl.5.

In 1997, PC home ownership had increased to over one-third of all households. ERIC C. NEWBURGER, U.S. DEP'T OF COMMERCE, COMPUTER USE IN THE UNITED STATES: 1997, at 1 (1999), *available at* http://www.census.gov/prod/99pubs/p20–522.pdf. But Internet use, no longer confined to tinkering PC owners in their homes, had grown to include 20 percent of all Americans. *Id.* at 9. Among adult Internet users, meanwhile, 65 percent connected from their homes, and most relied on the Net as an information resource. *Id.* at 10. Web browsing and e-mail now trailed only word processing among adult home users. *See* U.S. Census Bureau, Table 7: Purpose of Computer Use at Home by People 18 Years and Over: October 1997, http://www.census.gov/population/socdemo/computer/report97/tab07.pdf.

By 2003, 89 percent of home computer users browsed the Internet and used e-mail. Only the bare majority of users, 55.8 percent, engaged in word processing, the next most popular home activity. JENNIFER CHEESEMAN DAY ET AL., U.S. DEP'T OF COMMERCE, COMPUTER AND INTERNET USE IN THE UNITED STATES: 2003, at 12 tbl.F (2005), *available at* http://www.census.gov/prod/2005pubs/p23–208.pdf. Integration of the Internet into users' daily lives occurred at an accelerated pace between 1997 and 2003. The number of users who relied on the Net for daily news or personal communications increased by a factor of four during that period, and use of the Net for retail shopping increased by a factor of fifteen. *Id.* at 13 fig.8.

2. *See* Tim Wu, *Why Have a Telecommunications Law? Anti-Discrimination Norms in Com-*

munications, 5 J. TELECOMM. & HIGH TECH. L. 15, 31–35 (2006); *see also, e.g.,* Christopher S. Yoo, *Network Neutrality and the Economics of Congestion,* 94 GEO. L.J. 1847, 1878–79 (2006); Kevin Werbach, *The Federal Computer Commission,* 84 N.C. L. REV. 1, 18–22 (2005).

3. *See* Hush-A-Phone v. United States, 238 F.2d 266 (D.C. Cir. 1956).

4. *Id.* at 269.

5. *See* Use of the Carterfone Device in Message Toll Tel. Serv., 13 F.C.C. 2d 420 (1968). The FCC held that there was "no material distinction between a foreign attachment such as the Hush-A-Phone and an interconnection device such as the Carterfone . . . so long as the interconnection does not adversely affect the telephone company's operations or the telephone system's utility for others." *Id.* at 423–24.

6. Between 1985 and 1995, the percentage of American homes with answering machines increased from 13 percent to 52 percent. Peter Tuckel & Harry O'Neill, *A Profile of Telephone Answering Machine Owners and Screeners, in* AM. STATISTICAL ASS'N, PROCEEDINGS OF THE SURVEY RESEARCH METHODS, § 1157 (1995), *available at* http://www.amstat.org/sections/SRMS/Proceedings/papers/1995_201.pdf; *see also* Robert W. Oldendick & Michael W. Link, *The Answering Machine Generation: Who Are They and What Problem Do They Pose for Survey Research?,* 58 PUB. OPINION Q. 264, 268 tbl.2 (1994). The public's adoption of fax machines also accelerated during the 1980s; the number of fax machines in use increased from three hundred thousand to four million by the end of the decade. *See* Fax Machine History, http://www.ideafinder.com/history/inventions/fax.htm (last visited May 25, 2007).

7. *See Walled Gardens—A Brick Wall?,* Shosteck E-mail Briefing (Herschel Shosteck Assocs.), Mar. 2000 ("America Online (AOL) understands this. Originally conceived as a closed 'bulletin board' service, AOL gained market acceptance by creating a vast array of proprietary information which was regarded as superior to rivals of the day, including CompuServe and Prodigy. However, the arrival of the Internet forced AOL to open its doors. No matter how good the AOL proprietary content and services were, users demanded access to the millions of websites available on the World Wide Web, and Internet e-mail. Now, while AOL continues to gain revenue from its proprietary e-commerce services and advertising relationships, the firm's majority appeal is as an easy on-ramp to the Internet—in essence, an access provider with much less emphasis on specific content and services."); *see also* Josh Ramo, *How AOL Lost the Battles but Won the War,* TIME, Sept. 22, 1997, at 46 ("Retaining customers will become even harder as phone companies, cable companies, Microsoft, and Netscape make it even easier to use the Internet's open standards for browsing the Web, chatting and sending mail"); Frank Rose, *Keyword: Context,* WIRED, Dec. 1996, *available at* http://www.wired.com/wired/archive/4.12/ffaol.html ("AOL's strategy has been built on the notion that the Net would remain a cult attraction, unsuited to a mass market that can't handle anything more complicated than VCR . . . Yet as Wall Street and Madison Avenue fall increasingly under the Internet's spell, as tens of thousands of new websites blossom each month, and as the telcos and RBOCs muscle into the access business, the outlook for proprietary online services looks increasingly grim. CompuServe has been hemorrhaging 10,000 members a day.

General Electric's GEnie sank to 20,000 lonely members . . . Apple snipped the connection on its eWorld service. Could AOL be next?").

8. Amy Harmon, *Loyal Subscribers of Compuserve Are Fearing a Culture Clash in Its Takeover,* N.Y. TIMES, Feb. 16, 1998, at D8.

9. Peter H. Lewis, *A Boom for On-line Services,* N.Y. TIMES, July 12, 1994, at D1.

10. Harmon, *supra* note 8.

11. *See, e.g.,* Wikipedia, *Islands of Kesmai,* http://en.wikipedia.org/wiki/Islands_of_Kesmai (as of May 25, 2007 at 08:00 GMT).

12. Harmon, *supra* note 8.

13. Peter H. Lewis, *Adventures in Cyberspace,* N.Y. TIMES, Dec. 11, 1994, at A5. One variation was MCI Mail, which offered only e-mail (and, for a time, e-mail to postal mail) services and charged per e-mail sent. The service failed to, or at least chose not to, develop any services beyond its eponymous title. *See* L. R. Shannon, *MCI Mail Changes the Nature of Letters,* N.Y. TIMES, Nov. 9, 1993, at C13.

14. For instance, CompuServe featured the PROgramming area, which allowed subscribers to write and post software. *See, e.g.,* Ron Kovacs, *Editors Desk,* SYNDICATE zMAG., Feb. 7, 1989, *available at* http://www.atarimax.com/freenet/freenet_material/5.8-BitComputers SupportArea/11.Z-Magazine/showarticle.php?146.

15. For more on the ways in which the law treated services that chose different levels of intervention into user content, see Jonathan Zittrain, *The Rise and Fall of Sysopdom,* 10 HARV. J.L. & TECH. 495 (SUMMER 1997).

16. *See* Andrew Currah, Hollywood, the Internet and the Geographies of Disruptive Innovation (unpublished manuscript, on file with author); *see also* Mary J. Benner & Michael L. Tushman, *Exploitation, Exploration, and Process Management: The Productivity Dilemma Revisited,* 28 ACAD. MGMT. REV. 238, 239 (2003).

17. *See* Ross Rubin, *Players Scramble for Consumer Market,* INTERACTIVE HOME, Sept. 1, 1996; Steve Kovsky & Paula Rooney, *Online Service Providers Upgrade UIs,* PC WEEK, June 24, 1996, at 14.

18. A Little Microcomputer BBS History, http://www.portcommodore.com/bbshist.php?path=main-cbmidx-bbsidx (last visited June 1, 2007).

19. *See* HOWARD RHEINGOLD, THE VIRTUAL COMMUNITY, at xxiii–xxiv (1993), *available at* http://www.rheingold.com/vc/book/intro.html; Jack Rickard, *Home-Grown BBS,* WIRED, Sept.–Oct. 1993, at 42, *available at* http://www.wired.com/wired/archive/1.04/bbs.html.

20. *See* Tom Jennings, Fido and FidoNet, http://www.wps.com/FidoNet/index.html (last visited June 1, 2007); Living Internet, Bulletin Board Systems & FidoNet, http://www.livinginternet.com/u/ui_fidonet.htm (last visited June 1, 2007).

21. *Id.*

22. *See* Tom Jennings et al., FidoNet History and Operation (Feb. 8, 1985), http://www.rxn.com/~net282/fidonet.jennings.history.1.txt.

23. Some projects are exploring mesh networking technology as a way of networking devices together, and connecting them to the Internet backbone. *See, e.g.,* Nan Chen, *Wireless Mesh Networking for Developing Countries,* CONVERGE! NETWORK DIGEST, July 13,

2006, http://www.convergedigest.com/bpbbw/bp1.asp?ID=372&ctgy=; Neil Savage, *Municipal Mesh Network: Protocols Developed at MIT Are Helping the City of Cambridge to Go Wireless,* Tech. Rev., Feb. 27, 2006, http://www.technologyreview.com/InfoTech/wtr_16427,258,p1.html.

24. *See* Technology and Instruction, Accessing the Internet!, http://www.coastal.edu/education/ti/internetaccess.html (last visited June 1, 2007) ("In the late eighties and early nineties, [proprietary] online services enjoyed significant growth and prosperity, but today, they are a threatened industry, undermined significantly by the global push for standardization. Compuserve, GEnie, E-World, Podigy [*sic*] and many other online services all failed to recognize (or recognized too late) the dominance of HTML and other standard development languages for publishing Internet content.").

25. *See* ARPANET—The First Internet, http://livinginternet.com/i/ii_arpanet.htm (last visited June 1, 2007); IMP—Interface Message Processor, http://livinginternet.com/i/ii_imp.htm (last visited June 1, 2007).

26. *See* IMP—Interface Message Processor, *supra* note 25.

27. Press Release, Yahoo! Inc., Yahoo! Inc. Announces First Quarter Results (Apr. 22, 1996), *available at* http://yhoo.client.shareholder.com/press/ReleaseDetail.cfm?ReleaseID=173428.

28. Peter H. Lewis, *Yahoo Gets Big Welcome on Wall Street,* N.Y. times, Apr. 13, 1996, at 33 (reporting that the first day of trading "gave the young company a first-day market valuation of nearly $1 billion. . . . Goldman Sachs & Company set an offering price of $13 Thursday night on 2.6 million new shares, but the stock opened yesterday at $24.50 as demand outstripped supply. The shares rose quickly in very heavy trading to reach $43 before settling back to $33 at the end of the day"); Rose Aguilar, *Yahoo IPO Closes at $33 After $43 Peak,* CNET news.com, Apr. 12, 1996, http://news.com.com/Yahoo+IPO+closes+at+33+after+43+peak/2100–1033_3–209413.html ("Yahoo opened at about 8:45 a.m. PDT and shot up to $43 an hour later, which equals $1 billion for the company.").

29. *See* Barry M. Leiner et al., A Brief History of the Internet, http://www.isoc.org/internet/history/brief.shtml (last visited Dec. 2, 2007) ("[The Internet] started as the creation of a small band of dedicated researchers, and has grown to be a commercial success with billions of dollars of annual investment."); Barry M. Leiner et al., *The Past and Future History of the Internet,* Comm. ACM, Feb. 1997, at 102.

30. *See* Comm. on the Internet in the Evolving Info. Infrastructure, The Internet's Coming of Age 43 (2001).

31. *See* Richard T. Griffiths, The History of the Internet, Chapter Two: From ARPANET to World Wide Web, http://www.let.leidenuniv.nl/history/ivh/chap2.htm (last visited June 1, 2007) ("It is worth remembering, at this stage, that we are still [in the mid-1970s] in a World where we are talking almost exclusively about large mainframe computers (owned only by large corporations, government institutions and universities).").

32. *See* Leiner et al., A Brief History of the Internet, *supra* note 29 ("Internet was based on the idea that there would be multiple independent networks of rather arbitrary design, beginning with the ARPANET as the pioneering packet switching network. . . . In this

approach, the choice of any individual network technology was not dictated by a partic-ular network architecture but rather could be selected freely by a provider and made to interwork with the other networks through a meta-level 'Internetworking Architec-ture.'").

33. *See id.* ("Four ground rules were critical to [the early designs of the Internet]: [First, e]ach distinct network would have to stand on its own and no internal changes could be re-quired to any such network to connect it to the Internet. [Second, c]ommunications would be on a best effort basis. If a packet didn't make it to the final destination, it would shortly be retransmitted from the source. [Third, b]lack boxes would be used to connect the networks; these would later be called gateways and routers. There would be *no infor-mation retained by the gateways* about the individual flows of packets passing through them, thereby keeping them simple and avoiding complicated adaptation and recovery from various failure modes. [Fourth,] [*t*]*here would be no global control at the operations level*" (emphases added).).

34. DAVID D. CLARK, A CLOUDY CRYSTAL BALL 19 (1992), *available at* http://ietf20 .isoc.org/videos/future_ietf_92.pdf.

35. *See* COMM. ON THE INTERNET IN THE EVOLVING INFO. INFRASTRUCTURE, *supra* note 30, at 34–41 (discussing the design principles underlying the Internet that allowed for scal-able, distributed, and adaptive design); *see also* Leiner et al., A Brief History of the Inter-net, *supra* note 29 ("While there were other limited ways to interconnect different net-works, they required that one be used as a component of the other, rather than acting as a peer of the other in offering end-to-end service. In an open-architecture network, the individual networks may be separately designed and developed and each may have its own unique interface which it may offer to users and/or other providers, including [*sic*] other Internet providers.").

36. *See* Jay P. Kesan & Rajiv C. Shah, *Fool Us Once Shame on You—Fool Us Twice Shame on Us: What We Can Learn from the Privatizations of the Internet Backbone Network and the Domain Name System,* 79 WASH. U. L.Q. 89, 114 (2001).

37. *See id.* at 115–17. The new "border gateway protocol," or BGP, has proven central to In-ternet development.

38. *See* Trumpet Software Int'l, History, http://www.trumpet.com.au/history.html (last vis-ited June 1, 2007).

39. *See* John C. Dvorak, Winners for the 1995 Dvorak PC Telecommunications Excellence Awards, http://www.citivu.com/dvorak/95awds.html#winsock (last visited June 1, 2007).

40. Winsock experienced extremely wide distribution. *See* Trumpet Software Int'l, *supra* note 38 (discussing the "hundreds of thousands of Winsock packages to universities, government organisations, businesses, and domestic users around the world"); Tattam Software Enterprises About Us, http://www.tattsoft.com/aboutUs.htm (last visited Dec. 2, 2007) ("[S]ales grew exponentially and within months Peter had to leave his uni-versity job to nurture and grow the fledgling small business into a multi million dollar company"); CRISTINA CIFUENTES & ANNE FITZGERALD, COPYRIGHT IN SHAREWARE SOFTWARE DISTRIBUTED ON THE INTERNET—THE TRUMPET WINSOCK CASE, *in* PRO-CEEDINGS OF THE 19TH INTERNATIONAL CONFERENCE ON SOFTWARE ENGINEERING 456

(1997) (describing Winsock as gaining "an international reputation as the best available software for connecting to the Internet" and noting that guides to the Internet published during 1994 and 1995 invariably advised readers to use Trumpet Winsock for Internet connection.).

41. *See* Wikipedia, *Winsock,* http://en.wikipedia.org/wiki/Winsock (as of June 1, 2007, 11:00 GMT).

42. *See Walled Gardens—A Brick Wall?, supra* note 7 ("No matter how good the [America Online] proprietary content and services were, users demanded access to the millions of websites available on the world wide web, and Internet email."); *see also* Harmon, *supra* note 8 ("Compuserve's [*sic*] era as the home of choice for the technological elite really ended . . . when the service failed to quickly offer subscribers a path to the World Wide Web."); Robert Seidman, America Online's Elusive Exclusive with Time, Inc., IN, AROUND AND ONLINE, Jan. 6, 1995 ("America Online announced an expanded agreement with Time, Inc. that will bring the 'Entertainment Weekly' magazine to America Online. The press release from America Online also stated that the agreement extends their exclusive arrangement with *Time* Magazine—that *Time* couldn't be offered on any other online service.").

43. *See* Robert X. Cringely, *That Does Not Compute!,* PBS, Sept. 17, 1997, http://www.pbs.org/cringely/pulpit/1997/pulpit_19970917_000543.html ("Compuserve [*sic*], which couldn't decide whether it was a stodgy online service or a stodgy network provider doesn't have to be either. AOL, which couldn't decide whether it was an on-the-edge online service or an over-the-edge network provider, gets to stick to content and stop pissing off users by pretending to know what a modem is. . . . AOL not only becomes by far the largest online service, with almost 12 million users they will define what being an online service even means. Prodigy, Genie [*sic*], and the Microsoft Network will be lost in the noise: They mean nothing. From this point on, there will be only AOL and the Internet. But there is still a serious question of whether AOL can survive in the long term. . . . Unlike your local ISP, which spends nothing on content, AOL/Compuserve [*sic*] spend[s] a lot on content. And unlike the other emerging media companies like Yahoo, Excite, and even Netscape, which also spend a lot on content, AOL/Compuserve has to spend more money to maintain all those points of presence (PoPs) in every city.").

44. *See* Stephen C. Miller, *Point, Click, Shop till You Drop,* N.Y. TIMES, Apr. 20, 1995, at C2.

45. *See* Leiner et al., A Brief History of the Internet, *supra* note 29 ("The Internet has now become almost a 'commodity' service, and much of the latest attention has been on the use of this global information infrastructure for support of other commercial services. This has been tremendously accelerated by the widespread and rapid adoption of browsers and the World Wide Web technology, allowing users easy access to information linked throughout the globe. Products are available to facilitate the provisioning of that information and many of the latest developments in technology have been aimed at providing increasingly sophisticated information services on top of the basic Internet data communications.").

46. *See* J.H. Saltzer et al., *End-to-End Arguments in System Design,* 2 ACM TRANSACTIONS COMPUTER SYS. 277 (1984).

47. *See, e.g.,* Susan Brenner, *Private-Public Sector Cooperation in Combating Cybercrime: In Search of a Model,* 2 J. INT. COMM. L. & TECH. 58 (2007); Byron Hittle, *An Uphill Battle: The Difficulty of Deterring and Detecting Perpetrators of Internet Stock Fraud,* 54 FED. COMM. L.J. 165 (2001); K. A. Taipale, *Internet and Computer Crime: System Architecture as Crime Control* (Ctr. for Advanced Studies in Sci. & Tech. Policy Working Paper, 2003).
48. *See, e.g.,* Jerry Kang, *Information Privacy in Cyberspace Transactions,* 50 STAN. L. REV. 1193 (1998); Mark A. Lemley & Lawrence Lessig, *The End of End-to-End: Preserving the Architecture of the Internet in the Broadband Era,* 48 UCLA L. REV. 925 (2001); Joel R. Reidenberg, *Lex Informatica: The Formulation of Information Policy Rules Through Technology,* 76 TEXAS L. REV. 533 (1998).
49. Jonathan Zittrain, *Internet Points of Control,* 44 B.C. L. REV. 653 (2003).
50. Large Internet Service Providers peer with each other rather than paying for service, assuming that there is inherent shared value in the transfer of data. *See, e.g.,* Paul Milgrom et al., *Competitive Effects of Internet Peering Policies,* in THE INTERNET UPHEAVAL, 175–95 (Ingo Vogelsang & Benjamin M. Compaine eds., 2000); W. B. Norton, *The Evolution of the U.S. Internet Peering Ecosystem* (Equinix White Paper, 2004), *available at* http://www.nanog.org/mtg-0405/pdf/Norton.pdf.
51. David Clark, Address at Oxford Internet Institute on New Approaches to Research on the Social Implications of Emerging Technologies (Apr. 27, 2006).
52. *See* TSUKASA OGINO ET AL., STUDY OF AN EFFICIENT SERVER SELECTION METHOD FOR WIDELY DISTRIBUTED WEB SERVER NETWORKS (2000), http://www.isoc.org/inet2000/cdproceedings/1g/1g_1.htm ("In order to disperse the load on a Web server, generally the server cluster is configured to distribute access requests, or mirror servers are distributed geographically or situated on different networks."); *see also* Jonathan L. Zittrain, *The Generative Internet,* 119 HARV. L. REV. 1974, 1994 n.72 (2006) (mentioning companies that provide edge-caching services).
53. *See, e.g.,* Lemley & Lessig, *supra* note 48; Tim Wu, *Network Neutrality, Broadband Discrimination,* 2 J. TELECOMM. & HIGH TECH. L. 141 (2003).
54. *See* Burning Man, http://www.burningman.com/ (last visited Dec. 2, 2007); *see also* Xeni Jardin, *Burning Man Never Gets Old,* WIRED NEWS, Aug. 25, 2003, http://www.wired.com/culture/lifestyle/news/2003/08/60159.
55. *See* FCC, WIRELINE COMPETITION BUREAU, HIGH-SPEED SERVICES FOR INTERNET ACCESS: STATUS AS OF DECEMBER 31, 2004, at 6 (2005), *available at* http://www.fcc.gov/Bureaus/Common_Carrier/Reports/FCC-State_Link/IAD/hspd0705.pdf.

CHAPTER 3. CYBERSECURITY AND THE GENERATIVE DILEMMA

1. Bob Sullivan, *Remembering the Net Crash of '88,* MSNBC.COM, Nov. 1, 1998, *reprinted in* ZDNET.COM, http://news.zdnet.com/2100-9595_22-512570.html (last visited July 12, 2007).
2. *See* Joyce K. Reynolds, RFC 1135: The Helminthiasis of the Internet (Dec. 1989), http://www.ietf.org/rfcs/rfc1135; *see also* Internet Sys. Consortium, ISC Domain Survey: Number of Internet Hosts, http://www.isc.org/index.pl?/ops/ds/host-count-history

.php (last visited June 1, 2007) (cataloguing the number of Internet hosts from 1981 to present).

3. U.S. Gen. Accounting Office, GAO/IMTEC-89-57, Virus Highlights Need for Improved Internet Management (1989) [hereinafter GAO Report], *available at* www.gao.gov/cgi-bin/getrpt?IMTEC-89-57; *see generally* Mark W. Eichin & John A. Rochlis, With Microscope and Tweezers: An Analysis of the Internet Virus of November 1988 (1989) (paper presented at the IEEE Symposium on Security and Privacy) (providing a detailed analysis of the Morris worm and describing lessons learned by the Internet community in the immediate aftermath of the worm).

4. Sullivan, *supra* note 1.

5. Reynolds, *supra* note 2, § 1.1. For more on how worms behave, see generally Eugene H. Spafford, *Crisis and Aftermath,* 32 Comm. of the ACM 678 (1989), *available at* http://portal.acm.org/citation.cfm?id=63526.63527.

6. Reynolds, *supra* note 2, § 1.1.

7. Eugene H. Spafford, Purdue Tech. Rep. CSD-TR-933, The Internet Worm Incident (1991), *available at* http://homes.cerias.purdue.edu/~spaf/tech-reps/933.pdf; Eugene H. Spafford, Purdue Tech. Rep. CSD-TR-823, The Internet Worm Program (1988), *available at* http://homes.cerias.purdue.edu/~spaf/tech-reps/823.pdf.

8. Reynolds, *supra* note 2, § 1.2.

9. *Id.*

10. *See* Sullivan, *supra* note 1; *see also* Spafford, The Internet Worm Incident, *supra* note 7, § 3.3.

11. Sullivan, *supra* note 1; *see, e.g.,* James Bone, *Computer Virus at Pentagon,* The Times (London), Nov. 5, 1989; Philip J. Hilts, *'Virus' Hits Vast Computer Network; Thousands of Terminals Shut Down to Halt Malicious Program,* Wash. Post, Nov. 4, 1988, at A1; Tom Hundley, *Computer Virus Attack Called More Persistent Than Brilliant,* Chi. Trib., Nov. 7, 1988, at C4; John Markoff, *Author of Computer 'Virus' is Son of N.S.A. Expert on Data Security,* N.Y. Times, Nov. 5, 1988, § 1, at 1.

12. Ted Eisenberg et al., *The Cornell Commission: On Morris and the Worm,* 32 Comm. of the ACM 706, 707 (1989), *available at* http://portal.acm.org/citation.cfm?id=63526.63530 (publishing findings and dispelling myths about Morris and the worm).

13. GAO Report, *supra* note 3. The GAO used the occasion to make its report the first distributed over the Internet as well as on paper. The Internet was far smaller then: the GAO placed a quaint request on the report's cover page asking those who downloaded it to personally e-mail the author so he could manually tally the number of online readers.

14. Though there was initial discussion of legislation after the Morris incident, no federal legislation was passed. The Computer Abuse Amendments Act of 1994 was Congress's attempt to close loopholes identified in *United States v. Morris. See* Computer Abuse Amendments Act of 1994, Pub. L. No. 103-322, § 290001, 108 Stat. 1796 (1994); United States v. Morris, 928 F.2d 504, 506 (2d Cir. 1991); Michael W. Carroll & Robert Schrader, *Computer-Related Crimes,* 32 Am. Crim. L. Rev. 183, 196–97 (1995); John K. Markey & James F. Boyle, *New Crimes of the Information Age,* 43 Boston B.J. 10, 23 (1999). The Morris case remains a favorite example of those calling for more regulation

of cyber and computer crimes. *See, e.g.,* Michael Lee et al., *Electronic Commerce, Hackers, and the Search for Legitimacy: A Regulatory Proposal,* 14 BERKELEY TECH. L.J. 839, 872–73 (1999) (calling the expansion of the Computer Fraud and Abuse Act flawed); Joseph M. Olivenbaum, <CTRL><ALT><DEL>: *Rethinking Federal Computer Crime Legislation,* 27 SETON HALL L. REV. 574, 624–26 (1997).

15. GAO REPORT, *supra* note 3.

16. *Id.* § 3.1.

17. Spafford, *supra* note 5, at 685; *see* U.S. Department of Homeland Security Announces Partnership with Carnegie Mellon (Sept. 15, 2003), http://www.cert.org/about/US-CERT.html.

18. Eisenberg, *supra* note 12, at 709.

19. *Id.* at 709.

20. *Id.*

21. *Id.*

22. *See* U.S. v. Morris, 928 F.2d 504, 506 (2d Cir. 1991); Mathew Cain, *Morris Avoids Prison for Internet Worm,* MIS WEEK, May 7, 1990, at 1; *see generally* Susan M. Mello, Comment, *Administering the Antidote to Computer Viruses: A Comment on* United States v. Morris, 19 RUTGERS COMPUTER & TECH. L.J. 259 (1993).

23. Press Release, Yahoo! Media Relations, Yahoo! To Acquire Viaweb, June 8, 1988, http://docs.yahoo.com/docs/pr/release184.html.

24. *See* Robert Morris, Personal Web site, http://pdos.csail.mit.edu/~rtm/.

25. *See* Reynolds, *supra* note 2. Helminthiasis is an infestation of parasitic worms in the body. *See* Wikipedia, *Helminthiasis,* http://en.wikipedia.org/wiki/Helminthiasis (as of June 1, 2007, 08:00 GMT).

26. Reynolds, *supra* note 2, §§ 1.3–1.4.

27. *Id.* § 1.4.

28. Ron Rosenbaum, *Secrets of the Little Blue Box,* ESQUIRE, Oct. 1971, at 119. For accounts from an individual claiming to be an original "phone phreaker," see James Daly, *John Draper,* FORBES, June 3, 1996, at 138; John T. Draper, Cap'n Crunch in Cyberspace, http://www.webcrunchers.com/crunch/story.html (last visited June 1, 2007) (John T. Draper is also known as Cap'n Crunch).

29. Rosenbaum, *supra* note 28, at 120.

30. *Id.*

31. Amy Harmon, *Defining the Ethics of Hacking,* L.A. TIMES, Aug. 12, 1994, at A1.

32. Wikipedia, *Signaling System #7,* http://en.wikipedia.org/wiki/Signaling_System_7 (as of Aug. 15, 2007, 15:00 GMT).

33. Harmon, *supra* note 31.

34. *Id.*

35. Sullivan, *supra* note 1.

36. Spafford, *supra* note 5, at 678–81.

37. *Id.* at 680.

38. *Id.*

39. Matt Blaze, *Cryptography Policy and the Information Economy,* WINDOWSECURITY.COM,

Apr. 5, 2000, *available at* http://windowsecurity.com/whitepapers/cryptography_Policy _and_the_Information_Economy.html.

40. Increases in computer crime have received attention from the hacker community. *See* Harmon, *supra* note 31; *see also* PEKKA HIMANEN & LINUS TORVALDS, THE HACKER ETHIC (2001); BRUCE STERLING, THE HACKER CRACKDOWN: LAW AND DISORDER ON THE ELECTRONIC FRONTIER (2002), *available at* http://www.mit.edu/hacker/hacker .html; *cf.* Note, *Immunizing the Internet, Or: How I Learned to Stop Worrying and Love the Worm,* 119 HARV. L. REV. 2442 (2006) (introducing the idea of "beneficial cybercrime," which values system attacks for their tendency to draw attention to vulnerabilities in computer networks).

41. Eisenberg, *supra* note 12.

42. Reuters News Agency, *Latest MyDoom Outbreak Spreads,* TORONTO STAR, Feb. 26, 2004, at D5; Wikipedia, *Mydoom (Computer Worm),* http://en.wikipedia.org/wiki/Mydoom (as of June 1, 2007, 10:00 GMT); *see also* U.S. v. Morris, 928 F.2d 504, 506 (2d Cir. 1991) (quantifying the damage caused by the Morris worm by measuring the "estimated cost of dealing with the worm at each installation").

43. Wikipedia, *ILOVEYOU,* http://en.wikipedia.org/wiki/VBS/Loveletter (as of Apr. 6, 2007, 10:00 GMT); *see also* D. Ian Hopper, *'ILOVEYOU' Computer Bug Bites Hard, Spreads Fast,* CNN.COM, May 4, 2000, http://archives.cnn.com/2000/TECH/com puting/05/04/iloveyou.01/ ("Files associated with Web development, including '.js' and '.css' files, will be overwritten . . . . The original file is deleted. [The virus] also goes after multimedia files, affecting JPEGs and MP3s. Again, it deletes the original file and overwrites it . . . .").

44. *See* Wikipedia, *supra* note 43.

45. Robert Lemos, *Michelangelo Virus—Is It Overhyped or a Real Threat?,* ZDNET NEWS, Mar. 5, 1998, http://news.zdnet.com/2100-9595_22-508039.html. Amazingly, a few copies of the 1992 virus were still circulating in 1998.

46. *See, e.g.,* Paul W. Ewald, *Guarding Against the Most Dangerous Emerging Pathogens: In sights from Evolutionary Biology,* 2 EMERGING INFECTIOUS DISEASES, 245, 246 (Oct.– Dec. 1996) ("Like the traditional view of host/parasite coevolution, the modern view identifies host illness as a potential liability for the pathogen. When pathogens rely on the mobility of their current host to reach susceptible hosts, the illness caused by intense exploitation typically reduces the potential for transmission.").

47. *See generally* Randolph Court & Robert D. Atkinson, Progressive Pol'y Inst., How to Can Spam: Legislative Solutions to the Problem of Unsolicited Commercial E-mail (Nov. 1, 1999), http://www.ppionline.org/ndol/print.cfm?contentid=1349.

48. *See, e.g.,* JEFF FERRELL, CRIMES OF STYLE: URBAN GRAFFITI AND THE POLITICS OF CRIM INALITY (2005). Graffiti has been described as an example of artistic rather than financial entrepreneurship.

49. John Horrigan, Broadband Penetration on the Upswing: 55% of Adult Internet Users Have Broadband at Home or Work (Apr. 19, 2004), *available at* http://www.pewinternet .org/PPF/r/121/report_display.asp.

50. The respective numbers are 42 percent for broadband and 22 percent for dial-up. *See* John B. Horrigan, Home Broadband Adoption 2006, at 1, 9 (2006), http://www.pewinternet

.org/pdfs/PIP_Broadband_trends2006.pdf. Over the past year, there has been an almost 40 percent increase in the number of broadband lines worldwide. *See* Vince Chook, World Broadband Statistics: Q2 2006, at i–ii, 2 (2006), http://www.point-topic.com/content /dslanalysis/World + Broadband + Statistics + Q2 + 2006.pdf.

51. America Online & Nat'l Cyber Security Alliance, AOL/NCSA Online Safety Study 2 (Dec. 2005), http://www.staysafeonline.org/pdf/safety_study_2005.pdf.

52. *See, e.g.,* Jeremy Reimer, *Security Researchers Uncover Massive Attack on Italian Web Sites,* Ars Technica, June 18, 2007, http://arstechnica.com/news.ars/post/20070618-security -researchers-uncover-massive-attack-on-italian-web-sites.html (reporting on the compromise of Italian Web sites by malicious IFRAME code, made available for a fee by Russian crime organizations).

53. Tim Weber, *Criminals 'May Overwhelm the Web,'* BBC News, Jan. 25, 2007, http://news.bbc.co.uk/2/hi/business/6298641.stm.

54. *Id.*

55. Anestis Karasaridis et al., Wide-scale Botnet Detection and Characterization (2007), www.usenix.org/events/hotbots07/tech/full_papers/karasaridis/karasaridis.pdf. Existing studies attempting to identify compromised computers are hard-pressed to keep up. Operation Bot Roast, headed by the FBI, has uncovered only a comparatively tiny one million botnet computers in the United States. *See FBI Tries to Fight Zombie Hordes,* BBC News, June 14, 2007, http://news.bbc.co.uk/2/hi/technology/6752853.stm.

56. Posting of Bob Sullivan to The Red Tape Chronicles, Is Your Computer a Criminal?, http://redtape.msnbc.com/2007/03/bots_story.html (Mar. 27, 2007, 10:00 GMT).

57. Luke Dudney, Internet Service Providers: The Little Mans Firewall (2003), http://www.sans.org/reading_room/whitepapers/casestudies/1340.php.

58. *Id.* at 5.

59. According to IronPort, over 80 percent of the world's spam is currently sent by zombie computers. *See* Press Release, IronPort, Spammers Continue Innovation (June 28, 2006), http://www.ironport.com/company/ironport_pr_2006-06-28.html.

60. *Symantec's Top Threats, in* Symantec Home and Office Security Report 4 (2006), http://www.symantec.com/content/en/us/home_homeoffice/media/pdf/SHHOS _Dec06_NL_Final.pdf.

61. *See* Laura Frieder & Jonathan Zittrain, Spam Works: Evidence from Stock Touts and Corresponding Market Activity (Harv. Pub. L. Working Paper No. 135), *available at* http://ssrn.com/abstract=920553.

62. *See* Posting of Bob Sullivan to The Red Tape Chronicles, Virus Gang Warfare Spills onto the Net, http://redtape.msnbc.com/2007/04/virus_gang_warf.html (Apr. 3, 2007, 10:00 GMT).

63. *Id.*

64. *See* Deborah Radcliff, *When World of Warcraft Spreads to Your World,* ComputerWorld Security, Apr. 16, 2007, at http://computerworld.com/action/article.do?command =viewArticleBasic&articleId=9016684 (detailing recent exploits of the MMOG World of Warcraft, and noting that users' poor password practices—a study finds that 45 percent of respondents admitted to using one or very few passwords for multiple accounts—means one password stolen can allow access to multiple sites).

65. *See* Symantec Corp., W32.Sobig.F@mm, http://www.symantec.com/security_response/writeup.jsp?docid=2003-081909-2118-99 (last visited June 1, 2007) (providing a summary and removal details about the worm known as W32.Sobig.F@mm).

66. *See* John Leyden, *US State Department Rooted by 0-day Word Attack,* THE REGISTER, Apr. 19, 2007, http://www.theregister.co.uk/2007/04/19/us_state_dept_rooted/.

67. *See* Karasaridis, *supra* note 55.

68. *See* Sullivan, *supra* note 56.

69. *Id.*

70. CERT has also noted another threat, evidenced by the exploding number of incidents of application attacks as Web sites increasingly link Web pages to company databases. *See* Bee Ware, The Risk of Application Attacks Securing Web Applications (Jan. 7, 2005), http://www.securitydocs.com/library/2839.

71. IBM INTERNET SECURITY SYSTEMS, IBM INTERNET SECURITY SYSTEMS X-FORCE 2006 TREND STATISTICS 4 (2007), http://www.iss.net/documents/whitepapers/X_Force_Exec_Brief.pdf.

72. *Id.* at 7–8.

73. Internet Sys. Consortium, *supra* note 2.

74. THOMAS M. LENARD & DANIEL B. BRITTON, THE DIGITAL ECONOMY FACT BOOK 38 (8th ed. 2006), *available at* http://www.pff.org/issues-pubs/books/factbook_2006.pdf.

75. *Id.* at 8, 18.

76. *Id.* at 9.

77. *Id.* at 35–40.

78. *See, e.g.,* Common Malware Enumeration: Reducing Public Confusion During Malware Outbreaks, http://cme.mitre.org/ (last visited June 1, 2007).

79. Bill Gertz & Rowan Scarborough, *Inside the Ring—Notes from the Pentagon,* WASH. TIMES, Jan. 5, 2007, at A5, *available at* http://www.gertzfile.com/gertzfile/ring011207.html.

80. Ryan Naraine, *Microsoft Says Recovery from Malware Becoming Impossible,* EWEEK.COM, Apr. 4, 2006, http://www.eweek.com/article2/0,1895,1945808,00.asp.

81. Edu. Tech. Program, Costal Carolina Univ., Accessing the Internet, http://www.coastal.edu/education/ti/internetaccess.html (last visited Apr. 6, 2007); John B. Horrigan & Lee Rainie, The Broadband Difference: How Online Americans' Behavior Changes with High-Speed Internet Connections at Home (June 23, 2002), *available at* http://www.pewinternet.org/PPF/r/63/report_display.asp.

82. The first academic application of the term "virus" to computer software has been attributed to Leonard Adleman, a professor of computer science and molecular biology at the University of Southern California. *See* Wikipedia, *Computer Virus,* http://en.wikipedia.org/wiki/Computer_virus#Etymology (as of June 1, 2007, 10:05 GMT); *see also* Fred Cohen, *Computer Viruses: Theory and Experiments,* 6 COMPUTERS & SECURITY 22 (1987) (presenting research on the potential harm computer virus could cause and potential defenses).

83. *Cf.* WebMD, *What We Know About the Flu Virus,* http://www.webmd.com/cold-and-flu/flu-guide/how-do-flu-viruses-work (last visited June 1, 2007).

84. *See* Paul Ohm, *The Myth of the Superuser*, 41 U. C. DAVIS L. REV. (forthcoming 2008).

85. Susannah Fox et al., The Future of the Internet: In a Survey, Technology Experts and Scholars Evaluate Where the Network Is Headed in the Next Few Years, at i (Jan. 9, 2005), *available at* http://www.pewinternet.org/PPF/r/145/report_display.asp.

86. *See* Scott Berinato, *The Future of Security*, COMPUTERWORLD, Dec. 30, 2003, http://www .computerworld.com/printthis/2003/0,4814,88646,00.html (attributing the first use of "digital Pearl Harbor" to D. James Bidzos in 1991, later taken up by U.S. cybersecurity czar Richard Clarke); *see also* David Farber, *Balancing Security and Liberty*, 5 IEEE INTERNET COMPUTING 96 (2001) (discussing the possibility of a terrorist attack over the Internet in tandem with conventional terrorist attacks).

87. Mike Reiter & Pankaj Rohatgi, *Homeland Security*, 8 IEEE INTERNET COMPUTING 16, (2004), *available at* http://csdl2.computer.org/persagen/DLAbsToc.jsp?resourcePath =/dl/mags/ic/&toc=comp/mags/ic/2004/06/w6toc.xml&DOI=10.1109/MIC .2004.62; *see also* Drew Clark, *Computer Security Officials Discount Chances of 'Digital Pearl Harbor*,' NAT'L J. TECH. DAILY, June 3, 2003, *available at* www.govexec.com/ dailyfed/0603/060303td2.htm (reporting on experts' discounting of Internet viruses as a mode of terrorism, while acknowledging some of the risks of more run-of-the-mill security compromises).

88. E-mail from Christina Olson, Project Manager, StopBadware.org, to Jonathan Zittrain (Mar. 16, 2007, 22:12:20 EDT) (on file with the author, who is a principal investigator of the StopBadware project).

89. Niels Provos et al., The Ghost in the Browser (2007), http://www.usenix.org/events/ hotbots07/tech/full_papers/provos/provos.pdf.

90. The sheer magnitude of phishing activities suggests it is effective at seizing sensitive information. As one study monitoring a widely used antispam system reported, "In 2006 Symantec's Brightmail system blocked 2,848,531,611 phishing emails. Of these, 323,725 were unique phishing messages. On average, therefore, in 2006 there were 7.8 million blocked phishing attempts and 887 unique phishing messages *each day*." Zulfikar Ramzan & Candid Wüest, Phishing Attacks: Analyzing Trends in 2006 (2007), www.ceas.cc/2007/papers/paper-34.pdf (emphasis added).

91. Some early versions of two-factor authentication, such as identifying a preselected picture on a bank's Web site customized to the customer, are in fact not very secure. *See* Jim Youll, Why SiteKey Can't Save You (Aug. 24, 2006), http://www.cr-labs.com/publications /WhySiteKey-20060824.pdf. More promising versions require new hardware such as USB dongles or biometric readers on PCs—a fingerprint or retina scanner that can be used in addition to a password to authenticate oneself to a bank. It remains difficult to unambiguously authenticate the bank to the user.

92. StopBadware.org, Report on Jessica Simpson Screensaver, http://www.stopbadware .org/reports/reportdisplay?reportname=jessica (last visited June 1, 2007).

93. StopBadware.org, Report on FunCade, http://www.stopbadware.org/reports/reportdisplay?reportname=funcade (last visited June 1, 2007). For many programs, including FunCade and KaZaA, uninstalling the main program does not uninstall all the undesirable software originally installed along with it. Users must be knowledgeable enough to identify and remove the software manually.

94. *See* IntelliAdmin, Security Flaw in RealVNC 4.1.1 (last updated June 2006), http://www.intelliadmin.com/blog/2006/05/security-flaw-in-realvnc-411.html.

95. *See* Willie Sutton & Edward Linn, Where the Money Was: The Memoirs of a Bank Robber (1976).

96. Microsoft TechNet, 10 Immutable Laws of Security, http://www.microsoft.com/tech net/archive/community/columns/security/essays/10imlaws.mspx?mfr=true (last visited June 1, 2007).

97. *Id.*

98. *Id.*

99. *Cf.* Madeline Drexler, Secret Agents: The Menace of Emerging Infections (2002). For an excerpt, see http://www.pbs.org/wgbh/pages/frontline/shows/meat/safe/o157.html.

100. *Id.*

101. Philippe Biondi and Fabrice Desclaux were the two scientists. *See* Black Hat Europe 2006 Topics and Speakers, http://www.blackhat.com/html/bh-europe-06/bh-eu-06-speakers.html#Biondi (last visited June 1, 2007).

102. Philippe Biondi & Fabrice Desclaux, Presentation at Black Hat Europe: Silver Needle in the Skype 95 (Mar. 2–3, 2006). For slides, see http://blackhat.com/presentations/bh-europe-06/bh-eu-06-biondi/bh-eu-06-biondi-up.pdf.

103. *See* Microsoft Xbox, http://www.microsoft.com/xbox/ (last visited June 1, 2007).

104. *See* Tim Hartford, *Xbox Economics, Part 2,* slate, Dec. 21, 2005, http://www.slate.com/id/2132988/.

105. Microsoft was found to have abused its Windows monopoly for far less restrictive behavior that gave its own application writers an advantage against independent software producers. *See* United States v. Microsoft Corp., 97 F. Supp. 2d 59 (D.D.C. 2000) (order); United States v. Microsoft Corp., 87 F. Supp. 2d 30 (D.D.C. 2000) (conclusions of law); United States v. Microsoft Corp., 84 F. Supp. 2d 9 (D.D.C. 2000) (findings of fact); Commission Decision in Case COMP/C-3.

106. Tim Wu, *Wireless Carterfone,* 1 Int'l J. Comm. 389, 404–415 (2007), *available at* http://ijoc.org/ojs/index.php/ijoc/article/view/152/96.

107. *See* AMD, Telmex: Internet Box, http://www.amd.com/us-en/ConnectivitySolutions/ProductInformation/0,,50_2330_12264_14265,00.html (last visited June 1, 2007).

108. *See* MythTV, http://www.mythtv.org.

109. *See, e.g.,* Microsoft TechNet, Troubleshooting Windows Firewall Problems (last updated Mar. 28, 2005), http://technet2.microsoft.com/windowsserver/en/library/e5e9d65e-a4ff-405c-9a1d-a1135523e91c1033.mspx?mfr=true (offering advice to users encountering problems running software because of their firewalls); Victor Paulsamy & Samir Chatterjee, *Network Convergence and the NAT/Firewall Problems,* Proceedings of the 36th Hawaii International Conference on System Sciences (Jan. 2003), at http://doi.ieeecomputersociety.org/10.1109/HICSS.2003.1174338 (analyzing solutions to problems caused by firewalls in the deployment of VOIP software).

110. Reynolds, *supra* note 2.

111. U.S. GAO, *supra* note 3; *see also* Patricia Wallace, The Internet in the Workplace 33 (2004).

PART II. AFTER THE STALL

1. Benkler points out that, since 2002, IBM's revenues from Linux-related services have exceeded those for intellectual property transfer, licensing, and royalties. Yochai Benkler, The Wealth of Networks 47 (2006).

CHAPTER 4. THE GENERATIVE PATTERN

1. *See* Kevin Burns, TCP/IP Analysis and Troubleshooting Toolkit 5–28 (2003), *available at* http://www.wiley.com (search for ISBN "978-0-471-42975-3" and select "Read Excerpt 1") (describing the seven-layer OSI protocol model and the four-layer DOD protocol model, the two foundational network communications protocols).
2. Thus this book's earlier description, in Chapter One, of four layers: technology, including physical and protocol; application; content; and social.
3. *See infra* note 72.
4. Microsoft and Apple have both shown interest in becoming one-stop shops for applications that run on their respective platforms. Software packages like Office and iLife suggest the broad market that their respective makers hope to capture. *See* Apple, iLife, http://www.apple.com/ilife (last visited May 16, 2007); Microsoft, Office Products, http://www.microsoft.com/products (select "Office" from left-hand navigation bar) (last visited May 16, 2007). This all-in-one approach does carry some legal risks: for example, in a recent antitrust case, Microsoft was accused of putting a thumb on the scale for its own browser, not by designing its system to exclude new code, but by exploiting the power of system default options. *See* United States v. Microsoft Corp., 159 F.R.D. 318, 321 (D.D.C. 1995) (discussing the antitrust investigation against Microsoft and subsequent charges).
5. *See* John Markoff, *Apple Earnings Bolstered by iPod and Notebook Sales,* N.Y. Times, July 20, 2006, at C3 (reporting Apple's 4.6 percent share of the U.S. PC market).
6. *See* Donald A. Norman, The Invisible Computer 52 (1998) (arguing that the usefulness of a tool for a particular task is the key virtue of "information appliances"). Indeed, "the primary motivation behind the information appliance is clear: simplicity. Design the tool to fit the task so well that the tool becomes a part of the task . . . . The primary advantages of appliances come from their ability to provide a close fit with the real needs of their users, combined with the simplicity and elegance that arises from focus upon a simple activity." *Id.*
7. In fact, Norman argues that multifunction tools are not necessarily preferable to tools featuring fewer functions: "Take another look at the Swiss Army knife, one of those knives with umpteen blades. Sure, it is fun to look at, sure it is handy if you are off in the wilderness and it is the only tool you have, but of all the umpteen things it does, none of them are done particularly well." *Id.* at 71.
8. Historically, the adjective "plastic" has meant "moldable" or "sculptable," from Greek;

about a century ago it came to refer to a new class of materials capable of being molded in a soft or molten state, then hardened. *See* OXFORD ENGLISH DICTIONARY (2d ed. revised 2005) ("plastic: adjective . . . [of substances or materials] easily shaped or moulded: rendering the material more plastic; relating to moulding or modelling in three dimensions, or to produce three-dimensional effects: the plastic arts; [in science and technology] of or relating to the permanent deformation of a solid without fracture by the temporary application of force . . . from French plastique or Latin plasticus, from Greek plastikos, from plassein 'to mould'); *see also* Lawrence Lessig, *Social Norms, Social Meaning, and the Economic Analysis of Law,* 27 J. LEGAL STUD. 661 (1998).

9. GNU, The Free Software Definition, http://www.gnu.org/philosophy/free-sw.html (last visited May 16, 2007). This definition should not be confused with Franklin D. Roosevelt's Four Freedoms. *See* Franklin D. Roosevelt, President of the United States, Annual Message to Congress ("Four Freedoms Speech") (Jan. 6, 1941), *in* 87 Cong. Rec. 44, 46–47 (1941), *available at* http://www.ourdocuments.gov/doc.php?flash=true&doc=70&page=pdf.

10. Cooperative Linux is an example of a free, open source method for running Linux on Microsoft Windows. *See* coLinux, http://www.colinux.org (last visited May 16, 2007). Conversely, Wine is an open source implementation of Windows on top of Unix. *See* WineHQ, http://www.winehq.com (last visited May 16, 2007).

11. The Free Software Foundation is working to change its licenses to prohibit bolting a generative system inside a non-generative one. *See* Free Software Found., GPLv3, http://gplv3.fsf.org (last visited May 16, 2007) (discussing the rationale for the new provisions).

12. For a general discussion of objective affordances, see James J. Gibson, *The Theory of Affordances, in* PERCEIVING, ACTING, AND KNOWING (Robert Shaw & John Bransford eds., 1978). For a discussion of subjective affordances, see DONALD A. NORMAN, THE PSYCHOLOGY OF EVERYDAY THINGS (1998), which defines "affordance" as "the perceived and actual properties of the thing, primarily those fundamental properties that determine just how the thing could possibly be used." *Id.* at 9. For example, a "chair *affords* ('is for') support and, therefore, *affords* sitting." (emphasis added). *Id.*

13. *See, e.g.,* LAWRENCE LESSIG, THE FUTURE OF IDEAS: THE FATE OF THE COMMONS IN A CONNECTED WORLD (2002).

14. *See* Brett M. Frischmann, *An Economic Theory of Infrastructure and Commons Management,* 89 MINN. L. REV. 917, 918–19 (2005).

15. Tim Wu, *Network Neutrality, Broadband Discrimination,* 2 J. TELECOMM. & HIGH TECH. LAW 141, 145–47 (2003).

16. *See, e.g.,* CLAYTON M. CHRISTENSEN, THE INNOVATOR'S DILEMMA: WHEN NEW TECHNOLOGIES CAUSE GREAT FIRMS TO FAIL xiii–xvii (1997); Rebecca Henderson, *The Innovator's Dilemma as a Problem of Organizational Competence,* 23 J. PRODUCT INNOVATION MGMT. 5, 6–7 (2006).

17. *See* Cubby, Inc. v. CompuServe, Inc., 766 F. Supp. 135, 139–40 (S.D.N.Y. 1991) (discussing the nature of CompuServe's involvement in running the forums).

18. *See* ADVANCES IN BEHAVIORAL ECONOMICS (Colin F. Camerer, George Loewenstein & Matthew Rabin eds., 2003); Christine Jolls, Cass R. Sunstein & Richard Thaler, *A Be-*

havioral Approach to Law and Economics, 50 STAN. L. REV. 1471 (1998); Daniel Kahneman & Amos Tversky, *Prospect Theory: An Analysis of Decision Under Risk,* 47 ECONOMETRICA 263 (1979).

19. *See* Cass R. Sunstein, INFOTOPIA 80 (2006).

20. Tim Wu, *Wireless Carterfone,* 1 INT'L. J. COMM. 389, 404–15 (2007), *available at* http://ijoc.org/ojs/index.php/ijoc/article/view/152/96.

21. *See id.* at 419.

22. Andrew Currah, *Hollywood, the Internet and the World: A Geography of Disruptive Innovation,* 14 INDUSTRY & INNOVATION 359 (2007).

23. *Id.*

24. *See* CHRISTENSEN, *supra* note 16.

25. *Id.* at 15 (footnote omitted).

26. *Id.* at 24.

27. *See* Henderson, *supra* note 16.

28. *See* Mary J. Benner & Michael L. Tushman, *Exploitation, Exploration, and Process Management: The Productivity Dilemma Revisited,* 28 ACAD. MGMT. REV. 238, 240 (2003).

29. *See* Google Jobs, http://www.google.com/support/jobs/bin/static.py?page=about .html (last visited May 16, 2007).

30. *See supra* Ch. 2, p. 12.

31. *See* Intermatic, Inc. v. Toeppen, 947 F. Supp. 1227 (N.D. Ill. 1996) (discussing the actions of Dennis Toeppen, who registered over two hundred domain names associated with leading companies which had neglected to register those names themselves).

32. *See* Joshua Quittner, *Billions Registered,* WIRED NEWS, Oct. 1994, http://www .wired.com/wired/archive/2.10/mcdonalds.html.

33. According to Alexa.com, which monitors Internet traffic, as of March 2, 2007, Ebay.com was the seventh-most-visited Web site in the United States, and Craigslist.org was the tenth. *See* Alexa.com, http://www.alexa.com/site/ds/top_sites?cc=US&ts_ mode=country&lang=none (last visited Sep. 29, 2007).

34. *See* CHRIS ANDERSON, THE LONG TAIL: WHY THE FUTURE OF BUSINESS IS SELLING LESS OF MORE 50–51 (2006).

35. *See, e.g.,* ERIC VON HIPPEL, DEMOCRATIZING INNOVATION 19 (2005); ERIC VON HIPPEL, THE SOURCES OF INNOVATION 25 (1988); Eric Von Hippel, Christoph Hienerth, & Peter Kragh, Slides: Users as Innovators: Implications for Denmark's User-Centered Innovation Initiative Address at Copenhagen Business School (on file with author).

36. *See* William E. Splinter, *Center-pivot Irrigation,* 234 SCI. AM. 90 (June 1976); Eric von Hippel, Remarks at the Berkman Center for Internet and Society (Aug. 30, 2007) (notes on file with author).

37. Eric von Hippel, *supra* note 36; REI, CamelBak, http://www.rei.com/product/733668 (last visited Sep. 28, 2007).

38. *See* Mark Brogan, *Clock Speed: A Provenance Retrospective on Two Decades of Personal Computing,* PROVENANCE, Mar. 1996, http://www.netpac.com/provenance/vol1/no2/ features/clkspd3.htm.

39. *See* Laura Dunphy, *Star Search,* L.A. BUS. J., Mar. 13, 2000, at 1 (reporting that it costs

the recording industry approximately $1 million to launch a new recording artist); Jennifer Ordonez, *Behind the Music: MCA Spent Millions on Carly Hennessy—Haven't Heard of Her?—Pop Hopeful's Washout Is All-Too-Familiar Tune,* WALL ST. J., Feb. 26, 2002, at A1 (reporting that of the thousands of albums released in the United States each year by the five major recording companies, fewer than 5 percent become profitable).

40. *See* LARRY DOWNES & CHUNKA MUI, UNLEASHING THE KILLER APP: DIGITAL STRATEGIES FOR MARKET DOMINANCE (1998); *see also Simple Programs Make File Sharing Inevitable,* NEW SCIENTIST, Jan. 8, 2005, at 20, *available at* http://www.newscientist.com/article.ns?id=mg18524812.900 (discussing Tiny P2P, a peer-to-peer file-sharing program written by Edward Felten of Princeton University that consists of only fifteen lines of code).

41. *See generally* DAVID BOTH, A SHORT HISTORY OF OS/2 (2002), *available at* http://www.millennium-technology.com/HistoryOfOS2.html (providing a general history of the IBM OS/2 operating system).

42. *See* Frederic E. Davis, *Open Letter,* RED HERRING, Oct. 1, 1995, *available at* http://www.weblust.com/writing/herring2.html.

43. *See* Jay P. Kesan & Rajiv C Shah, *Deconstructing Code,* 6 YALE J. L. & TECH. 277, 292–97 (2004).

44. *See* Posting of Moorman to Forums: SourceForge.net, http://sourceforge.net/forum/forum.php?forum_id=425379 (Nov. 23, 2004) ("The viral nature of open source quickly became apparent when we first opened the site to the public. Since 1999 our biggest challenge has been trying to stay ahead of the growth curve. Today we have close to 1,000,000 users and 100,000 projects."). As of September 2007, the SourceForge front page reported that there were 158,761 projects. SourceForge.net, http://sourceforge.net (last visited Sep. 29, 2007).

45. *See generally* Yochai Benkler, *Coase's Penguin, or, Linux and the Nature of the Firm,* 112 YALE L.J. 369, 371 (2002) ("At the heart of the economic engine of the world's most advanced economies, . . . we are beginning to take notice of a hardy, persistent, and quite amazing phenomenon. A new model of production has taken root, one that should not be there, at least according to our most widely held beliefs about economic behavior. The intuitions of the late twentieth century American resist the idea that thousands of volunteers could collaborate on a complex economic project. . . . And yet, this is precisely what is happening in the software industry.").

46. *See, e.g.,* TrueCrypt: Free Open-Source On-The-Fly Encryption, http://truecrypt.sourceforge.net (last visited May 16, 2007).

47. *See, e.g.,* eMule, http://www.emule-project.net/home/perl/general.cgi?l=1 (last visited May 16, 2007).

48. *See, e.g.,* Citadel: The Groupware Server for Web 2.0, http://www.citadel.org (last visited May 16, 2007).

49. *See, e.g.,* Wikipedia, *Comparison of Web Browsers,* http://en.wikipedia.org/wiki/Comparison_of_web_browsers (as of May 5, 2007, 00:24 GMT).

50. *See, e.g.,* GIMP, http://www.gimp.org (last visited May 16, 2007) (providing access to, and assistance with, the GNU image manipulation program); MusE-Linux Music Edi-

tor, http://sourceforge.net/projects/lmuse (last visited May 16, 2007). A more comprehensive list of current SourceForge projects can be found on Wikipedia. *See* Wikipedia, *Category: SourceForge Projects,* http://en.wikipedia.org/wiki/Category:SourceForge_projects (as of Apr. 5, 2007, 17:51 GMT).

51. Eric Raymond refers in this regard to the concept of "indirect sale value." *See* ERIC S. RAYMOND, THE CATHEDRAL & THE BAZAAR: MUSINGS ON LINUX AND OPEN SOURCE BY AN ACCIDENTAL REVOLUTIONARY (1999); *see also* Mikko Välimäki, *Dual Licensing in Open Source Software Industry,* 8 SYSTEMES D'INFORMATION ET MANAGEMENT 63 (2003) (discussing the related phenomenon of software distributed under a "dual license" system).

52. In 1998, browser pioneer Netscape reacted to the dominance of rival Microsoft's Internet Explorer by releasing the code for its flagship software under a public license (the "Netscape Public License"), which enabled the public to freely use and develop the software, while allowing the company to continue publishing proprietary software based upon it. *See* Netscape Public License: Version 1.0, http://www.mozilla.org/MPL/NPL-1.0.html (last visited May 16, 2007); *see also* NETSCAPE, NETSCAPE COMMUNICATOR OPEN SOURCE CODE WHITE PAPER (2000), *available at* http://wp.netscape.com/browsers/future/whitepaper.html. This process marked the beginning of the Mozilla open source project. Today, the commercial imperative no longer exists; however, one of the most common Internet browsers, Mozilla Firefox, and a leading e-mail client, Mozilla Thunderbird, have their genesis in this process. Another example is OpenOffice.org, a set of freely available Microsoft Office–style applications, which is based on proprietary code released by its owners, Sun. Users continue to develop OpenOffice.org, which is freely available, while Sun markets the "StarOffice Office Suite," a "professional office productivity solution based on OpenOffice.org that provides enterprise value-add components including administration tools, commercial quality spellchecker and relational database." OpenOffice.org, http://www.sun.com/software/star/openoffice/index.xml (last visited May 16, 2007).

53. Even these organizations have made their content available to subscribers through the Web, whereas formerly it was accessible solely via their own proprietary software. *See* Terry Psarras, *Lexis & Westlaw: Proprietary Software Versus Browser Based,* LLRX.COM, Sept. 3, 2001, http://www.llrx.com/features/webvsoftware.htm; *see also* Linnea Christiani, *Meeting the New Challenges and LexisNexis: Post-SIIA Summit Interviews with Michael Wilens and Lisa Mitnick,* SEARCHER, May 2002, http://www.infotoday.com/searcher/may02/christiani.htm. Both Mitnick and Wilens noted that a key priority was expanding their stock of proprietary content that would not be available elsewhere. According to Mitnick, Senior Vice President of LexisNexis, "LexisNexis has focused on acquiring proprietary, value-added content, such as Shepard's and Matthew Bender, and signed exclusive licensing agreements with CCH, Tax Analysts, and Congressional Quarterly." *Id.* However, even these services are not without competition; there is a growing number of free legal information services including BAILII, which contains links to British and Irish law-related material; AsianLII, with databases covering twenty-seven Asian countries and territories; and WorldLII, which aggregates these and other

regional services. *See, e.g.,* BAILII, http://www.bailii.org (last visited May 16, 2007); AsianLII, http://www.asianlii.org (last visited May 16, 2007); AustLII, http://www .austlii.org (last visited Mar. 28, 2007); WorldLII, http://www.worldlii.org (last visited May 16, 2007); *see also* FindLaw, http://www.findlaw.com (last visited June 2, 2007); Cornell Legal Information Institute, http://www.law.cornell.edu (last visited June 2, 2007).

54. *See* The Hamster Dance, http://www.webhamster.com (last visited May 16, 2007).

55. *See* Ina Fried, *Apple: Widget Writers Wanted,* ZDNET NEWS, Dec. 9, 2004, http:// news.zdnet.com/2100-3513_22-5486309.html ("The Mac maker has launched a contest for developers who create programs in Dashboard—a part of Tiger, the update to Mac OS X. . . . The idea behind Dashboard, as well as a similar third-party program called Konfabulator, is that computer users want easy access to small programs that do things like showing stock quotes or displaying photos. . . . [T]he company wants to jump-start development of the widgets that work with Dashboard. Apple is hoping that the prospect of creating widgets will appeal to more than just the usual crop of Apple developers, given that only standard Web site skills are needed.").

56. *See* GEOFFREY A. MOORE, INSIDE THE TORNADO: MARKETING STRATEGIES FROM SILI-CON VALLEY'S CUTTING EDGE 101 (1995); GEOFFREY A. MOORE, INSIDE THE TOR-NADO: STRATEGIES FOR DEVELOPING, LEVERAGING, AND SURVIVING HYPERGROWTH MARKETS (2004). Both identify different classes of technology adopters, including, notably, a "late majority" which require a complete product, with appropriate support and training, as they lack the financial and organizational capacity to undertake such tasks themselves. *See generally* EVERETT ROGERS, DIFFUSION OF INNOVATIONS (5th ed. 2003).

57. One example is the continuing success of the commercial Red Hat Enterprise Linux, despite the many freely available Linux distributions, including Fedora Core, on which Red Hat is based.

58. *See* World Community Grid, http://www.worldcommunitygrid.org/index.html (last visited May 16, 2007) ("World Community Grid's mission is to create the largest public computing grid benefiting humanity. Our work is built on the belief that technological innovation combined with visionary scientific research and large-scale volunteerism can change our world for the better."). The site makes it easy to become involved: "Donate the time your computer is turned on, but is idle, to projects that benefit humanity!" *Id.*

59. *See* SETI@home, http://setiathome.berkeley.edu (last visited Dec. 1, 2007); *see also* Wikipedia, *SETI@home,* http://en.wikipedia.org/wiki/Seti_at_home (as of May 12, 2007, 02:06 GMT).

60. BitTorrent allows many people to download the same file without slowing down everyone else's download. This is possible because downloaders swap portions of the file with one another, instead of downloading it all from a single server. As each downloader uses up bandwidth, he also contributes bandwidth back to the swarm. This contribution is encouraged because those clients trying to upload to other clients gets the fastest downloads. *See* BitTorrent, What is Bit Torrent?, http://www.bittorrent.com/what-is-bittorrent (last visited May 16, 2007); *see also* Wikipedia, *BitTorrent,* http://en.wikipedia.org/wiki /Bittorrent (as of Mar. 28, 2007, 16:30 GMT).

61. JOHN STUART MILL, ON LIBERTY AND OTHER ESSAYS 75 (John Gray ed., 1998).

62. *Id.*

63. YOCHAI BENKLER, THE WEALTH OF NETWORKS 275 (2006).

64. *Id.* at 277; *see also* Yochai Benkler, *Freedom in the Commons: Towards a Political Economy of Information,* 52 DUKE L.J. 1245, 1248–49 (2003) ("Together these shifts can move the boundaries of liberty along all three vectors of liberal political morality. They enable democratic discourse to flow among constituents, rather than primarily through controlled, concentrated, commercial media designed to sell advertising, rather than to facilitate discourse. They allow individuals to build their own windows on the world, rather than seeing it largely through blinders designed to keep their eyes on the designer's prize. They allow passive consumers to become active users of their cultural environment, and they allow employees, whose productive life is marked by following orders, to become peers in common productive enterprises. And they can ameliorate some of the inequalities that markets have often generated and amplified.").

65. Yochai Benkler, *Sharing Nicely: On Shareable Goods and the Emergence of Sharing as a Modality of Economic Production,* 114 YALE L.J. 273 (2004).

66. *See* Yochai Benkler & Helen Nissenbaum, *Commons-based Peer Production and Virtue,* 14 J. POL. PHIL. 394 (2006) (arguing that socio-technical systems of commons-based peer production offer not only a remarkable medium of production for various kinds of information goods, but also serve as a context for positive character formation, as a society that provides opportunities for virtuous behavior is one that is more conducive to virtuous individuals, and suggesting that the practice of effective, virtuous behavior may lead to more people adopting the virtues as their own, or as attributes of what they see as their self-definition).

67. *See* JOHN FISKE, TELEVISION CULTURE (1988).

68. William W. Fisher III, *Theories of Intellectual Property, in* NEW ESSAYS IN THE LEGAL AND POLITICAL THEORY OF PROPERTY 169–73 (Stephen R. Munzer ed., 2001).

69. *See* Edward Tufte, THE COGNITIVE STYLE OF POWERPOINT: PITCHING OUT CORRUPTS WITHIN (2003).

70. NEIL POSTMAN, BUILDING A BRIDGE TO THE 18TH CENTURY: HOW THE PAST CAN IMPROVE OUR FUTURE (1999).

71. NEIL POSTMAN, TECHNOPOLY: THE SURRENDER OF CULTURE TO TECHNOLOGY (1992).

72. *See* Raaj Kumar Sah & Joseph E. Stiglitz, *The Architecture of Economic Systems: Hierarchies and Polyarchies,* 76 AM. ECON. REV. 716 (1986); Raaj K. Sah & Joseph E. Stiglitz, *The Quality of Managers in Centralized Versus Decentralized Organizations,* 106 Q.J. ECON. 289 (1991). These articles are summarized well in Tim Wu, *Intellectual Property, Innovation, and Decentralized Decisions,* 92 VA. L. REV. 123 (2006).

73. *See* Paul Freiberger & Michael Swaine, FIRE IN THE VALLEY 204 (2d ed. 2000).

74. *See* CVS Wiki, http://ximbiot.com/cvs/wiki/index.php (as of May 16, 2007, 12:00 GMT); *see also* Simson Garfinkel, *Super Sync,* TECH. REV., Nov. 11, 2001, at 11, *available at* http://www.technologyreview.com/Infotech/12642/.

75. *See* CERN, Basic Description of the CVS System, http://wwwasd.web.cern.ch/wwwasd/cvs/tutorial/cvs_tutorial_1.html#SEC1 (last visited May 16, 2007).

76. *See* About the World Wide Web Consortium (W3C), http://www.w3.org/Consortium (last visited May 16, 2007).

77. *See* COMM. ON THE INTERNET IN THE EVOLVING INFO. INFRASTRUCTURE ET AL., THE IN-
TERNET'S COMING OF AGE 408–10 (2001); World Wide Web Consortium, HTML
Converters, http://www.w3.org/Tools/Filters.html (last visited May 16, 2007) (providing information on various means to convert to and from HTML, as well as links to secondary sources).

78. *See I Made This!; New Tools and Services Make It Surprisingly Easy—Not to Mention
Cheap—to Build Your Own Website,* FORTUNE, Winter 2000 (Special Issue), at 229.

79. *See* DAVID KLINE & DAN BURSTEIN, BLOG!: HOW THE NEWEST MEDIA REVOLUTION IS
CHANGING POLITICS, BUSINESS, AND CULTURE (Arne J. De Keijzer & Paul Berger eds.,
2005).

80. *See* Fredrik Wacka, *Why Blogs Rank High in Search Engines,* WEBPRONEWS, Jan. 4, 2005,
http://www.webpronews.com/insiderreports/2005/01/04/why-blogs-rank-high-in-
search-engines (explaining that blog entries rank high because they are filled frequently
with relevant keywords, cut straight to the point, use entry titles as page titles, are coded
well, and usually stick to one topic per post).

81. *See* Lost Camera, http://lostcamera.blogspot.com.

82. *See* Peter Meyers, *Fact-Driven? Collegial? Then This Site Wants You,* N.Y. TIMES, Sept. 20,
2001, at G2.

83. *See* Ward Cunningham, Wiki Design Principles http://www.c2.com/cgi/wiki?Wiki
DesignPrinciples (as of Mar. 26, 2007, 12:00 GMT) (explaining that his goals for the
first release of Wiki included designing an "organic" system in which "[t]he structure
and text content of the site are open to editing and evolution," in which "[t]he mechanisms of editing and organizing are the same as those of writing so that any writer is automatically an editor and organizer," and in which "[a]ctivity within the site can be
watched and reviewed by any other visitor to the site"). Cunningham also notes that an
additional principle was that "[e]verybody can contribute; nobody has to." *Id.*

84. *See* Meyers, *supra* note 82; Wikipedia, *Ward Cunningham,* http://en.wikipedia.org/
wiki/Ward_Cunningham (as of May 10, 2007, 13:31 GMT); Wikipedia, *Wiki,* http://en.
wikipedia.org/wiki/WikiWiki (as of May 16, 2007, 23:11 GMT).

85. *See* Wikipedia, *Wiki, supra* note 84; Wikipedia, *Wikipedia,* http://en.wikipedia.org/
wiki/Wikipedia#History (as of May 16, 2007, 15:44 GMT).

86. For further discussion of commons-based peer production (including an examination of
free software and Wikipedia) as an alternate economic modality, see Benkler, *supra* note
65, at 334–36.

87. There is evidence this is, in fact, already occurring. *See* DON TAPSCOTT & ANTHONY D.
WILLIAMS, WIKINOMICS: HOW MASS COLLABORATION CHANGES EVERYTHING (2006);
Chrysanthos Dellarocas, *Strategic Manipulation of Internet Opinion Forums: Implications
for Consumers and Firms,* 52 MGMT. SCI. 1577 (2006), *available at* http://papers.ssrn
.com/sol3/papers.cfm?abstract_id=585404; Von Mathias Peer, *Wikipedia-Artikel, Die
Man Kaufen Kann,* WELTONLINE, Aug. 24, 2006, http://www.welt.de/data/2006/08/
24/1009086.html.

88. For a good discussion of the evolution of domain name disputes, see Archived Information for Domain Name Disputes, http://domains.org/archived_domain_disputes.html

(last visited Mar. 28, 2007) (providing links to discussions about domain name disputes); *see also* R. Lynn Campbell, *Judicial Involvement in Domain Name Disputes in Canada*, 34 REVUE DE DROIT DE L'UNIVERSITE DE SHERBROOKE 373 (2003); Jacqueline D. Lipton, *Beyond Cybersquatting: Taking Domain Name Disputes Past Trademark Policy*, 40 WAKE FOREST L. REV. 1361 (2005); Colby B. Springer, *Master of the Domain (Name): A History of Domain Name Litigation and the Emergence of the Cybersquatting Consumer Protection Act and the Uniform Dispute Resolution Policy*, 17 SANTA CLARA COMPUTER & HIGH TECH L.J. 315 (2003).

89. A fair unit of measurement, given creativity's role as an essential ingredient of the "good life." *See* William W. Fisher III, *Reconstructing the Fair Use Doctrine*, 101 HARV. L. REV. 1661, 1746–51 (1988). A "good society" encourages its members to live lives of self-determination and creativity by facilitating "conditions that increase and make more apparent people's opportunities for self-expression and communication," fostering a rich and shared artistic tradition, and encouraging and protecting the formation of communities and "constitutive group affiliations"—all of which are roles that the Internet increasingly fulfills. *Id.* at 1751–53.

90. *See* WILLIAM W. FISHER III, PROMISES TO KEEP: TECHNOLOGY, LAW, AND THE FUTURE OF ENTERTAINMENT 28–31 (2004).

91. Such a scenario need not be hypothetical. *See, e.g.,* Ken Silverstein, *The Radioactive Boy Scout*, HARPER'S MAG., Nov. 1998, at 59 (recounting the story of a child who created a nuclear reactor in his backyard shed).

92. *See* Ultramares Corp. v. Touche, Niven & Co., 174 N.E. 441 (N.Y. 1931).

93. The term is said to have been coined in 1991 by D. James Bidzos, the then-president of RSA Data Security, when he said that the government's digital signature standard provided "no assurance that foreign governments cannot break the system, running the risk of a digital Pearl Harbor." *See* Scott Berinato, *The Future of Security*, CIO.com, Dec. 30, 2003, www.cio.com/article/32033/The_Future_of_Security. The term has since become prominent in public debate, being employed most notably by former member of the National Security Council Richard A. Clarke. *See* Assoc. Press, *U.S. Cyberspace Chief Warns of 'Digital Pearl Harbor,'* CNN.COM, Dec. 8, 2000, http://archives.cnn.com/2000/TECH/computing/12/08/security.summit.ap/.

94. *See* BENKLER, *supra* note 1, *in* Notes to Introduction to Part II, note 1, at 23.

95. *See* MILL, *supra* note 61, at 75.

96. *See* Chapter Nine for a full discussion of this problem.

97. *See* MILL, *supra* note 61, at 73.

98. *See* Postini StatTrack, http://www.postini.com/stats (last visited May 16, 2007).

CHAPTER 5. TETHERED APPLIANCES, SOFTWARE AS SERVICE, AND PERFECT ENFORCEMENT

1. *See, e.g.,* Sharon E. Gillett et al., *Do Appliances Threaten Internet Innovation?*, IEEE COMMUNICATIONS, Oct. 2001, at 46–51.

2. *See, e.g.,* Nicholas Petreley, *Security Report: Windows vs. Linux*, THE REGISTER, Oct. 22,

2004, http://www.theregister.co.uk/security/security_report_windows_vs_linux/; Posting of Triple II to Mostly Linux, *10 Things a New Linux User Needs to Unlearn,* http://mostly-linux.blogspot.com/2006/06/10-things-new-linux-user-needs-to.html (June 17, 2006) ("Reboots are not SOP (Standard Operating Procedure).").

3. *See* Skype, Can I Call Emergency Numbers in the U.S. and Canada?, http://support .skype.com/index.php?a=knowledgebase&j=questiondetails&i=1034 (last visited June 1, 2007) ("Skype is not a telephone replacement service and emergency numbers cannot be called from Skype.").

4. Jim Davis, *TiVo Launches "Smart TV" Trial,* CNET NEWS.COM, Dec. 22, 1998, http://news.com.com/TiVo+launches+smart+TV+trial/2100-1040_3-219409 .html.

5. *See* Richard Shim, *TiVo, Gemstar End Lawsuit, Team Up,* CNET NEWS.COM, June 9, 2003, http://news.com.com/2100-1041-1014674.html; *see also* Jennifer 8. Lee, *Sonic-Blue Sues TiVo,* N.Y. TIMES, Dec. 13, 2001, at C3 (reporting patent lawsuits filed against TiVo by SonicBlue and Pause Technology).

6. *See, e.g.,* TrickPlay, U.S. Patent No. 6,327,418 (filed Apr. 3, 1998) (issued Dec. 4, 2001); Multimedia Time Warping System, U.S. Patent No. 6,233,389 (filed July 30, 1998) (issued May 15, 2001); *see also* Richard Shim, *Industry Ponders Impact of TiVo Patent,* CNET NEWS.COM, May 25, 2001, http://news.com.com/Industry+ponders+impact +of+TiVo+patent/2100-1040_3-258345.html.

7. Complaint for Patent Infringement, TiVo Inc. v. EchoStar Commc'ns Corp., 446 F. Supp. 2d 664 (E.D. Tex. Aug. 17, 2006) (No. 2:04-CV-1-DF), 2004 WL 3357025.

8. TiVo Inc. v. EchoStar Commc'ns Corp., No. 2:04-CV-1-DF, 2006 U.S. Dist. LEXIS 64293, at *22 (E.D. Tex. Aug. 17, 2006).

9. As of September 30, 2006, EchoStar reported 12,755,000 total DISH Network subscribers. EchoStar Commc'ns Corp., Quarterly Report for the Quarterly Period Ended September 30, 2006 (Form 10-Q), at 28 (Nov. 7, 2006), *available at* http://www .sec.gov/Archives/edgar/data/1001082/000095013406020645/d40946e10vq.htm.

10. Sharp-eyed readers of the *TiVo* injunction excerpt may have noticed something peculiar: the court's order spares 192,708 EchoStar units. Why? EchoStar was ordered to pay damages to TiVo for lost sales of DVRs that TiVo would have sold if EchoStar had not been a competitor, and the court found that exactly 192,708 more TiVos would have been sold. *See* TiVo Inc. v EchoStar Commc'ns Corp., No. 2:04-CV-1-DF, 2006 U.S. Dist. LEXIS 64293, at *4. Since the $90 million in damages paid by EchoStar already reimbursed TiVo for those units, it would have been double-dipping to kill those units. So 192,708 lucky EchoStar subscribers will get to keep their DVRs even if the court's order is implemented. How should EchoStar choose those subscribers? The order does not specify.

11. *See* 17 U.S.C. § 503 (2000). *Cf.* 35 U.S.C. § 283 (2000); 15 U.S.C. § 1116(a) (2000).

12. *See, e.g.,* Ben Barnier, *New York Ups Ante in Counterfeit Crackdown,* ABC NEWS, Feb. 2, 2006, http://www.abcnews.go.com/Business/story?id=1562460; *China Seizes 58 Million Illegal Publications in Three Months,* PEOPLE'S DAILY ONLINE, Nov. 27, 2006, http://english.peopledaily.com.cn/200611/27/eng20061127_325640.html.

13. EchoStar's customer service agreement has included what might be termed a "tethering rights clause": "[EchoStar] reserves the rights to alter software, features and/or function-

ality in your DISH Network receivers, provide data and content to Personal Video Recorder/Digital Video Recorder ('PVR/DVR') products, store data and content on the hard drives of PVR/DVR products, and send electronic counter-measures to your DISH Network receivers, through periodic downloads. DISH Network will use commercially reasonable efforts to schedule these downloads to minimize interference with or interruption to your Services, but shall have no liability to you for any interruptions in Services arising out of or related to such downloads." EchoStar Satellite L.L.C., Residential Customer Agreement, *available at* http://www.dishnetwork.com/content/about _us/residential_customer_agreement/index.shtml (last visited June 1, 2007). Such clauses are typical.

14. On October 3, 2006, the Federal Circuit granted an indefinite stay of the injunction pending the outcome of EchoStar's appeal. *TiVo Loses Ground on Appeals Court Ruling,* Business Week Online, Oct. 4, 2006, http://www.businessweek.com/investor/content /oct2006/pi20061004_960230.htm.

15. No case has tested whether consumers would have a remedy against EchoStar for their dead DVRs. On one hand, it might breach a manufacturer's warranty of fitness to produce a device that cannot lawfully be used for the purpose specified. On the other hand, "legal fitness" is distinct from functional fitness, and the consumer's ignorance of a patent (or of patent law) is no defense against consumer infringement. It is not clear that the seller of an infringing product owes indemnity to the user of it.

16. *See* PlayMedia Sys., Inc. v. America Online, Inc., 171 F. Supp. 2d 1094 (C.D. Cal. 2001).

17. *See* Lawrence Lessig, *The Limits in Open Code: Regulatory Standards and the Future of the Net,* 14 Berkeley Tech. L.J. 759, 761–62 (1999) [hereinafter *Limits in Open Code*]; *see generally* Lawrence Lessig, Code: Version 2.0, at 5 (2006) and its first edition, Code and Other Laws of Cyberspace (1999). Lessig elaborated the idea that "code is law," crediting Joel Reidenberg for the initial conception. *See* Joel R. Reidenberg, *Lex Informatica: The Formulation of Information Policy Rules Through Technology,* 76 Tex. L. Rev. 553 (1998).

18. "West coast code" refers to the code embedded in computer software and hardware, so dubbed because much of its development has occurred in West Coast locations such as Silicon Valley, California, and Redmond, Washington. This code has been contrasted with the more traditional regulatory "east coast code" that Congress enacts in Washington, D.C. *See* Lawrence Lessig, Code and Other Laws of Cyberspace 53 (1999).

19. *Id.* at 24–25 (describing the fallacy of "is-ism").

20. *See, e.g.,* Julie E. Cohen, *Some Reflections on Copyright Management Systems and Laws Designed to Protect Them,* 12 Berkeley Tech. L.J. 161, 163 (1997) (noting the possible negative effects of broad protection for copyright management systems). *Cf.* Lawrence Lessig, *Open Code and Open Societies: Values of Internet Governance,* 74 Chi.-Kent L. Rev. 1405, 1408–13 (1999) (discussing how open source software and freedom of participation were instrumental to the growth of the Internet).

21. *See generally* Mark Stefik, The Internet Edge: Social, Technical, and Legal Challenges for a Networked World 55–78 (2000); Jonathan L. Zittrain, Technological Complements to Copyright (2005).

22. For a discussion of the terminology used to describe intellectual property rights, see Pe-

ter K. Yu, *Intellectual Property and the Information Ecosystem,* 2005 MICH. ST. L. REV. 1, 4–6 (2005) (considering possible terms such as Wendy Gordon's GOLEM—"Government-Originated Legally Enforced Monopolies"—and IMP—"Imposed Monopoly Privileges").

23. *See* Apple, Sync Both Ways, http://www.apple.com/itunes/sync/transfer.html (last visited June 1, 2007).

24. *See, e.g.,* OPENNET INITIATIVE, INTERNET FILTERING IN CHINA IN 2004–2005 (2005), http://www.opennetinitiative.net/studies/china/; *see generally* Jack Linchuan Qui, *Virtual Censorship in China: Keeping the Gate Between the Cyberspaces,* 4 INT'L. J. COMM. L. & POL'Y 1 (Winter 1999/2000), *available at* http://www.ijclp.org/4_2000/pdf/ijclp _webdoc_1_4_2000.pdf (discussing efforts by the Chinese government to adapt—and censor—evolving Internet technologies).

25. *See* JACK GOLDSMITH & TIM WU, WHO CONTROLS THE INTERNET?, 113, 120 (2006) (characterizing most attempts at "sidestepping copyright" as mere phases and noting Steve Jobs's observation that users "would rather pay for music online than spend hours evading detection").

26. *See, e.g.,* Nart Villeneuve, Director, Citizen Lab at the Univ. of Toronto, Technical Ways to Get Around Censorship, http://www.rsf.org/article.php3?id_article=15013 (last visited June 1, 2007); Ethan Zuckerman, How to Blog Anonymously, http://www.rsf .org/article.php3?id_article =15012 (last visited June 1, 2007).

27. *See* BBC NEWS, Country Profile: North Korea, Feb. 14, 2007, http://news.bbc.co.uk/ 2/hi/asia-pacific/country_profiles/1131421.stm; Cathy Hong, *Puncturing a Regime with Balloons,* THE VILLAGE VOICE, Aug. 13–19, 2003, *available at* http://www.village voice.com/news/0333,hong,46013,1.html.

28. For a review of the places where interventions can be made to affect user behavior in the context of intellectual property enforcement, including through modification to endpoint devices, see Julie Cohen, *Pervasively Distributed Copyright Enforcement,* 95 GEO. L.J. 1 (2006).

29. Matt Richtel, *Apple Is Said to Be Entering E-Music Fray with Pay Service,* N.Y. TIMES, Apr. 28, 2003, at C1, *available at* http://query.nytimes.com/gst/fullpage.html?res= 9E0DEED7123DF93BA15757C0A9659C8B63; Peter Cohen, *iTunes Music Store Launches with 200K+ Songs,* MACWORLD, Apr. 28, 2003, http://www.macworld.com/ news/2003/04/28/musicstore/.

30. *See, e.g.,* Press Release, TiVo, TiVo Delivers New Service Enhancements for Series2 Subscribers, Introduces New Pricing for Multiple TiVo Households (June 9, 2004), *available at* http://web.archive.org/web/20041010143736/www.tivo.com/5.3.1.1.asp?article =210.

31. French copyright law recognizes at least a nominal right of withdrawal ("droit de retrait"). *See* Jean-Luc Piotraut, *An Authors' Rights–Based Copyright Law: The Fairness and Morality of French and American Law Compared,* 24 CARDOZO ARTS & ENT. L.J. 549, 608 (2006). Authors of software are not entitled to this right. *Id.*

32. *See* LESSIG, CODE: VERSION 2.0, *supra* note 17, at 128, 135.

33. Macrovision, Video Copy Protection FAQ, http://www.macrovision.com/webdocuments /PDF/acp_faq_videocopyprotection.pdf (last visited June 1, 2007); *see also* Macrovi-

sion, Secure DVD Content in Today's Digital Home, http://www.macrovision.com/pdfs/ACP_DVD_Bro_US.pdf (last visited June 1, 2007).

34. Zune.net, Beam Your Beats, http://www.zune.net/en-us/meetzune/zunetozunesharing.htm (last visited June 1, 2007).

35. *See* Assoc. Press, *TiVo Fans Fear Start of Recording Restrictions,* MSNBC.COM, Sept. 21, 2005, http://www.msnbc.msn.com/id/9430340/.

36. *See* posting of Brian Ashcraft to Kotaku, *China Rolls Out Anti-Addiction Software,* http://kotaku.com/gaming/china/china-rolls-out-anti+addiction-software-251955.php (Apr. 13, 2007).

37. TiVo Privacy Policy § 2.2 (May 2006), http://www.tivo.com/avouttivo/policies/tivoprivacypolicy.html ("The collection of Personally Identifiable Viewing Information is necessary for the use of certain advanced TiVo features. . . . If you expressly choose to allow TiVo to collect your Personally Identifiable Viewing Information, TiVo may use this information to provide the requested services as well as for surveys, audience measurement, and other legitimate business purposes.").

38. *See* Ben Charny, *Jackson's Super Bowl Flash Grabs TiVo Users,* CNET NEWS.COM, Feb. 2, 2004, http://news.com.com/2100-1041_3-5152141.html.

39. TiVo Privacy Policy, *supra* note 37, § 3.6 (noting that TiVo "may be legally obligated to disclose User Information to local, state or federal governmental agencies or Third Parties under certain circumstances (including in response to a subpoena)"). Other service providers, like antivirus software vendor Symantec, have been even less committal in their willingness to protect user privacy. They have stated that their products would not be updated to detect Magic Lantern, an FBI keystroke logging Trojan. *See* John Leyden, *AV Vendors Split over FBI Trojan Snoops,* THE REGISTER, Nov. 27, 2001, http://www.theregister.co.uk/2001/11/27/av_vendors_split_over_fbi/.

40. *See* 18 U.S.C. § 2518(4) (2000) (describing what orders authorizing or approving of the interception of wire, oral, or electronic communications must specify, and mentioning that the orders can be done ex parte). The carmaker complied under protest, and in 2004 a federal appellate court handed down an opinion titled *Company v. United States* (349 F.3d 1132 (9th Cir. 2003)), with the generic caption designed to prevent identification of the carmaker or the target of the investigation. The court found that the company could theoretically be ordered to perform the surveillance, but that, in this case, the FBI's surveillance had interfered with the computer system's normal use: a car with a secret open line to the FBI could not simultaneously connect to the automaker, and therefore if the occupants used the system to solicit emergency help, it would not function. *Id.* (Presumably, the FBI would not come to the rescue the way the automaker promised its customers who use the system.) The implication is that such secret surveillance would have been legally acceptable if the system were redesigned to simultaneously process emergency requests.

41. *See* Brian Wheeler, *'This Goes No Further . . . ,'* BBC NEWS, Mar. 2, 2004, http://news.bbc.co.uk/2/hi/uk_news/magazine/3522137.stm; *see also* United States v. Tomero, 462 F. Supp. 2d 565, 569 (S.D.N.Y. 2006) (holding that continuous mobile phone monitoring fits within the "roving bug" statute). The *Tomero* opinion is ambiguous about whether the bug in question was physically attached to the phone or effected through a remote update.

42. *See* Michael Adler, *Cyberspace, General Searches, and Digital Contraband: The Fourth Amendment and the Net-Wide Search,* 105 YALE L.J. 1093 (1996); *see also* LAWRENCE LESSIG, CODE: VERSION 2.0, at 20–23, 25–26; Lawrence Lessig, *Constitution and Code,* 27 CUMB. L. REV. 1, 6–7 (1996–97).

43. Dan Burk and Tarleton Gillespie have offered an autonomy-based argument against the deployment of trusted systems. *See* Dan Burk & Tarleton Gillespie, *Autonomy and Morality in DRM and Anti-Circumvention Law,* 4 TRIPLEC 239 (2006) ("State sponsorship of DRM in effect treats information users as moral incompetents, incapable of deciding the proper use of information products."). While few other scholars have analyzed the downsides of perfect enforcement in the context of the Internet or elsewhere, some have warned against assuming that perfect enforcement is desirable. *See, e.g.,* Cohen, *supra* note 28, at 43 ("The proper balance between enforcement and restraint is an age-old question in market-democratic societies, and solutions have always entailed compromise. It would be odd if the advent of digital networked technologies altered this dynamic so completely that middle-ground possibilities ceased to exist."); Mark A. Lemley & R. Anthony Reese, *Reducing Digital Copyright Infringement Without Restricting Innovation,* 56 STAN. L. REV. 1345, 1432–34 (2004); Alexandra Natapoff, *Underenforcement,* 75 FORDHAM L. REV. 1715, 1741 (2006); Eyal Zamir, *The Efficiency of Paternalism,* 84 VA. L. REV. 229, 280 (1998) ("[P]erfect enforcement is rarely the optimal level of enforcement.").

44. *See* David R. Johnson & David G. Post, *Law and Borders—The Rise of Law in Cyberspace,* 48 STAN. L. REV. 1367, 1367, 1383, 1387–88 (1996) (arguing that self-governance can and should be central to cyberspace regulation); John Perry Barlow, A Declaration of the Independence of Cyberspace (Feb. 8, 1996), http://homes.eff.org/~barlow/Declaration-Final.html ("Governments of the Industrial World, you weary giants of flesh and steel, I come from Cyberspace, the new home of Mind. On behalf of the future, I ask you of the past to leave us alone. You are not welcome among us. You have no sovereignty where we gather.").

45. *See* Note, *Exploitative Publishers, Untrustworthy Systems, and the Dream of a Digital Revolution for Artists,* 114 HARV. L. REV. 2438, 2455–56 (2001) (asserting that the No Electronic Theft (NET) Act's self-help mechanisms are likely to be ineffective because copy protections are "routinely cracked"); Eric Goldman, *A Road to No Warez: The No Electronic Theft Act and Criminal Copyright Infringement,* 82 U. OR. L. REV. 369 (2003) (discussing the history of the act and difficulties that have arisen when attempting to enforce it); Declan McCullagh, *Perspective: The New Jailbird Jingle,* CNET NEWS.COM, Jan. 27, 2003, http://news.com.com/2010-1071-982121.html (chronicling the NET Act's ineffectiveness).

46. For criticism of trusted system legislation, see Drew Clark, *How Copyright Became Controversial, in* PROC. 12TH ANN. CONF. ON COMPUTERS, FREEDOM & PRIVACY (2002), *available at* http://www.cfp2002.org/proceedings/proceedings/clark.pdf (criticizing the DMCA); Julie E. Cohen, *Lochner in Cyberspace: The New Economic Orthodoxy of "Rights Management,"* 97 MICH. L. REV. 462, 494–95 (1998) (characterizing support for DMCA and other legislation enlarging intellectual property rights as "Lochner pure

and simple"); Lisa J. Beyer Sims, *Mutiny on the Net: Ridding P2P Pirates of Their Booty,* 53 EMORY L.J. 1887, 1907, 1937–39 (2003) (describing objections to SBDTPA and DMCA § 1201 on grounds of overbreadth and interference with the fair use doctrine); Declan McCullagh, *New Copyright Bill Heading to DC,* WIRED, Sept. 7, 2001, http:// www.wired.com/news/politics/0,1283,46655,00.html (describing responses to the Security Systems Standards and Certification Act (SSSCA)); Letter from Shari Steele, Executive Dir., Elec. Freedom Found., to Senators Fritz Hollings and Ted Stevens (Nov. 5, 2001), *available at* http://www.eff.org/IP/DMCA/20011105_eff_sssca_letter .html (discussing the proposed SSSCA).

47. *See* Yochai Benkler, *Free as the Air to Common Use: First Amendment Constraints on Enclosure of the Public Domain,* 74 N.Y.U. L. REV. 354 (1999) (asserting that expansive intellectual property rights constrain the availability of information); Yochai Benkler, *Through the Looking Glass: Alice and the Constitutional Foundations of the Public Domain,* 66 LAW & CONTEMP. PROBS. 173, 216–18 (2003) (criticizing the NET Act and DMCA for expanding copyright protection in such a way that will chill expression); Neil Weinstock Netanel, *Locating Copyright Within the First Amendment Skein,* 54 STAN. L. REV. 1 (2001) (arguing that the expansion of copyright law limits the incentivizing effect of the regime and burdens speech); Pamela Samuelson, *Intellectual Property and the Digital Economy: Why the Anti-Circumvention Regulations Need to Be Revised,* 14 BERKELEY TECH. L.J. 519 (1999) (criticizing the DMCA as overly broad and describing some problems with expansive copyright protections).

48. *See, e.g.,* Dean F. Andal, *Read My E-Mail, No New Taxes!,* CAL-TAX DIG., Apr. 1997, *available at* http://www.caltax.org/MEMBER/digest/apr97/apr97-4.htm; *see generally* Charles E. McLure, Jr., *Taxation of Electronic Commerce: Economic Objectives, Technological Constraints, and Tax Laws,* 52 TAX L. REV. 269 (1997); William V. Vetter, *Preying on the Web: Tax Collection in the Virtual World,* 28 FLA. ST. U. L. REV. 649 (2001) (focusing on constitutional and jurisdictional issues).

49. According to a 2005 Pew Internet & American Life Project study, 27 percent of adult Internet users reported engaging in file-sharing. Pew Internet & American Life Project, Internet Activities (Jan. 11, 2007), http://www.pewinternet.org/trends/Internet_Activities _1.11.07.htm.

50. *See* William J. Stuntz, *The Substantive Origins of Criminal Procedure,* 105 YALE L.J. 393, 394–95 (1995). For a related discussion, which also draws on Stuntz, see LESSIG, CODE: VERSION 2.0, *supra* note 17, at 213.

51. Stuntz, *supra* note 50, at 395.

52. *Cf.* LESSIG, CODE: VERSION 2.0, *supra* note 17, at 309 (supporting exercise of free speech through democratic channels in societies observing the rule of law, rather than through "technological tricks").

53. *See* Marguerite Reardon, *Skype Bows to Chinese Censors,* CNET NEWS.COM, Apr. 20, 2006, http://news.com.com/2061-10785_3-6063169.html.

54. *See* Rebecca MacKinnon, *China's Internet: Let a Thousand Filters Bloom,* YALEGLOBAL ONLINE, June 28, 2005, http://yaleglobal.yale.edu/display.article?id=5928.

55. *See* Jonathan L. Zittrain & John G. Palfrey, Jr., *Reluctant Gatekeepers: Corporate Ethics on*

a Filtered Internet, in ACCESS DENIED: THE PRACTICE AND POLICY OF GLOBAL INTERNET FILTERING (Ronald J. Deibert et al. eds., 2008).

56. *See* James Boyle, *Foucault in Cyberspace: Surveillance, Sovereignty, and Hardwired Censors,* 66 U. CIN. L. REV. 177 (1997); *see also* Jonathan Zittrain, *A History of Online Gatekeeping,* 19 HARV. J.L. & TECH. 253, 295 (2006). Boyle believes the "Libertarian gotcha" to be contingent, not inherent. In other words, because code can be changed, it is possible to take a technology and then refashion it to make it easier to regulate.

57. FAREED ZAKARIA, THE FUTURE OF FREEDOM: ILLIBERAL DEMOCRACY AT HOME AND ABROAD 81–85, 91–92, 156 (reprint ed. 2004).

58. Ingrid Marson, *China: Local Software for Local People,* CNET NEWS.COM, Nov. 14, 2005, http://news.com.com/China+Local+software+for+local+people/2100-7344_3-5951629.html.

59. *See, e.g.,* Bantam Books, Inc. v. Sullivan, 372 U.S. 58, 70 (1963) ("Any system of prior restraints of expression comes to this Court bearing a heavy presumption against its constitutional validity."); *see also* LAWRENCE TRIBE, AMERICAN CONSTITUTIONAL LAW (1999).

60. *See* Lyombe Eko, *New Medium, Old Free Speech Regimes: The Historical and Ideological Foundations of French & American Regulation of Bias-Motivated Speech and Symbolic Expression on the Internet,* 28 LOY. L.A. INT'L & COMP. L. REV. 69, 123–24 (2006) (noting a possible connection between U.S. prior restraint doctrine and the U.S. conception of the Internet as a "free marketplace of ideas"); John G. Palfrey, Jr. & Robert Rogoyski, *The Move to the Middle: The Enduring Threat of "Harmful" Speech to the End-to-End Principle,* 21 WASH. U. J.L. & POL'Y 31, 52 (2006) (discussing a Pennsylvania law requiring ISPs to deny access to Web sites containing child pornography and a court decision that declared the law unconstitutional, partly on prior restraint grounds) (citing Ctr. for Democracy & Tech. v. Pappert, 337 F. Supp. 2d 606 (E.D. Pa. 2004)); *see also* Zieper v. Metzinger, 392 F. Supp. 2d 516 (S.D.N.Y. 2005), *aff'd,* 474 F.3d 60 (2d Cir. 2007).

61. Exetel Hosting Support Facilities, Frequently Asked Questions, http://www.exetel.com.au/a_support_hosting.php#webspace2 (last visited July 4, 2007).

62. *See* United States v. Am. Library Ass'n, 539 U.S. 194, 215–16 (Breyer, J., concurring) (2003) (arguing that the standard should have been heightened scrutiny for a law requiring libraries to use filtering systems in order to receive public funding and noting that "[t]he [filtering] technology, in its current form, does not function perfectly, for to some extent it also screens out constitutionally protected materials that fall outside the scope of the statute (*i.e.,* 'overblocks') and fails to prevent access to some materials that the statute deems harmful (*i.e.,* 'underblocks')"); ACLU v. Ashcroft, 322 F.3d 240, 266–67 (3d Cir. 2003), *aff'd and remanded by* 542 U.S. 656 (2004) ("We conclude that [the Child Online Protection Act (COPA)] is substantially overbroad in that it places significant burdens on Web publishers' communication of speech that is constitutionally protected as to adults and adults' ability to access such speech. In so doing, COPA encroaches upon a significant amount of protected speech beyond that which the Government may target constitutionally in preventing children's exposure to material that is obscene for minors."); Katherine A. Miltner, Note, *Discriminatory Filtering: CIPA's Effect*

on Our Nation's Youth and Why the Supreme Court Erred in Upholding the Constitutionality of the Children's Internet Protection Act, 57 FED. COMM. L.J. 555 (2005) (criticizing the Supreme Court's American Library Association decision on constitutional grounds, including overbreadth).

63. OpenNet Initiative, Unintended Risks and Consequences of Circumvention Technologies (May 5, 2004), http://www.opennetinitiative.net/advisories/001/.

64. Cf. LAWRENCE LESSIG, FREE CULTURE: HOW BIG MEDIA USES TECHNOLOGY AND THE LAW TO LOCK DOWN CULTURE AND CONTROL CREATIVITY 197 (2004) ("[F]air use in America simply means the right to hire a lawyer.").

65. See Dan L. Burk & Julie E. Cohen, Fair Use Infrastructure for Rights Management Systems, 15 HARV. J.L. & TECH. 41, 50–51 (2001) (discussing how technological controls interact with fair use principles); Mark Gimbel, Some Thoughts on Implications of Trusted Systems for Intellectual Property Law, 50 STAN. L. REV. 1671 (1998); see also Digital Rights Management Conference, https://www.law.berkeley.edu/institutes/bclt/drm/resources.html#bmcp (last visited June 1, 2007) (containing links to articles and news about DRM and fair use).

66. See Storage Tech. Corp. v. Custom Hardware Eng'g & Consulting, Inc., 421 F. 3d 1307, 1318–21 (Fed. Cir. 2005); Universal City Studios, Inc. v. Corley, 273 F.3d 429 (2d Cir. 2001); 321 Studios v. MGM Studios, Inc., 307 F. Supp. 2d 1085 (N.D. Cal. 2004).

67. See Universal City Studies, Inc. v. Corley, 273 F.3d 429 (2d Cir. 2001).

68. Cf. NEGATIVLAND, FAIR USE: THE STORY OF THE LETTER U AND THE NUMERAL 2 (1995) (describing how copies of the band Negativland's release U2 were impounded as part of a settlement agreement between the band and Island Records establishing that the releases were contraband).

69. Neb. Press Ass'n v. Stuart, 427 U.S. 539, 559 (1976).

70. Id.

71. In 1979, the U.S. government blocked publication of Progressive article "The H-Bomb Secret: How We Got It, Why We're Telling It," which included information on how nuclear weapons functioned. The case was later dropped. See United States v. Progressive, Inc., 467 F. Supp. 990 (W.D. Wis. 1979); see also A. DEVOLPI ET AL., BORN SECRET: THE H-BOMB, THE "PROGRESSIVE" CASE, AND NATIONAL SECURITY (1981).

72. See John M. Ockerbloom, Books Banned Online, http://onlinebooks.library.upenn.edu/banned-books.html (last visited June 1, 2007).

73. Charles Memminger, Law Enforcement Inc. Is Next Big Private Industry, HONOLULU STAR-BULLETIN, July 8, 2001, available at http://starbulletin.com/2001/07/08/features/memminger.html ("[The use of traffic light cameras] feels icky, hints at technology run amok and provides us with a glance into the future where, smile, we're constantly on some candid camera or another and privacy will be a concept as quaint as horse-drawn carriages and Nintendo 64.").

74. See, e.g., NICHOLAS J. GARBER ET AL., AN EVALUATION OF RED LIGHT CAMERA (PHOTO-RED) ENFORCEMENT PROGRAMS IN VIRGINIA 108–10 (Jan. 2005), available at www.thenewspaper.com/rlc/docs/05-vdot.pdf (discussing possible malfunctions of the cameras and possibility of false positives).

75. U.S. CONST. amend. II.

76. *See, e.g.,* Parker v. District of Columbia, 478 F.3d 370, 382–86 (D.C. Cir. 2007); Tony Mauro, *Scholar's Shift in Thinking Angers Liberals,* USA TODAY, Aug. 27, 1999, *available at* http://www.saf.org/TribeUSA.html.

77. *Parker,* 478 F.3d at 383.

78. *See* William J. Stuntz, *Local Policing After the Terror,* 111 YALE L.J. 2137, 2163, 2165–66 (2002).

79. *In re U.S. for an Order Authorizing the Roving Interception of Oral Communications,* 349 F.3d 1132 (9th Cir. 2003). Similar instances of burdenless yet extensive search made possible by the digital space have continued to emerge. In one recent case, the FBI remotely installed spyware via e-mail for surveillance purposes. *See* Declan McCullagh, *FBI Remotely Installs Spyware to Trace Bomb Threat,* CNET NEWS, July 18, 2007, http://news.com.com/8301-10784_3-9746451-7.html. Recent proposals by German officials would broadly legalize similar methods for counterterrorism efforts. *See* Melissa Eddy, *Germany Wants to Spy on Suspects via Web,* ASSOC. PRESS, Aug. 21, 2007, http://hosted.ap.org/dynamic/stories/G/GERMANY_TROJAN_HORSES?SITE=WDUN&SECTION=HOME&TEMPLATE=DEFAULT.

80. *See* Hepting v. AT&T Corp., 439 F. Supp. 2d 974 (N.D. Cal. 2006) (denying summary judgment motion in a class-action lawsuit where plaintiffs alleged that the defendant telecommunication carrier was collaborating with the National Security Agency in a massive warrantless surveillance program).

81. Richard Posner cites whistleblowers as the reason not to worry about routine automated government data mining of citizen communications. *See* Richard A. Posner, Editorial, *Our Domestic Intelligence Crisis,* WASH. POST, Dec. 21, 2005, at A31.

82. *See* Lior Jacob Strahilevitz, *"How's My Driving?" for Everyone (and Everything?),* 81 N.Y.U. L. REV. 1699 (2006).

83. For an elaboration of objections along these lines, including rights to engage in acts of conscience, see Burk & Gillespie, *supra* note 43.

84. *See* Tim Wu, *Does YouTube Really Have Legal Problems?,* SLATE, Oct. 26, 2006, http://www.slate.com/id/2152264; *see also* Cohen, *supra* note 28 ("Pervasively distributed copyright enforcement portends fundamental change in these processes. The linked regimes of authorization and constraint will constrict the 'breathing room' that is a critical constituent of each of them."); Tim Wu, Tolerated Use & the Return of Notice-Based Copyright (forthcoming) (on file with the author).

85. Pub. L. No. 105-304, 112 Stat. 2860 (1998) (codified in scattered sections of 17 U.S.C.).

86. 17 U.S.C. § 512(a) (2000). This is true at least so long as the ISPs have a policy for "terminating repeat infringers," which in practice has not affected the way they operate.

87. Copyright owners subsequently launched a comprehensive campaign to use the DMCA to take down content. *See, e.g.,* Chilling Effects, Chilling Effects Clearinghouse, http://chillingeffects.org (last visited June 1, 2007); Press Release, Recording Indus. Ass'n of Am., Worldwide Music Industry Coordinates Its Strategy Against Piracy (Oct. 28, 1999), *available at* http://riaa.com/news_room.php (follow "1999" hyperlink; then follow "Next" hyperlink; then select press release).

88. *See, e.g.,* Yochai Benkler, *Free as the Air to Common Use: First Amendment Constraints on Enclosure of the Public Domain,* 74 N.Y.U. L. Rev. 354, 414–29 (1999); Lawrence Lessig, *The Internet Under Siege,* 127 Foreign Pol'y 56 (2001), *available at* www.lessig .org/content/columns/foreignpolicy1.pdf; Note, *The Criminalization of Copyright Infringement in the Digital Era,* 112 Harv. L. Rev. 1705 (1999).

89. The pages would then be available only when those PCs were turned on, and when not too many other people were viewing them. Further, it would be much more difficult to publish anonymously.

90. Of course, publishers still might like to be able to designate a particular clip as infringing and see all instances of it automatically removed. That is a narrower demand than wanting any infringing clip to be identified automatically in the first instance.

91. Gun control would appear to be a policy designed to preempt violent crimes, but I have promised not to enter that debate here.

92. *See* Jessica Litman, Digital Copyright (2001).

93. *See* Clayton Collins, *Why Blockbuster Clings to Its DVDs and Rentals,* Christian Sci. Monitor, Feb. 24, 2005, *available at* http://www.csmonitor.com/2005/0224/p12s01 -stct.html (reporting that the U.S. video-rental business had $8.2 billion in rental revenue in 2003 and $14 billion in VHS and DVD sales). Jack Valenti, former head of the Motion Picture Association of America (MPAA), warned at a Congressional hearing that "the VCR is to the movie industry what the Boston Strangler was to a woman alone." *Home Recording of Copyrighted Works: Hearings on H.R. 4783, H.R. 4794, H.R. 4808, H.R. 5250, H.R. 5488, and H.R. 5705 Before the Subcomm. on Courts, Civil Liberties and the Admin. of Justice of the H. Comm. on the Judiciary,* 97th Cong., 2d Sess. 65 (1982) (statement of Jack Valenti, President, Motion Picture Association of America). (He later said that the MPAA did not want to prevent the VCR's deployment; it simply wanted to be able, through a favorable ruling, to withhold permission for sale of the technology until manufacturers agreed to a per-unit fee on VCRs and blank videocassettes that would be remitted to the publishers.)

94. *BBC Moves to File-sharing Sites,* BBC News, Dec. 20, 2006, http://news.bbc.co.uk/2/ hi/technology/6194929.stm.

95. Press Release, Apple, Apple Unveils Higher Quality DRM-Free Music on the iTunes Store (Apr. 2, 2007), http://www.apple.com/pr/library/2007/04/02itunes.html.

96. *Cf.* Specht v. Netscape Commc'ns Corp., 150 F. Supp. 2d 585, 594 (S.D.N.Y. 2001) ("The few courts that have had occasion to consider click-wrap contracts have held them to be valid and enforceable.").

97. *See* 17 U.S.C. § 107 (2000).

98. *See* Meir Dan-Cohen, *Decision Rules and Conduct Rules: On Acoustic Separation in Criminal Law,* 97 Harv. L. Rev. 625, 626–30 (1984).

99. Consider, for example, the penalties for copyright infringement. Under the U.S. copyright statutory damages provision, 17 U.S.C. § 504(c), a copyright plaintiff may collect between $750 and $30,000 per work infringed by a "regular" infringer. Courts have wide discretion to choose a number within this range, and may consider factors such as deterrence, harm to the plaintiff's reputation, and value of the work. Thus, if a peer-to-

peer user shares one hundred works and a court chooses a mid-range figure like $10,000, a typical downloader could be held liable for $1,000,000. This may be an example of an acoustic separation opposite from Dan-Cohen's model—penalties far harsher than what a citizen would anticipate.

100. This process appears to be at work when professors deal out harsh midterm grades, but then temper those grades by adjusting the final exam.

101. Law professor Randal Picker argues in *Rewinding Sony: The Evolving Product, Phoning Home and the Duty of Ongoing Design*, 55 CASE W. RES. L. REV. 749, 766–68 (2005), that legal liability for PC software authors ought to be structured so that producers are encouraged to be able to update a product from afar if it turns out that the product enables infringing uses and an update would stop them. This is a strong but dangerous argument. Indeed, gatekeeping responsibilities might not stop at a software author's own products. OS makers could be asked to become gatekeepers for applications running on their systems. Consider, for example, the technical ease with which an OS maker could disable functionality on a tethered PC of software such as DeCSS, which enables decryption of DVDs, and for which distributors of software have been successfully sued. Any vendor of tethered software could be pressured to take such action, possibly removing the capability of noninfringing uses at the same time. The core problem with Picker's proposal, even for those software producers who resemble traditional gatekeepers, is that it fails to take into account the generative loss from compelling software originators to retain control.

102. *See* Steve Sechrist, *Day of Reckoning for AACS Copyright Protection,* DISPLAY DAILY, Feb. 20, 2007, http://displaydaily.com/2007/02/20/day-of-reckoning-for-aacs-copy-protection/.

103. David Post, *Comment on the Generative Internet* (on file with the author).

104. *See, e.g.,* Tim O'Reilly, *What Is Web 2.0,* O'REILLY, Sept. 30, 2005, http://www.oreilly net.com/pub/a/oreilly/tim/news/2005/09/30/what-is-web-20.html.

105. *See* Wikipedia, *Web 2.0: Web-based Applications and Desktops,* http://en.wikipedia.org/wiki/Web_2#Web-based_applications_and_desktops (as of June 1, 2007, 09:00 GMT).

106. *See, e.g.,* Mapquest, Copyright Information, http://www.mapquest.com/about/copy right.adp (last visited Dec. 1, 2007); Windows Live ID Microsoft Passport Network Terms of Use, https://accountservices.passport.net/PPTOU.srf (last visited June 1, 2007); Gmail Terms of Use, http://mail.google.com/mail/help/intl/en/terms_of_use.html (last visited June 1, 2007).

107. Google Maps API, http://code.google.com/apis/maps/index.html (last visited Dec. 1, 2007).

108. *See id.*

109. Posting of Mike Pegg to Google Maps Mania, *25 Things to Do with Google,* http://googlemapsmania.blogspot.com/2006/11/25-things-to-do-with-google-maps.html (Nov. 11, 2006, 09:38).

110. *See* Google Maps API Terms of Service, http://code.google.com/apis/maps/terms .html (last visited June 1, 2007).

111. Brad Stone, *MySpace Restrictions Upset Some Users,* N.Y. TIMES, Mar. 20, 2007, at C3,

available at http://www.nytimes.com/2007/03/20/technology/20myspace.html?ex
=1332043200&en=8e52c7903cb71959&ei=5088&partner=rssnyt&emc=rss.

112. *See* Michael Liedtke, *Google to Stop Web Video Rentals, Sales,* Yahoo! News, Aug. 10,
2007, http://news.yahoo.com/s/ap/20070811/ap_on_hi_te/google_video_4 (last
visited Aug. 13, 2007); Posting of Cory Doctorow to BoingBoing, *Google Video Robs
Customers of the Videos They "Own,"* http://www.boingboing.net/2007/08/10/ google_
video_robs_cu.html (Aug. 10, 2007, 21:34).

113. One example of this would be BitTorrent, "a peer-assisted, digital content delivery platform" that distributes the cost of sharing files by breaking them down into smaller
pieces that are each supplied by separate peers in the network. BitTorrent, Company
Overview, http://www.bittorrent.com/about/companyoverview (last visited Dec. 1,
2007).

114. A variety of programs already allow users to contribute idle CPU time to far-flung projects. *See, e.g.,* Climateprediction.net, http://climateprediction.net/ (last visited June
1, 2007); Rosetta@home, What is Rosetta@home?, http://boinc.bakerlab.org/rosetta
/rah_about.php (last visited June 1, 2007); SETI@home, The Science of SETI@home,
http://setiathome.berkeley.edu/sah_about.php (last visited June 1, 2007); World
Community Grid, About Us, http://www.worldcommunitygrid.org/about_us/view
AboutUs.do (last visited June 1, 2007).

115. Christopher Lawton, *'Dumb Terminals' Can Be a Smart Move,* Wall St. J., Jan. 30,
2007, at B3, *available at* http://online.wsj.com/public/article/SB11701197127429
1861-oJ6FWrnA8NMPfMXw3vBILth1EiE_20080129.html?mod=blogs.

116. *See generally* Access Denied: The Practice and Policy of Global Internet Filtering (Ronald J. Deibert et al. eds., 2008).

117. Recursively generative applications are capable of producing not only new works, but
also new generative applications that can then be used to create new works.

118. *See* Jonathan Zittrain, *Normative Principles for Evaluating Free and Proprietary Software,* 71 U. Chi. L. Rev. 265, 272–73 (2004) (describing an open development model
for software).

CHAPTER 6. THE LESSONS OF WIKIPEDIA

1. *See* Matthias Schulz, *Controlled Chaos: European Cities Do Away with Traffic Signs,*
Spiegel Online Int'l, Nov. 16, 2006, http://www.spiegel.de/international/spiegel/
0,1518,448747,00.html.

2. In the United States, studies by the Federal Highway Traffic Safety Administration
(FTSA) have shown that motorists disobey speed limits on non-interstates 70 percent
of the time. Interview with Earl Hardy, Speeding Expert, Nat'l Highway Traffic Safety
Admin., and Elizabeth Alicandri, Dir. of Office of Safety Programs, Fed. Highway Admin., Washingtonpost.com (Mar. 30, 2006), http://www.washingtonpost.com/
wp-dyn/content/discussion/2006/03/23/DI2006032301185.html.

3. Schulz, *supra* note 1.

4. For a discussion of the differences between rules and standards, see, for example, Alan

K. Chen, *The Ultimate Standard: Qualified Immunity in the Age of Constitutional Balancing Tests,* 81 Iowa L. Rev. 261, 266–70 (1995); Wilson Huhn, *The Stages of Legal Reasoning: Formalism, Analogy, and Realism,* 48 Vill. L. Rev. 305, 377–79 (2003); Louis Kaplow, *Rules Versus Standards: An Economic Analysis,* 42 Duke L.J. 557 (1992); Russell B. Korobkin, *Behavioral Analysis and Legal Form: Rules vs. Standards Revisited,* 79 Or. L. Rev. 23, 29–31 (2000); Larry Lessig, *Reading the Constitution in Cyberspace,* 45 Emory L.J. 869, 896–97 (1996) (arguing that software code can act as a societal constraint); Joel R. Reidenberg, *Governing Networks and Rule-Making in Cyberspace,* 45 Emory L.J. 911, 917–18, 927–28 (1996) (discussing the role and establishment of information policy default rules); Joel R. Reidenberg, *Rules of the Road for Global Electronic Highways: Merging the Trade and Technical Paradigms,* 6 Harv. J.L. & Tech. 287, 301–04 (1993); Antonin Scalia, *The Rule of Law as a Law of Rules,* 56 U. Chi. L. Rev. 1175, 1176 (1989) (discussing how rules are more consistent with democracy than standards); Frederick Schauer, *Rules and the Rule of Law,* 14 Harv. J.L. & Pub. Pol'y 645, 650–51, 658 (1991) (discussing legal realist arguments regarding the distinction between rules and standards); Pierre J. Schlag, *Rules and Standards,* 33 UCLA L. Rev. 379 (1985) (discussing whether there is a coherent distinction between rules and standards); Cass R. Sunstein, *Problems with Rules,* 83 Cal. L. Rev. 953, 963–64 (1995).

5. *See, e.g.,* Lawrence Kohlberg, From Is to Ought: How to Commit the Naturalistic Fallacy and Get Away with It in the Study of Moral Development (1971); Lawrence Kohlberg, *Moral Stages and Moralization: The Cognitive-Developmental Approach, in* Moral Development and Behavior: Theory, Research and Social Issues (T. Lickona ed., 1976); Lawrence Kohlberg, *The Claim to Moral Adequacy of a Highest Stage of Moral Judgment,* 70 J. Phil. 630, 630–46 (1973).

6. *See generally* Robert Axelrod, The Evolution of Cooperation (1984); Robert Ellickson, Order Without Law (1991); Wikipedia, *Prisoner's Dilemma,* http://en .wikipedia.org/wiki/Prisoner%27s_dilemma (as of June 1, 2007, 11:00 GMT).

7. Law-and-order conservatives embrace such an idea when they argue that social programs should be largely funded by the private sector, and that in the absence of government redistribution the poor will still receive charity. They assert that higher taxes make it difficult for people to express their commitments voluntarily to each other through charitable contributions. *See, e.g.,* Larry Catá Backer, *Medieval Poor Law in Twentieth Century America: Looking Back Towards a General Theory of Modern American Poor Relief,* 44 Case W. Res. L. Rev. 871, 929–34 (1995); Alice Gresham Bullock, *Taxes, Social Policy and Philanthropy: The Untapped Potential of Middle- and Low-Income Generosity,* 6 Cornell J.L. & Pub. Pol'y 325, 327–31 (1997).

8. *See* Donald L. McCabe and Linda Klebe Trevino, *Academic Dishonesty: Honor Codes and Other Contextual Influences* 64 J. Higher Educ. 522 (1993).

9. *See, e.g.,* W. Bradley Wendel, *Regulation of Lawyers Without the Code, the Rules, or the Restatement: Or, What Do Honor and Shame Have to Do with Civil Discovery Practice?,* 71 Fordham L. Rev. 1567 (2003); James Q. Whitman, *Enforcing Civility and Respect: Three Societies,* 109 Yale L.J. 1279 (2000).

10. *See also* Jonathan Zittrain, *Internet Points of Control,* 44 B.C. L. Rev. 653 (2003).

11. Norman N. Holland, *The Internet Regression, in* THE PSYCHOLOGY OF CYBERSPACE (John Suler ed., 1996), *available at* http://www.rider.edu/~suler/psycyber/holland.html.

12. *See, e.g.,* Lawrence B. Solum & Minn Chung, *The Layers Principle: Internet Architecture and the Law,* 79 NOTRE DAME L. REV. 815 (2004); Kevin Werbach, *A Layered Model for Internet Policy,* 1 J. TELECOMM. & HIGH TECH. L. 37 (2002); Richard S. Whitt, *A Horizontal Leap Forward: Formulating a New Public Policy Framework Based on the Network Layers Model,* 56 FED. COMM. L.J. 587 (2004); *see also* AKASH KAPUR, INTERNET GOVERNANCE: A PRIMER 13, 17–19 (2005), *available at* http://www.apdip.net/publications/iespprimers/eprimer-igov.pdf (discussing the different layers and how their existence should affect Internet governance).

13. *See* Alexa, Global Top 500, http://www.alexa.com/site/ds/top_sites?ts_mode= global&lang=none (last visited June 1, 2007). While the sites' rankings tend to fluctuate, Wikipedia is consistently listed within the top 10.

14. For examples of attempts to create this library, see Internet Archive, Bibliotheca Alexandrina, http://www.archive.org/about/bibalex_p_r.php (last visited June 1, 2007); Alexandria Digital Library, http://www.alexandria.ucsb.edu/ (last visited June 1, 2007); Posting of Ionut Alex Chitu to Google Operating System, *Google's Digital Library of Alexandria,* http://googlesystem.blogspot.com/2006/08/googles-digital-library-of-alexandria.html (Aug. 13, 2006).

15. Wikipedia, *Encyclopaedia Britannica,* http://en.wikipedia.org/wiki/Encyclop%C3% A6dia_Britannica (as of June 1, 2007, 10:00 GMT).

16. *Id.*

17. The History Place, The Rise of Adolf Hitler, http://www.historyplace.com/worldwar2/riseofhitler/ (last visited June 1, 2007).

18. Cats That Look Like Hitler!, http://www.catsthatlooklikehitler.com/ (last visited June 1, 2007) (using the term "kitlers" to describe cats that look like Hitler).

19. Wikipedia founder Jimmy Wales underscores that Bomis, his dot-com search engine business, was not directly involved in pornography, pointing out that its content was R-rated rather than X-rated, like *Maxim* magazine rather than *Playboy.* This came to light when *Wired* reported that he had edited his own Wikipedia entry to make it more precise on the matter. *See* Evan Hansen, *Wikipedia Founder Edits Own Bio,* WIRED, Dec. 19, 2005, http://www.wired.com/news/culture/0,1284,69880,00.html.

20. GNE Is Not an Encyclopedia, GNE Help-Moderators, http://gne.sourceforge.net/eng/help/moderators.htm (last visited Mar. 9, 2007).

21. GNE Is Not an Encyclopedia, The GNE FAQ, http://gne.sourceforge.net/eng/faq.htm (last visited June 1, 2007).

22. Wikipedia, *Bomis,* http://en.wikipedia.org/wiki/Bomis (as of Apr. 11, 2007, 14:16 GMT).

23. Stacy Schiff, *Know It All: Can Wikipedia Conquer Expertise?,* NEW YORKER (July 21, 2006), *available at* http://www.newyorker.com/archive/2006/07/31/060731fa_fact.

24. Wikipedia, *Nupedia,* http://en.wikipedia.org/wiki/Nupedia (as of Apr. 30, 2007, 18:01 GMT).

25. *Id.*

26. Nupedia, The Free Encyclopedia, http://nupedia.8media.org (last visited June 1, 2007).

27. Posting of Timothy to Slashdot, *The Early History of Nupedia and Wikipedia: A Memoir,* http://features.slashdot.org/features/05/04/18/164213.shtml (Apr. 18, 2005, *updated* Apr. 20, 2005 19:19 GMT).

28. Also known as the "robustness principle." *See* INFO. SCI. INST., UNIV. OF S. CAL., TRANS- MISSION CONTROL PROTOCOL: DARPA INTERNET PROGRAM PROTOCOL SPECIFICATION (Jon Postel ed., Sept. 1981), *available at* http://rfc.sunsite.dk/rfc/rfc793.html.

29. *See* Wikipedia Meta-Wiki, *Wikipedia,* http://meta.wikimedia.org/wiki/Wikipedia (as of June 1, 2007, 08:15 GMT).

30. Wikipedia Meta-Wiki, *Three-Revert Rule,* http://en.wikipedia.org/wiki/Wikipedia: Three-revert_rule (as of June 1, 2007, 08:15 GMT).

31. Wikipedia policy prohibits "wheel wars"—cases in which a Wikipedia administrator re- peatedly undoes the action of another—just as it prohibits edit wars. *See* Wikipedia, *Wheel War,* http://en.wikipedia.org/wiki/Wikipedia:Wheel_war (as of May 30, 2007 at 21:40 GMT). A meta-meta-rule is that while administrators do not second-guess each others' actions without good reason, some restrictions require persistent consensus among admins—nearly any admin may unprotect a page or remove a block.

32. *See* Wikipedia, *Wikipedia: No Legal Threats,* http://en.wikipedia.org/wiki/Wikipedia: No_legal_threats (as of May 30, 2007 at 21:41 GMT).

33. *E.g.,* Wikipedia Meta-Wiki, Editing with Tor, http://meta.wikimedia.org/wiki/Tor (as of June 1, 2007, 08:15 GMT) ("English Wikipedia tends to block every Tor node.").

34. Wikipedia, *Barnstar,* http://en.wikipedia.org/wiki/Barnstar (as of June 1, 2007, 08:20 GMT).

35. There are many different Wikipedia barnstars that connote different things. For exam- ple, General Barnstars are awarded to describe "contributions or editing along a specific theme." The Barnstar of High Culture, Epic Barnstar, and Ancient Ruin History Barn- star are examples of barnstars awarded "in recognition of excellent contributions" that are within one of seven major categories listed on the Main Page. Wikimedia Commons, *Barnstar,* http://commons.wikimedia.org/wiki/Barnstar (as of June 1, 2007, 08:30 GMT) (describing different barnstars awarded to Wikipedia contributors).

36. Wikipedia, *English Wikipedia,* http://en.wikipedia.org/wiki/English_Wikipedia (as of June 1, 2007, 08:25 GMT).

37. *See* Eric S. Raymond, *Release Early, Release Often, in* THE CATHEDRAL AND THE BAZAAR: MUSINGS ON LINUX AND OPEN SOURCE BY AN ACCIDENTAL REVOLUTIONARY (2001), *available at* http://www.catb.org/~esr/writings/cathedral-bazaar/cathedral-bazaar/ ar01s04.html.

38. *See supra* note 2.

39. Jim Giles, *Internet Encyclopaedias Go Head to Head,* NATURE NEWS, Dec. 14, 2005, http://www.nature.com/news/2005/051212/full/438900a.html (last updated Mar. 28, 2006).

40. Except for those younger users that shun it for more instantaneous forms of messaging.

See Nate Anderson, *Teens: E-mail Is for Old People,* Ars Technica, Oct. 2, 2006, http://arstechnica.com/news.ars/post/20061002-7877.html.

41. Gregg Keizer, *Spam Sets Record, Accounts for 94 Percent of E-mail,* IT News, Jan. 11, 2007, http://www.itnews.com.au/newsstory.aspx?CIaNID=44188.

42. *See supra* Ch. 3.

43. *See* Wikipedia, *Wikipedia: Counter-Vandalism Unit,* http://en.wikipedia.org/wiki/Wikipedia:Counter-Vandalism_Unit (as of May 30, 2007, at 17:40 GMT); Wikipedia, *Wikipedia: Barnstars,* http://en.wikipedia.org/wiki/Wikipedia:Barnstars (as of Sep. 30, 2007, 00:18 GMT) ("The Defender of the Wiki may be awarded to those who have gone above and beyond to prevent Wikipedia from being used for fraudulent purposes. It was created after the 2004 Indian Ocean earthquake, when a fraudulent charity tried to take advantage of the widespread media coverage of the article.").

44. *See, e.g.,* Wikipedia, *User:MartinBot,* http://en.wikipedia.org/wiki/User:MartinBot (as of May 30, 2007, 17:41 GMT).

45. The actual Wikipedia entry stated: "For a brief time, [Seigenthaler] was thought to have been directly involved in the Kennedy assassinations of both John, and his brother, Bobby. Nothing was ever proven." John Seigenthaler, *A False Wikipedia 'Biography,'* USA Today, Nov. 29, 2005, *available at* http://www.usatoday.com/news/opinion/editorials/2005-11-29-wikipedia-edit_x.htm.

46. Wikipedia, *Seigenthaler Controversy,* http://en.wikipedia.org/wiki/John_Seigenthaler_Sr._Wikipedia_biography_controversy (as of June 1, 2007, 09:00 GMT).

47. Wikipedia, Deletion Log, http://en.wikipedia.org/w/index.php?title=Special%3ALog&type=delete&user=Essjay&page=John+Seigenthaler+Sr (as of June 1, 2007, 09:00 GMT) (allowing user to look at deletions for a given Wikipedia page).

48. *See* 47 U.S.C. § 230 (c)(1) (2000); Seigenthaler, *supra* note 45.

49. 47 U.S.C. § 230 (c)(1) (2000); *see also* Ken S. Myers, *Wikimmunity: Fitting the Communications Decency Act to Wikipedia,* 20 Harv. J.L. & Tech. 163 (2006) (concluding that Wikipedia would be immune under CDA § 230 provisions). There is an unexplored doctrinal issue with CDA § 230: Wikipedia's unusual structure makes it difficult to ascertain whether a Wikipedia editor should be deemed an agent of Wikipedia for liability purposes, just as a reporter for an online newspaper, as the newspaper's agent, can make statements that give rise to liability for the paper, CDA § 230 notwithstanding.

50. Michael Snow, Article Creation Restricted to Logged-in Editors (Dec. 5, 2005), http://en.wikipedia.org/wiki/Wikipedia:Wikipedia_Signpost/2005-12-05/Page_creation_restrictions.

51. *See supra* note 19.

52. Wikipedia, *Congressional Staffer Edits to Wikipedia,* http://en.wikipedia.org/wiki/Congressional_staffer_edits_to_Wikipedia (as of June 1, 2007, 09:00 GMT).

53. *Time on Wikipedia Was Wasted,* Lowell Sun, Jan. 28, 2006.

54. *See generally* James Surowiecki, The Wisdom of Crowds (2004).

55. Centiare, Directory: MyWikiBiz, http://www.centiare.com/Directory:MyWikiBiz (as of June 1, 2007, 09:05 GMT).

56. *Id.*

57. Wikipedia, *User Talk:MyWikiBiz,* http://en.wikipedia.org/wiki/User_talk:MyWikiBiz /Archive_1 (as of June 1, 2007, 09:05 GMT).

58. E-mail from Jimmy Wales, founder, Wikipedia, to WikiEN-1 mailing list, *about My WikiBiz* (Aug. 9, 2006, 02:58 PM), http://www.nabble.com/MyWikiBiz-tf2080660 .html.

59. Wikipedia, *User:Essjay/RFC,* http://en.wikipedia.org/wiki/User:Essjay/RFC (as of June 1, 2007, 09:00 GMT).

60. *See* Noam Cohen, *After False Claim, Wikipedia to Check Degrees,* N.Y. TIMES, Mar. 12, 2007, at C8, *available at* http://www.nytimes.com/2007/03/12/technology/12wiki.html.

61. Wikipedia, *User_talk:Essjay,* http://en.wikipedia.org/wiki/User_talk:Essjay (as of Apr. 18, 2007, 18:11 GMT).

62. *See, e.g.,* Wikipedia, *Wikipedia: Requests for Arbitration/Pedophilia Userbox Wheel War,* http://en.wikipedia.org/wiki/Wikipedia: Requests_for_arbitration/Pedophilia_userbox _wheel_war#Jimbo_as_the_ultimate _authority (as of May 30, 2007, 21:58 GMT), in which Wikipedia editors and administrators warred over whether to permit a Wikipedia user to identify himself as a pedophile on his Wikipedia user page. Jimbo ultimately cut the debate short by removing the label and banning its return, and the Wikipedia arbitration committee recognized Jimbo's powers, subject to review by the Wikimedia Foundation's board of trustees, to pretermit what would otherwise be a decision handled through other processes. On the other hand, Jimbo's creation of a new Wikipedia article for Mizoli's Meats, a South African butcher shop, was deleted by a sysop twenty-two minutes later, deemed manifestly unworthy of inclusion. *See* David Sarno, *Wikipedia Wars Erupt,* L.A. TIMES, Sept. 30, 2007, *available at* http://www.latimes.com/entertainment /news/newmedia/la-ca-webscout 30sep30,1,6497628.story.

63. *See* A. Michael Froomkin, *Habermas@Discourse.net: Toward a Critical Theory of Cyberspace,* 116 HARV. L. REV. 749 (2003).

64. Jon Postel was the RFC editor for twenty-eight years, choosing which drafts of requests for comment to publish as IETF RFCs. RFC Editor et al., RFC 2555; 30 Years of RFCs (Apr. 7, 1999), http://www.ietf.org/rfc/rfc2555.txt. He was also the Internet Assigned Numbers Authority, a name given to the functions he performed in allocating blocks of IP addresses. *See* Jonathan Zittrain, *ICANN: Between the Public and the Private,* 14 BERKELEY TECH. L.J. 1071 (1999); Todd Wallack & Ellen Messmer, *Industry Asks: Who Is Jon Postel?,* NETWORK WORLD (Apr. 21, 1997), http://www.networkworld.com/ news/0421postel.html.

65. *See* RACHEL KLEINFELD BELTON, COMPETING DEFINITIONS OF THE RULE OF LAW (Jan. 2005), *available at* http://www.carnegieendowment.org/files/CP55.Belton.FINAL .pdf; *see also* DEMOCRACY AND THE RULE OF LAW (Adam Przeworski & Jose Maria Maravall eds., 2003); ALBERT VENN DICEY, INTRODUCTION TO THE STUDY OF THE LAW OF THE CONSTITUTION 175–336 (5th ed. 1897); FRIEDRICH A. HAYEK, THE CONSTITUTION OF LIBERTY 162–76 (1960); CHARLES DE MONTESQUIEU, MONTESQUIEU: THE SPIRIT OF THE LAWS (Anne M. Cohler et al. eds., 1989); SAMUEL RUTHERFORD, LEX, REX, OR THE LAW AND THE PRINCE (1998); Philip Selznick, *American Society and the Rule of Law,* 33 SYRACUSE J. INT'L L. & COM. 29 (2005); Barry R. Weingast, *The Politi-*

cal Foundations of Democracy and the Rule of Law, 91 Am. Pol. Sci. Rev. 245 (1997); Anthony M. Kennedy, Assoc. Justice, U.S. Supreme Court, Speech at the American Bar Association Annual Meeting (Aug. 9, 2003)(revised Aug. 14, 2003), *available at* http:// www.supremecourtus.gov/publicinfo/speeches/sp_08–09–03.html; Wikipedia, *Rule of Law,* http://en.wikipedia.org/wiki/Rule_of_law (as of June 1, 2007, 08:30 GMT).

66. Wiki Truth, *Jimbo Found Out,* http://www.wikitruth.info/index.php?title=Jimbo_ Found_Out (last visited June 1, 2007).

67. Wikipedia, *Articles for Deletion/Angela Beesley,* http://en.wikipedia.org/wiki/Wikipedia: Articles_for_deletion/Angela_Beesley (as of Jan 6. 2007, 19:17 GMT).

68. Wikipedia, *Articles for Deletion/Angela Beesley (3rd nomination),* http://en.wikipedia .org/wiki/Wikipedia:Articles_for_deletion/Angela_Beesley_(3rd_nomination) (as of May 3, 2007, 16:46 GMT).

69. 17 U.S.C. § 512 (2000); *see also* Wikipedia, *Online Copyright Infringement Liability Limitation Act,* http://en.wikipedia.org/wiki/Online_Copyright_Infringement_Liability _Limitation_Act (providing a summary of the § 512 provisions of the DMCA) (as of June 1, 2007, 09:00 GMT); *supra* Ch. 5, note 83 and accompanying text.

70. RU Sirius, *Jimmy Wales Will Destroy Google,* 10 Zen Monkeys (Jan. 29, 2007), http://www.10zenmonkeys.com/2007/01/29/wikipedia-jimmy-wales-rusirius-google-objectivism/.

71. Communitarianism is a social theory that rejects the devaluation of community. In asserting that family, friends, and social groups are important to the good life, communitarians focus on three themes: the importance of social context and tradition for meaning-making, the self's social nature, and the community's normative value. Each of these themes suggests the importance of allowing individuals to participate freely in various aspects of society and to shape the society in which they live. *See* Alasdair MacIntyre, *Concept of a Tradition,* in Liberalism and its Critics 125, 142 ("We all approach our own circumstances as bearers of a particular social identity. I am someone's son or daughter, someone else's cousin or uncle; I am a citizen of this or that city, a member of this or that guild or profession; I belong to this claim, that tribe, this notion. Hence what is good for me has to be the good for one who inhabits these roles."); Michael J. Sandel, *Justice and the Good,* in *id.,* 159, 165 (Sandel ed., 1984) ("[I]n so far as our constitutive self-understandings comprehend a wider subject than the individual alone, whether a family or tribe or city or class or nation or people, to this extent they define a community in the constitutive sense. And what marks such a community is not merely a spirit of benevolence, or the prevalence of communitarian values, or even 'shared final ends' alone, but a common vocabulary of discourse and a background of implicit practices and understandings within which the opacity of the participants is reduced if never finally dissolved."); Michael Walzer, Thick and Thin 27 (1984) (arguing that meaning is made with reference to particular social contexts that are "shared across a society, among a group of people with a common life"); *see generally* Daniel Bell, Communitarianism and Its Critics (1993); Robert Nisbet, The Quest for Community (1953); Cass R. Sunstein, *Beyond the Republican Revival,* 97 Yale L.J. 1539 (1988); Robert J. Condlin, *Bargaining with a Hugger: The Weakness and Limitations of a Communitarian Conception*

of Legal Dispute Bargaining, Or Why We Can't All Just Get Along (Berkeley Press Legal Series, Working Paper No. 1194), *available at* http://works.bepress.com/cgi/viewcontent .cgi?article=1000&context=robert_condlin.

72. *See* Europa Glossary, Subsidiarity, http://europa.eu/scadplus/glossary/subsidiarity _en.htm (last visited June 1, 2007); Wikipedia, *Subsidiarity,* http://en.wikipedia.org/ wiki/Subsidiarity (as of June 1, 2007, 09:00 GMT).

73. *See* IDG News Serv., *Chinese Censors Block Access to Wikipedia,* ITWORLD.COM, June 14, 2004, http://www.itworld.com/Tech/2987/040614wikipedia/; Wikipedia, *Blocking of Wikipedia in Mainland China,* http://en.wikipedia.org/wiki/Blocking_of_Wikipedia _in_mainland_China (as of June 1, 2007, 08:45 GMT).

74. Not every version of Wikipedia has the same policies. The German Wikipedia recently instituted a test project to have concurrent versions of pages—stable and unstable—so that the edits would need to be approved by a Wikipedian of a certain stature before going live. The plan was designed to address vandalism problems and allow edits to previously protected pages. *See* Daniel Terdiman, *Can German Engineering Fix Wikipedia,* CNET NEWS.COM, Aug. 23, 2006, http://news.com.com/2100–1038_3–6108495 .html.

75. *See supra* note 1 and accompanying text.

76. Wikipedia is licensed under the GNU Free Documentation License. This license allows anyone to copy, redistribute, or modify the work for commercial or noncommercial purposes, as long as the author is properly attributed and that any resulting derivative works are also under the same license. *See* GNU Project, Free Documentation License, http://www.gnu.org/licenses/fdl.html (last visited June 1, 2007). The latter provision is often referred to as "copyleft." *Id.* There is currently some debate surrounding the state of Wikipedia's license. The GFDL is not currently compatible with the Creative Commons Attribution-Sharealike (BY-SA), a similar and more widely used license. There is interest in making Wikipedia available under the CC BY-SA or compatible license, which would make Wikipedia's content better able to be incorporated into other works. Such a process would likely require an update by the creators of the GFDL (the Free Software Foundation) to allow for compatibility with the CC BY-SA license.

77. Wales may be reconsidering: "'When we're turning down millions and millions of dollars in advertising revenue that could be used, to for example, put computers in schools in Africa . . . we have to [be] very thoughtful and responsible about why we're doing it,' he said in an interview." Wendell Roelf, *Wikipedia Founder Mulls Revenue Options,* REUTERS, Apr. 20, 2007, http://reuters.com/internetNews/idUSL1964587420070420.

78. Wikipedia, *Mirrors and Forks/Abc,* http://en.wikipedia.org/wiki/Wikipedia:Mirrors _and_forks/Abc (as of June 1, 2007, 09:10 GMT).

79. Wikipedia, *Talk:Gracenote,* http://en.wikipedia.org/wiki/Talk:Gracenote (as of June 1, 2007, 09:10 GMT).

80. Dove, Dove Cream Oil Body Wash (online broadcast), http://dovecreamoil.com/ (displaying results of Dove Cream Oil contest where users were asked to make their own commercials); *Video: Angry Attack Ads Roll In,* CNET NEWS.COM, Mar. 31, 2006. http://news.com.com/1606-2-6056633.html (showing a medley of user-submitted commercials criticizing the Chevy Tahoe).

81. *But see* Louise Story, *The High Price of Creating Free Ads,* N.Y. TIMES, May 26, 2007, at http://www.nytimes.com/2007/05/26/business/26content.html (explaining the downsides of relying on user-generated content for advertising).

82. Rebecca Popuch, Yelp Elite Status, http://www.yelp.com/user_details_reviews_self ?userid=-4XnJXO0YQhcl7Dz2Yir_g&rec_pagestart=10&review_sort=time, Feb. 4, 2007. Popuch notes that Yelp does not permit users to delete their own profiles, so changes of heart cannot be promptly reflected by initiating a mass deletion of one's contributions to the system. See *infra* Ch. 9 for further discussion of this policy.

83. *See supra* Ch. 4, note 72 and accompanying text.

84. *See, e.g.,* Posting of Rebecca Mackinnon to RConversation, *Google in China: Degrees of Evil,* http://rconversation.blogs.com/rconversation/2006/01/google_in_china.html, (Jan. 25, 2006, 12:49); Press Release, Reporters Without Borders, Google Launches Censored Version of Its Search Engine (Jan. 25, 2006), *available at* http://www.rsf.org/ article.php3?id_article=16262; Amnesty Int'l, Amnesty International Launches Global Campaign Against Internet Repression, http://web.amnesty.org/library/Index/ENGACT 300162006 (last visited June 1, 2007); Curbing Corporate Complicity in Internet Filtering and Surveillance: Tech Firms Pursue Code of Conduct, Open Net Initiative (Feb. 1, 2007), http://www.opennetinitiative.net/blog/?p=137.

85. *See* SUROWIECKI, *supra* note 54, at 15–17, 72, 85.

86. Ilse Arendse, 'MySpace Will Fail . . . ', News24, Apr. 20, 2007, http://www.news24 .com/News24/Technology/News/0,,2-13-1443_2102112,00.html.

87. *See* Deciphering the Mystery of Bee Flight, PhysOrg.com, Nov. 30, 2005, http://www .physorg.com/news8616.html.

PART III. SOLUTIONS

1. *See, e.g.,* Placeopedia, http://www.placeopedia.com/ (last visited May 30, 2007) (linking Wikipedia articles to specific locations and showing them on a map) Soup Soup Augmented News, http://www.soup-soup.net/ (last visited May 30, 2007) (featuring news, links to Wikipedia articles that give background on the places in the news, and blogs and photos on similar topics in one place).

2. *See* Joyce K. Reynolds, RFC 1135: The Helminthiasis of the Internet (Dec. 1989), http://www.ietf.org/rfc/rfc1135.txt.

3. *See* John Borland, *See Who's Editing Wikipedia,* WIRED.COM, Aug. 15, 2007, http:// www.wired.com/politics/onlinerights/news/2007/08/wiki_tracker (explaining the mechanics of Wikiscanner); Posting of Kevin Poulsen to meat level, *Vote on the Most Shameful Wikipedia Spin Jobs,* WIRED.COM, http://blog.wired.com/27bstroke6/wikiwatch/ (Aug. 13, 2007, 23:03 GMT) (curating a user-contributed library of particularly notable instances of organizational censorship on Wikipedia).

4. *See generally* James Surowiecki, THE WISDOM OF CROWDS (2004). For a discussion of communitarian views of democratic citizenship and participatory meaning-making, see, for example, Michael Walzer, *Response,* in PLURALISM, JUSTICE, AND EQUALITY 282 (David Miller & Michael Walzer eds., 1993).

5. Communitarians have championed citizens' role in shaping their communities. *See, e.g.,*

MICHAEL WALZER, THICK AND THIN: MORAL ARGUMENT AT HOME AND ABROAD (rev. ed. 2006); Michael J. Sandel, *Justice and the Good*, in LIBERALISM AND ITS CRITICS 159 (Michael Sandel ed., 1984). For more on communitarianism, see generally ALASDAIR C. MACINTYRE, AFTER VIRTUE: A STUDY IN MORAL THEORY (2d ed. 1984); MICHAEL J. SANDEL, DEMOCRACY'S DISCONTENT: AMERICA IN SEARCH OF A PUBLIC PHILOSOPHY (reprint ed. 1998); MICHAEL WALZER, SPHERES OF JUSTICE: A DEFENSE OF PLURALISM AND EQUALITY (reprint ed. 1984).

CHAPTER 7. STOPPING THE FUTURE OF THE INTERNET

1. For a sketch of such a machine, see Butler Lampson, Microsoft, Powerpoint on Accountability and Freedom 17–18 (Sept. 26, 2005), http://research.microsoft.com/lampson/slides/accountabilityAndFreedomAbstract.htm.

2. *See* Dan Griffin, *Create Custom Login Experiences with Credential Providers for Windows Vista*, MSDN MAG., Jan. 2007, http://msdn.microsoft.com/msdnmag/issues/07/01/CredentialProviders/?topics=/msdnmag/issues/07/01/CredentialProviders (detailing ways in which an organization can customize the Windows Vista logon screen and implement various authentication methods).

3. Some have suggested that the Internet ought to be zoned in a parallel fashion, thereby distinguishing it in an analogous fashion to the scenario involving Red and Green PCs. *See* Riva Richmond, *Software to Spot 'Phishers' Irks Small Concerns,* WALL ST. J., Dec. 19, 2006, at B1, *available at* http://online.wsj.com/public/article/SB116649577602354120-5U4Afb0JPeyiOy1H_j3fVTUmfG8_20071218.html (describing a feature in Internet Explorer 7 that turns the Internet address bar green when entering an e-commerce site that Microsoft has certified as legitimate); *see also* David S. Isenberg, *The Internet Experiment Is Not Finished,* VON MAG., Mar. 2006, at 64, *available at* http://www.vonmag-digital.com/vonmag/200603/?pg=66 (suggesting that the red-green divide I outline in this book will be exploited by "control-freak incumbents" seeking to wall off generativity).

4. *Cf.* David Talbot, *The Internet Is Broken—Part 2,* TECH. REV., Dec. 20, 2005, *available at* http://www.technologyreview.com/printer_friendly_article.aspx?id=16055 (describing "middleman" technologies that authenticate Internet communications by receiving identification information from senders and routing certain attributes of this information on to recipients).

5. *See, e.g.,* Granma's Rules of POLA, http://www.skyhunter.com/marcs/granmaRulesPola.html (last visited June 1, 2007) (outlining six rules for desktop security based on the Principle of Least Authority); Sudhakar Govindavajhala & Andrew W. Appel, Windows Access Control Demystified 2 (Jan. 31, 2006) (unpublished manuscript under submission), *available at* http://www.cs.princeton.edu/~sudhakar/papers/winval.pdf (detailing how the "fine-grained and expressive" character of Windows access control makes it difficult to evaluate the consequences of commercial access-control configurations, which leads to misconfigurations and "privilege-escalation vulnerabilities"); Introduction to Capability Based Security, http://www.skyhunter.com/marcs/capabilityIntro/index.html (last visited June 1, 2007).

6. *See Wikipedia Qatar Ban 'Temporary,'* BBC News, Jan. 2, 2007, http://news.bbc.co.uk/ 1/hi/technology/6224677.stm; *see also* Wikipedia User Page, User talk:82.148.97.69, http://en.wikipedia.org/wiki/User_talk:82.148.97.69 (as of Mar. 23, 2007, 00:10 GMT) (explaining, on the user talk page of an IP address used by many people in Qatar, why the IP address was blocked).

7. *See Web Users to 'Patrol' US Border,* BBC News, June 2, 2006, http://news.bbc.co.uk/1/ hi/world/americas/5040372.stm.

8. I am a principal investigator of StopBadware.

9. This distributed approach to resolving generative social problems has begun to see greater use and experimentation. One example is the U.S. Department of Homeland Security's proposed Cell-All program, which would outfit cell phones with sensors for biological and chemical weapons and report "hits" to a central database. *See* Mimi Hall, *Phones Studied as Attack Detector,* USA TODAY, May 3, 2007, http://www.usa today.com/tech/news/techpolicy/2007-05-03-cellphone-attack-detector_ N.htm?csp=34.

10. *See* L. Jean Camp & Allan Friedman, Good Neighbors Can Make Good Fences: A Peer-to-Peer User Security System (Sept. 24, 2005) (conference paper, presented at Research Conference on Comm'cn, Info. and Internet Pol'y), http://web.si.umich.edu/tprc/ papers /2005/453/tprc_GoodNeighbors.pdf.

11. *See* YOCHAI BENKLER, THE WEALTH OF NETWORKS 285–87 (2006).

12. *Cf.* Alasdair MacIntyre, *Seven Traits for the Future,* 9 HASTINGS CTR. REP. 5, 6–7 (1979) (discussing the importance of "cooperative and rational" planning, celebrating "non-manipulative relationships," and describing the ideal society as one in which citizens do not "fence around unpredictability wherever it is to be found").

13. When done well, community initiatives can serve to mitigate the less egalitarian outcomes which the move toward private policing has caused. *See, e.g.,* Clifford Shearing & Jennifer Wood, *Governing Security for Common Goods,* 31 INT. J. SOC. L. 205 (2003). However, there are criticisms of such community initiatives. In this view, there need to be structures in place to protect minority views within the communities, otherwise their rights can be trampled.

14. John Perry Barlow, A Declaration of Independence of Cyberspace (Feb. 8, 1996), http:// homes.eff.org/~barlow/Declaration-Final.html.

15. *See, e.g.,* Kevin R. Pinkney, *Putting Blame Where Blame Is Due: Software Manufacturer and Customer Liability for Security-Related Software Failure,* 13 ALB. L.J. SCI. & TECH. 43, 46 (2002) (arguing that software makers should be liable for exploited security vulnerabilities).

16. In the American legal system, the main reason for this is because the harm from bad software is usually only economic, and liability for a defective product requires some form of physical harm arising from the defect. *See* RAYMOND T. NIMMER, THE LAW OF COMPUTER TECHNOLOGY § 10:32 (3d ed. 2006).

17. That might be the only remedy owed the consumer, rather than, for example, emotional damages from missing one's favorite shows. This arises from the difference between damages in contract and tort. *See generally* W. PAGE KEETON, PROSSER AND KEETON ON THE LAW OF TORTS 962 (1984).

18. *See* Wikipedia, *Blue Screen of Death,* http://en.wikipedia.org/wiki/Blue_screen_of_ death (as of June 1, 2007, 09:30 GMT).

19. *See supra* Ch. 5, at 119.

20. *See* Jonathan Zittrain, *A History of Online Gatekeeping,* 19 HARV. J.L. & TECH. 253 (2006).

21. *See* David P. Reed et al., *Active Networking and End-to-End Arguments,* IEEE NETWORK, May/June 1998, at 69–71, *available at* http://web.mit.edu/Saltzer/www/publications/ endtoend/ANe2ecomment.html.

22. *See* Marjory S. Blumenthal, *End-to-End and Subsequent Paradigms,* 2002 L. REV. M.S.U.-D.C.L. 709, 717 (2002) (remarking that end-to-end arguments "interact with economics, public policy, and advocacy dynamically to shape access to communication and information and to influence innovation").

23. *See infra* Ch. 8, note 8.

24. *See* Jonathan Zittrain, *The Generative Internet,* 119 HARV. L. REV. 1974, 1988–89 (2006).

25. *See* Saul Hansell, *Spam Fighters Turn to Identifying Legitimate E-Mail,* N.Y. TIMES, Oct. 6, 2003, at C1 (discussing authentication and other possible solutions for limiting spam); Yakov Shafranovich, *2004: The Year That Promised Email Authentication,* CIR- CLEID, Dec. 27, 2004, http://www.circleid.com/posts/2004_the_year_that_promised_ email_authentication (discussing various e-mail authentication proposals to limit spam on the receiving end); *see also* Saul Hansell, *4 Rivals Near Agreement on Ways to Fight Spam,* N.Y. TIMES, June 23, 2004, at C1 (discussing approaches toward authentication proposed by major ISPs).

26. *See, e.g.,* JOHANNES ULLRICH, INTERNET SERVICE PROVIDERS: THE LITTLE MAN'S FIRE- WALL (2003), http://www.sans.org/reading_room/special/index.php?id=isp_blocking (providing a case study of traffic filtering by ISPs).

27. *See* John Markoff, *Attack of the Zombie Computers Is a Growing Threat, Experts Say,* N.Y. TIMES, Jan. 7, 2007, § 1, at 1.

28. *See* Ryan Naraine, *Microsoft Says Recovery from Malware Becoming Impossible,* EWEEK .COM, Apr. 4, 2006, http://www.eweek.com/article2/0,1895,1945808,00.asp.

29. *See, e.g.,* StopBadware.org Identifies Companies Hosting Large Numbers of Websites That Can Infect Internet Users with Badware, StopBadware.org, May 3, 2007, http:// stopbadware.org/home/pr_050307 (discussing the top five hosting providers in their clearinghouse and pointing out that while providers were often quick to help Web site owners clean the code, they were unprepared to answer customers' questions about vul- nerabilities that permitted hacks in the first place).

30. *See* Reinier H. Kraakman, *Gatekeepers: The Anatomy of a Third-Party Enforcement Strat- egy,* 2 J.L. ECON. & ORG. 61 (1986) (identifying four criteria for the appropriateness of legal intervention: "(1) serious misconduct that practicable penalties cannot deter; (2) missing or inadequate private gatekeeping incentives; (3) gatekeepers who can and will prevent misconduct reliably, regardless of the preferences and market alternatives of wrongdoers; and (4) gatekeepers whom legal rules can induce to detect misconduct at reasonable cost").

31. Paul Festa, *Hotmail Uses Controversial Filter to Fight Spam,* CNET NEWS.COM, Nov. 9, 1999, http://news.com.com/Hotmail+uses+controversial+filter+to+fight+spam/2100-1040_3-232706.html.

32. *Id.* ("MAPS has used the RBL primarily to pressure server administrators to mend their policies, according to supporters. 'The RBL is an educational tool for applying pressure more than a technical tool,' said John Mozena, vice president of CAUCE, which has ties to both Hotmail and MAPS. 'The wider implementation it has, the more important it becomes, because that increases the number of people your users can't reach if you're not playing well with others.'").

33. *See* Kieren McCarthy, *Anti-Spammers Turn Guns on Each Other,* THE REGISTER, July 19, 2000, http://www.theregister.co.uk/2000/07/19/antispammers_turn_guns_on_each/.

34. *See* Class Notes from Matt Anestis, Internet & Society 1999, Class 10: Barbed Wire on the Electronic Frontier: Private Armies & Their Private Weapons, *available at* http://cyber.law.harvard.edu/is99/scribes10.html.

35. *See* Kiri Blakeley, *Spam Warfare,* FORBES, Sept. 18, 2000, at 230.

36. *See* Laura Frieder & Jonathan Zittrain, *Spam Works: Evidence from Stock Touts,* 2007, Berkman Center Research Publication No. 2006-11, *available at* http://ssrn.com/abstract=920553.

37. The same problem arises when states attempt to compel Internet Service Providers to block faraway content such as child abuse images. The blocks are usually permanently implemented using tools developed in the fight against hackers, and they block IP addresses that can later belong to an entirely innocent party. *See* Jonathan Zittrain, *Internet Points of Control.,* 44 B.C. L. REV. 653 (2003).

38. *See supra* Ch. 3, & text accompanying note 101.

39. For example, one iframe exploit was: [iframe src="http://isecurepages.net/out.php?s_id=11" width=0 height=0] [/iframe].

40. *See* Stopbadware.org, Frequently Asked Questions, Questions About Websites That Are the Subject of Google Warnings, http://www.stopbadware.org/home/faq#partner-warnings-search.

41. Per Chapter 3: Google and StopBadware.org, which collaborate on tracking and eliminating Web server exploits, report hundredfold increases in exploits between August of 2006 and March of 2007. In February of 2007 alone, Google reported that 11,125 servers believed to be infected.

42. By visiting a site like www.webtong.com, which searches WHOIS records lodged by domain name registrants, and typing in a domain name, one can find the contact information a domain owner provided. For example, a search for google.com provided the e-mail address "contact-admin@google.com." *See* Search Domain Name Data, http://www.webtong.com/services/domain/whois.html (last visited May 11, 2007).

43. In an e-mail, the Web site owner stated, "I believe the problem that brought this issue up was on . . . [a] bulletin board that was in .php. . . . We turned off the bulletin board. Someone had hacked us and then installed something that ran an 'Active X' something or rather. It would be caught with any standard security software like McAfee. What is unfortunate is that the bulletin board is rarely used at all, no one uses it actually. So we

turned it off and killed the links from our website and saved the database of posts for the future. It was fixed within 20 minutes of noticing the Search Engine link re-direct." E-mail from Web site owner to StopBadware (Jan. 14, 2007) (on file with the author).

44. A snapshot of the dialog box can be found at Steps for Installing Microsoft AntiSpyware, http://support.moonpoint.com/security/spyware/MS-Antispyware/ms-antispyware-install.html (last visited Nov. 23, 2007).

45. *See, e.g.,* SARAH PERCY, MERCENARIES: THE HISTORY OF A NORM IN INTERNATIONAL RELATIONS (2007).

46. *See* Marsh v. Ala., 326 U.S. 501 (1946).

47. *See, e.g.,* Molly Shaffer Van Houweling, *Sidewalks, Sewers, and State Action in Cyberspace,* http://cyber.law.harvard.edu/is02/readings/stateaction-shaffer-van-houweling.html (last visited Nov. 18, 2007).

48. *See* FIND, http://www.nets-find.net (last visited Nov, 23, 2007).

CHAPTER 8. STRATEGIES FOR A GENERATIVE FUTURE

1. Microsoft is widely reported to have employed this strategy with the Xbox 360. At the time of its release, it was estimated that its total cost was $715, including parts, assembly, et cetera. BusinessWeek calculated that Microsoft was losing up to $126 per unit. *See* Arik Hesseldahl, *Microsoft's Red-Ink Game,* BUSINESSWEEK, Nov. 22, 2005, http://businessweek.com/technology/content/nov2005/tc20051122_410710.htm.

2. For opposing sides of this debate, compare Paul A. David, *Clio and the Economics of QWERTY,* 75 AM. ECON. REV. 332 (1985), with Stan J. Liebowitz & Stephen E. Margolis, *Should Technology Choice Be a Concern of Antitrust Policy?,* 9 HARV. J. L. & TECH. 283 (1996) (arguing that it is difficult for "inappropriate" technology to become established as a standard and that antitrust policy should not be used to improve on even imperfect results). *See also* Seth Schoen, Trusted Computing: Promise and Risk, http://www.eff.org/Infrastructure/trusted_computing/20031001_tc.php (last visited May 15, 2007).

3. *See* 15 U.S.C.A. §§ 41–58 (West Supp. 2006); FTC, Enforcing Privacy Promises: Section 5 of the FTC Act, http://www.ftc.gov/privacy/privacyinitiatives/promises.html (last visited May 15, 2007).

4. For example, a spreadsheet created in Microsoft Excel can be exported to the common .csv format and imported into another program. A photo file can be saved in Adobe Photoshop in the .jpg format and opened in any other photo editing program. Software such as VmpegX can translate video files from one format, such as .avi, to another, such as .mov. *See* About FfmpegX, http://Vmpegx.com/index.html (last visited May 15, 2007).

5. One might imagine the law providing the same strong protections for data portability against the changing interests of service providers as is given in private contracts against interference from shifting political circumstances. *See* Fletcher v. Peck, 10 U.S. 87 (1810) (affirming the validity of contract even in the wake of popular legislative attempts to revoke land claims); Dartmouth College v. Woodward, 17 U.S. 518 (1819) (protecting the pre–Revolutionary War charter of Dartmouth College against the state's attempt to invalidate it).

6. Wikipedia's content is licensed under the GNU Free Documentation License, which allows licensees to copy, modify, and distribute the content as long as they release the modified version under the same license. *See* Wikipedia, Wikipedia:Copyrights, http://en .wikipedia.org/wiki/Wikipedia:Copyrights (as of May 15, 2007, 05:15 GMT); GNU Free Documentation License, http://www.gnu.org/licenses/fdl.html (last visited May 15, 2007).

7. In June 2006, the popular site couchsurfing.com experienced a massive data failure, from which the founder believed the site could not recover. He issued a statement to his community saying goodbye. *See* Posting of Michael Arrington to TechCrunch, *Couch- Surfing Deletes Itself, Shuts Down,* http://www.techcrunch.com/2006/06/29/couch surfing-deletes-itself-shuts-down (June 29, 2006). Several days later, after much cajoling from Arrington's community, the CouchSurfing site was back up, although some data had been permanently lost. In December 2006 some Gmail users logged on to find their inboxes empty and all their contacts deleted. That data was not recoverable. *See* Hari K. Gottipati, *GMail Disaster, Google Confirmed the Mass Email Deletions. Even Backups Are Gone?,* O'REILLY XM, Dec. 28, 2006, http://www.oreillynet.com/xml/blog/2006/12/ gmail_disaster_google_confirme.html. Outages at the domain registration site Register- Fly caused that site to be taken down indefinitely. *See* Posting of Rich Miller to Netcraft, *RegisterFly Site Goes Offline,* http://news.netcraft.com/archives/2007/03/06/registerfly _site_goes_offline.html (Mar. 6, 2007, 20:07 GMT) (reporting RegisterFly's outages and subsequent shutdown, and ICANN's fears about the status of the domain names registered with RegisterFly).

8. For an overview of different perspectives on the debate, see, for example, *"Network Neutrality": Hearing Before the S. Comm. on Commerce, Sci. & Transp.,* 109th Cong. (2006) (statement of Lawrence Lessig, Professor of Law, Stanford Law School), *available at* http://commerce.senate.gov/pdf/lessig-020706.pdf; Tim Wu, Network Neutrality FAQ, http://timwu.org/network_neutrality.html (last visited May 15, 2007); Christopher S. Yoo, *Would Mandating Broadband Network Neutrality Help or Hurt Competition? A Comment on the End-to-End Debate,* 3 J. TELECOMM. & HIGH TECH. L. 71 (2004); David Farber & Michael Katz, *Hold Off on Net Neutrality,* WASH. POST, Jan. 19, 2007, at A19. For a more detailed discussion of the network neutrality debate, compare Tim Wu, *Network Neutrality, Broadband Discrimination,* 2 J. TELECOMM. & HIGH TECH. L. 141 (2003), and Mark A. Lemley & Lawrence Lessig, *The End of End-to-End: Preserving the Architecture of the Internet in the Broadband Era,* 48 UCLA L. REV. 925 (2001), with Christopher S. Yoo, *Beyond Network Neutrality,* 19 HARV. J.L. & TECH. 1 (2005). *See also Legal Affairs Debate Club—Keeping the Internet Neutral? Christopher S. Yoo and Tim Wu Debate,* LEGAL AFFAIRS, May 1, 2006, http://www.legalaffairs.org/webexclusive/ dc_printerfriendly.msp?id=86. For articles noting the centrality of end-to-end, see for example, Marjory S. Blumenthal, *End-to-End and Subsequent Paradigms,* 2002 L. REV. M.S.U.-D.C. L. 709 (describing end-to-end as the current paradigm for understanding the Internet); and Lawrence Lessig, *The Architecture of Innovation,* 51 DUKE L.J. 1783 (2002) (arguing that end-to-end establishes the Internet as a commons). For the perspective of a number of economists, see William J. Baumol et al., *Economists' Statement on Network Neutrality Policy* (AEI-Brookings Joint Ctr., Working Paper No. RP07–08,

2007). For an argument about why competition alone does not preclude network discrimination, see Brett M. Frischmann & Barbara van Schewick, *Network Neutrality and the Economics of an Information Superhighway: A Reply to Professor Yoo,* 47 JURIMETRICS (forthcoming 2007) (manuscript at 7–8), *available at* http://papers.ssrn.com/abstract=1014691. *See also* Jonathan L. Zittrain, *The Generative Internet,* 119 HARV. L. REV. 1974, 1988–89, 2029–30 & n.208 (2006).

9. *See* Written Ex Parte of Professor Mark A. Lemley & Professor Lawrence Lessig, *In re* Application for Consent to the Transfer of Control of Licenses MediaOne Group, Inc. to AT&T Corp., No. 99–251 (F.C.C. 1999), *available at* http://cyber.law.harvard.edu/works/lessig/cable/fcc/fcc.html; Joseph Farell, *Open Access Arguments: Why Confidence Is Misplaced,* in NET NEUTRALITY OR NET NEUTERING: SHOULD BROADBAND INTERNET SERVICES BE REGULATED? 195 (Thomas M. Lenard & Randolph J. May eds., 2006); Barbara van Schewick, *Towards an Economic Framework for Network Neutrality Regulation,* 5 J. TELECOMM. & HIGH TECH. L. 329, 368–77 (2007) (noting the existence of switching costs and other factors).

10. Skype has petitioned the U.S. Federal Communications Commission to require mobile phone network providers to allow the use of Skype—and any other application chosen by the user—over their networks. Petition to Confirm a Consumer's Right to Use Internet Communications Software and Attach Devices to Wireless Networks, in the Matter of Skype Communications, FCC Petition RM-11361 (2007), *available at* http://svartifoss2.fcc.gov/prod/ecfs/retrieve.cgi?native_or_pdf=pdf&id_document=6518909730.

11. *See* Robert E. Kahn, *The Role of Government in the Evolution of the Internet,* 37 COMM. ACM 15 (1994); Barry M. Leiner et al., *The Past and Future History of the Internet,* 40 COMM. ACM 102 (1997); Andrew Orlowski, *Father of Internet Warns Against Net Neutrality,* REGISTER, Jan. 18, 2007, *available at* http://www.theregister.com/2007/01/18/kahn_net_neutrality_warning; Video: An Evening with Robert Kahn, http://archive.computerhistory.org/lectures/an_evening_with_robert_kahn.lecture.2007.01.09.wmv (last visited Nov. 30, 2007); *see also* David Farber & Michael Katz, Editorial, *Hold Off on Net Neutrality,* WASH. POST, Jan. 19, 2007, at A19; Adam D. Thierer, *"Net Neutrality": Digital Discrimination or Regulatory Gamesmanship in Cyberspace?,* at 17–19 (CATO Policy Analysis No. 507, 2004), http://www.cato.org/pubs/pas/pa507.pdf; Robert Pepper, *Network Neutrality: Avoiding a Net Loss,* TECHNEWSWORLD, Mar. 14, 2007, *available at* http://www.technewsworld.com/story/Ii1IJ10PgRjmkt/Network-Neutrality-Avoiding-a-Net-Loss.xhtml; Christopher Yoo, *Beyond Network Neutrality,* 19 HARV. J.L. & TECH. 1 (2005), *available at* http://jolt.law.harvard.edu/articles/pdf/v19/19HarvJLTech001.pdf.

12. *See* Declan McCullagh, *FAQ: Wi-Fi Mooching and the Law,* CNET NEWS.COM, July 8, 2005, http://news.com.com/FAQ+Wi-Fi+mooching+and+the+law/2100-7351_3-5778822.html; Paul Festa, *Free Wireless Net Access for the Masses,* CNET NEWS.COM, Sept. 26, 2001, http://news.com.com/Free+wireless+Net+access+for+the+masses/2100-1033_3-273516.html; EFF Wireless-Friendly ISP List, http://www.eff.org/Infrastructure/Wireless_cellular_radio/wireless_friendly_isp_list.html (last visited May 15, 2007).

13. One such product is the Nessus Vulnerability Scanner. *See* Nessus, Nessus Vulnerability Scanner, http://www.nessus.org (last visited May 15, 2007).

14. *See* Rajiv Shah & Christian Sandvig, *Software Defaults as De Facto Regulation: The Case of Wireless APs* 9 (Sept. 23, 2005), (unpublished manuscript, presented to Conference on Comm. Info. and Internet Pol'y), *available at* http://web.si.umich.edu/tprc/papers/2005/427/TPRC%20Wireless%20Defaults.pdf.

15. *See* John Markoff, *Venture for Sharing Wi-Fi Draws Big-Name Backers,* N.Y. TIMES, Feb. 6, 2006, at C3; What's FON?, http://www.fon.com/en/info/whatsFon (last visited May 15, 2007).

16. *See, e.g.,* Verizon Online, Terms of Service, http://www.verizon.net/policies/vzcom/tos_popup.asp (last visited May 15, 2007).

17. *See, e.g.,* Wireless Service Theft Prevention Law, 720 ILL. COMP. STAT. ANN. §§ 5/16F-1 to -6 (West 2006); S.B. 1646, 92 Gen. Assembly, (Ill. 2003), *available at* http://www.ilga.gov/legislation/publicacts/pubact92/acts/92-0728.html; *Man Arrested for Stealing Wi-Fi,* CBS NEWS, Apr. 4, 2007, http://www.cbsnews.com/stories/2005/07/07/tech/main707361.shtml; Jane Wakefield, *Wireless Hijacking Under Scrutiny,* BBC NEWS, July 28, 2005, http://news.bbc.co.uk/2/hi/technology/4721723.stm.

18. Most users do not use a steady amount of bandwidth all the time, and ISP service-delivery models reflect this. That is why many users of one access point, all streaming videos, will slow each other down. *See* Akamai Technologies, *Internet Bottlenecks* (White Paper, 2000), *available at* www.akamai.com/dl/whitepapers/Akamai_Internet_Bottlenecks_Whitepaper.pdf; Beat Liver & Gabriel Dermler, *The E-Business of Content Delivery* (IBM Research Paper), http://www.tik.ee.ethz.ch/~cati/paper/isqe99c.pdf.

19. *See, e.g.,* Dynamic Platform Standards Project, Facing Reality on "Network Neutrality," http://www.dpsproject.com (last visited May 15, 2007); Dynamic Platform Standards Project, Legislative Proposal: The Internet Platform for Innovation Act, http://www.dpsproject.com/legislation.html (last visited May 15, 2007).

20. Circumvention tools include anonymizers, VPNs, and Psiphon. *See, e.g.,* Reporters Without Borders, Technical Ways to Get Around Censorship, http://www.rsf.org/article.php3?id_article=15013#2 (last visited May 15, 2007) (providing an overview of different technologies that can be used to avoid censorship); Anonymizer: Free Web Proxy, Free Anonymizers and the List of Web Anonymizers List, http://www.freeproxy.ru/en/free_proxy/cgi-proxy.htm (last visited May 15, 2007). For some skepticism that users can circumvent network neutrality restrictions, see William H. Lehr et al., *Scenarios for the Network Neutrality Arms Race,* 1 INT'L J. COMMC'NS 607 (2007) (describing "technical and non-technical countermeasures" ranging from letter-writing campaigns to end-to-end encryption that prevents an ISP from discerning the activity in which a user is engaging).

21. *See* Skype, http://skype.com (last visited May 15, 2007); Wikipedia, *Skype,* http://en.wikipedia.org/wiki/Skype (as of May 15, 2007, 17:45 GMT).

22. Notably, the Nintendo Wii has been configured in this manner. Although its Internet Channel software allows users to browse the entire Internet using the Wii, to date user-configurability of the home page and other features has been limited. *See* Wikipedia, *Internet Channel,* http://en.wikipedia.org/wiki/Internet_Channel (as of May 15, 2007,

07:00 GMT); Wii, The Developers Talk About the Internet Channel, http://us.wii .com/story_internet.jsp (last visited May 15, 2007). The Playstation 3 has similar features. *See* Network-internetbrowser, http://www.us.playstation.com/PS3/network/ internetbrowser (last visited May 15, 2007).

23. Cable Televison Consumer Protection and Competition Act of 1992, Pub. L. No. 102-385, 106 Stat. 1460 (codified as amended in scattered sections of 47 U.S.C.).

24. A large, but far from comprehensive, list of community public access television organizations that have used the provisions of the 1992 Act is available through the Google Directory. *See* Google Directory, Public Television, http://www.google.com/Top/ Arts/ Television/Networks/North_America/United_States/PBS/(last visited May 15, 2007). *See generally* Turner Broadcasting Sys., Inc. v. FCC, 520 U.S. 180 (1997); Laura Linder, Public Access Television: America's Electronic Soapbox (1999); Nancy Whitmore, *Congress, The U.S. Supreme Court and Must-Carry Policy: A Flawed Economic Analysis,* 6 Comm. L. & Pol'y 175 (2001); Harris J. Aaron, Note, *I Want My MTV: The Debate Over Digital Must-Carry,* 80 B.U. L. Rev. 885 (2000); C-Span, Must Carry, http://www.mustcarry.org/mustcarry.asp (providing short updates on the status of FCC action regarding proposals. regarding must-carry); C-Span, About Us, http:// 12.170.145.161/about/index.asp?code=About (last visited May 15, 2007); Wikipedia, *Must-Carry,* http://en.wikipedia.org/wiki/Must-cary (as of May 15, 2007, 07:00 GMT).

25. *See* James C. Goodale, All About Cable 2-62 (2006); Benjamin M. Compaine & Shane M. Greenstein, Communications Policy in Transition 410–17 (2001); Reply Comments of the Staff of the FTC, *In re* Satellite Carrier Compulsory License, Docket No. RM 98-1 (1998), *available at* http://www.ftc.gov/be/v980004.shtm. To be sure, the impact of must-carry (and what would happen without it) was hotly debated through years of constitutional litigation and thousands of pages of data and expert testimony. *See* Turner Broadcasting System, Inc., v. Federal Communications Commission, 520 U.S. 180 (1997). The district court majority opinion in the case concluded that a number of broadcasters could be threatened in the absence of must-carry, Turner Broadcasting v. FCC, 910 F. Supp. 734 755 (D.D.C. 1995), but Judge Williams's dissent is persuasive that much of the data offered was conclusory and self-interested.

26. Use of the Carterfone Device in Message Toll Tel. Serv., 13 F.C.C.2d 420 (1968).

27. *See* Tim Wu, *Wireless Net Neutrality: Cellular Carterfone on Mobile Networks* (New Am. Found. Wireless Future Working Paper No. 17, Feb. 2007), *available at* http:// ssrn.com/abstract=962027; Petition to Confirm a Consumer's Right to Use Internet Communications Software and Attach Devices to Wireless Networks, *supra* note 10. For a description of Steve Jobs's claim of safety as a reason for the iPhone to remain tethered, see Katie Hafner, *Altered iPhones Freeze Up,* N.Y. Times, Sep. 29, 2007, *available at* http://www.nytimes.com/2007/09/29/technology/29iphone.html.

28. The U.S. Telecommunications Act of 1996 sought to create a market in third-party cable boxes, but these boxes would not be able to make use of the cable network to provide independent services—and even allowing third-party vendors to provide boxes functionally identical to the ones offered by the cable companies has proven difficult, as the Federal Communications Commission has tried to balance cable company requests for

delays with a desire to implement competition. *See* Posting of Art Brodsky to Public Knowledge Policy Blog, *Consumer and Public Interest Groups Ask FCC to Enforce Set-Top Box Choices* (Nov. 15, 2006, 15:30), http://www.publicknowledge.org/node/718. The FCC has granted some waivers. *See* FCC, Memorandum Opinion and Order *in re* Cablevision Systems Corporation's Request for Waiver of Section 76.1204(a)(1) (Jan. 10, 2007), *available at* http://hraunfoss.fcc.gov/edocs_public/attachmatch/DA-07-48A1.pdf; FCC, Memorandum Opinion and Order *in re* Bend Cable Communications, LLC Request for Waiver of Section 76.1204(a)(1) (Jan. 10, 2007), *available at* http://hraunfoss.fcc.gov/edocs_public/attachmatch/DA-07-47A1.pdf. However, others have been denied. FCC, Memorandum Opinion and Order *in re* Comcast Corporation, LLC Request for Waiver of Section 76.1204(a)(1) (Jan. 10, 2007), *available at* http://hraunfoss.fcc.gov/edocs_public/attachmatch/DA-07-49A1.pdf; Posting of Cowboy Neal to Slashdot, *FCC Opens Market for Cable Boxes* (Jan. 11, 2007, 21:51), http://hardware.slashdot.org/article.pl?sid=07/01/12/0043249. See Press Release, FCC, Media Bureau Acts on Requests for Waiver of Rules on Integrated Set-Top Boxes and Clarifies Compliance of Downloadable Conditional Access Security Solution (Jan. 10, 2007), *available at* http://hraunfoss.fcc.gov/edocs_public/attachmatch/DOC-269446A1.pdf, for information regarding decisions on integrated boxes, and Todd Spangler, *FCC: Set-Top Fines Capped at $325K,* Multichannel News, Feb. 15, 2007, http://www.multichannel.com/article/CA6416753.html, for general information about the rulings.

29. United States v. Microsoft Corp., 84 F. Supp. 2d 9, 19 (D.D.C. 1999).
30. *See id.* at 43–98.
31. *See* Jonathan Zittrain, *The Un-Microsoft Un-Remedy: Law Can Prevent the Problem That It Can't Patch Later,* 31 Conn. L. Rev. 1361 (1999). Microsoft was also found to be maintaining its OS monopoly by disadvantaging the JAVA programming environment, which is meant to allow code to be platform-independent.
32. This does not mean that appliance makers can legally punish those who figure out how to tinker with their products. *See* Lexmark Int'l, Inc., v. Static Control Components, Inc., 387 F.3d 522 (6th Cir. 2004); Static Control Components, Inc. v. Lexmark Int'l, Inc., 2006 U.S. Dist. LEXIS 94438 (E.D. Ky. 2006) (holding that a microchip created to enable a competitor's print cartridges to work with the original manufacturer's printer did not violate the manufacturer's copyright).
33. *See* Brett Frischmann, *An Economic Theory of Infrastructure and Commons Management,* 89 Minn. L. Rev. 917, 1015–20 (2005); Barbara Van Schewick, *Towards an Economic Framework for Network Neutrality Regulation,* 5 J. Telecomm. & High Tech. L. 329, 378–82 (2007).
34. *See, e.g.,* N.Y. Real Prop. Acts Law § 522 (Consol. 2007).
35. *See, e.g.,* Di Leo v. Pecksto Holding Corp., 109 N.E.2d 600 (N.Y. 1952).
36. *See* Restatement (Second) of Contracts § 90 (1981).
37. *See generally* Joseph William Singer, *The Reliance Interest in Property,* 40 Stan. L. Rev. 611 (1988).
38. Posting of Ryan Block to Engadget, A Lunchtime Chat with Bill Gates, http://www.engadget.com/2007/01/08/a-lunchtime-chat-with-bill-gates-at-ces/ (Jan. 8, 2007, 14:01).

39. However, Microsoft's End User License Agreement limits damages to the amount paid for the software. *See, e.g.,* EULA for Windows XP, § 18, http://www.microsoft.com/windowsxp/home/eula.mspx; EULA for Vista, § 25, http://download.microsoft.com/documents/useterms/Windows%20Vista_Ultimate_English_36d0fe99-75e4-4875-8153-889cf5105718.pdf.

40. *See* Google, Google Desktop—Features, http://desktop.google.com/features.html#searchremote (last visited May 15, 2007).

41. Matthew Fordahl, *How Google's Desktop Search Works,* MSNBC.COM, Oct. 14, 2004, http://www.msnbc.msn.com/id/6251128/.

42. 467 U.S. 735 (1984).

43. *Id.* at 743.

44. *See, e.g.,* Declan McCullagh, *Police Blotter: Judge Orders Gmail Disclosure,* CNET NEWS.COM, Mar. 17, 2006, http://news.com.com/Police+blotter+Judge+orders+Gmail+disclosure/2100-1047_3-6050295.html (reporting on a hearing that contested a court subpoena ordering the disclosure of all e-mail messages, including deleted ones, from a Gmail account).

45. Orin Kerr, *Search and Seizure: Past, Present, and Future,* OXFORD ENCYCLOPEDIA OF LEGAL HISTORY (2006).

46. *Cf.* Orin S. Kerr, *Searches and Seizures in a Digital World,* 119 HARV. L. REV. 531, 557 (2005) ("Under Arizona v. Hicks (480 U.S. 321 (1987)), merely copying information does not seize anything." (footnote omitted)).

47. *See, e.g.,* Google, Google Privacy Policy, http://www.google.com/privacypolicy.html (last visited Apr. 6, 2007) (noting that Google discloses personal information only when it has "a good faith belief that access, use, preservation or disclosure of such information is reasonably necessary to (a) satisfy any applicable law, regulation, legal process or enforceable governmental request, . . . (d) protect against imminent harm to the rights, property or safety of Google, its users or the public as required or permitted by law").

48. *See* Orin S. Kerr, *A User's Guide to the Stored Communications Act, and a Legislator's Guide to Amending It,* 72 GEO. WASH. L. REV. 1208, 1208–09 (2004).

49. *See* 50 U.S.C. § 1861(a) (Supp. III 2003).

50. *See id.* § 1861(c)–(d).

51. *See* Letter from William E. Moschella, Assistant Att'y Gen., to L. Ralph Mecham, Dir., Admin. Office of the U.S. Courts (Apr. 30, 2004), *available at* http://www.fas.org/irp/agency/doj/fisa/2003rept.pdf; Letter from William E. Moschella, Assistant Att'y Gen., to J. Dennis Hastert, Speaker, U.S. House of Repres. (Apr. 1, 2005), *available at* http://www.fas.org/irp/agency/doj/fisa/2004rept.pdf; Letter from William E. Moschella, Assistant Att'y Gen., to Nancy Pelosi, Speaker, U.S. House of Repres. (Apr. 27, 2007), *available at* http://www.fas.org/irp/agency/doj/fisa/2006rept.pdf; *see also* OFFICE OF THE INSPECTOR GEN., A REVIEW OF THE FEDERAL BUREAU OF INVESTIGATION'S USE OF NATIONAL SECURITY LETTERS (2007), *available at* http://www.usdoj.gov/oig/special/s0703b/final.pdf. Some have suggested that the Justice Department may have misused the authority granted to it by FISA. *See, e.g.,* Dan Eggen & Susan Schmidt, *Secret Court RebuVs Ashcroft,* WASH. POST, Aug. 23, 2002, at A01, *available at* http://www.washingtonpost.com/ac2/wp-dyn/A51220-2002Aug22?language=printer; Carol D. Leonnig,

Secret Court's Judges Were Warned About NSA Spy Data, WASH. POST, Feb. 9, 2006, at A01, *available at* http://www.washingtonpost.com/wp-dyn/content/article/2006/02/08/AR2006020802511_pf.html.

52. *See* USA PATRIOT Improvement and Reauthorization Act of 2005, 18 U.S.C. § 2709(c) (2006). This provision has been found unconstitutional in *Doe v. Gonzales,* 500 F.Supp.2d 879 (S.D.N.Y. 2007).

53. *See* 12 U.S.C. § 3414(a)(5)(A), (D) (2000 & Supp. IV 2004); 15 U.S.C. §§ 1681u, 1681v(a) (2000 & Supp. IV 2004); 18 U.S.C. § 2709(a) (2000 & Supp. IV 2004); 50 U.S.C. § 436 (2000).

54. *See* 18 U.S.C. § 2709(a) (2000).

55. *See id.* § 2709(b).

56. *See* Barton Gellman, *The FBI's Secret Scrutiny,* WASH. POST, Nov. 6, 2005, at A1.

57. *See* John Solomon, *FBI Finds It Frequently Overstepped in Collecting Data,* WASH. POST, June 14, 2007, at A1.

58. *See* The Company v. United States, 349 F.3d 1132, 1133 (9th Cir. 2003) (establishing that eavesdropping on vehicle operators could not be allowed, primarily because it disabled the proper functioning of the company's communication with the vehicle if there were to be an emergency); *see also* Doe v. Ashcroft, 334 F. Supp. 2d 471, 475 (S.D.N.Y. 2004) (holding that prohibiting an ISP from communicating its receipt of a national security letter is an impermissible prior restraint on speech); *supra* Ch. 5, Regulability and the Tethered Appliance.

59. 365 U.S. 610 (1961).

60. *See id.* at 610, 615–18.

61. *See* Warshak v. United States, 490 F.3d 455 (6th Cir. 2007); United States v. D'Andrea, 2007 WL 2076472, *3 (D. Mass. July 20, 2007) (quoting Warshak v. United States, 490F.3d 455); *cf.* LaFave, 1 SEARCH AND SEIZURE § 2.6 at 721 (4th ed. 2006). *But cf.* U.S. v. Lifshitz, 369 F.3d 173, 190 (2d Cir. 2004) (noting that individuals "may not, however, enjoy such an expectation of privacy in transmissions over the Internet or e-mail that have already arrived at the recipient," in a suit involving a probationer); U.S. v. Hambrick, 225 F.3d 656 (4th Cir. 2000) (holding that consumers have no legitimate expectation of privacy in noncontent consumer information, such as name and billing address, provided to their ISP).

62. Orin Kerr, The Volokh Conspiracy, A Series of Posts on Warshak v. United States, http://volokh.com/posts/1182208168.shtml (last visited June 23, 2007).

63. *See* Posting of Jacobson to Free Software Found. Blog on GPL Compliance and Licensing, *Employers: Don't Panic,* http://www.fsf.org/blogs/licensing/nopanicing (Feb. 17, 2006, 15:52).

64. *See* 17 U.S.C. § 512 (2000) (defining the DMCA safe harbor protections).

65. *See* James Bessen & Robert M. Hunt, *An Empirical Look at Software Patents,* 16 J. ECON. & MGMT. SCI. 157 (2007).

66. *Id.*

67. *See* James Bessen & Robert M. Hunt, *The Software Patent Experiment,* 14–15 (Research on Innovation Working Paper, 2004), *available at* http://www.researchoninnovation .org/softpat.pdf. Software companies that assert strong intellectual property rights can

also deter the work of standards-setting organizations by claiming ownership of some part of a standard. *See* Mark Lemley, *Intellectual Property Rights and Standard-Setting Organizations* (Boalt Working Papers in Public Law, Paper No. 24, 2002), *available at* http://repositories .cdlib.org/boaltwp/24/.

68. *See* Carl Shapiro, *Navigating the Patent Thicket: Cross Licenses, Patent Pools, and Standard Setting, in* INNOVATION POLICY AND THE ECONOMY 12 (2001), *available at* http://faculty .haas.berkeley.edu/shapiro/thicket.pdf.

69. In *Mazer v. Stein,* 347 U.S. 201, 217 (1954), a distinction was made between copyright and patent: "Unlike a patent, a copyright gives no exclusive right to the art disclosed; protection is given only to the expression of the idea—not the idea itself." Over-patenting can be seen in U.S. Patent & Trademark Office, Questions and Answers—USPTO, http://www.uspto.gov/main/faq/index.html (last visited May 15, 2007). One manifestation of the breadth of what can be patented is the famous patent issued in 2002 for swinging sideways while on a swing. That patent was issued to a five-year-old child. *See* U.S. Patent No. 6,368,227 (issued Apr. 9, 2002).

70. *See* Posting of Adrian Kingsley-Hughes to Gear for Geeks, *Ballmer: Linux "Infringes our intellectual property"* http://blogs.zdnet.com/hardware/?p=154 (Nov. 17, 2006, 06:55), discussing Steve Ballmer's assertion that Linux infringes Microsoft's patents at the Professional Association for SQL Server conference in Seattle on November 16, 2006); Roger Parloff, *Microsoft Takes on the Free World,* FORTUNE, May 14, 2007, http://money .cnn.com/magazines/fortune/fortune_archive/2007/05/28/100033867/index .htm?source=yahoo_quote; Posting of Cory Doctorow to BoingBoing, *Ballmer: Linux Users Are Patent-Crooks* http://www.boingboing.net/2006/11/17/ballmer_linux_users _.html (Nov. 17, 2006, 07:44). For more information on the third version of the General Public License, see GPLv3 Final Discussion Draft Rationale, http://gplv3.fsf.org/ rationale,pdf, at 24, and GPLv3 Process—March update, http://gplv3.fsf.org/process-definition.

71. Ronald J. Mann, *Do Patents Facilitate Financing in the Software Industry?,* 83 TEX. L. REV. 961, 978–82 (2005).

72. *See* 17 U.S.C. § 507 (2000); 35 U.S.C. § 286 (2000). For patents, the statute of limitations applies only to monetary damages; injunctions may be prevented through the doctrines of estoppel and laches. *See* A. C. Aukerman Co. v. R. L. Chaides Constr. Co., 960 F.2d 1020, 1040–43 (Fed. Cir. 1992). Other countries set different time limits for their statute of limitations. *See, e.g.,* Doerte Haselhorst, *German IP Law Update,* IP INTELLIGENCE: EUROPE, Winter 2002, http://www.howrey.com/europe/newsletter/Winter 2002a/10.html; Posting of Patent Hawk to Patent Prospector, Patent Litigation in China, http://www.patenthawk.com/blog/2006/04/patent_litigation_in_china.html (Apr. 30, 2006, 14:17).

73. *See* Zittrain, *supra* note 31.

74. Laches is defined as "[u]nreasonable delay in pursuing a right or claim—almost always an equitable one—in a way that prejudices the party against whom relief is sought," or as "[t]he equitable doctrine by which a court denies relief to a claimant who has unreasonably delayed in asserting the claim, when that delay has prejudiced the party against whom relief is sought," BLACK'S LAW DICTIONARY 891 (8th ed. 2004). The use of the

laches defense to prevent sandbagging is seen, for example, in *Webster Electric Co. v. Splitdorf Electrical Co.*, 264 U.S. 463 (1924) (denying claims of patent infringement where the rights-holder "stood by and awaited developments" for eight years), and *Woodbridge v. United States,* 263 U.S. 50 (1923) (rendering patent rights unenforceable where an inventor made claims after a nine-year delay to maximize profits). However, the bounds of the laches doctrine remain largely unclear. *See, e.g.,* Lynda Calderone & Tara Custer, *Prosecution Laches as a Defense in Patent Cases,* Flaster Greenberg Newsletter (Nov. 2005), *available at* http://www.flastergreenberg.com/pdf/PatentArtic_prf3.pdf; Symbol Technologies v. Lemelson, 422 F. 3d 1378 (Fed. Cir. 2005) (showing that courts may be reluctant to accept laches except under extreme circumstances).

75. Claims might allege that proprietary code infringes a free software license by incorporating free software. Much free software is copylefted, a licensing scheme that allows anyone to freely modify and copy it, but not to incorporate it into proprietary code. *See* GNU Project, What Is Copyleft?, http://www.gnu.org/copyleft/ (last visited May 15, 2007); Wikipedia, *Copyleft,* http://en.wikipedia.org/wiki/Copyleft (as of May 15, 2007, 06:00 GMT).

76. *See, e.g.,* Lawrence Lessig, Free Culture: How Big Media Uses Technology and the Law to Lock Down Culture and Control Creativity (2004).

77. Yochai Benkler, The Wealth of Networks 278 (2006).

78. *Id.* at 275.

79. 17 U.S.C. § 504 (West 2006).

80. *See* Creative Commons, Choose a License *available at* http://www.creativecommons.org/license/ (last visited Mar. 22, 2007).

81. One example of such an authentication system is Microsoft's Sender ID. *See* Microsoft, Sender ID, http://www.microsoft.com/mscorp/safety/technologies/senderid/default.mspx (last visited May 15, 2007).

82. *See, e.g.,* David R. Johnson et al., *The Accountable Internet: Peer Production of Internet Governance,* 9 Va. J.L. & Tech. 9 (2004), *available at* http://www.vjolt.net/vol9/issue 3/v9i3_a09-Palfrey.pdf (discussing the imperfections of filtration).

83. *See* Yochai Benkler, *Some Economics of Wireless Communications,* 16 Harv. J.L. & Tech. 25 (2002) (suggesting that open wireless networks will be more efficient at optimizing wireless communications capacity than spectrum property rights will be).

84. *See* Michel Marriott, *Hey Neighbor, Stop Piggybacking on My Wireless,* N.Y. Times, Mar. 5, 2006, § 1, at 11 (explaining some of the dangers of open wireless networks).

85. *See, e.g.,* 4 Melville B. Nimmer & David Nimmer, Nimmer on Copyright § 12.04[3] (2005).

86. As noted in Chapter 6, one might argue in Wikipedia's case that anyone editing Wikipedia is actually an agent of Wikipedia, and therefore not "another" service provider under 47 U.S.C. § 230(c). *See* Ch. 6, note 49.

87. Geoff Goodell et al., Blossom: A Perspective Access Network, http://afs.eecs.harvard.edu/~goodell/blossom (last visited May 15, 2007) (describing the philosophy, design objectives, and implementation of the Blossom network, which seeks to allow users to specify the perspective from which they view Internet resources).

88. *See* Owen Gibson, *New York Times Blocks UK Access to Terror Story,* Guardian, Aug. 30,

2006, at 4, *available at* http://www.guardian.co.uk/terrorism/story/0,,1860876,00
.html; Tom Zeller Jr., *Times Withholds Web Article in Britain,* N.Y. TIMES, Aug. 29,
2006, at C7, *available at* http://www.nytimes.com/2006/08/29/business/media/
29times.html. For the original *New York Times* article, see Don Van Natta Jr. et al., *Details Emerge in British Terror Case,* N.Y. TIMES, Aug. 28, 2006, http://www.nytimes
.com/2006/08/28/world/europe/28plot.html.

89. For most arguments of this type, one implication is that "grassroots"-style democracy in
the form of mass public participation will be more democratic on the Internet than in
traditional governmental settings. *But see* Neil Weinstock Netanel, *Cyberspace Self-Governance: A Skeptical View from Liberal Democratic Theory,* 88 CAL. L. REV. 395 (2000).
Netanel argues that the sorts of principle-based checks in most democracies, such as antidiscrimination principles and equality in the basic rights of citizenship, are not sustainable in an unregulated cyberspace environment. As applied in this case, Netanel's
argument might cast doubt on the net worth of "tricks" or technologies that seem to simultaneously promote democracy and undermine state sovereignty. *See id.* at 412–27
(discussing cyberpopulism); *cf.* Andy Kessler, *Network Solutions,* WALL ST. J., Mar. 24,
2007, at A11 (describing the communities enabled by Facebook, in which user-specified
preferences and privacy are carefully maintained in order to facilitate user openness).

90. LAWRENCE LESSIG, CODE: VERSION 2.0, 309 (2006).

91. In this case, the distinction is not between conduct rules and decision rules, but between
conduct rules and enforcement. MEIR DAN-COHEN, HARMFUL THOUGHTS: ESSAYS ON
LAW, SELF, AND MORALITY 125–72 (2002); *see also* Gautham Rao, *The Federal Posse
Comitatus Doctrine: Slavery, Compulsion, and Statecraft in Mid-Nineteenth Century
America,* 26.1 L. & HIST. REV. (forthcoming 2008) (describing the difficulties of persuading U.S. citizens in the North to assist in the return of escaped slaves to the South
before the Civil War), *available at* http://www.press.uillinois.edu/journals/lhr/rao26_1
.pdf.

92. *See* Tim Wu, *When Code Isn't Law,* 89 VA. L. REV. 679, 707 (2003) (disputing Lessig's argument and suggesting that instead of looking at code as law, society should understand
code as a mechanism for *avoiding* and thus shaping law, in a similar fashion to how tax
lawyers look for loopholes); *id.* at 689 (analyzing law-following behavior using an economic compliance model, which states that people obey laws when disobedience yields
greater harms than benefits, and therefore concluding that code—and, by extension,
code's ability to circumvent regulation—can easily be understood as a productive part of
the process of law).

93. In May 2007, anonymous browsing services had the following use levels as studied by
Hal Roberts of Harvard's Berkman Center for Internet & Society. Anonymizer: no data;
dynaweb: 24 mil hit/day/700k users/day est.; ultrareach: 70 mil hits/day/1mil users/
day est.; circumventor: 30 installs/day; psiphon: 8,000 servers/80,000 users est.; jap:
6,000 concurrent clients; tor: 1 Gbps. E-mail from Hal Roberts to Jonathan Zittrain
(May 31, 2007 at 21:44 EDT) (on file with the author).

94. *See, e.g.,* File Pile, http://www.filepile.org (last visited May 15, 2007).

95. Oink, http://oink.me.uk (last visited May 15, 2007).

96. *See* Doug Lichtman & David Jacobson, *Anonymity a Double-Edged Sword for Pirates Online,* CHICAGO TRIB., Apr. 13, 2000, at N25 (describing the music industry's attempt to "take aim at the pirates' ships" by flooding file-sharing sites with thousands of decoy files with names similar to popular songs).

97. For one such proposal, see WILLIAM W. FISHER III, PROMISES TO KEEP 199–259 (2004). *But see* Salil Mehra, *The iPod Tax: Why the Digital Copyright System of American Law Professors' Dreams Failed in Japan,* 79 U. COLO. L. REV. (forthcoming 2008), *available at* http://ssrn.com/abstract = 1010246 (noting that a digital recording tax in Japan similar to the proposals made by Fisher and others failed to produce its intended result).

98. *See, e.g.,* Terry Frieden, *27 Charged in Child Porn Sting,* CNN.COM, Mar. 16, 2006, http://www.cnn.com/2006/LAW/03/15/childporn.arrests/index.html (describing a child pornography bust by the U.S. Department of Justice in early 2006 and the use of Internet security measures to try to keep file-sharing out of the eye of the law, and showing that the eventual infiltration of this group by law enforcement was due to the fact the group was open—even if only a little—to new members not personally known by existing members).

99. *See, e.g.,* ROBERT J. BUNKER, NETWORKS, TERRORISM AND GLOBAL INSURGENCY 150 (2006) (noting, in the context of a general analysis of the effects of networks on terrorism and global conflict, that Al Qaeda has been "increasing its use of the Internet for propaganda, recruiting and training purposes"); GUS MARTIN, UNDERSTANDING TERRORISM 406–12 (2003) (describing how the Internet facilitates the interests of terrorists, such as through their use of chat rooms, which improve communication with new recruits and existing members, especially when members are separated by a large distance); D. WHITTAKER, TERRORISTS AND TERRORISM IN THE CONTEMPORARY WORLD 39 (2004) (discussing Internet use by the Liberation Tigers of Tamil Elam, in Sri Lanka, to "pump out propaganda and to recruit their ranks"). *See generally* GABRIEL WEIMANN, TERROR ON THE INTERNET (2006);

100. BENKLER, *supra* note 77, at 287–88.

101. *See* Isaiah Berlin, *Two Concepts of Liberty, in* FOUR ESSAYS ON LIBERTY 122 (1969).

CHAPTER 9. MEETING THE RISKS OF GENERATIVITY

1. ADVISORY COMM. TO THE SEC'Y OF HEALTH, EDUC. & WELFARE, RECORDS, COMPUTERS AND THE RIGHTS OF CITIZENS, at § II (1973), *available at* http://aspe.hhs.gov/datacncl/1973privacy/tocprefacemembers.htm.

2. *See* Daniel J. Solove, *Privacy and Power: Computer Databases and Metaphors for Information Privacy,* 53 STAN. L. REV. 1393 (2001) (examining the dangers to personal privacy posed by electronic databases).

3. *See generally id.*

4. U.S. S. COMM. ON GOV'T OPERATIONS & U.S. H. GOV'T OPERATIONS SUBCOMM. ON GOV'T INFO. & INDIVIDUAL RIGHTS, LEGISLATIVE HISTORY OF THE PRIVACY ACT OF 1974, at 9–28, 97–150, *available at* http://www.loc.gov/rr/frd/Military_Law/LH_

privacy_act-1974.html (reporting that Senate Bill 3418 initially covered all organizations that collected personal information, but the Senate Committee on Government
Operations limited the bill's scope to the federal government).

5. Fair Credit Reporting Act § 602, 15 U.S.C.A. § 1681 (West 2006).

6. 18 U.S.C. § 2710 (2000).

7. Elec. Privacy Info. Ctr., The Video Privacy Protection Act, http://www .epic.org/privacy
/vppa/ (last visited June 1, 2007).

8. SIMSON GARFINKEL, DATABASE NATION 1–37 (2000).

9. Polly Sprenger, *Sun on Privacy: "Get Over It,"* WIRED NEWS, Jan. 26, 1999, http://
www.wired.com/news/politics/0,1283,17538,00.html.

10. *Id.*

11. E-mail from Jim Waldo, engineer, Sun Microsystems, to Jonathan Zittrain (Apr. 18,
2007, 23:02) (on file with author).

12. FREEDOM OF INFO. COMM., AM. SOC'Y OF NEWSPAPER EDS. & FIRST AMENDMENT CTR.,
FREEDOM OF INFORMATION IN THE DIGITAL AGE 10–12, 15 (2001), *available at*
http://www.freedomforum.org/publications/first/foi/foiinthedigitalage.pdf (finding that
89 percent of adults surveyed were concerned about personal privacy, and that nearly identical percentages reported that they were concerned with crime, access to quality health
care, and the future of the social security system); Humphrey Taylor, Most People Are
"Privacy Pragmatists" Who, While Concerned About Privacy, Will Sometimes Trade It Off
for Other Benefits, Mar. 19, 2003, http://www.harrisinteractive.com/harris_poll/index
.asp?PID=365 (discussing Harris Poll #17, which found that 69 percent of adults believe
consumers have "lost all control of how personal information is collected and used by companies" and that 53 percent disagreed that "existing laws and organizational practices provide a reasonable level of protection for consumer privacy policy").

13. Jerry Kang & Dana Cuff, *Pervasive Computing: Embedding the Public Sphere,* 62 WASH.
& LEE L. REV. 93 (2005) (discussing privacy concerns that emerge as mobile, wireless
devices expand Internet connectivity); Jeffrey Rosen, *A Watchful State,* N.Y. TIMES,
Oct. 7, 2001, at A1, *available at* http://www.nytimes.com/2001/10/07/magazine/07
SURVEILLANCE.html?ex=1172466000&en=6b3f27c506e13d53&ei=5070 (ex-
amining the possible effects of biometric identification technology on personal privacy);
Daniel J. Solove, *Identity Theft, Privacy, and the Architecture of Vulnerability,* 54 HAST-
INGS L.J. 1227 (2003) (considering identity theft and privacy in the context of public
identification systems and information-storage architectures).

14. CAL. CIV. CODE § 1798.82 (West 2003). California legislators are currently considering
a variety of different proposals to amend or even repeal portions of this statute.

15. StrongAuth, Inc., maintains a compendium of such disclosures, including those by MasterCard International, Polo/Ralph Lauren, Bank of America, and several universities.
See Washington's SSB 66043—On the Heel of CA's SB 1386, Newsletter (StrongAuth,
Inc.), May 5, 2005, http://www.strongauth.com/index.php?option=com_content&
task=view&id=36&Itemid=42.

16. Robert Lemos, *Bank of America Loses a Million Customer Records,* CNET NEWS.COM,
Feb. 25, 2005, http://news.com.com/Bank+of+America+loses+a+million+customer
+records/2100-1029_3-5590989.html?tag=st.rc.targ_mb. This type of data loss is not

uncommon. As one study noted, "60 percent of [compromised record] incidents involved organizational mismanagement: personally identifiable information accidentally placed online, missing equipment, lost backup tapes, or other administrative errors." Kris Erickson & Philip N. Howard, *A Case of Mistaken Identity?: News Accounts of Hacker and Organizational Responsibility for Compromised Digital Records, 1980–2006,* 12 J. COMPUTER-MEDIATED COMM. (2007), *available at* http://jcmc.indiana.edu.

17. Joris Evers, *Credit Card Breach Exposes 40 Million Accounts,* CNET NEWS.COM, June 20, 2005, http://news.cnet.co.uk/software/0,39029694,39190155,00.htm.

18. Hiawatha Bray, *BC Warns Its Alumni of Possible ID Theft After Computer Is Hacked,* BOSTON GLOBE, Mar. 17, 2005, at E3, *available at* http://www.boston.com/business/ technology/articles/2005/03/17/bc_warns_its_alumni_of_possible_id_theft_ after_computer_is_hacked/.

19. *See* Privacy Rights Clearinghouse, A Chronology of Data Breaches, http://www.privacy rights.org/ar/ChronDataBreaches.htm (last visited June 1, 2007).

20. *Amazon's Old Customers "Pay More,"* BBC NEWS, Sept. 8, 2000, http://news.bbc.co.uk/ 2/hi/business/914691.stm.

21. For more on price discrimination for information goods, see William Fisher, When Should We Permit Differential Pricing of Information? (2007) (working draft, on file with author).

22. *See* Paul Saffo, Sensors: The Next Wave of Infotech Innovation, http://www.saffo.com/ essays/sensors.php (last visited June 1, 2007).

23. *See* Gordon E. Moore, *Cramming More Components onto Integrated Circuits,* ELECTRONICS, Apr. 19, 1965, *available at* http://download.intel.com/research/silicon/moores paper.pdf.

24. Michael McCahill & Clive Norris, *CCTV in London* 6–7 (Urban Eye Project, Working Paper No. 6, 2002), *available at* http://www.urbaneye.net/results/ue_wp6.pdf.

25. More information on the original project's results and further efforts is available at the clickworkers site. *See* Clickworkers, http://clickworkers.arc.nasa.gov/top (last visited June 1, 2007).

26. YOCHAI BENKLER, THE WEALTH OF NETWORKS 69 (2006).

27. *See supra* note 25 and accompanying text.

28. Luis von Ahn, Presentation for Google TechTalk on Human Computation (Oct. 26, 2006), *available at* http://video.google.com/videoplay?docid=-8246463980976635143.

29. *Cf.* BENKLER, *supra* note 26, at 81 (discussing the potential for digital proofreading).

30. BENKLER, *supra* note 26, at 33, 76; *see also* Jessica Litman, *Sharing and Stealing,* 27 HASTINGS COMM. & ENT. L.J. 1, 39–50 (2004) (examining the concept of public activity derived from compiling private activity in the context of online media sharing and P2P networks).

31. *See* SearchEngines.com, Click Popularity—DirectHit Technology Overview, http:// www.searchengines.com/directhit.html (last visited June 1, 2007); *see also* Google, Google Searches More Sites More Quickly, Delivering the Most Relevant Results, http://www.google.com/technology/ (last visited June 1, 2007) (explaining Google's PageRank search system).

32. For a detailed discussion of captchas, see Luis von Ahn et al., CAPTCHA: Using Hard

AI Problems for Security, *available at* http://www.cs.cmu.edu/~biglou/captcha_crypt .pdf.

33. For a detailed discussion of captchas, spammers' workarounds, and human computation, see von Ahn, *supra* note 28. For his slides, see http://www.cs.cmu.edu/~biglou/ cycles.ppt.

34. *Id.*

35. E-mail from Luis von Ahn to Jonathan Zittrain (May 22, 2007) (on file with author).

36. The use of pornography in motivating individuals to fill in captchas has been suggested but not proven.

37. *See* von Ahn, *supra* note 28.

38. *See* Brad Stone, *Captchas, Online Gatekeepers Against Spam, Need an Overhaul,* INT'L HERALD TRIB., June 11, 2007, *available at* http://www.iht.com/articles/2007/06/11/ business/codes.php.

39. *See* Posting of Ben Maurer to *Exploring, reCAPTCHA: A New Way to Fight Spam,* EXPLORING (May 23, 2007), http://bmaurer.blogspot.com/2007/05/recaptcha-new-way-to-fight-spam.html (May 23, 2007, 16:31).

40. JEFFREY ROSEN, THE NAKED CROWD: RECLAIMING SECURITY AND FREEDOM IN AN ANXIOUS AGE 23 (2004); Jeffrey Rosen, *The Naked Crowd: Balancing Privacy and Security in an Age of Terror,* 46 ARIZ. L. REV. 607, 610 (2004) ("[I]t was proposed after September 11 to engage in ambitious forms of what Roger Clarke has called 'mass dataveillance' to consolidate and analyze public and private data in the hope of unearthing unusual patterns that might predict suspicious activity.").

41. *See, e.g.,* FRED H. CATE, PRIVACY IN THE INFORMATION AGE 113 (1997) (proposing how notice could be used to protect privacy).

42. *See, e.g.,* JEFFREY ROSEN, THE UNWANTED GAZE: THE DESTRUCTION OF PRIVACY IN AMERICA 172–73 (2001) (explaining how, with the help of encryption, "individual Internet users could come close to realizing Louis Brandeis and Samuel Warren's ideal" of privacy).

43. ShotSpotter is a company that offers some examples of this technology. *See* ShotSpotter, ShotSpotter Gunshot Location System (GLS) Overview, http://www.shotspotter.com/ products/index.html (last visited June 1, 2007) (providing an overview of the company's products); Ethan Watters, *Shot Spotter,* WIRED MAGAZINE, Apr. 2007, at 146–52, *available at* http://www.shotspotter.com/news/news.html (discussing the use and effectiveness of this technology); *see also* ShotSpotter, ShotSpotter in the News, http://www .shotspotter.com/news/news.html (last visited June 1, 2007) (providing links to articles discussing the company and its products).

44. Sig Christenson, *Border Webcams Rack Up Millions of Hits in a Month,* SAN ANTONIO EXPRESS-NEWS, Dec. 10, 2006, http://www.mysanantonio.com/news/metro/stories/ MYSA121106.01A.border_webcam.323e8ed.html.

45. *Id.* ("[S]tate officials Sunday tout[ed] it as a success beyond anyone's dreams.").

46. Assoc. Press, *Texas Border Cam Test Catches 10 Illegal Immigrants,* CHI. SUN-TIMES, Jan. 8, 2007, http://www.suntimes.com/news/nation/201613,CST-NWS-bord08.article ("It seems to me that $20,000 per undocumented worker is a lot of money" (quoting state Rep. Norma Chavez) [internal quotation marks omitted]); Editorial, *Virtual Wall*

a Real Bust That Didn't Come Cheap, San Antonio Express-News, Jan. 19, 2007, at 6B ("[T]he results are in: The plan bombed.").

47. *See* David Brin, The Transparent Society: Will Technology Force Us to Choose Between Privacy and Freedom? 52–54, 149–78 (1999).

48. *See* Neal Feigenson & Meghan A. Dunn, *New Visual Technologies in Court: Directions for Research,* 27 L. & Human Behav. 109 (2003) (discussing how recent advances in visual technologies will affect legal decision-making, with reference to many cases that have altered the way courtrooms incorporate new technologies).

49. The Anderson County jailcam was discontinued as of November 27, 2006; the Web site no longer discusses its removal. It was formerly accessible at http://www.tnacso.net/cont/jailcam.php.

50. Assoc. Press, *Tenn. Jail Web Cam Jeopardizes Security,* Boston Globe, Nov. 25, 2006, http://www.boston.com/news/odd/articles/2006/11/25/tenn_jail_web_cam_jeopardizes_security/ (noting that Maricopa County, Arizona, also shut down its camera after losing a lawsuit by inmates alleging abuse of their rights).

51. In the aftermath of the September 11 attacks and the passing of the USA PATRIOT Act, the government has been increasingly likely to take an active role in issues of electronic surveillance. For an overview of surveillance law and its shifting usage by the government, see Daniel J. Solove, *Reconstructing Electronic Surveillance Law,* 72 Geo. Wash. L. Rev. 1264, 1278–80 (2004).

52. *See* Daniel J. Solove, The Digital Person: Technology and Privacy in the Information Age 2–7, 13–26 (2004) (expressing concern about the collection of information held in commercial databases, public records, and government files).

53. *See* Kang & Cuff, *supra* note 13, at 134–42.

54. The largest difference may arise from the fact that invasions of privacy implicate the dignity of individuals rather than firms' profits, and thus there is no natural lobby to organize against this personal intrusion.

55. *Expert: LAPD Officers' Behavior Not Unreasonable,* ABC News, Nov. 11, 2006, http://abcnews.go.com/GMA/story?id=2646425; Video: LA Police Brutality (posted by 3101010 on YouTube, Nov. 10, 2006), http://www.youtube.com/watch?v=7_gFJJXLv28.

56. Video: Bus Uncle (posted by beautyjeojihyun on YouTube, May 11, 2006), http://www.youtube.com/watch?v=RSHziqJWYcM.

57. *Id.*

58. *Hong Kong's "Bus Uncle" Beaten Up by Three Men,* Channel NewsAsia, June 8, 2006, http://www.channelnewsasia.com/stories/eastasia/view/212671/1/.html.

59. Jonathan Krim, *Subway Fracas Escalates into Test of the Internet's Power to Shame,* Wash. Post, July 7, 2005, at D1, *available at* http://www.washingtonpost.com/wp-dyn/content/article/2005/07/06/AR2005070601953.html.

60. For details on Star Wars Kid, see Wikipedia, *Star Wars Kid,* http://en.wikipedia.org/wiki/Star_Wars_kid (as of June 1, 2007, 10:00 GMT).

61. *Star Wars Kid Is Top Viral Video,* BBC News, Nov. 27, 2006, http://news.bbc.co.uk/2/hi/entertainment/6187554.stm.

62. *See, e.g.,* Heather Adler, *Stephen Colbert Aims His Lightsaber at Star Wars,* Dose.ca,

Aug. 24, 2006, http://www.dose.ca/celeb/story.html?id=10261eb6-0469-4198-a16a-1f302275b2a9 (describing the Comedy Central show host's mocking of the Star Wars Kid); Video: White & Nerdy (Google Video, Sept. 19, 2006), http://video.google.com/videoplay?docid=1384277706451157121 ("Weird Al" Yankovic's music video from his album "Straight Outta Lynwood," which includes a scene imitating the Star Wars Kid). For a list of other pop-culture references, see Wikipedia, *Star Wars Kid, supra* note 60.

63. Mark Twain, Mark Twain's Autobiography, Part 2, at 10 (2003).

64. This was a lesson learned by George Allen, a Republican candidate in the 2006 U.S. Senate campaign who was caught on camera calling an Indian supporter of his opponent by the derogatory epithet "macaca." Carl Hulse, *Senator Apologizes to Student for Remark,* N.Y. Times, Aug. 24, 2006, at A20, *available at* http://www.nytimes.com/2006/08/24/washington/24allen.html; *see also* Dale Eisman, *Others Will Have "Macaca Moments," Pundits Say,* Virginian-Pilot, Dec. 1, 2006, http://www.redorbit.com/news/technology/751673/others_will_have_macaca_moments_pundits_say/index.html.

65. Such places, while private, are sometimes treated by the law as places of "public accommodation," in recognition of their hybrid status. This classification imposes some responsibility on their owners for equal treatment of patrons. *See* 42 U.S.C. § 12181(7) (2000) (defining a public accommodation as a restaurant and inn, among other things, for purposes of the Americans with Disabilities Act); 42 U.S.C. § 2000a(b)(1)–(2) (2000) (classifying inns and restaurants as places of public accommodations for the purposes of the 1964 Civil Rights Act).

66. *See* Eric A. Posner & Cass R. Sunstein, *The Law of Other States,* 59 Stan. L. Rev. 131, 162 (2006) ("In a reputational cascade, people think that they know what is right, or what is likely to be right, but they nonetheless go along with the crowd in order to maintain the good opinion of others. Suppose that Albert suggests that global warming is a serious problem and that Barbara concurs with Albert, not because she actually thinks that Albert is right, but because she does not wish to seem, to Albert, to be ignorant or indifferent to environmental protection. If Albert and Barbara seem to agree that global warming is a serious problem, Cynthia might not contradict them publicly and might even appear to share their judgment, not because she believes that judgment to be correct, but because she does not want to face their hostility or lose their good opinion. It should be easy to see how this process might generate a cascade."). New and unique ideas can have important effects, *see generally* Malcolm Gladwell, The Tipping Point: How Little Things Can Make a Big Difference (2000), but unless widely held views are consistently challenged, incorrect ideas can become deeply ensconced. *See* Cass R. Sunstein, *A New Progressivism,* 17 Stan. L. & Pol'y Rev. 197, 210–11 (2006); *see also* Irving L. Janis, Groupthink (2d ed. 1982) (discussing how group pressure can lead members to agree to a result that they personally think is wrong).

67. *See* McIntyre v. Ohio Elections Comm'n, 514 U.S. 334, 360–61 (1995) (Thomas, J., concurring) ("There is little doubt that the Framers engaged in anonymous political writing. The essays in the Federalist Papers, published under the pseudonym of 'Publius,' are only the most famous example of the outpouring of anonymous political writing that occurred during the ratification of the Constitution. . . . [T]he historical ev-

idence indicates that Founding-era Americans opposed attempts to require that anonymous authors reveal their identities on the ground that forced disclosure violated the 'freedom of the press.'").

68. TMZ Staff, *Elisha: The B*tch Next Door!,* TMZ.COM, Nov. 14, 2006, http://www.tmz.com/2006/11/14/elisha-the-b-tch-next-door/.

69. Gawker Stalker, http://gawker.com/stalker/ (last visited June 1, 2007).

70. DAVID WEINBERGER, SMALL PIECES LOOSELY JOINED: A UNIFIED THEORY OF THE WEB 104 (2002).

71. Traditionally, retailers, television networks, and movie theaters were forced to try to identify mainstream, popular choices. They had to favor middle-ground material because they had only a limited amount of shelf space, prime-time hours, or screens, respectively, and needed to maximize their sales. Online marketplaces do not have that limitation: "A hit and a miss are on equal economic footing, both just entries in a database called up on demand, both equally worthy of being carried. Suddenly, popularity no longer has a monopoly on profitability." Chris Anderson, *The Long Tail,* WIRED, Oct. 24, 2004, http://www.wired.com/wired/archive/12.10/tail.html.

72. Flickr had approximately five hundred million photos as of May 2007. E-mail from Meagan Busath, Public Relations Representative, Flickr, to Jonathan Zittrain (May 24, 2007, 15:17 EDT) (on file with author).

73. DAVID WEINBERGER, EVERYTHING IS MISCELLANEOUS: THE POWER OF THE NEW DIGITAL DISORDER (2007).

74. *See* Posting of Loren Baker to Search Engine Journal, *Google, Neven Vision & Image Recognition,* http://www.searchenginejournal.com/google-neven-vision-image-recognition/3728/ (Aug. 15, 2006); Jacqui Cheng, *Facial Recognition Slipped into Google Image Search,* ARS TECHNICA, May 30, 2007, http://arstechnica.com/news.ars/post/2007 0530-facial-recognition-slipped-into-google-image-search.html.

75. Adam Liptak, *Driver's License Emerges as Crime-Fighting Tool, but Privacy Advocates Worry,* N.Y. TIMES, Feb. 17, 2007, at A10, *available at* http://www.nytimes.com/2007/02/17/us/17face.html.

76. The Nuremberg Files, http://www.christiangallery.com/atrocity/ (last visited June 1, 2007).

77. *See* Planned Parenthood of Columbia/Willamette Inc. v. Am. Coal. of Life Activists, 422 F.3d 949 (9th Cir. 2005).

78. Abortion Cams: Shame Deters Abortion, http://www.abortioncams.com/ (last visited June 1, 2007). The Web site is premised on the belief that showing the images of clinic patients will either shame or scare women away from having an abortion. *See* How to Deter Abortion, http://www.abortioncams.com/deter.htm (last visited June 1, 2007) ("Would a preacher want to be photographed going into a whore house, would a Priest want to be photographed going into a sex chat room with grade school kids? Neither would a mother want to be photographed going in to kill her baby.").

79. *See* Posting of Tom Owad to Applefritter, *Data Mining 101: Finding Subversives Within Amazon Wishlists,* http://www.applefritter.com/bannedbooks (Jan. 4, 2006, 19:37); *see also* Paul Marks, *"Mashup" Websites Are a Dream Come True for Hackers,* 190 NEW SCIENTIST, May 12, 2006, at 28, *available at* http://www.newscientisttech.com/channel/

tech/electronic-threats/mg19025516.400-mashup-websites-are-a-hackers-dream-come-true.html.

80. Handschu v. Special Serv. Div., No. 71 Civ. 2203 (S.D.N.Y. Feb. 15, 2007), *available at* http://graphics.nytimes.com/packages/pdf/nyregion/20070215_nycruling.pdf.

81. *Home Video: Utah Mall Shooting,* FOX News, Feb. 16, 2007, http://www.foxnews.com/story/0,2933,252395,00.html.

82. Glenn Chapman, *Internet Users Transformed into News Reporters,* Middle E. Times, Feb. 11, 2007, http://news.yahoo.com/s/afp/20070211/tc_afp/uscanadaitinternetmedia companynowpublicyahoo ("You have tens of millions of people around the world with cell phones with cameras connected to providers. It's like having an army of stringers out." (quoting Scott Moore, head of Yahoo News) (internal quotation marks omitted)).

83. Witness.org was founded with the idea that it would be easier to bring perpetrators to justice if there was photographic or video evidence of their crimes. Its mission is to use "video and online technologies to open the eyes of the world to human rights violations." Witness.org, About Witness, http://witness.org/index.php?option=com_content&task=view&id=26&Itemid=78 (last visited June 1, 2007).

84. Urs Gasser, *Regulating Search Engines: Taking Stock and Looking Ahead,* 8 Yale J.L. & Tech. 201, 202 (2006) ("Since the creation of the first pre-Web Internet search engines in the early 1990s, search engines have become almost as important as email as a primary online activity. Arguably, search engines are among the most important gatekeepers in today's digitally networked environment."); Stephen E. Arnold, Google: Search Becomes an Application Platform 1 (2005) (unpublished position paper), *available at* http://islandia.law.yale.edu/isp/search_papers/arnold.pdf ("Just as calculations were one of the reasons for mainframes, search is one of the reasons why distributed, parallel, commodity-based network systems are the next computing platforms. The smartphone, the desktop computer, the Xbox game machine, and even the mainframe gain greater utility when linked to a computer similar to one built, owned, and operated by Google."); Memorandum from Deborah Fallows et al., Pew Internet & Am. Life Project, on The Popularity and Importance of Search Engines 3 (2004), *available at* http://www.pew internet.org/pdfs/PIP_Data_Memo_Searchengines.pdf ("The availability of reliable, easy-to-use search engines has transformed people's connection to information. For some, search engines are indispensable. Many people deeply rely on search engines to deliver vitally important information to them: 44% of searchers say that all or most of the searches they conduct are for information they absolutely need to find.").

85. Pay-for-placement has existed from the first days of the Web's commercialization. *See* Jeff Pelline, *Pay-for-Placement Gets Another Shot,* CNET News.com, Feb. 19, 1998, http://news.com.com/Pay-for-placement+gets+another+shot/2100-1023_3-208309.html. Until early 2007, Yahoo's search engine placed the highest bidders' ads before the most relevant ads. Yahoo, however, switched to ranking based on relevance only, a change driven by significant competitive pressures. *See* Sara Kehaulani Goo, *Yahoo Retools Ad Technology; Ranking System Ends Pay-for-Placement Ads in Search Results,* Wash. Post, Feb. 6, 2007, at D2 ("The whole notion that I can buy my way to the top [of spon-

sored links] is something we do want to move beyond" (quoting Tim Cadogan, Vice President, Yahoo Search Marketing)). Of course, advertisers routinely pay for placement among sets of sponsored links included alongside search results in search engines like Yahoo and Google.

86. BENKLER, *supra* note 26, at 76.

87. *Id.* at 76–80.

88. *See* Paul Resnick et al., *The Value of Reputation on eBay: A Controlled Experiment,* 9 EXPERIMENTAL ECON. 79, 96, 98–99 (2006), *available at* http://www.si.umich.edu/~presnick/papers/postcards/PostcardsFinalPrePub.pdf.

89. *See, e.g.,* Paul Resnick et al., *Reputation Systems,* 43 COMMS. ACM 45–48 (2000), *available at* http://www.si.umich.edu/~presnick/papers/cacm00/reputations.pdf (noting that reputation systems protect anonymity while fostering reliable transactions); Paul Resnick & Richard Zeckhauser, *Trust Among Strangers in Internet Transactions: Empirical Analysis of eBay's Reputation System,* 11 ADVANCES APPLIED MICROECON. 127 (2002), *available at* http://www.si.umich.edu/~presnick/papers/ebayNBER/RZNBERBodega Bay.pdf (noting that eBay's system and others appear to work, probably with help from norms drawn from outside the online context); Chrysanthos Dellarocas, *The Digitization of Word-of-Mouth: Promise and Challenges of Online Feedback,* 49 MGMT. SCI. 1407, 1417–21 (2003), *available at* http://ssrn.com/abstract=393042 (noting several ways that users can game the system, including changing their user name after receiving a bad rating).

90. Ina Steiner, *eBay "Feedback Farms" Planted with One-Cent eBooks,* AUCTIONBYTES.COM, Oct. 3, 2006, http://www.auctionbytes.com/cab/abn/y06/m10/i03/s02.

91. Google did de-list BMW for creating dummy Web pages with key words in order to raise the ranking of its central Web site. *BMW Given Google "Death Penalty,"* BBC NEWS, Feb. 6, 2006, http://news.bbc.co.uk/2/hi/technology/4685750.stm. Google, however, quickly showed mercy and relisted the site just three days later, casting some doubt on the effectiveness of the system when the perpetrator is an influential and important Web site. *See* Posting of Danny Sullivan to Search Engine Watch Blog, *Welcome Back to Google, BMW—Missed You These Past Three Days,* http://blog.searchenginewatch.com/blog/060208-104027 (Feb. 8, 2006, 10:40).

92. Cyworld allows its users to decorate their pages by renting various digital accoutrements. While one's home page has the metaphor of a physical home, every digital item within the home is rented rather than purchased. For example, a frame cover for a picture in the room costs $1.72 and lasts thirty days. *See* Cyworld, http://us.cyworld.com/main/index.php (last visited June 1, 2007); Wikipedia, *Cyworld,* http://en.wikipedia.org/wiki/Cyworld (as of June 1, 2007, 19:00 GMT).

93. Cho Jin-seo, *Cyworld Members Reach 20 Mil.,* KOREA TIMES, Feb. 5, 2007, http://search.hankooki.com/times/times_view.php?term=cyworld++&path=han kooki3/times/lpage/tech/200702/kt2007020519364411810.htm&media=kt.

94. Jennifer Park, *"I Was a Cyholic, Cyworld Addict,"* OHMYNEWS, July 26, 2004, http://english.ohmynews.com/articleview/article_view.asp?menu=c10400&no=179108&rel_no=1&back_url.

95. Lior Jacob Strahilevitz, *"How's My Driving?" for Everyone (and Everything?),* 81 N.Y.U. L. Rev. 1699 (2006).

96. For example, dodgeball.com combines online friend lists and cell-phone text messaging to allow users to advertise their whereabouts to friends, see when they are near friends of friends, and even see when their crushes are nearby. *See* Dodgeball.com, http://www.dodgeball.com/ (last visited June 1, 2007). Loopt offers a similar service. *See* Loopt.com, Your Social Compass, https://loopt.com/loopt/sess/index.aspx (last visited Dec. 1, 2007); Meetro.com helps users chat over the Internet and connect with other Meetro users who live nearby. *See* Meetro, What Is Meetro?, http://meetro.com/ (last visited June 1, 2007).

97. One prominent recent example is found in the Seattle-based start-up Avvo, which provides ratings for attorneys. An opaque system that generated low ratings for some prompted offended lawyers to consider pressing for damages to their practices. *See* Posting of John Cook to John Cook's Venture Blog, *Avvo's Attorney Rating System Draws Fire,* http://blog.seattlepi.nwsource.com/venture/archives/116417.asp#extended (June 8, 2007, 14:53).

98. Gasser, *supra* note 84, at 232–33 (observing that search algorithms are often trade secrets).

99. *See* Judit Bar-Ilan, *Web Links and Search Engine Ranking: The Case of Google and the Query "Jew,"* 57 J. Am. Soc'y for Info. Sci. & Tech. 1581 (2006).

100. Google, An Explanation of Our Search Results, http://www.google.com/explanation.html (last visited June 1, 2007) ("If you recently used Google to search for the word 'Jew,' you may have seen results that were very disturbing. We assure you that the views expressed by the sites in your results are not in any way endorsed by Google.").

101. Advisory Comm. to the Sec'y of Health, Educ. & Welfare, *supra* note 1.

102. *See* Pamela Samuelson, *Five Challenges for Regulating the Global Information Society, in* Regulating the Global Information Society 321–22 (Chris Marsden ed., 2000) (describing how technological developments threaten existing means for protecting traditional values such as "privacy, innovation, and freedom of expression").

103. It does not just happen on social networking sites; constitutional law scholar Laurence Tribe was distressed when a statement he posted on a family Web site became the subject of public attention. Rosen, The Naked Crowd: Reclaiming Security and Freedom in an Anxious Age, *supra* note 40, at 164–65.

104. Nancy Blachman & Jerry Peek, How Google Works, http://www.googleguide.com/google_works.html (last visited June 1, 2007).

105. *See* Samuelson, *supra* note 102, at 323–24 (arguing that given the tediously slow nature of the harmonization process, nations may generally be better off seeking not complete harmonization but "policy interoperability," broad agreement on goals that allow room for flexible implementation of those goals at a later date).

106. Martijn Koster, A Standard for Robot Exclusion, http://www.robotstxt.org/wc/norobots.html (detailing the genesis of robots.txt) (last visited June 1, 2007).

107. *Id.*

108. *See, e.g.,* Yahoo!, Search Help, How Do I Prevent You from Indexing Certain Pages?, http://help.yahoo.com/lus/yahoo/search/webcrawler/slurp-04.html (last visited Dec.

1, 2007); Microsoft Live Search, Site Owner Help: Control Which Pages of Your Website Are Indexed, http://search.msn.com.sg/docs/siteowner.aspx?t=SEARCH_WEB MASTER_REF_RestrictAccessToSite.htm (last visited Dec. 1, 2007); Baidu, http://www.baidu.com/search/robots.html (last visited June 1, 2007); Google, Webmaster Help Center: How Do I Request that Google Not Crawl Parts or All of My Site?, http://www.google.com/support/webmasters/bin/answer.py?answer=33570 &topic=8846 (last visited June 1, 2007). *See generally* Posting of Dan Crow to the Official Google Blog, *Controlling How Search Engines Access and Index Your Website,* http://googleblog.blogspot.com/2007/01/controlling-how-search-engines-access .html (Jan. 26, 2007, 11:36).

109. Though this is not to say that the robots.txt standard has indeed proved to be legally vulnerable in practice. In March 2007, German courts affirmed with *A Painter v. Google* that electing *not* to use robots.txt in fact granted an implied license for search engines to index a page. *See* Ben Allgrove, *The Search Engine's Dilemma,* 2 J. INTELL. PROP. L. & PRAC. 437 (2007).

110. *See* Jody Freeman, *The Private Role in Public Governance,* 75 N.Y.U. L. REV. 543 (2000); Mark A. Lemley, *Intellectual Property Rights and Standard-Setting Organizations,* 90 CAL. L. REV. 1889 (2000); Pamela Samuelson, *Questioning Copyright in Standards,* 48 B.C. L. REV. 193 (2007) (describing the uniform standards underpinning the information society as "an integral part of the largely invisible infrastructure of the modern world," and offering a thorough analysis of why and how courts should resist placing these standards under the scope of U.S. copyright protection).

111. *See* A. Michael Froomkin, *Habermas@Discourse.net: Toward a Critical Theory of Cyberspace,* 116 HARV. L. REV. 749, 777–96 (2003) (discussing the evolution of Internet standards setting).

112. ebay, Inc. v. Bidder's Edge, 100 F. Supp. 2d 1058 (N.D. Cal. 2000).

113. 17 U.S.C. § 512(d) (2000).

114. Google prevailed, on a particularly favorable fact pattern, against one author-plaintiff challenging the search engine's copying and distribution of his copyrighted works. Field v. Google, 412 F. Supp. 2d 1106 (D. Nev. 2006) (finding Google's copying and distribution of the copyrighted works through cached links to be a fair use on grounds that offering access through its cache serves important social purposes and transforms rather than supersedes the original author's use).

115. *See* Complaint, McGraw-Hill Companies, Inc. v. Google, No. 05-CV-8881 (S.D.N.Y. Oct. 19, 2005).

116. *See* Complaint, Author's Guild v. Google, No. 05-CV-8136 (S.D.N.Y. Dec. 20, 2005).

117. Creative Commons Legal Code, http://creativecommons.org/licenses/by-nc-sa/2.5/ legalcode (last visited June 1, 2007).

118. In a case brought by Adam Curry against a Dutch tabloid after the tabloid attempted to republish several CC-licensed photos that Curry had posted on Flickr, the District Court of Amsterdam found that "[i]n case of doubt as to the applicability and the contents of the License, [Audax, the tabloid,] should have requested authorization for publication from the copyright holder of the photos (Curry). Audax has failed to perform such a detailed investigation, and has assumed too easily that publication of the pho-

tos was allowed. Audax has not observed the conditions stated in the [Attribution-Noncommercial-Sharealike] License [. . .]." *See* Posting of Pamela Jones to Groklaw, *Creative Commons License Upheld by Dutch Court,* http://www.groklaw.net/article.php ?story=20060316052623594 (Mar. 16, 2006, 06:05 EST). However, American law is not nearly so clear. Some commentators have suggested that in the interest of clarifying the enforceability of these rights in the United States, Creative Commons licensors, when faced with some infringement of the rights they have chosen to retain, should file cease and desist letters and force a legal decision on this issue. *See* Posting of John Palfrey, *Following up on the RSS/Copyright Debate,* http://blogs.law.harvard.edu/palfrey/ 2006/07/28/following -up-on-the-rsscopyright-debate (July 28, 2006, 17:02 EST). Until then, content publishers may have no way to grapple with the "widespread abuse" and piracy of works published under Creative Commons licenses. *See* Posting of Ethan Zuckerman to My Heart's in Accra, *Can Creative Commons and Commercial Aggregators Learn to Play Nice?,* http://www.ethanzuckerman.com/blog/?p=900 (July 21, 2006, 15:32). *But see* Posting of Mia Garlick to Creative Commons Weblog, *Creative Commons Licenses Enforced in Dutch Court,* http://creativecommons.org/weblog/entry /5823 (Mar. 16, 2006) (questioning whether the legitimacy of Creative Commons licenses should depend on judicial validation).

119. To be sure, it may be easy for the wishes expressed in a Creative Commons license to be respected, since nearly every variant of the license is designed to emphasize sharing among peers rather than restrictions. Variants that do not contemplate such sharing— for example, the Founder's Copyright that asserts regular copyright protection but only for a limited term, or Developing Nations, which only relaxes copyright's restrictions for certain states—are used hardly at all. *See* Creative Commons, License Statistics, http://wiki.creativecommons.org/License_statistics (last visited June 1, 2007).

120. *See, e.g.,* Pamela Samuelson, *Privacy as Intellectual Property?,* 52 STAN. L. REV. 1125, 1170–73 (2000).

121. Wikipedia, *Metadata,* http://en.wikipedia.org/wiki/Metadata (as of June 1, 2007, 20:30 GMT).

122. Flickr allows users to record data such as shutter speed, exposure, date, photographer, geotagging data, and viewer comments. *See, e.g.,* Flickr Camera Finder, http://www .flickr.com/cameras (last visited June 1, 2007). However, no convenient process exists for ensuring that this metadata remains attached to a photo when someone saves it to a hard drive or reposts it on a different site.

123. Some experiments have also attempted to empower individuals to make their preferences clear at the point an image or video is initially captured. An example is Miguel Mora's Identity Protection System, which would allow a sticker or badge to function as a signal for surveillance cameras to block an individual from their recording. *See* Miguel.Mora.Design, http://www.miquelmora.com/idps.html (last visited July 28, 2007).

124. TED NELSON, LITERARY MACHINES (1981); Wikipedia, *Transclusion,* http://en .wikipedia.org/wiki/Transclusion (as of June 1, 2007, 10:30 GMT).

125. Consider, for example, the Internet Archive. Proprietor Brewster Kahle has thus far

avoided what one would think to be an inevitable copyright lawsuit as he archives and makes available historical snapshots of the Web. He has avoided such lawsuits by respecting Web owners' wishes to be excluded as soon as he is notified. *See* Internet Archive FAQ, http://www.archive.org/about/faqs.php (last visited June 1, 2007).

126. Moore v. Regents of the Univ. of Cal., 793 P.2d 479 (Cal. 1990).

127. Daniel Goleman, *Normal Social Restraints Are Weakened in Cyberspace,* Int'l Herald Trib., Feb. 20, 2007, *available at* http://www.iht.com/articles/2007/02/20/business /email.php.

128. *See* John Suler, *The Online Disinhibition Effect,* 7 CyberPsychology & Behav. 321, 322 (2004) (noting how not having facial feedback with those we are addressing online allows us to ignore any negative emotional responses to our statements).

129. Yochai Benkler, *Sharing Nicely: On Shareable Goods and the Emergence of Sharing as a Modality of Economic Production,* 114 Yale L.J. 273 (2004).

130. *See* John Naughton, *Our Changing Media Ecosystem, in* United Kingdom Office of Communications—The Next Decade 61 (Ed Richards, Robin Foster & Tom Kiedrowski eds., 2006).

131. *Cf., e.g.,* Local Loan Co. v. Hunt, 292 U.S. 234, 244 (1934) (noting that providing debtors with a clean slate is "[o]ne of the primary purposes of the Bankruptcy Act"); Thomas H. Jackson, *The Fresh-Start Policy in Bankruptcy Law,* 98 Harv. L. Rev. 1393 (1985).

132. Such proscriptions may also prove difficult to reconcile with constitutional frameworks. *See, e.g.,* Eugene Volokh, *Freedom of Speech and Information Privacy: The Troubling Implications of a Right to Stop People from Speaking About You,* 52 Stan. L. Rev. 1049 (2000).

133. *See* Jeffery Rosen, *Privacy in Public Places,* 12 Cardozo Stud. L. & Literature 167, 189 (2000) ("[W]e have fewer opportunities to present ourselves publicly in all of our complexity; and, therefore, as more of our private lives are recorded in cyberspace, the risk that we will be unfairly defined by isolated pieces of information that have been wrenched out of context has increased dramatically."); *see also* Rosen, The Naked Crowd: Reclaiming Security and Freedom in an Anxious Age, *supra* note 40, at 55–57 (2001) (describing how Larry Lessig was hurt by an e-mail discussing Microsoft that was taken out of context and then used against him).

134. *See, e.g.,* Richard Delgado & Jean Stefancic, Understanding Words That Wound 207 (2004).

135. This kind of compelled speech would not be unprecedented. For much of the twentieth century, the FCC's Fairness Doctrine forced broadcasters to air controversial public interest stories and provide opposing viewpoints on those issues. *See* Steve Rendall, *The Fairness Doctrine: How We Lost It and Why We Need It Back,* Extra!, Jan./Feb. 2005, http://www.fair.org/index.php?page=2053. Under President Reagan, the FCC repealed this doctrine in 1987. *Id.* Despite this administrative change, the Supreme Court has consistently interpreted the First Amendment to include the right *not* to speak in a line of compelled speech cases. *See, e.g.,* Keller v. State Bar of Cal., 496 U.S. 1 (1990) (holding that lawyers could not be forced to pay bar association fees to sup-

port political messages with which they disagreed); Abood v. Detroit Bd. of Educ., 433 U.S. 915 (1977) (holding that teachers could not be forced to pay union fees to support political messages with which they disagreed).

136. Posting of Joseph Nye to The Huffington Post, *Davos Day 3: Internet Privacy and Reputational Repair Sites,* http://www.huffingtonpost.com/joseph-nye/davos-day-3-internet -pri_b_39750.html (Jan. 26, 2007, 18:14 EST).

137. Posting of Dan Meredith & Andy Golding to The Google News Blog, *Perspectives About the News from People in the News,* http://googlenewsblog.blogspot.com/2007/ 08/perspectives-about-news-from-people-in.html (Aug. 7, 2007, 22:32).

138. ReputationDefender, http://www.reputationdefender.com (last visited June 1, 2007). ReputationDefender was started by a former student of mine, and I once served on its advisory board. The firm has itself been the subject of some controversy. *See, e.g.,* Posting of Ann Bartow to Feminist Law Professors, *Well, Those "ReputationDefender" Guys Certainly Are Well Connected,* Anyway, http://feministlawprofs.law.sc.edu/?p=1671 (Apr. 8, 2007, 17:47).

139. Emily Nussbaum, *Say Everything,* N.Y. MAG., Feb. 12, 2007, *available at* http://nymag .com/news/features/27341/index1.html.

140. People aged fifty to sixty-four are almost twice as likely as young people to worry about privacy online. PEW RESEARCH CTR. FOR THE PEOPLE & THE PRESS, ONLINE NEW-COMERS MORE MIDDLE-BROW, LESS WORK-ORIENTED: THE INTERNET NEWS AUDIENCE GOES ORDINARY 24 (1999) *available at* http://people-press.org/reports/pdf/ 72.pdf.

141. Memorandum from Amanda Lenhart & Mary Madden, Research Fellows, Pew Internet & Am. Life Project, on Social Networking Websites and Teens: An Overview 2–5 (Jan. 7, 2007), *available at* http://www.pewinternet.org/pdfs/PIP_SNS_Data_Memo _Jan_2007.pdf; *see also* AMANDA LENHART & MARY MADDEN, TEENS, PRIVACY & ONLINE SOCIAL NETWORKS, at v (Apr. 18, 2007), *available at* http://www.pewinternet .org/pdfs/PIP_Teens _Privacy_SNS_Report_Final.pdf (noting that 53 percent of parents of online teens have installed filtering software on home computers).

142. AMANDA LENHART & MARY MADDEN, TEEN CONTENT CREATORS AND CONSUMERS, at i–iii, 4–5 (2005), *available at* http://www.pewinternet.org/pdfs/PIP_Teens_Content _Creation.pdf.

143. Justin Berton, *The Age of Privacy; Gen Y Not Shy Sharing Online—But Worries About Spying,* S.F. CHRON., May 20, 2006, at A1.

144. LENHART & MADDEN, TEENS, PRIVACY, & ONLINE SOCIAL NETWORKS, *supra* note 141, at v (finding that "40% of teens with profiles online think that it would be hard for someone to find out who they are from their profile, but that they could eventually be found online.").

145. 15 U.S.C. §§ 6502–6506 (2000).

146. The FTC provides updates on COPPA enforcement on its Web page. The agency has filed twelve cases since COPPA was enacted, and only one in the past three years. *See* FTC, Privacy Initiatives, http://www.ftc.gov/privacy/privacyinitiatives/childrens_enf .html (last visited June 1, 2007). According to one source, 77 percent of children aged eight to seventeen who were surveyed said they would lie about their age in order to do

something they were restricted from doing on a Web site. Isabel Walcott, Online Privacy and Safety Survey, *available at* http://web.archive.org/web/20001202110700/http://www .smartgirl.com/press/privacyfindings.html (last visited June 1, 2007).

147. The U.S. Children's Online Protection Act and its predecessors also struggled with how to protect kids from receiving information that could be harmful to them, such as pornography, that adults have a right to see. The most restrictive approach has been to ask providers of information online to assume that kids are receiving it unless each person accessing can demonstrate possession of a valid credit card. *See* 47 U.S.C. § 231(c)(1) (2000). This approach was struck down as unconstitutional. ACLU v. Ashcroft, 322 F.3d 240 (3d Cir. 2003), *aff'd and remanded,* 542 U.S. 656 (2004).

148. Children's Internet Protection Act (CIPA), Pub. L. No. 106-554, §§ 1701–1741, 114 Stat. 2763, 2763A-335 to 2763A-352 (2000) (codified as amended at 20 U.S.C. § 9134 and 47 U.S.C. § 254). While one federal court held that the CIPA is unconstitutional, see Am. Library Ass'n, Inc. v. United States, 201 F. Supp. 2d 401 (E.D. Pa. 2002), the Supreme Court subsequently reversed that decision and affirmed the Act's constitutionality. United States v. Am. Library Ass'n, Inc., 539 U.S. 194 (2003).

149. *See, e.g.,* Vodafone, Content Control: Restricted Access, http://www.vodafone-i .co.uk/contentcontrol/restrictedaccess.htm (last visited June 1, 2007); Vodafone, Content Control, http://online.vodafone.co.uk/dispatch/Portal/appmanager/voda fone/wrp?_nfpb=true&_pageLabel=template11&pageID=PAV_0024&redirect edByRedirectsImplServletFlag=true (last visited June 1, 2007) (providing an overview of the content control service).

150. Posting to Furd Log, *Lessig and Zittrain—Pornography and Jurisdiction,* http://msl1 .mit.edu/furdlog/?p=332 (June 30, 2003, 19:09:54 EST).

151. Alexa, Traffic Rankings for Myspace.com, http://www.alexa.com/data/details/traffic_details?q=&url=myspace.com/ (last visited June 1, 2007).

152. *See* MySpace.com, How Do I Add Color, Graphics, & Sound to My Profile Page?, http://www.myspace.com/Modules/Help/Pages/HelpCenter.aspx?Category =4&Question=7 (last visited June 1, 2007); David F. Carr, *Inside MySpace.com,* Baseline Mag., Jan. 16, 2007, http://www.baselinemag.com/print_article2/0,1217, a=198614,00.asp (discussing the history of MySpace.com and its customizability).

153. *See* Margaret J. Radin, *Property and Personhood,* 34 Stan. L. Rev. 957, 959–60 (1982) ("Most people possess objects they feel are almost part of them. These objects are closely bound up with personhood because of the way we constitute ourselves as continuing personal entities in the world. They may be different as people are different, but some common examples might be a wedding ring, a portrait, an heirloom, or a house. . . . The opposite of holding an object that has become part of one-self is holding an object that is perfectly replaceable with other goods of equal market value. One holds such an object for purely instrumental reasons.").

154. Advisory Comm. to the Sec'y of Health, Educ. & Welfare, *supra* note 1, at § II.

155. PledgeBank, for example, encourages people to take action by exchanging commitments to undertake an activity. PledgeBank, http://www.pledgebank.com/ (last visited June 1, 2007). Meetup helps people find and arrange events with others who share common interests. *See* Meetup, http://www.meetup.com/ (last visited June 1, 2007).

156. *See* Alison Doyle, *To Blog or Not to Blog?*, ABOUT.COM, http://jobsearch.about.com/ od/jobsearch blogs/a/jobsearchblog.htm (last visited June 1, 2007); Ellen Goodman, Editorial, *The Perils of Cyberbaggage,* TRUTHDIG, Feb. 21, 2007, http://www.truthdig .com/report/item/20070221_the_perils_of_cyberbaggage/; Ellen Goodman, Editorial, *Bloggers Get Caught Between the Real and the Cyber,* PITTSBURGH POST-GAZETTE, Feb. 23, 2007, at B7; *MySpace Is Public Space When It Comes to Job Search: Entry Level Job Seekers—It's Time to Reconsider the Web,* COLLEGEGRAD.COM, July 26, 2006, http://www.collegegrad.com/press/myspace.shtml.

157. John Perry Barlow, A Declaration of the Independence of Cyberspace (Feb. 8, 1996), http://homes.eff.org/~barlow/Declaration-Final.html.

CONCLUSION

1. The XO organization reports that the United Nations Development Programme will partner with them to assist governments in distribution and support of the machines as they are made available. *See* United Nations Development Programme, $100 Laptop Project Moves Closer to Narrowing Digital Divide (Jan. 28, 2006), http://content .undp.org/go/newsroom/january-2006/100-dollar-laptop-20060128.en?category ID=349425&lang=en; OLPC, One Laptop per Child http://wiki.laptop.org/go/ One_Laptop_per_Child.

2. *See* One Laptop Per Child (OLPC), Progress, http://www.laptop.org/en/vision/ progress/index.shtml; Tim Bloomberg, *Quanta to start "One Laptop" Project in Sept.,* THE CHINA POST, May 16, 2007, *available at* http://www.chinapost.com.tw/news/ archives/business/2007516/109813.htm. The post-launch phase is planned to include Mexico, all of Central America, Ethiopia, Angola, Pakistan, Vietnam, Indonesia, and the Philippines. OLPC, Map, http://www .laptop.org/map.en_US.html.

3. *See* Assoc. Press, *Laptop Detractors Shrugged Off,* WIRED NEWS, Apr. 4, 2006, http:// www.wired.com/news/technology/0,70584-0.html?tw=rss.index.

4. *See Constructionism,* http://wiki.laptop.org/go/Constructivism. *See generally* Seymour Papert & Idit Harel, *Situating Constructionism, in* CONSTRUCTIONISM (1991); SEYMOUR PAPERT, MINDSTORMS: CHILDREN, COMPUTERS, AND POWERFUL IDEAS (1980). It should be noted that constructivism and constructionism are two distinct concepts—the first was conceived by Jean Piaget and is based on children's interests and perceptions. The second was conceived by Seymour Papert and has more to do with how children learn. Both concepts are important for experience-based learning, and OLPC itself invokes both ideas.

5. *See* Posting of Evan Blass to Engadget, *Microsoft Will Sell $3 Software to Developing Countries,* http://www.engadget.com/2007/04/20/microsoft-will-sell-3-software-to-developing-countries/ (Apr. 20, 2007, 11:40), Michael Kannellos, *Five Countries to Get Cheap Windows XP,* CNET NEWS.COM, Aug. 10, 2004, http://news.com.com/ Five+countries+to+get+cheap+Windows+XP/2100-1016_3-5304023.html.

6. OLPC posted a request for content in October 2006. *See OLPC Request for Content,* OLPC Wiki, http://wiki.laptop.org/index.php?title=Request_for_content&oldid= 13244 (as of Oct. 3, 2006, 19:14 GMT).

7. *See, e.g.,* Posting of Wayne Hodgins to Off Course-On Target, *Opportunities in Our Laps?* http://waynehodgins.typepad.com/ontarget/science/ (Apr. 19, 2007, 01:14); Posting of Atanu Dey to Deeshaa, *OLPC—Rest in Peace—Part 2,* http://www.deeshaa .org/2006/08/04/olpc-rest-in-peace-part-2/ (Aug. 4, 2006).

8. Ryan Singel, *High Security for $100 Laptop,* WIRED, Feb. 7, 2007, http://www.wired .com/news/technology/0,72669-0.html.

9. *OLPC Bitfrost,* http://wiki.laptop.org/go/OLPC_Bitfrost (as of Feb. 1, 2007) ("The Bitfrost platform governs system security on the XO laptops. Given that 'objectionable content' lacks any kind of technical definition, and is instead a purely social construct, filtering such content lies wholly outside of the scope of the security platform and this document."); OLPC Code Browser, http://dev.laptop.org/git.do?p=security;a=commit ;h=HEAD.

10. *OLPC Bitfrost,* http://wiki.laptop.org/go/OLPC_Bitfrost (as of Feb. 1, 2007) ("The OLPC project has received very strong requests from certain countries considering joining the program to provide a powerful anti-theft service that would act as a theft deterrent against most thieves . . . the anti-theft daemon will shut down and lock the machine if its cryptographic lease ever expires. In other words, if the country operates with 21-day leases, a normal, non-stolen laptop will get the lease extended by 21 days each day it connects to the Internet. But if the machine does not connect to the Internet for 21 days, it will shut down and lock.").

11. *See* Caslon Analytics, http://www.caslon.com.au/volkscomputernote1.htm#morphy (last visited May 22, 2007).

12. Bruce Sterling, *The Year in Ideas: A to Z; Simputer,* N.Y. TIMES, Dec. 9, 2001, §6, *available at* http://www.nytimes.com/2001/12/09/magazine/09SIMPUTER.html?ex= 1171429200&en=9383e00b97332584&ei=5070.

13. *See* Jason Overdorf, *The $100 Un-PC,* NEWSWEEK.COM, Feb. 12, 2007, http:// www.newsweek.com/id/42955; Nitya Varadarajan, *Cheap, Cheaper, Cheapest,* BUSINESSTODAY, Mar. 26, 2006, *available at* www.india-today.com/btoday/20060326/features3html. Reports of a $10 PC in the idea phase have also been released recently. Akshaya Mukul, *HRD Hopes to Make $10 Laptops a Reality,* THE TIMES OF INDIA, May 4, 2007, *available at* http://timesofindia.indiatimes.com/Business/HRD_hopes_to_make _10_laptops_a_reality/articleshow/1999828.cms.

14. *Guerrilla Warfare and the OLPC,* OLPC Wiki, http://wiki.laptop.org/go/Guerrilla _Warfare_and_the_OLPC (as of May 22, 2007, 01:34 GMT).

15. Gene Spafford, *Re: [IP] $10 Laptops from HRD Ministry, India,* IP Listserv (May 6, 2007), http://www.listbox.com/member/archive/247/2007/05/sort/time_rev/page/ 2/entry/23:91/20070506140410:307417BE-FBFC-11DB-A2B9-C8C92BEBA671/.

16. RFC Editor et al., RFC 2555: 30 Years of RFCs (1999), http://www.ietf.org/rfc/ rfc2555.txt.

17. *See, e.g.,* Tools, Technology & Solutions, http://www.plagiarism.org.

18. Middlebury College's History Department banned the use of Wikipedia as a source in early 2007. *See A Stand Against Wikipedia,* INSIDE HIGHER ED., Jan. 26, 2007, http:// insidehighered.com/news/2007/01/26/wiki; Noam Cohen, *A History Department Bans Citing Wikipedia as a Research Source,* N.Y. TIMES, Feb. 21, 2007, at B8, *available at*

http://www.nytimes.com/2007/02/21/education/21wikipedia.html. Other schools are frowning upon Wikipedia as a source as well. Matt Reilly, *Source of the Problem,* THE DAILY ORANGE, Apr. 2, 2007, *available at* http://www.dailyorange.com/home/index.cfm?event=displayArticle&ustory_id=fe593637-958b-44e6-9f03-b8cba4264ec6.

19. SAGrader, IdeaWorks, http://www.ideaworks.com/sagrader/index.html (last visited May 22, 2007).

20. InnoCentive Frequently Asked Questions, http://www.innocentive.com/faqs.php (last visited Sept. 30, 2007); Darren J. Carroll, Chief Executive Officer, InnoCentive, Distributed R&D Case Study: Innocentive (Mar. 3, 2005), http://ocw.mit.edu/NR/rdonlyres/Sloan-School-of-Management/15-352Spring-2005/2F3996A5-1852-419E-8EB8-6C4354266BA2/0/mit_mar07_2005.pdf.

21. InnoCentive Frequently Asked Questions, http://www.innocentive.com/faqs.php (last visited Sept. 30, 2007) ("If your solution is selected as 'best' by the Seeker, prior to receiving a financial award you must transfer your intellectual property rights in the solution.").

22. Amazon's Mechanical Turk, http://www.mturk.com/mturk/welcome (last visited Sept. 30, 2007); *see also* Posting of Elinor Mills to Tech News Blog, *Amazon's Mechanical Turk Lets You Make $$$, Sort Of,* http://www.news.com/8301-10784_3-9782813-7.html (Sept. 21, 2007, 12:35 PDT).

Index

15; and endpoint control, 125; Mill on, 98–99, 100; post hoc scrubs, 116; retroactive, 109

CERT/CC (Computer Emergency Response Team Coordination Center), 39, 147–48

chaos, in absence of law, 128

Chapman v. United States, 188

Chickasaw, Alabama, ownership of, 172

child abuse, online images of, 111

children: Children's Internet Protection Act (CIPA), 325n148; Children's Online Privacy Protection Act of 1998 (COPPA), 232; One Laptop Per Child, 235–41, 244; restricted online use by, 232–33

China: Google in, 113, 147; information regulation in, 105, 108, 114, 147, 180, 196; surveillance in, 113; Wikipedia in, 144

Christensen, Clayton, *The Innovator's Dilemma,* 83–84, 86

Christian Gallery News Service, 215

chuckroast.com, 170–71

Citizendium, 145

citizen reporters, 216

Clark, David, 31, 156

Clarke, Richard, 51

clickworkers, 206

code: abstract concepts in, 190; and copyright infringement, 189–92; corruption of, 4, 43, 44; and cyberlaw, 104–8, 197, 310n92; data paths separate from, 40–41; easy to write, 19; embedded into hardware, 13; good and useful, 31; outside, 4, 16–17, 56; poisoned, 189; proprietary, 192; renegade, 36–38; sharing of, 16; transmission of, 14; view source, 121; "west coast," 105. *See also* worms and viruses

code-backed norms, 223–28

code-based enforcement mechanisms, 105

code thickets, 188–92

collaboration, online, 95–96

commercial filtering programs, 114–15

common law, 110

commons, 78–79, 90

Communications Decency Act, 195

communitarianism, 293n71

CompuServe, 23, 24, 27; central control by, 3, 7, 57, 74, 81, 82, 106–7; data paths of, 40–41; and Digital Millennium Copyright Act, 119; and dumb terminals, 41, 101–2; "Electronic Mall" of, 29–30; era at an end, 34, 174, 255n7, 256n24; and hyperlinks, 89; measurement in, 157

computers: customized to user's needs, 17, 30; "dumb" terminals, 15, 20, 41, 101–2; hardware and software bundled in, 9; mainframes, 12, 15, 24, 57; minicomputers, 15; professional management of, 17, 44; rogue applications for, 24; unbundling of, 12, 14; vendor programming, 8–9, 17

conduct rules, 122–23

Constitution, U.S.: and anonymous speech, 213; and free speech, 114, 230; and gun control, 117; and privacy policies, 112, 185–86, 188; and private property, 172

constructionism (constructivism), 236–37

consumer protection law, 177

content layer, 67

contextualization, 229–31

coordinate coexistence producing information, 207

COPPA (Children's Online Privacy Protection Act of 1998), 232

copyright infringement, 111, 119–20, 175; and code production, 189–92; and content thickets, 192–93; and Creative Commons licenses, 225; and "creative cultural bricolage," 192; and employment agreements, 189; patent thicket, 190–92; and peer-leveraging

compared to, 73–76; limitations of, 177; and network neutrality, 178–85; PCs as, 4, 59–61, 102, 185–88; PCs vs., 18, 29, 57–59; and perfect enforcement, 161; and privacy, 185–88; regulatory interventions in, 103–7, 125, 197; remote control of, 161; remote updates of, 106–7, 176; security dilemma of, 42, 106–7, 123–24, 150, 176–88; specific injunction, 108–9; variety of designs for, 20; Web 2.0 and, 102; *See also specific information appliances*

information overload, 230

information services, early forms, 9

InnoCentive, 246

innovation: blending models for, 86–90; generativity as parent of, 80–84, 90; group, 94; and idiosyncrasy, 90–91; inertia vs., 83–84; "sustaining" vs. "disruptive," 83–84, 87, 97

intellectual property: and code thickets, 188–92; and contraband rules, 103–4; cross-licensing of, 190; fair use defense, 115, 121–22; illegal online file sharing, 111–12, 197; inadequate protection for, 217; licensing of, 79; and patent thicket, 190–92; principle of tolerated uses, 119–22, 190–91; and privacy law, 210; statutes of limitations, 191; value of, 98. *See also* cyberlaw

Interface Message Processors (IMPs), 27

Internet: application layer, 67–69; assumption of equality in, 33–34; assumptions of user trustworthiness, 20–21, 30–32, 130, 227; as "best efforts" network, 33; browsers, 121; bundled proprietary model defeated by, 30; channels of communication and control in, 42; collaboration in design of, 34; competitors, 9; connectivity of, 32; consumer applications of, 28; content layer of, 67; design of, 27–28, 30–35,

41, 130, 243; economic value as a commons, 79, 85; entrance of, 26–30; expansion and growth of, 43, 102; first message on, 27; flexibility vs. security of, 9, 40, 42–43; generative technology of, 3, 5, 8, 34, 72, 152, 178, 242; goodwill subsidy assumed, 9; hourglass architecture of, 67–69; and market forces, 20–21; modularity of, 41; motives of creators, 28; numbers of users, 36, 157–58; outside code on, 4; personal identity management on, 32–33; physical layer of, 67–69; Postel's Law, 134; protocol compatibility in, 28–29; protocol layer of, 39, 67–69; and quality of service, 33; quiet development of, 7–8, 243; regulability of, 8, 9, 103, 105, 107, 196–97; regulatory interventions of, 20, 98, 103, 245; research environment as source of, 34, 38–39; RFCs for, 243; security problems of, 97, 130, 168, 195; shared access to, 32; simplicity as core value of, 31–32, 33; social layer of, 67; standards of, 39, 224, 225; as terrorist recruiting tool, 198; and tethered appliances, 8–9; transmission speed of, 32, 33; trusted systems in, 105; unexpected success of, 7, 20, 33, 34; untenable status quo of, 43–51; users as consumers vs. participants, 161; as what we make it, 242, 244–46; wireless access points of, 69, 179–80, 194; worms and viruses in, 36–54

Internet Engineering Task Force (IETF), 39, 141, 148; RFC 1135 on Morris worm, 60, 151

Internet Governance Forum, 242–43

iPhone, 1, 2–3, 5, 101, 106, 182

iPod, 1, 101, 233

Iran, censorship in, 114–15

ISPs (Internet Service Providers): and Digital Millennium Copyright Act, 119–20; early on-ramps to, 29, 30;

Timex/Sinclair Z-1000, 13
TiVo, 59, 64, 71, 77, 101, 123, 162, 184;
    and preemption, 108; and regulator
    control, 107; and surveillance, 109
TiVo v. EchoStar, 103–4, 107, 108
tolerated uses, 119–22, 190–91
traffic lights: cameras at, 116–17; and
    verkeersbordvrij, 127–28
tragedies of the commons, 158
transclusion, use of term, 226–27
transferability, 73
transmission speed, irregularity of, 32
trial and error, learning by, 236
Trumpet Winsock, 29
trust: assumptions of, 20–21, 30–32,
    39–40, 134, 135, 147; trade-offs with,
    33
trusted systems, 105
Tushman, Michael, 24
Twain, Mark (Samuel Clemens), 212, 213
two-factor authentication, 53
typewriters, "smart," 15, 19, 20, 34

unitary rights holder, 189
United States v. Am. Library Ass'n, 282–
    83n62
Unix operating system, 39, 132, 190
U.S. Census, 11
user-generated content, 146, 147
user ID, 32, 195
U.S. General Accounting Office (GAO),
    38–39
U.S. government, research funding from,
    27, 28
U.S. Telecommunications Act (1996),
    304–5n28

values, 79
VCRs, 121
verkeersbordvrij ("free of traffic signs" ex-
    periment), 127–28, 130; lessons of,
    128, 211, 228; "unsafe as safe" experi-
    ment, 129; Wikipedia experiment
    with, 133–34, 144, 146

video games: emergence of, 15; as infor-
    mation appliances, 20, 57, 58, 101; li-
    censing of, 58, 177; remote updating
    of, 176; third-party code for, 183;
    Xbox, 3–4, 184
video rental industry, 121, 202
virtual machine technology, 155, 156
virtual worlds, 47
viruses. *See* worms and viruses
VisiCalc, 2
Vixie, Paul, 168–69, 172, 173
VNC, 54
Von Ahn, Luis, 206–7

Wales, Jimbo: and Bomis search engine,
    133, 289n19; and Essjay, 141; and
    MyWikiBiz, 140; and Nupedia, 133;
    and Wikia, 141; and Wikipedia, 133,
    136, 138, 139, 142, 145, 147–48
Warhol, Andy, 214
warranty, law of, 162
Warshak v. United States, 188
Web 2.0: bottom-up tagging on, 214; de-
    cision-making control ceded to, 167;
    and end of generativity, 123–26; and
    peer production, 206–16; usability of
    older versions with, 125; use of term,
    102, 123
webcams, 158, 210–12
Web sites: accessibility of, 4; blacklists of,
    114–15; fake "link farms," 207; and
    information appliances, 102; and pri-
    vacy, 177, 203, 226; and spam, 170–
    72; surveillance of, 109
Weinberger, David, 214
Westlaw, 89
whistleblowers, 118
wi-fi access points, 69, 179–80, 194
Wikipedia, 74, 130, 226; barnstar
    awards, 136, 145; biographies of living
    persons in, 138; blocks of, 136, 140;
    "Bureaucrats" of, 135–36; as central-
    ized service, 157; community-devel-
    oped standards of, 139, 143, 146–48,